Books by Milton Lomask

Andrew Johnson: *President on Trial* (1960)

Seed Money: *The Guggenheim Story* (1964)

Aaron Burr: *The Years from Princeton to Vice President* (1979)

Aaron Burr: *The Years of Exile* (*in progress*)

AARON BURR

Milton Lomask

AARON BURR

The Years from Princeton to Vice President 1756-1805

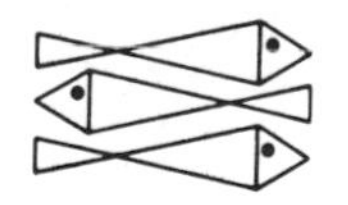

Farrar • Straus • Giroux

NEW YORK

Printed in the United States of America
Published simultaneously in Canada by McGraw-Hill
Ryerson Ltd., Toronto
Designed by Guy Fleming

Library of Congress Cataloging in Publication Data
Lomask, Milton.
Aaron Burr, the years from Princeton to Vice President,
1756–1805.
Bibliography: p.
Includes index.
1. Burr, Aaron, 1756–1836. 2. United States—Politics
and government—1783–1809. 3. Vice-Presidents—United
States—Biography. I. Title.
E302.6.B9L7 1979 973.4'6'0924 [B] 78-31142

FOR RAY NEVILLE

WITH THANKS

CONTENTS

ILLUSTRATIONS

FOLLOWING PAGE 190

PREFACE

A YEAR AFTER AARON BURR DIED IN 1836 in a small hotel on Staten Island, New York, John Quincy Adams wrote that "Burr's life, take it altogether, was such as in any country of sound morals his friends would be desirous of burying in profound oblivion."

The former President's remark, recorded in his monumental diary, reflected the opinion of many contemporaries in an age that had watched Burr's spectacular rise to "within a hair's breadth of the Presidency of the United States," and his equally spectacular decline to "within a hair's breadth of a gibbet and a halter for treason." Many Americans shuddered when on the dueling grounds of Weehawken, New Jersey, he fired the bullet that killed Alexander Hamilton. They learned with mingled reactions about his filibuster into the Southwest with the intent, so Burr himself said, of freeing the Mexicans from their Spanish overlords. They listened to the forensics in a Virginia courtroom where a jury, bowing to the instructions of the Chief Justice of the United States, pronounced him innocent of having tried to separate the Western half of the country from the East. They more or less forgot him when, after the trial, he exiled himself in Europe to escape his creditors.

When he returned to America a few years later, it was to practice law and to become a legendary figure on the streets of New York, a slender, elegant, piercing-eyed man, with a touch of brimstone in his glance and a dry smile on his lips, often alone and visibly aging. Local tradition holds that mothers sometimes called him to the attention of their children, as a horrible example of what happens to the wicked. By this time he had lost everything dear to him, including his daughter and his only grandchild; but to the last breath of his eighty years, he never lost the reputation of being a libertine. Only once during the closing decades of his life did his name resume its once wonted place in the public consciousness. That was in his seventy-eighth year when the rich and notorious widow who had recently become his second wife sued him for "absolute divorce," accusing him of adultery with a twenty-one-year-old woman and "divers other females."

However well John Quincy Adams's epitaph conformed to prevailing sentiment, it was valueless as prophecy. The oblivion he wished for Burr has not materialized. Few Americans have enjoyed a more intensive posthumous career. Not neglect but controversy has been his portion from posterity. According to his critics, he was at best a *génie manqué*, at worst an unscrupulous adventurer, ambitious without principle, charming without substance. His defenders have detected in him a bud of greatness that failed to unfold only because of the malevolence of others. The objective of critics and apologists alike has been to place before us the real man. But who *was* the real Aaron Burr? That his mistakes were on the grand scale, both sides concede. But where were they rooted—in the man himself, or in the circumstances of his time and place?

This first volume of my biography of Aaron Burr—which covers the period from his birth in 1756 to his farewell remarks as Vice President of the United States, in the Senate on 2 March 1805—is an attempt to provide some of the answers to these difficult questions. (The second and final volume, still in progress at this writing, will complete the story of the events leading up to his trial for treason, his exile and final years.) For their help in this effort to understand Aaron Burr, I am greatly indebted to the late Allan Nevins; to Dr. Mary-Jo Kline, editor of *The Papers of Aaron Burr* for The New-York Historical Society; to many members of the staff of the Library of Congress, especially Peter Petcoff and Eileen Donahue; to Ray Allen Billington, the Henry E. Huntington Library; Alexander P. Clark, the Princeton University Library; Kate Mearns, the Senate House Museum, Kingston, New York; Samuel Engle Burr, Jr., President General of the Aaron Burr Association; Mrs. Gilbert W. Norwood and Alex J. Hurst, Jr., the Friends of the Hermitage, Ho-Ho-Kus, New Jersey; Jared Banta, the Historical and Preservation Society of Paramus, New Jersey; Nan C. Fahy, Bethlehem, Pennsylvania; Jack and Irene Rice, Menands, New York; Mrs. Jane Durgin, New York City; the late Esther Douty, Washington, D.C.; Suzanne Burr Geissler, Florham Park, New Jersey; Hannah R. Landon, Newport, Rhode Island; J. Merton England, the National Science Foundation; the late J. W. Marino, Weehawken, New Jersey; and my friend and collaborator in spirit, Ray Neville, to whom the book is dedicated.

MILTON LOMASK

McLean, Virginia
March 1978

The Fates never decreed that I should go anywhere,
but someone should be the worse for it.

Aaron Burr *to* Sally Burr Reeve

17 January 1774

AARON BURR

I

Visible Saints

According to his mother, he began life as he lived it —"unexpectedly." Less than twenty-four hours before the event, Esther Edwards Burr noted in her dairy the departure of her husband, the Reverend Aaron Burr, on a trip connected with his duties as pastor of the First Presbyterian Church of Newark, New Jersey, and as president of the College of New Jersey, later known as Princeton. His absence left Esther "ready to imagine ye Sun does not give so much light as it did when my best Self was at home," and she "proposed to visit as much as I can" to keep her spirits up.

"P.M.," she wrote on 5 February 1756, "Made a visit to Mrs. Ogdens, & she has been worrying of me to go with her tomorrow to make a Wedding visit. I said yt women in my circumstances had no business to go Sticking themselves up at Weddings. Well she would leve it to the company (for there was a number of young women by) & they Said I was right, so Mrs. Ogden left off at last."

The "circumstances" were more advanced than Esther knew. Next morning she could add only a few words to her diary: "Very poorly unable to write—Febry the 6 day."

Some time that Thursday—"unexpectedly," she revealed later—she became the mother of her second child, a son whom a London magazine would someday apostrophize as the "famous, infamous Aaron Burr, Vice President of the United States."

2

THE BOY BORN in the Newark manse that winter day would go through life aware that his maternal grandfather was the great Jonathan Edwards, and his father a preeminent figure in the religious and educational circles of his era. Aaron Burr had come into the world with a pedigree second to none by colonial standards. And this was, perhaps, the first of his misfortunes.

At the time of his birth, Grandfather Edwards was best known as the pastor of the Congregational Church in Northampton, Massachusetts. He became more widely known as the author of the Edwardsean Theology, last holdout of the swiftly thinning ranks of American believers in the stricter tenets of John Calvin; still later he was recognized as one of the most original minds of pre-revolutionary America.

On the infant's paternal side there were no ancestors of comparable magnitude but many of above-average competence and character. The first American Burr, a carpenter named Jehu, reached Massachusetts Bay Colony in 1630 on one of the seventeen vessels of Governor John Winthrop's fleet, vanguard of the great Puritan immigration. For five generations Jehu's people had lived in England. Remotely they were Celtic, possibly borrowing the family name from the village of Birr in Ireland. Jehu's first wife (he was twice married) and first son came with him, or so it seems from blurry ancient records. From Roxbury on the Boston Neck they forged west to help found Agawam, later Springfield, Massachusetts. After eight years in that place they moved to Unquowa on the shores of Long Island Sound. There, at the time of his death in 1672, the first American Burr was discharging a variety of civic duties for what meanwhile had become Fairfield, Connecticut.

Rapidly his descendants impressed the family name on militia rolls and magisterial registers; on indentures to wood-lots, "home-lots," "long-lots," pastures and fields; on stubby slate headstones, ornamented with angels' wings and angels' faces, in burying grounds throughout New England and beyond. One of Jehu's sons took part in the first and unsuccessful effort to establish a public-school system in Connecticut. Another served on the court that found "Mercy Desborough, wife of Thomas," guilty of "suckling black pigs," and other witcheries "contrary to the peace of our Sovereign Lord and Lady, the King and Queen, their Crown and dignity." During the early years of the eighteenth century, few men were better known in Connecticut than Jehu's grandson, Peter Burr, lawyer, educator, presiding officer of the colonial assembly, and chief judge of the superior court when he died on Christmas Day 1724. Quite likely, one of the mourners who accompanied his coffin to "God's Acre," the Fairfield cemetery, was his half brother Daniel's son, the slight and broad-faced boy who would become the Reverend Aaron Burr, father of the "famous, infamous" Aaron.

The first Aaron grew up on a farm in the hills above Fairfield. Townspeople spoke of his father as Daniel Burr of Upper Meadow, to distinguish him from a local cousin of the same name. Before her marriage, his mother was Elizabeth Pinkney, daughter of a Fairfield settler who had moved on to Eastchester, New York. She was Daniel's third wife, mother of eight of his eleven children. Of these, Aaron, born on 4 January 1716, was the last. He was six when his father died, leaving him, the youngest offspring, five hundred forty-five pounds and ten shillings.

3

The senior Aaron Burr's America was as preoccupied with religion as his son's America would be with politics.

Generations later Americans, looking back on this period, would find it easy to think of early New England as a solid block of Calvinism, but in fact fissures and deeper cracks had attacked the structure long before Aaron Burr of Fairfield, the father of our subject, was born.

As the primeval forest moved back, as the long drudgery-filled day of the first-generation pioneers gave way to the more leisurely pace of their sons and grandsons, worldly pleasures and moneymaking attracted more and more adherents. Most people continued to observe the forms of religion, but the fervor ebbed. Well before the end of the seventeenth century, the first Puritan century in America, a prominent minister was complaining that many New Englanders had become "sermon-proof." The local Congregational or Presbyterian meeting-house continued to dominate the community, but tavern and counting room ran it a close second. The law required all to attend services, but it was a rare town that had constables enough to catch or stocks enough to punish those who stayed away.

Originally church membership and the civic voting privileges that went with it were open only to "visible saints," those who had knowingly undergone "conversion." Starting in 1657, many churches tried to cope with a spreading religious indifference by adopting the "half-way covenant," an arrangement permitting the unsanctified to enjoy limited church membership and have their children baptized. Even this and other departures from orthodoxy failed to stem the swelling tide of rebellion. In the first Aaron Burr's day, the paradox of preachers exhorting their listeners to be virtuous, while admitting that the practice of virtue would not necessarily save them, gave rise to a popular jingle:

> You can and you can't
> You shall and you shan't.
> You will and you won't.
> You'll be damned if you do on't. [sic]

Competition from other creeds, all heretical in Puritan eyes, intruded even earlier. Only seven years after the first boatload of English Puritans disembarked at Salem in 1630, a synod of the Massachusetts churches pointed to the existence within the commonwealth of "eighty-two opinions, some blasphemous" and "others erroneous," along with "nine unwholesome expressions." The delegates assigned these apostasies "to the devil of hell from whence they came," but they refused to stay consigned. In 1722 Connecticut had only eighty Episcopalians; in 1737 it had twelve hundred. Of the four richest congregations in Boston in 1740, two were Episcopalian, one was Arminian, and one was the liberal Brattle Street Church.

When in the early 1730's Aaron Burr of Fairfield took up residence in Yale's recently built College House in New Haven, the winds of dissent were blowing through its halls. As an undergraduate, he leaned toward Arminianism. Whereas Calvinism conceived of the human being as totally dependent on the mercy of God and incapable of participating in his own salvation, Arminianism held that the grace of God was open to all and that the individual could accept or reject it as he saw fit. Young Burr had received his A.B. degree in 1735 and was doing further study on a Berkeley scholarship before he abandoned this Dutch-born canon, made his peace with the dominant religion, and determined to enter the ministry.

For this turning point in his life his future father-in-law was indirectly responsible. In 1735 Jonathan Edwards was at the zenith of his ministerial career at Northampton. Late that year he delivered a series of sermons against the moral decay and spiritual apostasy around him. The results exceeded his hopes. In November of 1736 he wrote a friend in Scotland that within recent months "three hundred souls," a large number in a community of two hundred families, had been "savingly brought home to Christ." So fast had "the number of true saints multiplied" that Northampton "seemed to be full of the presence of God . . . full of love . . . of joy," with the minds of the people so "wonderfully taken off from the world that it has come to be treated amongst us as a thing of very little consequence."

The Northampton revival was a forerunner of the Great Awakening of a few years later. The elated Edwards quoted the Bible: "A city that is set upon a hill cannot be hid." The brightness that was Northampton from 1735 to 1737 was soon perceived at New Haven, where it created a stir among the black-gowned inhabitants of College House.

Aaron Burr was one of those affected. "This year," he wrote in 1736, "God saw fit to open my eyes . . . Though before I had been . . . driven to a form of religion, yet I knew nothing as I ought to know. But then I was brought to the footstool of sovereign grace, saw myself polluted by nature and practice, had affecting views of the Divine wrath I deserved, was made to despair of help in myself, and almost concluded that my day of grace was past. It pleased God at length to reveal His Son to me in the Gospel, as an all-sufficient Saviour . . ."

The Reverend Burr began his "trials," his preaching apprenticeship, in two small churches. He was at Hanover, New Jersey, when he received a call from the First Church at Newark, a congregation approximately as prominent in the Jerseys as the Northampton church in Massachusetts. His predecessor had proved too "meek and unoffending" to halt a leakage of members to the recently established Episcopalian church in Newark. Aware of these conditions and of his inexperience, twenty-two-year-old Burr was genuinely surprised when after a year of probation the Newark parishioners asked that he be ordained as their settled minister.

Urbane, lenient, and inordinately charming, he handled his pastoral duties with aplomb. But it was as an educator that he shone. In 1746 he helped found America's fourth college, the College of New Jersey, at Elizabethtown. The school was only four and a half months old when death removed its first president, the local Presbyterian pastor, Jonathan Dickinson. The Reverend Burr at once took over, moving the students to Newark. For three years he discharged his presidential duties without salary, a productive period, it would seem, for soon he was writing a friend abroad that the enrollment had grown from but "8 students when the Care of the college was . . . committed to me to between 40 and 50 . . . now."

"Now" was 1751. Burr was in his thirty-fifth year, a man of "lenient byass," in the words of one friend; "a little small man as to body but of great and well improved mind," in the words of another. Pastor of a flourishing church, head of a growing college, he could complain of only one lack in his life. Slaves and servants tended his hip-roofed house standing between the church and the jail under the elms and buttonwoods of Newark. No hostess stood by his side to welcome the dignitaries arriving for meetings of the college board. When in the fall of 1751 his affairs took him to Boston, he found his historian-friend, the Reverend Thomas Prince of Old South Church, prepared to play Cupid. Sally, the Boston minister's daughter, had spent part of the summer with the Jonathan Edwardses in Northampton. She and Esther Edwards had met before but only briefly. In the massy clapboard parsonage on King Street, acquaintance ripened into profound friendship, and in the late summer Esther returned the visit. During a month at the Prince home in Boston, her "engaging deportment and conversation" delighted Sally's father. When soon after her departure he learned that Burr was in town, he hastened to tell his bachelor colleague that were he hunting a mistress for his manse he need look no further than Esther Edwards.

The Newark minister-educator could not have been unacquainted with Esther. He, too, had visited the Edwardses at Northampton. Five years had passed, however, since his last journey there. In his mature eyes the thirteen-year-old Esther he saw then was simply another child among the many

Edwards daughters, though there is a legend that even then he singled her out and resolved to remain celibate until this enchanting creature achieved nubility. If so, he was scarcely the impatient lover his son would be. A late-May sun was greening New England hills before the Reverend Aaron saddled up and rode north to have another look at Esther Edwards.

4

HIS DESTINATION was not Northampton but Stockbridge, a forest-bound village on the Massachusetts frontier. Thence Jonathan Edwards had moved after his Northampton congregation, angered by his handling of a doctrinal matter, had relieved him of his pulpit.

Today Jonathan Edwards seems best remembered for a few blazing sermons on the once popular subject of hell and damnation. Actually, these pulpit exercises were only a fragment of his literary output and a far from typical one. When early in a life that began in 1703 in East Windsor (now South Windsor), Connecticut, he found his vocation in Calvinism, religion's gain was science's loss. So impressive were his occasional forays into natural philosophy that one twentieth-century student of his mind credits him with an "insight into science and psychology so much ahead of his time that our own can hardly be said to have caught up with him."

There was a strain of homicidal madness in the family on his father's side, but his father, the Reverend Timothy Edwards, was merely dull and Jonathan was a genius. He was not at first drawn to the predestinarian aspect of his father's beliefs. "From my childhood up," he would recall as a young man, "my mind had been full of objections against the doctrine of God's . . . choosing whom he would to eternal life, and rejecting whom he pleased, leaving them to . . . be everlastingly tormented in hell. It used to appear like a horrible doctrine to me. But I remember the time very well when I seemed to be convinced . . . as to the sovereignty of God . . ." After that, it seemed to Edwards that he saw the "excellency of God" wherever he turned—"in the clouds and blue sky; in the grass, flowers, trees; in the water and all nature . . ." Religion, he decided, had little to do with rule and creed. It was primarily a personal inner experience, "not a means to an end"—for God alone dictated the end—but an end in itself.

In his fourteenth year, his second as a student at Yale College, he discovered the works of John Locke and Isaac Newton. Over Locke's *An Essay Concerning Human Understanding* he hovered as a miser over his "handfuls of silver and gold." He read Newton's *Optics* in the same spirit. Other New England youths of his time found in these apostles of the Enlightenment a brutal rebuke to everything they had been taught. Jonathan found a challenge: he would spend the rest of his life in an effort to fashion from the man-centered theories of Locke and Newton an intellectual scaffolding for the God-centered theories of John Calvin. The attempt was beyond even his superb abilities, but his writings transcended the purpose that inspired them. Dealing brilliantly with ageless questions, the nature of human freedom among them, they would be read long after the validity of orthodox Calvinism had ceased to interest large numbers of people.

In 1727 he became colleague-minister at Northampton to his grandfather, Solomon Stoddard, a man of such influence along the Connecticut River that the Boston ministers spoke of him enviously as the "Pope of the Valley." In 1729 Stoddard died, and Edwards took his place. Tall and slender, with a wedge-shaped face notable for its gentle, almost womanly beauty, he was loving and lovable in his home, but elsewhere said to be "proud, overbearing and rash." He lectured his parishioners now on the "Infinitely Glorious Perfection of God," now on the fires of hell, over which he pictured the Deity dangling them like "some loathesome insect." Whatever the words, the manner was always the same: the voice thin and languid, the gestures minimal, the mild eyes fixed on the bell rope hanging at midchurch, causing parishioner Gideon Clark to imagine that Brother Edwards had stared it off.

It was a point of pride with him not to visit the sick. Nor did he permit his followers to engage him overmuch in small talk. Ministerially speaking, the Reverend Jonathan Edwards had no bedside manner. For twenty-three years his flock admired and tolerated him, hopefully aware, without necessarily knowing that they were, that someday the oracle would slip. He did, finally.

Suddenly he announced the suspension of a popular rule that allowed saints and sinners alike to partake of the Last Supper. Henceforth, only visible saints could approach the sacred table. There was a protracted hullabaloo. Hell hath no fury like a congregation scorned. Edwards's people outtalked him in church and out, and in June 1750 they dismissed him. Fifteen months later, at the request of the Congregational Commissioners for Indian Affairs at Boston, he assumed charge of the little Indian mission at Stockbridge.

Early in his Northampton career he had married Sarah Pierrepont of New Haven, Connecticut. She brought him beauty, wit, and eleven children. For Edwards, head of a "large and chargeable family," exile to a lonely Indian mission in the wilderness was a financial strain, but for Edwards, the scholar, it had compensations. At Stockbridge his clerical duties were on the whole lighter than they had been in Northampton, his opportunities for thought and study greater. At a six-sided desk in the four-by-eight study of his farmhouse-parsonage, he produced some of his most important works.

While he wrote, the women of his family supplemented a shrunken income by making paper fans and selling them. It was a household much reduced in material goods that greeted the Reverend Aaron Burr on his arrival in the spring of 1752.

What was Esther like, the young woman whom the thirty-six-year-old college president had traveled so far to court? The one known portrait provides an incomplete answer. Its artist, whoever he was, chose to present Esther as a premature dowager; but Samuel Hopkins, an intimate of the Edwards household in Stockbridge, found her "formed to please," exceeding "most of her sex in the beauty of her person, and in a decent and easy gesture, behaviour and conversation; not stiff and starch on the one hand, nor mean and indecent on the other." Granted she had a "peculiar smartness in her make and temper," and before the Reverend Aaron came with his proposal she had tartly turned down several much younger men. Obviously the middle-aged minister from Newark encountered no difficulties. He stayed in Stockbridge only three days—"in which short time," one of his students at the College of New Jersey exclaimed, "he accomplished his whole design!"

As if this efficiently dispatched romance were not unorthodox enough, the marriage did not take place in the Edwards home. According to the incredulous student, Mr. Burr was no sooner back at his own home than he sent a recent graduate of the college to fetch Esther and her mother to Newark. There, on a Monday evening, 29 June 1752, "the nuptial ceremonies were celebrated." A month later the student observer, obviously in a more resigned frame of mind, was jotting down his impressions of the president's bride. She was "amiable in her person, of great affability and agreeableness in conversation, and a very excellent economist."

5

SOME OF THE local reactions to the union were less benign. To students and townspeople alike, the sixteen-year spread between bride and groom was fodder for gossip. During Sunday services in the square stone meetinghouse with its box-like roof and long hard benches, the eyes of some parishioners rested censoriously on the new occupant of the raised pew reserved for the pastor's family under the "wine-cup" pulpit. Esther had lived too long in a parson's household to miss the import of these stares.

"Sabbath . . . ah!" she ruminated. "Religion, thou gettest many a stab from thy *professed friends!*" Her husband warned her to "expect to hear, & bare a great deal of ill nature . . . One thing they Say is yt I am very proud but you would laugh to hear what they bring to prove it."

A fierce pride flamed through the Edwards family. It would reappear in Esther's son, who in his eventful adulthood would refuse to comment publicly on criticism of his conduct. "No apologies or explanations," he would say. "I hate them!" Esther neglected to mention what it was her Newark neighbors cited to prove her a proud woman—her love of finery, perhaps. In an account book kept with her husband, she listed the treasures of her wardrobe: "a suit of black Paduasoy," "a brown Calimanco gown," a "Corded Dimity with flowered border," "a mask" to protect her complexion when rough winds off the Passaic River or the Jersey salt meadows sheared across the open fields of Newark.

Others could speak as they wished of her marriage, but "do you think I would exchange my *good Mr. Burr* for any person or thing on Erth!" she asked. "*No Sire!* not for a Million Such worlds as this yt had no Mr. B—r in it!"

Sally Prince of Boston was the recipient of this confession. The two women corresponded furiously. Esther posted her letters in batches, numbering the batches consecutively. Collectively these were her diary, depository for the canny observations and flights of fancy of a buoyant and outspoken young woman. Its thickly scribbled pages yield many glimpses of its author. We see her, on a visit to Stockbridge during the French and Indian War, bowing to her father's order that she stay with him a couple of weeks as planned instead of fleeing at once from the ever present likelihood of an Indian attack on that exposed outpost. But external obedience was accompanied by inward protest. She could not argue with her father's reminder that one should be ready at all times to meet his maker, "but I am not willing to be Butchered by a barbarous enemy nor can't make my Self willing." However, she added, "if the Indians get me, they get me." We see her unimpressed with New York City: "I would not live here a fortnight for any money." We see her assaulting the ramparts of male chauvinism even as her son would do after her. Off to Boston went her report of "a Smart combat with Mr. Ewing about our sex." Then a tutor at the College of New Jersey, John Ewing would make his mark as the longtime provost of the University of Pennsylvania. Although Esther considered him a "man of Good Parts & lerning," it grieved her that he harbored "mean thoughts about women." He said they were incapable of "anything so cool and rational" as friendship. "I talked him quite Silent," Esther boasted. "He got up and said Your Servant & went off . . . My Tongue you know hangs prety loose."

It has been written of Jonathan Edwards that his religious tracts contain as much Freud as Calvin. Esther shared her father's appreciation of the waywardness of the human mind. Resentment and annoyances, she decided, should not be left "*grumbling* within until they are forced to belch out all at once like a cloud."

To her Boston friend she grumbled copiously. At times she found the duties of a clergyman's wife a "Tedious Round." The parsonage was the meeting place for synod and presbytery. These gatherings called for long hours "in ye citchen, making Mince-pyes & Cocoa-nut-Tarts." There were always guests. "Know sooner is the house emty'd but filled again." One day it was "30 to 31 visitors"; on another, "a parcel of triflers" and "little Flirting Misses." On still another, "an Army to breakfast" drove a tuckered Mrs. Burr to rhyme:

> How happy is the holy Hermit's lot!
> The world forgetting, by the world forgot.

"Pray what do you think every body marrye in or about winter for?" she mused. "I really believe tis for fear of lying cold, & for want of a bedfellow. Well, my advice to such is ye Same with ye Apostle, Let them Marry . . . tis better to Marry than to———!" It is interesting to find the daughter of a Calvinist minister touching so lightly on such a topic. She was not alone; to the Puritans of eighteenth-century America the cardinal sins were not the pleasures of the flesh but blasphemy, irreverence, and sabbath-breaking. In a sparsely settled land where there were never enough working hands, childbearing was regarded as an absolute virtue. The rulers of a colonial church might spend weeks investigating a report that a parishioner had laughed aloud during worship service. More often than not, these same worthies would go along with a policy known as "the seven-months rule." Under this unwritten law of the church, a woman who acquired a wedding ring by the seventh month of pregnancy was received without question into the communion of the saints. Jonathan Edwards and many other New England religious leaders of his day viewed the practice of "bundling" with tolerance. There is extant the diary of a divinity student of the time who, during the year before ordination, had five love affairs in succession, and "bundled with the fourth of his inamoratas *magna cum voluptate*." Historically, the view of sex as the paramount and all-inclusive sin belongs not to Puritanism but to its vulgar successor, Victorianism.

When, on the eve of the French and Indian War, Newark learned of the bloody rout of British General Braddock on the Pennsylvania frontier, the Reverend Aaron Burr mounted his pulpit to thunder sorrow and apprehension. His wife echoed him in letters to Sally Prince: "General Braddock . . . killed & his Army defeated. O my dear what will . . . become of us! Our *Sins*, our *Sins*—they . . . call aloud for Vengeance . . . Tis just, tis right—I haven't a word to Say against the ordering of God—for I know I have been guilty enough to procure the Judgment of heaven."

Jonathan Edwards's daughter had the Puritan's abiding sense of personal unworthiness. Yet gloom was not her natural métier. Merrily, unabashedly, her letters mingled piety and gossip. With her quill she informed Sally in one sentence that today "Mr. Burr preached against whoredom & never did people need it more"; in the next that "Cousin Billy Vance is going to be Married—Did you ever hear the like? pray what can he do with a Wife? He is more of a woman than of a man."

The passing years provided new subjects for her spirited pen. In 1754 came Sarah, her first child. The little girl's father was convinced that the bright-eyed baby would grow up to be a "numbhead." Esther considered her "above middling in all accounts." Aaron, arriving two years later, inspired no encomiums. Indeed, his mother became the first of his many detractors. She described him as "a little dirty Noisy Boy . . . very sly and mischievous," sprightlier "than Sally and most say handsomer, but not so good tempered . . . he requires a good governor to bring him to terms."

6

From 1754 on, the letters brimmed with news of impending change. A permanent home was being erected at Princeton for the College of New Jersey. On 17 September 1754 the cornerstone of the college building, Nassau Hall, was laid. In late 1756 the building stood complete, and in the last month of that year the Burrs moved into the adjoining house that Robert Smith, architect of the Pennsylvania Statehouse (Independence Hall), had built for the president and his family.

Esther wrote enthusiastically of her new surroundings. She reported that Nassau Hall was "the most commodious" of any American college, the largest man-made structure "upon the Continent." Of uncut native stone, 176 feet one way and 54 feet the other, the shapely three-story-and-basement pile gave off "a grandure & yet a simplicity yt cant well be expressed." She was "well pleased" with her new house and neighbors. Cheerful words went to Boston in the chatty letters of a woman not yet aware of the shadows gathering around her.

Her husband was working hard to meet the expenses flowing from the relocation of his school. When he was not writing begging letters to Europe, he was on the road giving sermons, making speeches, playing the prototype of a thousand fund-raising American college presidents to come.

In September 1757 he returned from a tiring trip to learn that the royal governor of New Jersey, Jonathan Belcher, had died. Belcher had been a good friend to the college. It was only fitting that its president prepare the funeral sermon. Ill on his arrival home, the forty-two-year-old Reverend Burr worsened during an afternoon spent at his desk. Written in a state of "intermittent fever" and delivered in near-delirium, his funeral oration for Belcher was the prelude to his own. On the twenty-fourth of the month the engaging sophisticate, who had guided what is now Princeton University through its formative years, was dead.

Now the Puritan in Esther took over. For the second time her infant son fell critically ill, narrowly escaping death. From this ordeal, coming so swiftly after the loss of her husband, Esther took refuge in her faith. She wrote her father on 2 November 1757 that she had entered "into a renewed and explicit covenant with God," and had received assurances that she would not live much longer. She found "transporting" this "foretaste of Heaven," this certainty that she would soon share in the "glorious state my dear departed must be in." The modern mind may cringe at this eagerness of a mother to abandon her children, but so far as we know, Esther's daughter never saw this letter. As for Aaron, he was in his sixties when a copy of portions of it was sent him by a well-meaning friend, hopeful that the example of his mother's piety would wean him from his wicked ways.

Two days after the Reverend Burr's death, the college board invited Jonathan Edwards to take his place as president of Princeton. Edwards protested that his "vapid, sizzy" constitution and "contemptibleness of speech, presence, and demeanor" ill-fitted him to succeed a man "so remarkably well qualified in these respects." We need not take this exercise in modesty too seriously. Behind it lay the understandable unwillingness of a scholar and a writer to exchange the quiet of his Stockbridge farmhouse for the turmoil of supervising the education of a hundred lively young minds. Edwards was planning several books, including a major effort to be entitled *The History of the Work of Redemption.* It is said that he wept when on 4 January 1758 a council of the Stockbridge Church, enlarged by two representatives sent northward by the trustees of Nassau Hall, accepted the conditions he had proposed and recommended him to the presidency of Princeton. Reluctantly he accepted, arriving at the New Jersey college on 16 February, accompanied by his daughter Lucy. The understanding was that the rest of his family would follow in the spring. But this was not to be.

Smallpox was epidemic in Princeton. Dr. William Shippen of Philadelphia, friend of the Burr and Edwards families, was in town, giving inoculations. Vaccinated in February, Edwards seemed at first to be recovering. Then he developed a "secondary fever" that, as Dr. Shippen wrote his wife in Stockbridge, "proved too strong for his feeble frame."

His death on 22 March 1758 stripped Esther of the two men she had most loved and leaned on. She, too, was successfully inoculated, only to die on 17 April, "seemingly without any disease." In Boston, Sally Prince grieved. So great had been her esteem for Esther that she had long "scrupled" in her mind "whether I cou'd love one of the other Sex as I ought to . . . while my Burrissa held the empire of my breast." She remembered "Burrissa" as the possessor of "every tender and generous passion . . . her person . . . handsome . . .

her manners easy . . . her ideas clear, strong & bright." In Esther's death, at twenty-seven, Miss Prince saw fate's "inexorable hand."

7

DR. SHIPPEN took the orphaned children to Philadelphia. His ample brick house on the southwest corner of Fourth and Locust Streets would be their home for two years. Plans called for Grandmother Edwards to pick them up there and take them to her place in Stockbridge. But the family tragedy was not yet finished. Reaching the Quaker City in good health, Sarah Pierrepont Edwards fell ill a few days later of a violent dysentery. On 2 October 1758 she, too, was dead.

The two children, Aaron and Sally, lost father, mother, grandfather, and grandmother—all within thirteen months. Not an easy situation for such young children to understand. Aaron was two and a half, his sister not quite five. It is reasonable to assume that the suddenness of it all was almost impossible for them to take in. Only yesterday they had had around them a loving and protective family, a mother and father and at least the awareness, if not always the physical presence, of grandparents. Now, suddenly, nothing. The ensuing sense of loss, of incompletion, may have contributed to Sally's almost lifelong invalidism and to Aaron's tendency, in his later years, to reach out repeatedly for impossible goals, as though striving to fill an inner void.

It is not known why, after the death of Grandmother Edwards, their care fell to Timothy Edwards, oldest of the Jonathan Edwardses' three sons. At that time Timothy was only twenty-one and a bachelor. Perhaps the mother of the Reverend Burr, still living at the time of his death in 1757, had meanwhile died. In any event, on 22 March 1760, the guardianship papers were issued to Timothy, and by the late fall the Burr children were living in his recently established home on the shores of the little tidal river in Elizabethtown, New Jersey.

2

Resolute Boy

THE FREE BOROUGH of the town of Elizabeth," as King George II called the oldest English community in New Jersey when he chartered it in 1740, had by 1760 acquired four hundred buildings and a profitable leather-treatment industry. Most of the buildings stood near the stone bridge over the Elizabeth River, three miles northwest of the landing site on the Arthur Kill where travelers boarded the ferry for the leisurely twenty-seven-mile sail via Staten Island to New York City. Low-lying hills and windmills broke the horizon north and west of the town. Salt meadows glistened among tall elms in the town itself.

Here Timothy Edwards settled, following his marriage in the fall of 1760 to Rhoda Ogden, member of a large local family long prominent in colonial affairs. The oldest son of Jonathan Edwards was a stolid, thoughtful, self-sacrificing man. During his student days at Princeton his ambition was to be a lawyer. Then came the multiple deaths in his family. Burdened at twenty-one with the Burr children and three or four of his younger brothers and sisters, he turned instead to a mercantile career as more immediately remunerative. Starting their married life with a ready-made family, he and Rhoda eventually added fifteen children of their own. Nine were born in the house on the southern shores of the Elizabeth River.

Esther Burr had spoken of her son as a "resolute boy." That he was, and a doughty battler against the forces of adult rectitude. At any rate, so Aaron chose to remember himself when as an old man he repeatedly related three little tales about his childhood. He was fond of recalling how at the age of four he "took offense" at something his guardian-uncle said or did, ran away from home, and for "three or four days" baffled all efforts to find him. At the age of eight "the prim behavior and severe morality" of a woman guest of the house aroused the rebel in him. Seeing the old lady strolling in the orchard, dressed in costly silks, he ascended a cherry tree and bombarded her with ripe fruit. At ten he ran away again.

This time he headed for the docks of New York, where he signed aboard an outward-bound vessel as a cabin boy. Uncle Timothy tracked him down. Spotting his guardian on deck, Aaron shinnied up the shrouds to the head of the topgallant mast. From there he refused to budge "until all the preliminaries of a treaty of peace were agreed upon." Doubtless, one of the boy's conditions was that his guardian abstain from whipping him "like a sack" as had once happened. Years later, when Burr's bizarre activities were the talk of the country, Uncle Timothy reproached himself for not having done this more often.

Some of Burr's biographers have taken these childhood escapades to mean that Timothy was a harsh and insensitive mentor, and that his lively ward reacted with loathing and defiance. This picture is hard to accept in view of the cordial relations between nephew and uncle after Aaron left the Edwards home, when he and the older man kept in touch by correspondence. Respect and affection characterized the letters on both sides. An ardent patriot during the Revolutionary War, Timothy often scanted his own interests to furnish the Continental Army with badly needed hard money. When a decade after the war he went broke, his nephew, by then a well-paid lawyer, came to his aid. A surviving legal document shows

Aaron undertaking to satisfy his guardian's creditors at "ten shillings on the pound."

Growing up in a crowded foster home could not have been a blissful experience for Esther Burr's resolute son. No wicked guardian is needed to explain his restlessness, his eagerness to get away. Not that Elizabethtown was lacking in activities of interest to a growing boy. There were the waters of the Arthur Kill to sail his skiff on, the Jersey swamps to fish and hunt. There was big-boned, fair-haired Mathias Ogden, one of Aunt Rhoda Edwards's younger brothers, for a companion; gun or rod or tiller in hand, the two boys developed a friendship that would last until Matt's death, at the age of thirty-seven, during a yellow fever epidemic in 1791.

Uncle Timothy saw to it that his orphaned wards were properly educated. Sally attended a girls' school in Boston. Aaron learned "bravely," as a classmate observed, at the Presbyterian Academy in Elizabethtown, where his uncle was a member of the Board of Visitors and where later Alexander Hamilton, newcome to the mainland from his native West Indies, would get his first taste of American education. There were also private tutors. One of them, Princeton-graduate Tapping Reeve, fell in love with Sally, married her, and took her to Litchfield, Connecticut, where he practiced law a few years before opening his famous law school in 1784.

Sally, an invalid much of her life, became the mother of a son, Aaron Burr Reeve, and died in her forty-third year. Litchfielders credited her with a "noble and commanding face and figure" and a gracious manner, but her brother's letters spoke of flaws in her behavior distressing to those who loved her. On one occasion Aaron told his sister bluntly that he would visit her more often if she would refrain from endlessly complaining. In the same letter he expressed pleasure that she had recovered her health, and added, "I hope you are at length convinced that the continuation of it depends on your own conduct." He rebuked her for assuming that nobody was interested in her troubles. He assured her that her friends were "much concerned." He hoped this knowledge would induce her to "use some self-denial." "Do, dear Sister, put the case to yourself," he lectured, "how could you bear to see Mr. Reeves [sic] writhing with Agony from Day to Day, and tortured every night with the severest Pain; and should join to this the reflection, that as soon as he recovered he would by his own Imprudence put himself in the same situation . . . ?" What "imprudence"? The affectionate letter writer gave his sister's problem no name.

2

IN HIS ELEVENTH YEAR Aaron decided that the time had come to enroll in the college at Princeton. Accordingly, he presented himself to the "President and Tutors," an undersized child with tiny fawn-like ears, a nose too thin at the bridge for the wide space between the refulgent eyes—dark hazel in color but seemingly black because of the shade provided by "his projecting eye-bones and brows"—a narrow head, and a delicate oval face of unbelievable prettiness. Apparently the black-robed dignitaries did not even bother to give him the examination his father had drafted nineteen years before. Too small and too young, they told him, and sent him home.

Back in Elizabethtown he studied the curriculum for the first two years at Princeton on his own. No great task for a bright boy, for, according to a traveler from across the sea, the course work at eighteenth-century Princeton was only a little more demanding than that of an English grammar school. Aaron conned Greek and Latin grammar; read Horace, Cicero, the Greek Testament, Lucian and Xenophon; dipped into geography, rhetoric, logic and mathematics; and tried his hand at composition in an essay on the capacity of music to relieve the anxieties of "the meanest Mechanick" and "cheat away the time."

He was thirteen when in the fall of 1769 he returned to Nassau Hall, only to find that again he had overreached himself. Citing the reading he had done at home, he requested admission on the third-year or junior level. His request might have been honored had he been able to make it two years earlier. Meanwhile, Princeton had acquired its sixth president in the person of strong-minded and rock-featured John Witherspoon, longtime pastor of the Laigh Kirk in Paisley, Scotland, and leader of the "popular" or traditional branch of Presbyterianism there. On taking over at Princeton, Witherspoon detected laxities in the admission procedures, and at once resolved to stiffen them. In a notice, published in the spring of 1769, he announced that henceforth a candidate for one of the upper classes must prove his fitness in one of two ways. He must either pass the public examination given just before the fall commencement to the members of the next-lower class; or, if that were inconvenient, he must be tested along with three members "ballotted from the class he desired to enter, and by a fair comparison with them . . . be admitted or degraded." It is not known to which of these ordeals Aaron submitted. Whatever the process, the verdict of the examiners was that if he wished to enter Princeton he must do so, not on the junior level, but on the sophomore level.

Mortified by this blow at his self-esteem, Aaron set out to show the Princeton authorities that they had underrated his abilities. During his first year as a collegian he studied sixteen hours a day. When he discovered that his powers of concentration waned in the early afternoon, he began omitting the midday meal or eating next to nothing at that hour. In the years to come, he would often fast or abstain in this manner. He would refuse to trod the religious pathway of his forebears, but their influence on him was far from negligible. Restraint in the matter of food and drink, a meticulousness bordering on fussiness in the conduct of his affairs as a professional man—these puritanical traits would remain with him throughout life.

When his first examination period at Princeton arrived, he received such high grades that he concluded that little or no further study was necessary. He passed the remainder of his college career in "idleness, negligence and . . . dissipation." So we read in *The Memoirs of Aaron Burr* by Matthew L. Davis, Burr's official biographer. But what "dissipation," one wonders. The college in those days consisted of Nassau Hall, the president's house, the steward's house, the outhouse, the kitchen building, and the shed for the fire engine and its leather buckets. The brash new walls of the main building looked out over a bald-looking campus to the single street of a village that was little more than a clearing in the Jersey forest. There was a tavern—The Hudibras—kept by Colonel Jacob Hyer. There was a general store, a few tinkers' shops, a tinsmith's establishment. The potential for sinning in these places was limited, and the routine of the college left little time for it.

At five in the morning the awakening bell clanged through Nassau Hall's high-ceilinged corridors. Any scholar not out of bed by five-thirty was dragged out by a servant who made the rounds and pounded on every door. The academic day began with communal prayers in the big first-floor chapel with its "small tho' exceeding good organ—the first to be used in any American Presbyterian house of worship—" and its life-size portrait of King George II. The morning prayers gave way to an hour of study, pursued during the winter months by candlelight. Breakfast at eight saw the students at three long tables in the basement dining room. The hours between nine and one were for classroom recitation. After dinner, everybody was free to wander where he pleased for all of two hours. Next came more study, more prayers, supper at five, and still more study after that. At nine all candles went out, all students retired. On Sunday every boy had to attend a church in the morning, a sermon at the college in the afternoon. "Bill-keepers" maintained a relentless watch. Appointed by the president or one of the tutors, these functionaries jotted down the names of boys who absented themselves from prayer or worship service, or otherwise infringed on the rules. Suspected culprits were summoned to Dr. Witherspoon's office. Those found guilty received fines or worse. One offender was expelled for "stealing hens," and was thereafter remembered by a horrified classmate as an "earth-born, insatiate Helluo . . ."

To get into trouble under this regimen, a student had to be enterprising. In afteryears the Princeton townspeople whispered about Aaron Burr, pointing to the lonely grave of a young woman named Catherine Bulluck, said to have died of a broken heart after student Burr seduced and abandoned her. Fed by Burr's then growing reputation as a ladies' man, this macabre tale persisted in the face of evidence, unearthed by a Princeton librarian, that Miss Bulluck had died in the home of an aunt, "quite virtuously," of tuberculosis.

3

Aaron was immensely popular with his fellow scholars. They called him "Little Burr." The nickname was more an endearment than a reference to his size. He had, even then, what the religious writers of the Middle Ages called "charism" and what journalists today call "charisma."

Several of the friends he made at Princeton would remain so as long as they lived. One of them was William Paterson—Judge Paterson at the time of his death in 1806. Of this genial and diffident gentleman, a contemporary remarked that "Mr. Paterson is one of those kind of Men whose powers break in upon you, and create wonder and astonishment." No one could have been physically less impressive; he was slight of build, with a beveled and even-featured face, but Paterson's bland external sheltered a first-rate mind and a glowing spirit. At the time Burr arrived at Princeton, the future judge was just beginning the legal career that would carry him to the attorney generalship of New Jersey, to the convention called to frame the federal constitution, to the United States Senate, to the governorship of his state, and finally to the Supreme Court. A busy career; too busy, he once confided to Burr, confessing that "I have always been fond of solitude, and, as it were, of *stealing* through life."

Growing up in the town of Princeton, an immigrant from Ireland, William Paterson had watched Nassau Hall being built, had spent four happy years there as a student. Since taking his degree in 1763, he had become a sort of unofficial dean of alumni, avuncularly eager to assist and encourage any student, and especially one in whom he saw the promise of a future that would shed glory on his alma mater. "To do you any little services in my power will afford me great satisfaction," he assured Burr in a letter enclosing a few "notes on dancing" that he hoped the young man would be able to use in the preparation of one of his college essays. A century later one of the judge's grandsons, a New Jersey lawyer of the same name, stated flatly that Aaron Burr wrote none of his college essays, that Paterson wrote them all. As after Burr's death several of the essays were published as examples of his youthful precocity, one almost longs to believe this accusation with its ironic overtones. But the "proof" advanced by the younger Paterson—the presence among his grandfather's papers of some of Burr's essays in his grandfather's "chirography"—is too equivocal by far.

Among the other lasting friends whom Aaron acquired at college were Allen Moses of Georgia and Samuel Spring of Massachusetts, both on their way to distinguished ministerial careers. Many other associates of his Princeton days would figure in his life on a less intimate basis. Among them were Brockholst Livingston of the influential New York–New Jersey family, Henry (Light-Horse Harry) Lee of the Virginia Lees, and James Madison of Virginia, future President.

Much of the intellectual life of eighteenth-century Princeton centered in two literary clubs. One was the American Whig Society, founded by Madison, Scottish-born Hugh Henry Brackenridge, and Philip Freneau, subsequently celebrated as the "poet of the Revolution." The other was the Cliosophic Society. Of this group William Paterson was the principal founder and Burr a dedicated member.

Two small rooms on the top floor of Nassau Hall served as meeting places. Tucked under the eaves, low-ceilinged and small-windowed, these chambers became a little stuffy when the "bewigged and beruffled" members gathered. The two clubs regularly flailed at one another in rhyme. Whig-founder Madison versified that the "Clios" were "screech owls, monkeys and baboons" and likely to remain so until they

> . . . skulk within their dens together
> Where each one's stench will kill his brother.

It is easy to understand the future President's reputation at Princeton as "the worst of the Whig poets." How bad the Clios were remains unknown, their rhymed diatribes having succumbed to the merciful erosion of time.

As in all literary societies, the members composed and read papers. Aaron, in one of his, touched on a subject with which his name would someday be sensationally connected. "I . . . shall conclude," he orated on this occasion, "with the single reply of that valiant and honorable personage, Colonel Gardiner, to a person who challenged him . . . to . . . a duel; to whom the colonel replied, with all the boldness and intrepidity of a warrior, and all the god-like reverence of a Christian: 'You know . . . that I have courage to fight with feeble man, but I am afraid to sin against Almighty God.' "

Having found during his sophomore year that he could master the course work at Princeton, Burr in his last two years did not overwork. Neither did he altogether neglect his studies. His essays demonstrate a familiarity with the classical authors on the shelves of the college library. The faculty awarded him first honors for "reading the English language . . . and answering questions on Orthography." They gave him second honors for "reading the Latin and Greek languages with propriety," and graduated him neither at the top nor at the second-from-the-top of his class of twenty-two, but at a respectable level.

The topic of his commencement address, in September 1772, was "Building Castles in the Air." His staccato delivery displeased William Paterson. His message—that a man should not waste his time on dreams—was one that he himself would steadfastly ignore.

4

HE DID NOT LEAVE Princeton immediately after graduation. For slightly more than a year he hung about, idly reading and brooding. His patrimony from his parents was a modest one, but Uncle Timothy had husbanded it well. Aaron had money enough for the time being, and felt under no compulsion to plunge into gainful occupation; he could afford a fallow spell. Occasionally he visited Elizabethtown to sail and hunt with Matt Ogden and flirt with the girls. The Timothy Edwardses were no longer in their New Jersey home. Aunt Rhoda's health, always fragile, had worsened in the moist coastal air. Obligingly Uncle Timothy had moved back to Stockbridge, where the air was drier and where for some years his porch-fronted store on Main Street would be the commercial center of that Massachusetts hamlet.

At Princeton, Aaron's thoughts were beginning to probe the future: what should he do with his life? As an educated man and a gentleman's son, his choices were limited to what was regarded as the approved vocational trinity: medicine, the ministry, or the law. No action on his part, no written word exists to indicate that he felt inwardly impelled toward any of these fields. Even at this early date, one seems to detect at the core of his being a certain noncommitment, an almost paralyzing reluctance to bind himself to a given course, eschewing all others.

Samuel Spring, studying theology in Rhode Island, urged him to prepare for the ministry, reminding him that such "was the prayer of your dear father and mother." Burr did not take this suggestion lightly. No less than fourteen of his classmates were already embarked on religious careers, and his friends took it for granted that as the inheritor of "an almost suffocating odor of sanctity" he would eventually do likewise. During his senior year, practically the entire student body at Princeton had been visited by a religious awakening. Troubled at his inability to join this outburst of piety, he had called on Dr. Witherspoon, and had come away relieved to learn from that stout Presbyterian that what he was witnessing was not religion but fanaticism.

Reading back from coming events, it is clear that in the summer of 1773 his mind was on one of the major themes of his grandfather's writings. Could he commit himself to Jonathan Edwards's contention that the destiny of the human being lies wholly in the hands of God, that whoever thinks otherwise is deluded, that what is called "free will" is only ignorance of cause? In the fall Aaron moved northward in search of an answer to that question. His destination: Bethlehem, Connecticut. There his grandfather's friend and disciple, the Reverend Joseph Bellamy, had established a school of divinity in his home.

Under Dr. Bellamy he studied hard and seriously. On the whole, he liked his situation in the middle-aged minister's household, although, as he pointed out in one of his letters to sister Sally Reeve, "we must always have our Plagues, and you know I am pretty much of a quiddle." What his "plagues" were can be guessed. A well-built man of "commanding appearance," Dr. Bellamy was known for his pungent sermons and resounding voice. He was equally known for his "domineering temper" and for a manner so "abrupt and dogmatical" that it was not uncommon for a prospective student, having reached the parsonage-school in the morning, to pack his bags and depart before the day was done. We can also guess what Aaron "quiddled" about. It was the Bethlehem minister's practice to subject his students to the Socratic method. They were encouraged to state and defend their objections to the tenets of Calvinism. Apparently Burr's objections were numerous and his support of them vehement, for not long after the start of his studies he was bragging to Matt Ogden that he had "the doctor completely under" his thumb.

From time to time he broke off his reading to take tea with Sally and her husband in nearby Litchfield or to record for the Reeves his impressions of life in Bethlehem. "Just been over to the Tavern to buy candles," he reported one snow-bright winter afternoon. "There I saw six Slayloads of Bucks and Bells from Woodberry [Woodbury], and a happier Company I believe there never was; it really did me good to look at them. They were drinking Cherry-Rum . . . and I perceived both Males and Females had enough to keep them in Spirits—the Females especially looked too immensely good-natured to say NO to anything—and I doubt not the Effects of this Frolic will be very visible a few months hence."

These words were written in January 1774. In February, Aaron told Uncle Timothy that he had decided on a legal career. Should he study with Timothy's lawyer-brother, Pierpont Edwards, or with Sally's husband? Timothy replied, "I would have you act your pleasure therein," and in May Aaron moved to his brother-in-law's stolid, pillar-fronted house in sycamore-shaded Litchfield.

Was Burr's rejection of the pulpit tantamount to a rejection of religion? No answer to that query can be essayed without reference to the zeitgeist of late-eighteenth-century America. The drift away from Puritanism had been marked in recent years. Any number of Americans, and especially those who were young and college-bred, were turning to the theories of deism. Inspired by the Enlightenment in Europe, this creed, as could be said of all systems of religious thought, meant different things to different individuals. At the heart of it, however, lay the assumption that "in principle the one true God can be discovered by man's unaided reason." From this fundamental sprang other departures from the prevailing orthodoxy —for one, an aversion to the doctrines of original sin and predestination; for another, a refusal to regard a special revelation from on high as a precondition to the living of a virtuous life; for still another, a belief that "man is congenitally quite capable of knowing and conforming with the will and purpose of his maker." What the deism of his time and place meant to Burr is implicit in the only explanation he ever voiced for choosing the bar over the pulpit. Seven months of close inspection of his grandfather's teachings had convinced him, he said, that "the road to Heaven was open to all alike."

Having chosen the law as his profession, eighteen-year-old Burr appeared in no hurry to master it. His letters from his sister's house in Litchfield to Matt Ogden in Elizabethtown said nothing of Blackstone or Coke. They said a great deal about the young women of the vicinity, enough to give the impression that the little Connecticut town was populated exclusively with luscious girls and that Aaron was in love with all of them and vice versa.

His scholarly cousin, Thaddeus Burr, lived in Fairfield, forty miles away. Aaron took horse there frequently, ostensibly to see his kinsman, actually to spend time with Dorothy Quincy of Boston, passing the summer at Thaddeus's home. Pert, petulant, pretty "Dolly" was already spoken for—by John Hancock, the wealthy Boston merchant, soon to be president of the Continental Congress. This circumstance did not prevent Miss Quincy from complaining that her chaperone seldom allowed her "a moment alone" with this "handsome young man" from Litchfield.

With or without "moments alone," the relationship was conspicuous enough to alarm cousin Thaddeus. He was after all a close friend of the Boston merchant, and so long as Hancock's fiancée rested under his roof his responsibilities as a host were clear. Archly he called the attention of his young cousin to the presence in the Fairfield environs of "a certain Miss———," said to be the owner of a large fortune. Aaron wondered what Matt thought of a man marrying for money. "*Steadily*, Aaron," Matt advised. "Money is alluring . . . but let not fortune buy your peace, nor sell your happiness."

For Aaron these were halcyon days, soon to give way to more troubled ones. During his first summer at Litchfield, twelve of the American colonies named delegates to the First Continental Congress in Philadelphia. The Stamp Act, the Townshend duties, and now a British embargo on rebellious Boston—the Revolution rumbled near. Litchfield was remote from the centers of anti-British turmoil, but in August 1774 the winds of revolt eddied in the Berkshires of adjoining Massachusetts. At Barrington "several hundred persons tore down the house of a man who was suspected of being unfriendly to the liberties of the people." Among the patriot ringleaders were some Connecticut men. The local sheriff had rounded up eight of them and had brought them to Litchfield.

Even as Burr described these events for Matt Ogden's eyes, half a hundred other rebels, "armed each with a white club," were riding into town, seemingly bent on freeing the arrested patriots. "I shall here leave a blank," Aaron wrote, "to give you a few sketches of my unexampled valour, should they proceed to hostilities." But there were no hostilities. Aaron was compelled to complete his letter with the sorry intelligence that the arrested patriots had refused to be snatched from the hands of the law. The "*sneaks*," he lamented, "all gave bonds . . . to appear at the next court for committing a riot."

A few months later the names Lexington and Concord were on local lips. Ablaze with patriotism, Aaron wrote his friend that the two of them must go at once to Massachusetts to join the American army mustering at Cambridge. Matt replied that his affairs held him at home for the time being. Aaron contained himself only until the news arrived of the first full-scale encounter of the Revolution, the Battle of Bunker Hill in June 1775. At this point he rushed to Elizabethtown to pick up Matt. In late July the friends were en route to Cambridge, where George Washington had recently taken over as commander in chief. With them went a letter from Elias Boudinot of Elizabethtown to Washington's aide, Joseph Reed of Philadelphia. Writing as a member of the Continental Congress, lawyer Boudinot recommended Matt for military preferment.

"The young Gentleman . . . that accompanies him," he added, "will be equally taken notice of by you, as the only Son of our old worthy Friend President Burr. He is on the same errand in the hopes of improving his youth to the advantage of his country."

3

Gentleman Soldier

IN THE SUMMER OF 1775 the American camp at Cambridge was a frustrating place for a young man burning to improve "his youth to the advantage of his country." After the skirmishes at Lexington and Concord, some sixteen thousand New England farmers had poured into the area, bringing with them "democratical" notions suitable to a Boston town meeting but out of place in a military setting. Officers elected by their men exercised indifferent control, and the camp was a clutter of verminous huts and tents and whimsically distributed latrines. Chaos confronted Washington when he took over in July. Under those conditions it is easy to understand his failure to act on a request from John Hancock, writing as president of the Continental Congress, that the commander in chief find room on his staff for a couple of inexperienced youngsters named Aaron Burr and Mathias Ogden.

Entrenched at Boston on the far side of the Charles River was the might of Britain. But His Majesty's generals had neither the manpower nor the heart to take the offensive. At Cambridge the supply of ammunition was inadequate, amounting in late summer to "not more than 9 rounds a man." Of artillery, without which an assault on the British occupants of the city was out of the question, there were only a few small fieldpieces, all "pitifully . . . light."

3 / *Gentleman Soldier*

It was not then the stir of battle that Aaron and Matt encountered when they reached Cambridge on the first day of August, but the boredom of military stalemate and disorganization. Brawny riflemen, rushing up from rural Pennsylvania and the backcountry South and spoiling for a chance to shoot at redcoats, relieved the tedium by fighting among themselves. Aaron took to his bed with a "fever."

There he languished, immobilized by disgust, until one morning his ears picked up the excited chatter of soldiers in an adjoining room. Congress, he learned, had decreed an attack on Canada. An army incapable of carrying the war to Boston a few miles to the east had been told to seize the key cities of England's fourteenth colony in the New World, hundreds of miles to the north. One American contingent under Brigadier General Richard Montgomery of New York was about to move on Montreal. Now a call was out for volunteers to follow Colonel Benedict Arnold of Connecticut through the wilderness of Maine to Quebec.

Young Burr was on his feet at once, cured by the prospect of adventure. Matt Ogden, who had already volunteered for the expedition, demurred when his friend announced his intention of going along. At nineteen, Aaron had attained his full height, five feet six inches. Slender and delicately formed, he was much too frail, in husky Matt Ogden's view, to survive the rigors of the impending mission. Little Burr remained undeterred. When during the second week of September the eleven hundred members of the expedition left Cambridge for their port of embarkation at Newburyport, Massachusetts, most of them went by carriage. Aaron gathered a few kindred souls about him and walked the sixty miles.

He was in his element at Newburyport. Every house in town, he wrote sister Sally, was open to a soldier, especially one "join'd with anything of the gentleman." Aaron never forgot his aristocratic origins. He had come into the army as a "gentleman volunteer," and he would serve in this capacity until his receipt two years later of his only regular commission, that of lieutenant colonel. Congress, in the summer of 1775, had authorized Washington "to Victual" volunteers "at continental Expence"; and an order promulgated years later by the General of the Armies further clarifies their status. "The Establishment which Cadets [unattached volunteers] hold in the army," it reads, "gives them a title to the Consideration of Gentlemen, and the General expects they will be treated as such, so long as they meet the character . . . These young gentlemen will however do well to bear in mind that they are to rise by their merits . . ." So long as the volunteer remained unattached, no pay came to him; but promotions in the field by brevet or warrant were possible and those who moved from cadet to subaltern (second lieutenant) or above usually drew compensation accordingly.

At Newburyport, Aaron smiled at a note from a friend begging him after he had conquered Quebec to refrain from turning "Papist" for the sake of the French girls there. He told Sally not to worry on that score. He intended to return to her "as sound as I left you, both in the Head & Heart way."

From Newburyport the expedition moved by sea to the mouth of the Kennebec River on the shores of Maine. Aaron sailed on the sloop *Sally*. "The very name is prosperous," he told his sister. "My next letter will I hope be from Quebec." But his next letter was from Fort Weston, only fifty miles up the Kennebec. Here, too, he was struck by the eagerness of the inhabitants of two blockhouses and a lonely private home to be "obliging" to a soldier. He wrote Sally that he was "falling on roast chickens and wallowing, if you please, in a good feather bed." A cheery, chatty letter, obviously designed to allay the fears of his sister, who had recently vowed that if any harm befell him, neither "the frightful nois of great guns nor the tho'ts of being in a Camp" would prevent her from coming to nurse him in person. "But adieu to these soft Scenes," Aaron wrote her from Fort Weston. "Tomorrow I traverse the woods. You would laugh heartily to see me accoutred in my traveling Dress." He gave her a "scetch" of it: "over a pr of Boots I draw a Pr of Woolen Trousers of coarse coating. A short double breasted Jacket of the same. Over this comes a short coat curiously fringed with a belt as curious. My blanket slung over my back as that's a thing I never trust from me. To these add a Tommahawk, Gun, Bayonet, etc." He observed that his "small round Hat with a snap-up brim" was a gift. It was topped by "a large Fox Tail with a black Feather curl'd up together. The Donor I suppose meant to help my Deficiency in Point of Size."

Notwithstanding his "Deficiency," he held up well on a six-hundred-mile journey so scourged with hardships that the term "March to Quebec" at that time became synonymous with fortitude. From the head of navigation at Fort Weston the troops moved up the Kennebec, some in heavy tub-like bateaux, others on foot. In his journal of the expedition Mathias Ogden wrote of "winter approaching in hasty strides" as the soldiers left the Kennebec in the mountains of upper Maine and pushed west by land to the Dead River. Dying vegetation discolored bleak waters as they struggled across a web of lakes and morasses to the Chaudière, an erratic stream that rises in the hills above Lake Megantic to churn northward a hundred ninety miles to the St. Lawrence.

Three disheartened companies turned back. As the others labored on, food dwindled. Starving men shot dogs and ate them. Strong men gave up. Little Burr swung along as though on a Sunday outing. Fishing and hunting in the Jersey badlands had inured him to the discomforts of marsh and swamp. Plying his skiff on the Jersey waterways had prepared him for handling a 400-pound bateau. On one occasion he and his boatmates failed to understand frenzied signals from companions on the banks of a river, warning them of an impending waterfall. The hurtling craft plunged them twenty feet into lashing foam. One man drowned. Aaron and the others made shore with difficulty. Three decades later a fellow marcher would remember Cadet Burr's uncomplaining endurance and refuse to believe that he "ever intended any ill to his country."

By mid-November the survivors—about six hundred seventy-five—had crossed the St. Lawrence and were at Point aux Trembles (now Neuville), twenty miles above Quebec. Montreal had fallen to the Americans, and Montgomery, utilizing a captured British flotilla, was hastening downriver with clothing and additional troops. At month's end Burr was moving upriver with instructions to accompany him to Arnold's headquarters. The communications he presented to the general included a plea from Arnold that Montgomery make a place for him on his staff. A product of the British army, Montgomery had been complaining about the lack of "gentlemen" among the officers of his "scantily-clad and ill-equipped" army. Apparently Burr measured up in this regard, for by the time of his return to Point aux Trembles he was no longer an unattached cadet; he was a captain and aide-de-camp to Montgomery.

The reinforcements from Montreal raised the invading troops to a strength of about nine hundred. Enough to storm the strongest citadel in North America, guarded by sixteen hundred men? None could say. On 4 December the Americans broke camp to march for the Plains of Abraham adjoining the western walls of Quebec. A council of war produced plans. Two bodies, one under Montgomery and the other under Arnold, were to move simultaneously on the southern gates of the citadel from different sections of the Lower Town lying along the rocky river shore three hundred feet below the fortress.

On the twenty-seventh orders to attack were hastily rescinded, "the weather not being thought proper." Montgomery and Arnold wanted conditions more likely to cloak their activities. These materialized in the early morning hours of the last day of 1775 in the form of a blinding snowstorm.

Burr marched beside Montgomery at the head of the general's column. Bulky scaling ladders and cannon trailed behind them. Thick ice under the snow hampered the advance. Their first destination was a barricade across a rock-bound defile in the Près-de-Ville section of the Lower Town. No resistance there, but it was a different story at the next and higher strongpoint, a cottage equipped with four small cannon. At the approach of the Americans, its defenders, mostly inexperienced citizen volunteers, took fright. Some threw down their arms. All were preparing to flee when a drunken sailor among them decided, before taking off, to touch a match to one of the primed and loaded cannon.

Grapeshot pouring into the imperfect light of the dawn mortally wounded Montgomery and two of his aides. The general's last words were to Burr. "We shall be in the fort in two minutes," he said, even as "he received the grapeshot & fell in his arms." Of those in the front row, only Burr and a French guide remained alive, and Burr's earnest efforts to rally the men behind him and push on were countermanded by an order to retreat from the slain general's successor in command. Aaron's Princeton classmate, Samuel Spring, had come north as chaplain of the expedition. It is from Spring that we have the memorable story of Burr's final actions at Près-de-Ville that morning. As the other Americans fled before the pursuing Canadians, Aaron lingered behind in a futile effort to carry off the body of Montgomery and ensure it a proper burial. The minister's story, as told years later, had Little Burr hoisting the general, a big man, to his shoulders, and then stumbling through deep snow for several yards before dropping his burden to avoid capture.

The repulse of Montgomery's column and the subsequent overwhelming of Arnold's followers at the other end of town doomed this first of what would be two unsuccessful efforts by the Americans to separate the fourteenth colony from Mother England. During the dismal winter of 1776, Arnold and the remnants of his army hung on the fringes of the

Canadian citadel, waiting for reinforcements that when they came were too little and too late against the larger reinforcements reaching the British commander at Quebec. For Aaron the winter was the nadir of his army career. He functioned as brigade major to Arnold, now a brigadier general. He disliked Arnold and described his situation, in a letter to Sally, as "Dirty, ragged, moneyless and friendless."

The "friendless" was heartfelt. Soon after the attack on Quebec, Matt Ogden went home to seek a berth for himself in the New Jersey Line. The friends vowed to keep in touch, and as the months passed with no word from the south, Aaron fretted like a lovesick schoolgirl. When a letter did reach him in May, it told him little more than that Matt had received a commission as lieutenant colonel and would soon be serving in upstate New York with his regiment. The conviction that his chum had deserted him led Burr to dilate on how "promotion, the caresses of the great and the flatteries of the low are sometimes fatal to the noblest minds"; how the "fickle heart, tiptoe with joy, as from an eminence, views with contempt its former joys, connexions and pursuits." Still he stood ready to forgive. "Should fortune ever frown upon you, Matt," he wrote, "should those you now call friends forsake you; should the clouds gather force on every side, and threaten to burst upon you, think then upon the man who never betrayed you; rely on the sincerity you never found to fail; and if my heart, my life, or my fortune can assist you, it is yours."

What the disconsolate major did not know was that his absent friend was not only striving to improve his own lot but Aaron's as well. Burr's valor during the Quebec expedition had already been mentioned in the hall of Congress. On a visit to Philadelphia in the early spring, Matt further touted his friend's abilities. During his stay in the Quaker City he learned from Colonel Joseph Reed that there was a vacancy on the commander in chief's secretarial staff. Reed offered to recommend Ogden, but Matt's heart was set on active duty. He asked Reed to suggest Burr for the position instead. Reed did so, but Aaron was not yet aware of this development when on 26 May he wrote his sister from Fort Chambly in Canada that he was planning soon to "start . . . Southward." His official biographer, Matthew L. Davis, would have us believe that General Arnold objected strenuously to this plan, and that Burr's departure a short time later was an act of disobedience. It is clear, however, that he left Canada with Arnold's blessing, for in his 26 May letter to Sally he pointed out that "I go on public business." It is also clear that his purpose in leaving was essentially personal. Like Matt, he was hopeful of finding to the south a military connection more satisfying than his brigade majorship under Arnold. He had reached Albany, New York, before he learned—not from Matt but from others—that General Washington had reserved a place for him on his staff.

2

A FEW WEEKS after the British evacuation of Boston in May, Washington had hastened to New York City, knowing that the enemy would direct its first major thrust at that seaport. By early June he had accumulated some twenty thousand soldiers, and was struggling to put Manhattan Island and its environs into a posture of defense. At the time of Aaron's arrival, the commander in chief was making his headquarters two miles north of the city limits in a square and imposing mansion on the shores of the Hudson that Burr himself would someday occupy; it was generally spoken of as Richmond Hill. Some historians trace Burr's uneasy relations with Washington to this, their first encounter. If so, it appears to have been a case of instant dislike on Washington's part. The correspondence covering Aaron's journey from Canada shows that he could not possibly have reached Richmond Hill before 12 June—and he was gone from there ten days later. This same correspondence indicates that, even before reporting to Washington, he had told John Hancock of his dissatisfaction with his military situation, and had threatened to resign from the service. Hancock had been a friend to Aaron's father. Acting *in loco parentis*, he advised the young man, instead of abandoning a well-begun army career, to look for a post congenial to his eager temperament. There was a vacancy on the staff of Washington's second in command in New York City, Major General Israel Putnam. Hancock offered to recommend Aaron if he were interested. He was. On 22 June the necessary orders were drawn, and the major transferred his luggage to "Old Put's" headquarters in the large brick structure known as the Warren House at the bottom of Broadway adjoining the Battery.

Some sprightly tales have been written of Burr's service on the staff of the commander in chief: how he offended the stately Virginian by telling him how to run the war, how he examined documents meant only for the general's eyes and undertook an "affair of gallantry" that the general indignantly discovered. These stories all assume that the young major was at Washington's headquarters far longer than he was. None is supported by a shred of evidence, and the thought of Washington's objecting to an "affair of gallantry" is laughable. One gathers from the diary of another of his aides, James McHenry, that most of the general's aides carried on such affairs most of the time.

Still, there is reason to believe that something happened between Washington and Burr during the latter's short stay at Richmond Hill headquarters—something that, were we to know its nature, might explain Washington's frequently ungracious treatment of Burr in the years to come. Clearly something in the manner of the younger man annoyed the older one. Perhaps it was Burr's innate air of superiority, derived from his family background, his habit of holding himself different from other men, an attitude that U.S. Senator William Plumer of

New Hampshire would have occasion to note and record some two and a half decades later. One thing can be confidently asserted. To the romantic stripling, fresh from his moment of glory before Quebec, the company of the methodical, realistic, and apparently disapproving Virginia squire was less than stimulating.

His new boss was of a different stripe. Old Put, a Connecticut farmer in his late fifties and a veteran of the French and Indian War, was rough-spoken, warmhearted, and colorful. His abilities as a military leader were unimpressive, but his roaring ways comported with Major Burr's notions of how a great war should be conducted. "My good old general," Aaron called him.

3

NOT LONG AFTER Burr's shift of assignment, General Putnam welcomed into his headquarters in the Warren House a young woman named Margaret Moncrieffe, a happenstance worthy of a few words because it has given rise to the story of "the pretty spy," a typical example of the many half-factual, half-fanciful tales that have attached themselves to the memory of Aaron Burr. Prior to the Revolution, Putnam and Margaret's father, an American-based major in the British army, were on friendly terms. When the exigencies of war compelled the major to report to his regiment on Staten Island, he left his daughter with strangers in Elizabethtown, New Jersey, and from there Margaret, lonely and friendless, wrote to the general in the hopes that Putnam could make it possible for her to rejoin her father. Unable to help her immediately, Putnam invited Margaret to live in his household in New York until arrangements could be made for sending her to Staten Island.

Margaret has been described as being "a girl of fourteen" at that time, "but a woman in development and appetite, witty, vivacious, piquant and beautiful." At Putnam's headquarters she soon tired of spinning flax with the general's wife and daughters. In search of diversion she took to retiring to the roof of the house. There she entertained herself, sometimes by painting pictures of flowers, sometimes by watching the military activities along the nearby Battery with the aid of a telescope. The story goes that it was Major Burr who, on examining one of her artistic efforts, decided that this pretty child was playing the spy. Obviously her paintings were meant for her father's eyes; just as obviously, that seasoned soldier would find, hidden among the posies, a circumstantial depiction of the American defenses on the New York waterfront.

Burr mentioned his suspicions to Putnam, who mentioned them to Washington, and the commander in chief took them seriously enough to have Margaret transferred to the American encampment at Kingsbridge, some nineteen miles to the north. From there, one morning, a barge supplied by the Continental Congress bore her through Spuyten Duyvil Creek, down the Hudson, and across the Bay of New York to the waiting arms of her father aboard a British vessel anchored off Staten Island. With her went one of Putnam's always eclectically inscribed messages. "*Ginrale* Putnam's compliments to Major Moncrieffe," it read, "has made him a present of a fine daughter, if he don't *lick* her he must send her back again, and he will previde her with a good *twig* husband."

Margaret would be back, although not in the flesh. Twenty years later her memoirs appeared in two volumes. In England she had married a Mr. Coglan, had found him cruel and brutish, and had sought solace in the beds of sundry peers and other notables in London. In *The Memoirs of Mrs. Coglan, Daughter of the late Major Moncrieffe* (London, 1795), she told all. Titillating to American readers was her revelation that she might never have taken the primrose path had she not been forcibly separated from the only true love of her life, a "colonel" encountered during her short stay at Kingsbridge, New York. Aaron Burr? Margaret failed to give a name to the man to whom "I plighted my virgin vow." But who else had a sufficiently wide enough reputation as a Casanova to deserve the compliment? Never mind that Burr was not yet a colonel when he and Margaret met. A year after his death, his Victorian biographer, M. L. Davis, stated flatly that Burr seduced the fourteen-year-old girl. As evidence Davis quoted parts of Mrs. Coglan's memoirs; but Davis's quotes were selective, and a reading of the full text shows that Margaret did not go as far as he. Her story was that she and her American colonel wished to marry. Indeed, they would have done so had not General Putnam refused permission on the grounds that her father would not want her joined to "a good *twig*," who might someday have to train his musket on the major himself.

This fable would outlive its villain. Burr had been in his grave for a decade when an American newspaper saw fit to resurrect the old tale with embellishments. "Miss Moncrieffe, the celebrated British spy," the *New York Sun* informed its readers on 9 July 1846, "was arrested near West Point . . . held in custody as a prisoner of war . . . permitted to enjoy the largest liberty, and indulged freely in her favorite occupations of drawing and painting. Every one admired the beautiful productions of her genius, which she desired to send to her father, but they accidentally passed through the hands of Aaron Burr who [detected] . . . under the paintings, accurate plans of the American fortifications, intended as a guide to the British in their proposed attack on West Point! Burr was up to all sorts of devilment and intrigue, and this fortunate discovery insured him a passport to the acquaintance of the young Amazon. The heartless Burr seduced her—probably she was a willing victim, as she knew enough of human nature to know that a wretch who would betray a female would betray his country . . . But she was disappointed. Burr's property, in this instance at least, held him to his allegiance . . . her father, to make her appear a mere child, represented her to be only 14 at the time of her capture by the Americans—a deception, as she afterwards confessed. She was nearer twenty-two . . ."

4

As General Putnam's aide-de-camp, Burr could not complain of dullness. He was sent into New Jersey and elsewhere on recruiting trips, and was to tell sister Sally that all of their old girlfriends in Elizabethtown had married and were doing their "patriotic duty" by enlarging the population. He crossed the East River to inspect the distribution of American troops and defenses on Long Island, and reported back, accurately enough, that they could not hold against an invading army. He was at Old Put's side on Long Island when the forces of British General William Howe came ashore there and the Americans fell back in disarray. He was in the thick of the operations on the dark, rainy August night when Washington rescued the third of his army that the British victory on Long Island had entrapped behind the flimsy earthworks on Brooklyn Heights. He and his good old general were fleeing the city when, on 15 September 1776, the long-anticipated British investiture of Manhattan took place. Landing from the East River, the enemy deployed along a line roughly parallel with New York's Twenty-third Street. This region was country then, rocky, hilly, and intermittently wooded, with the city standing a couple of miles to the south.

The imminence of the attack had been evident since dawn when heavily burdened English transports were sighted gliding up the river. Washington spent the morning moving from place to place, overseeing the retreat of his troops to Harlem Heights. The actual landing of the British began about 1 p.m., and at approximately this hour Putnam and Burr met the commander in chief near what is now the New York Public Library on Forty-second Street. The aftermath of their brief conference provides some idea of what it was about. Most of the American soldiers were thought to be safely above the British invasion line, but a brigade commanded by Colonel Gold Sellek Silliman was known to be still below it. Apprised of this situation, Putnam sent Burr riding southward in search of the endangered brigade.

5

SLIGHTLY TO THE north and east of the city limits in those days a hill, subsequently leveled, occupied the area now marked by the confluence of Grand and Centre Streets. Here, in the early afternoon, Burr came upon Silliman and his troops, dug in behind the mud walls of a little fortress called Bayard's Hill Redoubt.

There must be twenty versions of what happened next. Some have it that Burr reported not to Silliman but to his artillery officer, Colonel Henry Knox. These versions say that Knox told the troops to stay where they were, and that Major Burr disobediently countermanded his order and led them off. Some accounts make much of the presence among the entrapped soldiers of a young New York artillery captain, the implication being that at Bayard's Hill Redoubt, on that bewildering afternoon, Aaron Burr and Alexander Hamilton took the measure of each other for the first time.

Hamilton's latest biographer, James Thomas Flexner, questions whether the incident ever occurred. He reasons that if during the war Burr had saved Hamilton from capture or worse he would have bragged about it afterwards. But, in what seems to have been his only recorded recollection of the incident, Burr did not mention Hamilton at all. Unfolded many years after the event, his story was that he reported directly to Colonel Silliman and urged him to leave immediately. Since coming to New York, Burr had been a frequent guest at a country home, on the bank of the Hudson, owned by a Major Thomas Clarke and his wife.* Coming and going from the Clarkes' place in what was then the village of Chelsea, he had made a point of reconnoitering the area. He knew every hidden wagon road and path, and was certain he could lead the brigade to safety. None of these statements impressed Colonel Silliman, who pronounced escape impossible and expressed a determination to defend his position "to the last man."

Having failed to lure the colonel out with argument, Burr resorted to ruse. Withdrawing a short distance, he abruptly reversed direction, put spurs to his horse, and galloped back to the redoubt, calling out that orders just received commanded Silliman to abandon fort. Perhaps the colonel fell for this trick; or perhaps, in the interval, he had decided that risky flight was preferable to certain capture. The troops moved out at once, striking westward across the island and then northward, following Burr's directions. A skirmish or two with small parties of the enemy impeded their progress, but by nightfall all of the fleeing troops, save for a few stragglers, were encamped with the rest of the American army on Harlem Heights. Practically an entire brigade had been saved from the filthy and suffocating holds of Great Britain's prison ships. Aaron was proud of his part in this maneuver, and understandably shocked when in the general orders of the following day, the commander in chief neglected to mention it—an omission that Burr would ever after regard as an "intentional slight."

6

LATE SEPTEMBER found the chagrined major at the American camp at Kingsbridge, in the southeast corner of Westchester County, writing another of those letters that dem-

* Mrs. Thomas Clarke, née Mary Stillwell, was an aunt of the woman who later became Burr's wife, Mrs. Theodosia Bartow Prevost. The Clarkes' daughter, Charity, later became the wife of Benjamin Moore, second Protestant Episcopal Bishop of New York and president of Columbia College. It was Bishop Moore who received Hamilton into the Church shortly before the latter's death. (John E. Stillwell, *The History of Captain Richard Stillwell, Son of Lieutenant Nicholas Stillwell*, 45.)

onstrate his talent for putting at ease the minds of the folks back home. Aunt Rhoda Edwards had written of her terror at the fall of New York. Aaron assured her that "the most important revolution that ever took place" was far from lost, that on balance the abandonment of New York City was all to the good. "Our present situation," he explained to his worried foster-mother, "renders their [the British] navy of less service to them, and less formidable to us . . . Add to these . . . the effect the very appearance of success on the part of the enemy has upon our leading men. It arouses them from the lethargy which began to prevail, convinces them that their measures are unequal to their grand design; that the present is the important moment, and that every nerve must now be exerted."

A month later, at White Plains, New York, the major was taking time out from his military duties to ask sister Sally to send him a "Pr of Leathern Drawers" and some "plain Metal Buttons." He had some "cloath" on hand but could not "make it up for want of the Same." In early November all the forces under Putnam were crossing the Hudson, heading south. By early December, Old Put and his staff were in Philadelphia. Here for a few weeks Burr helped carry out his general's efforts to strengthen the defenses of that city, threatened by the British advance across New Jersey—a threat lifted on the day after Christmas by Washington's surprise capture of the enemy outpost at Trenton.

He was at Princeton with his general when, in the spring of 1777, he received a letter from Matt Ogden, registering concern at the slowness of Aaron's rise in rank. Burr's reply to this kindly inquiry tells us a good deal about its author's peculiar makeup.

"As to 'Expectations of promotion,' " he wrote his old friend, "I have not the least, either on the line or staff. You need not express any surprise at it, as I have never made any applications, and as you know me, you know I never shall. I should have been fond of a berth in a regiment, as we proposed when I last saw you. But, as I am at present happy in the esteem and entire confidence of my good old general, I shall be piqued at no neglect, unless particularly pointed, or where silence would be want of spirit. Tis true, indeed, my former equals, and even inferiors in rank, have left me. Assurances from those in power I have had unasked, and in abundance; but of these I shall never remind them. We are not to judge of our own merits, and I am content to contribute my mite in my station."

"Ambitious" is the word most often associated with Aaron Burr, but this letter to Matt Ogden would seem to be that of a man disdainful of ambition, as though, having been born at the top of the heap, he regarded himself as under no compulsion to fight for what he wanted as ordinary mortals must. Was his personal demon at work—the hubris inherited from his Edwards side? One is impelled to assume so. At any rate, he continued to contribute his mite as Putnam's aide-de-camp until at length the promotion he was too proud to seek sought him. When it came, he wrote another and even haughtier letter, probably the only one of its kind ever sent by a junior officer to George Washington.

The word "thanks" does not appear in it, only a formal acknowledgment of the "honour done me," followed by these imperious *obiter dicta:* "I am . . . constrained to observe that the late date of my appointment subjects me to the command of many who were younger in the service, and junior officers the last campaign . . . I would beg to know whether it was any misconduct in me . . . which entitled the gentlemen lately put over me to that preference? Or, if a uniform diligence and attention to duty has marked my conduct since the formation of the army, whether I may not expect to be restored to that rank of which I have been deprived, rather, I flatter myself, by accident than design?" The icy tone could hardly have endeared him to Washington, and we know of no reply.

Burr was in Peekskill when his commission took effect. Dated 29 June 1777, it made him a lieutenant colonel in the Continental establishment. As such, he was assigned to an unnumbered organization designated as Colonel Malcolm's Additional Continental Regiment. At that time the "Malcolms" were encamped near the high bridge over the Croton River four miles south of Peekskill. William Malcolm, their commander, was a wealthy New York City merchant who had organized and equipped the unit as a patriotic duty but who had little military experience and no interest in acquiring more. The fat, easygoing merchant was looking forward to relinquishing the reins to his second in command when, in late July, Aaron reported for duty and gave him a bad moment. Malcolm had expected a seasoned officer. Instead, he found himself shaking hands with what appeared to be a mere boy. The puzzled merchant's first impulse was to remain with his regiment. Within a few days, however, twenty-one-year-old Aaron's obvious capacity for leadership had reassured him.

The regiment meanwhile had crossed the Hudson. By early September it was lying along the Ramapo River in a rock-walled valley known as the Clove on the site of what is now the village of Suffern in Orange County, New York. Here two lines of entrenchments and a blockhouse guarded the southern opening of the pass through the Ramapo Mountains, a fourteen-mile-long declivity regarded by the patriots as the back door to the American forts along the upper Hudson and one that must be kept closed to the enemy at all times. At the Clove, Colonel Malcolm made ready to remove himself and his family to a country home some twenty miles away. "You shall have the honor of disciplining and fighting the regiment," he told Aaron as he departed, "while I will be its father." These words were the New York merchant's last order to his second in charge. For the remainder of Burr's stay with the regiment, he was its de facto commander.

He found the unit badly undermanned, and launched a recruiting drive that within a few months lifted his force of effectives from under three hundred to over five hundred. Discovering the Malcolms to be innocent of discipline, he instituted a draconian regime, lightened by a close attention to the comforts of his men and an often exhibited willingness to care for their needs out of his own pocket. There was no dearth of activity. In late September a contingent of loyalists out of New York overran Bergen County, New Jersey. Spreading across the rich farmlands just south of the Clove, the invaders were devastating orchards, wrecking fences, and driving off cattle and horses. A dispatch from Putnam, alerting Burr to the invasion, emphasized the size of the marauding force, about two thousand men, and urged him to pull back with the regiment into the Ramapo Mountains. Burr sent word to the general that he had no intention of running from an enemy he had not seen. He then moved a picked portion of his troops, not north into the hills, but south into Bergen County.

Not far from Hackensack, he learned that the enemy pickets were less than a mile away. Darkness had come, ushering in what the farmers of the region would later recall as a "night of terror." On the march since early morning, Burr's men were exhausted. Leading them into a sheltering stand of trees along the Hackensack River, he instructed them to rest, and then pressed on alone to reconnoiter. Late that night he stumbled onto an enemy picket of thirty men. All were asleep save two marching sentinels. Having satisfied himself that the outpost was too far from its main body to be heard, Burr sped back to the river, awakened his soldiers, and hustled them forward. As they approached the picket, one of the enemy sentinels challenged. Burr shot the man dead. Simultaneously he gave the order to attack. Within minutes the rest of the picket—an officer, a corporal, and twenty-seven privates—were his prisoners.

News of this coup, racing across the countryside, had a heartening effect on the frightened local farmers. By the time Burr got his captives to the village of Paramus, hundreds of New Jersey militiamen were converging there and calling on the colonel to lead them against the invader. He was making preparations to do so when word arrived that there was no longer an enemy to attack. Alarmed by the seizure of their picket and the rising of the militia, the loyalists had already taken off for New York, leaving most of their plunder behind them. In the midst of these excitements, another dispatch came in from Putnam. It directed the regiment to join Washington and his army, then engaged in a futile effort to dislodge the enemy from British-held Philadelphia. Two and a half months later the Malcolms were at Valley Forge, where one winter night Colonel Burr's reputation as a disciplinarian came close to costing him his life.

7

SIX MILES SOUTH of the raddle of ramshackle huts and open graves that was Valley Forge that bitter winter, a small stony-bottomed stream parted the encircling hills to form a convenient passageway known as the Gulph. On the assumption that if the British came out of Philadelphia they would approach the camp at this point, the Gulph was heavily manned.

Throughout much of the winter the craggy and wooded outpost was a trouble spot. Often, for several nights running, the militiamen on guard there would raise false alarms, spreading the word that the redcoats were coming, and forcing the officers at the Forge to turn out their troops and spend the night preparing for an enemy who never appeared. Washington's aides puzzled over the cause of these irruptions. Some attributed them to the desolation of the spot, arguing that the frequent false alarms at the Gulph represented nothing more than the efforts of bored and lonely men to entertain themselves. At least one officer, General Alexander McDougall of New York, blamed the difficulty on the lax discipline often found at remote outposts. Impressed by the good order prevailing among the Malcolms, he persuaded Washington to detach Colonel Burr to the Gulph as the commanding officer there.

Burr at once imposed a rigorous discipline. During the daylight hours, drills were frequent and regular. At night, the colonel slept little. Men assigned to outlying posts and accustomed to resting on them, or even walking away, discovered that the new officer in charge had a habit of appearing on the scene when least expected. At first, resentment confined itself to mutterings. Then threats were heard. Then Burr was told of a plot. Some of the malcontents, banding together, were planning to remedy what they considered an intolerable situation by murdering the man responsible for it. Having ascertained the night set for this attempt, Burr saw to it that the guns of his men were relieved of cartridges before calling them out for a late parade. The night was brilliantly moonlit, the inspecting officer's eyes alert as he passed down the line. Suddenly a man stepped from the ranks, leveling his musket point-blank at the colonel. "Now is the time, my boys," he shouted as the click of his emptied gun rang out sharply but harmlessly in the cold, still darkness. As it did so, Burr drew his sword. With a swift downward movement he all but severed the man's arm above the elbow. There were no more mutinies or false alarms at the Gulph.

8

By spring 1778, when the British left Philadelphia and Washington's army dogged them across New Jersey, the Malcolms had become an instrument in Burr's hands. Few regimental commanders were more respected by their men, few more unquestioningly obeyed. At the battle of Monmouth Courthouse near what is now Freehold, New Jersey, the regiment went into action as a part of the American left wing under Major General William Alexander Lord Stirling of New Jersey. Sometime that afternoon Burr espied a detached party of enemy troops emerging from a copse at the far end of the miry ravine below him. Signaling his men to change course, he was riding hard in the direction of the isolated redcoats and would ever be convinced that he would have taken all of them, when one of Washington's aides rode up with orders that, pending further word, he was to hold his troops where they were.

For a considerable period the Malcolms had no choice but to remain in the muddy ravine. It was a dangerously exposed position. A cannonball smashed and killed Burr's second in command. The colonel's horse fell dead beneath him, and he himself scrambled free, unhurt, only because, seconds before, he had moved his leg from its accustomed place alongside the animal's saddle girth. If Burr ever harbored any kind thoughts toward George Washington, they dissolved forever at Monmouth Courthouse. In the battlefield region that Sunday, 28 June 1778, the thermomcter stood at 96 degrees. The glowering sun and the leaden air accounted for almost as many deaths as ball and scattershot. Aaron's constitution had faltered under the strain of the preceding months, and at Monmouth he experienced the onset of the distressing symptoms—nausea and prolonged headaches—that would plague him off and on for years to come.

A dramatic outgrowth of the battle was the court-martial of Major General Charles Lee, Washington's English-born second in command. Fleshless, scarecrow-like Lee had begun the attack on the British that Sunday. Few incidents of the Revolutionary War have been the source of more controversy than his decision not to engage the enemy when he found him in the late morning. Some authorities say his retreat was precipitate and unnecessary, and that it robbed Washington of an opportunity to demolish the main British army and end the war then and there. Others contend that, had Lee not acted as he did, even the partial American victory at Monmouth would have been impossible.

When in the early afternoon of that day of heat and horror,

Washington encountered Lee near the causeway over Middle Spotswood Brook, he upbraided him in the presence of his staff—a reprimand so sprinkled with profanity, according to one of several highly varying stories of it, that "the leaves shook on the trees, charming, delightfully." Lee afterwards declared that his superior had uttered false accusations, detrimental to his character. In an indiscreetly phrased letter, he demanded an opportunity to justify himself "to the army, to Congress, to America, and to the world in General." Washington obliged by authorizing a court-martial, which pronounced the defendant guilty on three charges and suspended him from his command.

Disenchanted with the commander in chief, Burr found it easy to side with the disgraced officer. His letter on the subject to Lee has not been found. It is a safe guess, however, that like many top Americans of his day, and several subsequent historians, he regarded the downgrading of Lee as deliberately engineered to protect Washington's status as a military leader. All that remains of Burr's post-Monmouth correspondence with Lee is the latter's reply, with its plaintive assertion of Lee's intention to retire to his Virginia plantation "and learn to hoe tobacco, which I find is the best school to form a consummate *general*."

Burr was not present at any of the twenty-six sessions of the court-martial in July and August. On instructions from Washington, he was shifting from point to point along the shores of the Hudson, gathering information on the movements of the British in and above New York City. This assignment completed, he rejoined the main army in time to put his regiment on the road, the Malcolms having been ordered to occupy the little forts at West Point in the Hudson River Highlands.

Burr did not accompany them, for by fall his health had so deteriorated that he was forced to take leave for several weeks. Part of this period he spent with friends in Elizabethtown, part of it at a country home called the Hermitage in

Paramus, where one of his companions was a Mrs. Theodosia Bartow Prevost.

It was during this interval of rest and attempted recuperation that he wrote Washington, asking permission "to retire from pay and duty" until his health returned. "My anxiety to be out of pay arises in no measure from intention or wish to avoid any requisite service," he explained. "But too great a regard to malicious surmises, and a delicacy perhaps censurable, might otherwise hurry me unnecessarily into service, to the prejudice of my health."

Burr's letter was dated 24 October 1778, His Excellency's stern answer two days later. "You . . . carry your ideas of delicacy too far," Washington wrote, "when you propose to drop your pay while the recovery of your health necessarily requires your absence from the service. You therefore have leave to retire until your health is so far reestablished as to enable you to do your duty."

One of Burr's biographers writes that, on receipt of this letter in late October, the colonel nobly "repaired forthwith to West Point, being unwilling to accept a furlough unless his pay was intermitted." In fact, he took his time about it. On the first Thursday of November he was resting at Mrs. Prevost's home in Paramus and writing sister Sally of his plans to pay her a visit in the near future. "I shall bring a French master with me—a slovenly old French priest," he informed her, "and one or two servants." Much of November had gone before he reported to his regiment at West Point. There, two months later, he bade the Malcolms farewell and crossed the Hudson to White Plains, to begin what was to be his last regular military assignment.

9

Throughout the war the Continental Army controlled the tree-darkened Highlands that flank the Hudson

River for some sixteen miles northward of Peekskill. Just below Peekskill, the American outposts east of the Hudson stretched along the upper reaches of Westchester County. Fifteen miles farther south, the forward pickets of the British, anchored at Kingsbridge, extended in a southeasterly direction across what is now the upper Bronx of New York City.

In between these two often shifting lines lay the "Neutral Ground." To people acquainted with the wartime activities in this rolling country of lush pastures and little mills on brisk streams, the term "neutral ground" conjured up nights illuminated by burning barns, scenes of women and children fleeing in fright from ransacked farmhouses, of grazing lands stripped of livestock by gangs of roving banditti, some known as "skinners" and riding under the patriot banner, others as "cowboys" and riding under the Union Jack. Writing of the Neutral Ground soon after the war, Washington Irving recalled how, in "the zeal of service," both skinners and cowboys "were apt to make blunders, and confound the property of friend and foe. Neither of them in the heat and hurry of a foray, had time to ascertain the politics of the horses and cows which they were driving off into captivity; nor when they wrung the neck of a rooster, did they trouble their heads whether he crowed for Congress or King George."

At White Plains, at the center of this no-man's-land, stood the headquarters of the American officer in charge of the Westchester Lines. It would be interesting to know why in January 1779 George Washington approved the appointment of twenty-three-year-old Burr to this post. Always extremely sensitive to criticism, the commander in chief must have been aware that Burr was not numbered among his admirers, and was probably in sympathy with the so-called Conway Cabal, whose adherents were in favor of replacing the Virginia squire with General Horatio Gates or some other high-ranking officer. If Washington's objective was to put the critical colonel outside the main thrust of the war, he could not have found a better way of doing so. Command of the Westchester Lines offered difficulties and challenges, but little or no opportunity for deeds of glory. In truth, it came near to being what was known in American military parlance as a "granny's post."

At White Plains, Aaron faced no known and visible enemy, but that shadow play of changing loyalties and guerrilla warfare common to areas never wholly secured by either party to a war. His mission was to protect the Westchester County farmers—but from whom? He had barely arrived at White Plains, in a heavy snowstorm, when he discovered that the American camp was filled with stolen goods and animals, and that his horsemen were "infatuated with the itch for scouting," from which excursions they returned laden with spoil.

To General McDougall, his superior at Peekskill, the new commandant wrote that never before had he "wished for arbitrary power," but at this moment he "could gibbet half a dozen *good* whigs with all the venom of an inveterate Tory." After he took over on the thirteenth, his first official act was to see to it that every heap of stolen bedding, every head of cattle and "fat horse" was returned to its owner, irrespective of whether the owner adhered to the patriot or to the Tory cause. He then reformed his command and strengthened and tightened his outposts.

In short, the son of stern Puritan divines tolerated no nonsense on the Westchester Lines. "Van Tassel and Fisher of the Militia," his order book reads for 18 February 1779, ". . . tried . . . for Plundering, found guilty and sentenced to receive Van Tassel 50 and Fisher 25 lashes. The Commanding Officer approves the foregoing Sentences and Orders them to be Inflicted Immediately, the Plunderers to be whipped at the Plundered House, to Ask Pardon of the Injured Party and be kept in Confinement till they make satisfaction."

In afteryears Samuel Young, one of the men who served under Burr at White Plains, used strong words to describe the qualities the young officer brought to his duties there. When the colonel assumed the command, Young recalled, the troops were "negligent and discontent," but in a "few days these very men were transformed into brave and honest defenders . . . After the first ten days there was not a single instance of robbery . . . The inhabitants, to express their gratitude, frequently brought presents . . . but Colonel Burr would accept no present. He . . . paid in cash for everything that was received, and sometimes, I know . . . these payments were made with his own money . . . His diet was simple and spare . . . Seldom sleeping more than an hour at a time, and without taking off his clothes . . . between midnight and two o'clock in the morning . . . he visited the quarters of all his captains, and their picket-guards . . . the distance which he thus road [sic] every night must have been from *sixteen* to *twenty-four* miles; and . . . he never omitted these excursions even in the severest . . . weather; and except the short time necessarily consumed in hearing . . . complaints and petitions from persons both above and below the lines, Colonel Burr was constantly with the troops."

Not quite "constantly." Samuel Young himself noted that on two nights the colonel disappeared, and Burr's order book records his absence from the lines for a brief period in late February 1779. Tradition says that on these occasions he stole from camp on a horse named Old Put, and crossed the Hudson, then alive with British shipping, to spend a few hours with Mrs. Prevost at the Hermitage in Paramus. So viable was this tradition that as late as 1887 *Harper's Magazine* was telling the story of "Aaron Burr's Wooing" in energetic verse:

> Eight miles to the river he gallops his steed,
> Lays him bound in the barge, bids his escort make speed,
> Loose their swords, sit athwart, through the fleet
>   reach yon shore;
> Not a word! not a plash of the thick-muffled oar!
> Once across, once again in the seat, and away—
> Five leagues are soon over when love has the say;
> And "Old Put" and his rider a bridle-path know
> To the Hermitage Manor of Madame Prevost.

10

AARON WAS still unwell when he took charge of the Westchester Lines. On 10 March 1779 he informed Washington that his condition had become "unequal" to his responsibilities, and expressed a wish to resign from his command and the army sometime "before the 15th of March." In his reply, granting permission, Washington expressed regret both at "the loss of a good officer" and at the ill health which occasioned it. One gathers from this exchange of polite notes that the dominant emotion on both sides was relief—Washington's at being rid of a troublesome officer, Burr's at being freed from an assignment that promised no military advancement. Not that his resignation put a total stop to his contributions to the war effort. During the next few months, wandering restlessly from place to place in search of health, he often carried verbal orders for Generals McDougall and Arthur St. Clair. He was in New Haven in July 1779 when an enemy force attacked that Connecticut community. Placing himself at the head of an improvised army of militia and Yale College students, he helped hold back the burning and plundering invaders long enough to let most of the women and children flee the town.

With this action he ended his Revolutionary War career. In the years ahead he would speak of it often, always proudly and in the manner of a man who felt that he had given a good account of himself. Colonel Burr had earned his credentials as a patriot and a dutiful son of his country. There would come a time in the closing years of his life, a troubled time, when this vision of his younger self would help to sustain him. It was of no small importance to him that he had earned the right to be called "Colonel," a title that would cling to his name the whole of his life and beyond. After New Haven, he fastened his attention on civilian matters. There were his interrupted law studies—these must now be completed as rapidly as his health permitted. There was also the matter of Madame Prevost.

4

Love and Law

After the battle of Monmouth in the summer of 1778, Washington's army, moving northward through New Jersey, rested a few days in the sprawling and largely Dutch-inhabited settlement of Paramus. The general and his "family," his staff, arrived on 10 July. Arrangements had been made for them to establish headquarters in the house of a Mrs. Watkins, but at midday the commander in chief changed his plans after being handed a note from Theodosia Bartow Prevost, wife of a British colonel fighting in the West Indies, and sister-in-law of the British general who even then was assembling in East Florida the forces that a few months later overran Georgia and crushed the rebellion in that state.

"Mrs. Prevost," Theodosia wrote, "Presents her best respects to His Excellency . . . requests the Honour of his Company as she flatters herself the accomodations will be more Commodious than those to be procured in the Neighborhood. Mrs. Prevost will be particularly happy to make her House Agreeable to His Excellency and Family—Hermitage Friday Morning eleven o'clock."

The general and his staff remained only long enough at the Watkins house to dine with its mistress and her two daughters. They then rode on to the more "commodious" Hermitage. There, according to the diary of one of Washington's young aides, they found, in addition to Mrs. Prevost and her family, some "fair refugees from New York." And there "we talked and walked and laughed away the leisure hours of four days and four nights and would have gallanted and talked with them till now, had not the General given orders for our departure."

Standing well back from the post road, a Gothic-style house built of the red sandstone native to the vicinity, the Hermitage was the scene of numerous such revels during the Revolution. Its latchstring was always out to American officers traveling in the area. General Charles Lee, Colonel James Monroe, Commissary General Jeremiah Wadsworth, and Colonel Robert Troup were among the many who found in the company of its engaging occupants and in its spacious rooms a respite from the rigors of camp and battlefield. Patriot officers were not its only distinguished guests. In the late summer of 1780 Peggy Shippen Arnold, en route from Philadelphia to join her husband at West Point, spent a night there. A month later, Arnold's treason having meanwhile come to light, Peggy stopped there again. It is on this occasion that she is alleged to have confessed to Theodosia—who as the wife of a British officer could be expected to be sympathetic—that she had known of her husband's defection to the enemy from the beginning and had encouraged and abetted his schemes.

Living with Mrs. Prevost during the Revolution were some of her children, her mother, Mrs. Ann De Visme, and her half sister, Catherine De Visme. Mrs. Prevost, born toward the end of 1746, was the only child of her mother's marriage to Theodosius Bartow, an attorney in Shrewsbury, New Jersey. Her mother was one of the six daughters of Richard and Mercy Sands Stillwell, of Shrewsbury, all noted for their beauty. On her side of the family, the American line went back four generations to Nicholas Stillwell. He arrived in the New World from England in 1638; he lived first in Virginia, and then in and around New York City, while it was still New Amsterdam, where his exploits as an Indian fighter earned him a nickname, "Valiant," and a lieutenancy in the militia. On the paternal side the line traced to Theodosia's grandfather, the Reverend John Bartow, sent to America in 1702 by the Propagation Society of London to establish the Church of England in Westchester County, New York. Theodosia never knew her father. His death, on 5 October 1746, preceded her birth by several weeks.

She was five when her mother became the wife of Captain Philip De Visme of the British army, a union that, by the time of the captain's death in 1762, had given Theodosia three half brothers and two half sisters. Her own first marriage, in 1763, was to Captain—later Lieutenant Colonel—James Mark Prevost. Then commander of the British forces in New Jersey, James Mark (anglicized from Jacques Marc) was a native of Switzerland, he and his older brother, known to history as Brigadier General Augustine Prevost, having left that country to join the English army when Parliament authorized His Majesty to grant commissions to foreign Protestants. Five children were born to Theodosia and the colonel. Little is known of the daughters—Sally, Anna Louisa, and Mary Louisa—and the absence of their names from a will left by one of Theodosia's aunts in 1815 suggests that by that date all three were dead. Although the sons, Augustine James Frederick and John Bartow—commonly addressed as Frederick and Bartow—were mere boys when the Revolution began, they were ensigns in the British army when it ended and had served in Jamaica with their father.

As was common among British officers stationed in the colonies, James Mark Prevost acquired property. One of his purchases included two hundred forty acres in Bergen County, listed on the books as "the Provost Patent in the Ramapo Tract." On the eve of the war he sold this parcel to Robert Morris of Philadelphia and two other land speculators. It is not known what then remained of his New Jersey estate, although family letters indicate that the Hermitage was not a part of it and that the colonel's holdings consisted chiefly of a different house and a lot. When in the early 1770's Prevost's orders took him to the West Indies with his regiment, the 60th Foot, his wife and children and some of the De Vismes were residing at the Hermitage. Local tradition says Aaron Burr paid his first visit there in the fall of 1777, while he and his regiment were encamped only fifteen miles away at the Clove. And at some unrecorded moment during his many ensuing visits Colonel Burr fell in love with Colonel Prevost's wife.

2

SHE WAS ten years his senior. In the eyes of a man deprived of his mother in infancy, her maturity was no doubt an attraction, to say nothing of her amply confirmed status as a parent. Not unnaturally, some of the neighbors saw the situation in a different light, the daughters of Governor William Livingston of New Jersey, for example. As Burr's visits to the Hermitage grew more frequent, Sarah (Mrs. John Jay) and Susanna Livingston assumed that the dashing young officer was interested in Catherine, Theodosia's younger half sister. Colonel Robert Troup, their friend—and Burr's—put them straight. "I have had the opportunity," that enterprising young man reported to Aaron, "of removing entirely the suspicion that they had of your courting Miss De Visme. They believe nothing of it now, and attribute your visits to Paramus to motives of friendship for Mrs. Prevost and the family. Wherever I am, and can with propriety . . . I shall represent this matter in its true light." For obvious reasons, propriety was of the essence. Theodosia supplied it, taking care, as long as her husband lived, to keep the increasingly warm relationship with Burr on an intellectual plane.

She was not accounted a beauty by her familiars, although the disfiguring scar on her face, often mentioned by contemporaries, was not there when Colonel Burr met her, being the result of a burn suffered later. The only extant likeness, a tiny head engraved on an old watch, suggests a certain fine-drawn daintiness, and James Monroe's epithet for her, "my dear little friend," suggests petiteness.

Whatever her externals, they were of no moment to Aaron. He loved the inner woman. "She had the truest heart," he said, "the ripest intellect, and the most winning and graceful manners of any woman [I] ever met." She was educated beyond most of the women of her day—no trifling consideration to the son of the second president of Princeton. She spoke French fluently, and was given to quoting the French and Latin poets. Like Aaron, she was an avid reader. Jean-Jacques Rousseau's *The Social Contract, or Principles of Political Right* stood on the Hermitage bookshelves, alongside the works of most of the other literary greats of the day.

Great was the colonel's pleasure at finding this "winning and graceful" woman as well acquainted as himself with the *Letters to His Son and Others* by the fourth earl of Chesterfield. As Grandfather Edwards had feasted on Newton and Locke, so Burr—ever since the appearance of the *Letters* in 1774—had feasted on Chesterfield. What the *Letters* meant to him was brought out over a century ago by James Parton, the first of Burr's biographers to treat his life and character *in extenso.* It was Parton's feeling that when Burr abandoned the faith of his fathers he found a substitute in "the gospel according to Philip Dormer Stanhope, Lord Chesterfield." As Parton wrote, "Chesterfield himself was not a more consummate Chesterfieldian than Aaron Burr. The intrepidity, the self-possession, the consideration for others, the pursuit of knowledge, which Chesterfield commends, were all illustrated in the character of the young American, who also availed himself of the *license* which that perfect man of the world allowed himself and recommended to his son." Burr seems to have taken everything in the *Letters* at face value, from Chesterfield's advice to his son to clean his teeth regularly, to his lordship's graphically supported contention that a gentleman is free to do whatever he pleases so long as he does it with style. Theodosia was more discriminating. "The indulgence you applaud in Chesterfield," she told Aaron, "is the only part of his writings I think reprehensible. Such lessons from so able a pen are dangerous to a young mind, and ought never to be read till the judgment and the heart are established in virtue." To which she added, cunning charmer that she was, "You have, undoubtedly, a mind superior to the contagion."

3

For more than a year after his resignation from the army, Colonel Burr was a nomad: now in New Haven, now at the Hermitage, now a guest of cousin Thaddeus in Fairfield, now with the Reeves in Litchfield, now in Middletown, Connecticut, staying at the home of Titus Hosmer, the leading lawyer of that place and one of Connecticut's delegates to the Continental Congress. For many months the goal of these wanderings, the recovery of his health, remained a *fata morgana*. Far from disappearing, the symptoms that had shortened his military career first intensified so rapidly and then abated so slowly that at times he despaired of ever resuming his interrupted law studies on a systematic basis. His medical bulletins to his friends during this period picture a man swinging wildly from elation to despondency and back again. The tone of one letter is euphoric, with its author confident that a cure is at hand, thanks to the restorative effects of a mineral spring near Paramus. In another he describes himself as so low in spirits that he sees no one and partakes of no amusement. In still another, he tells William Paterson that his health "will bear no imposition. I am obliged to eat, drink, sleep, and study as it directs." As late as the fall of 1780, Robert Troup was convinced that his friend was not long for "this wrangling world."

It has been suggested that the dilemma in which the colonel now found himself, a man in love with a married woman, contributed to the breakdown of his health—a possibility he himself may have recognized when he admitted to Paterson that "I am often a little inclined to *hypo*." Certain it is that during that always trying adjustment, the move from military life to civilian life, he had his share of worries.

Among other things, Mrs. Prevost was in trouble. As the wife of an officer fighting with the enemy, her situation in Bergen County was at all times a ticklish one. It grew more so toward the end of 1778 when the New Jersey legislature passed the so-called "forfeiting act," setting up machinery whereby the property of "certain fugitives" and other "offenders" against the patriot cause, British army officers included, could be confiscated by the state. Theodosia had long been concerned over the fate of her husband's property, and the succeeding months brought further reason for apprehension. Hitherto, Colonel Prevost had served in distant Jamaica. Now he was on American soil, participating in the subjugation of Georgia by the army commanded by his brother, General Augustine Prevost. On 4 March 1779, at "Miller's-burnt-out-bridge on Briar Creek," a detachment led by Theodosia's husband provided "His Majesty's troops" with their "final victory . . . over the Rebels" in Georgia. The same issue of the Savannah newspaper that described this engagement carried a proclamation designating the colonel as lieutenant governor of the state's newly formed royal administration. Obviously this was a temporary arrangement, for by the end of the year James Mark Prevost was in England, and by the spring of 1780 he was again in Jamaica.

As these threatening developments took form, Theodosia's friends rallied to her support. William Paterson, attorney general of New Jersey since 1776, wrote on her behalf to the Commissioners for Forfeited Estates in Bergen County. James Monroe and Robert Troup exerted what influence they could. It was true, Troup pointed out, that Theodosia "is the wife of an enemy. What then? Must we abandon human nature in order to manifest our patriotism? I can affirm that Mrs. Prevost is a sincere and cordial wellwisher to the success of our army . . ."

In the fall of 1779 the Bergen County commissioners served Theodosia with an inquisition. This document put her on notice that the procedures leading to a possible seizure of her husband's holdings were already in process. In a petition to the legislature, praying that the further procedures of the commissioners be stayed, Theodosia stated that "as a British subject" her husband had taken "no decisive part in the Revolution" until His Majesty's troops "possessed themselves" of Georgia, "and a summons from their commander-in-chief left him no alternative what line of conduct to pursue." The action of the House of Assembly in ordering her petition filed for consideration at its next sitting gave her a breather, time in which to consider what defensive strategy to pursue. Through members of the family, her husband suggested that she and her daughters join him. Theodosia gave his plea some thought. In the end, however, she sent him a ring containing a lock of her hair, and stayed where she was, fearful that, were she to join Prevost at this point, the commissioners would move against his estate at once. In addition, her little girls were delicate, and she herself was not well.

Burr was often at her side during these trying months. His hand is visible in all her decisions. In the summer of 1780 she got in touch for the first time with his sister in Litchfield. "Your health, my Dear Madam," she wrote Sally Reeve, "has given me the utmost concern . . . Though I have not the happiness of a personal acquaintance, as the sister of my inestimable friend, you are justly entitled to my highest regard . . ." Theodosia invited Sally and her husband to visit the Hermitage, saying that there Mrs. Reeve "would find a sympathizing friend who would feel a singular pleasure to be in the smallest degree conducive to your recovery."

Writing to Troup from Paramus a few months later, Burr

announced his intention in the near future of visiting his sister. He did not journey alone. By mid-December Theodosia and her daughters were living temporarily in Sharon, Connecticut, only a short ride from Sally's house—and well beyond the reach of the Bergen County commissioners. Apparently this flight was in some way instrumental in saving her husband's holdings, for his house and lot did not appear among the some five hundred estates eventually confiscated under the New Jersey forfeiting act.

4

THROUGHOUT THIS TIME of troubles, Burr was in steady correspondence with his fellow officer and "particular friend," Robert Troup. The young men had served together during the futile attempt of the rebels to hold New York City in the summer of 1776. Captured by the British in August of that year and exchanged in December, Troup had later fought in one of the battles leading to the surrender of Burgoyne at Saratoga. A year younger than Aaron, bright and genial, with a good head for figures, Troup in 1778 was selected by the Congress as secretary of the newly formed board of war. When only a year later that body was dissolved, he was given the same position on the board of treasury, only to resign in disgust on 8 February 1780. His duties had become so heavy, he complained to Aaron, that he had to work "even on Saturday nights, which places me below the level of a negro in point of liberty." As Troup prepared to put behind him the "cursed slavish life" of the board of treasury, he proposed that he and Aaron find a competent mentor and complete their reading for the bar together. In retrospect, one has to smile at the effusions of the letters in which the disgruntled treasury official urged this course of action: his statement that he felt he would learn more in "three years" with Burr than in "six years without him," his hope that the two of them would live together "during life." In later years, as a staunch Federalist, Troup would be one of Burr's most outspoken political critics.

Partly because of Burr's faltering health, partly because of his preoccupation with Theodosia's problems, the young candidates for the bar had trouble in arriving at a mutually agreeable plan. In a desultory way, Burr had already started reading in the office of Titus Hosmer in Middletown. Troup had nothing but praise for that respected attorney. He pointed out, however, that both of them would probably wish to practice in New York or New Jersey, and the law of Connecticut was far different from that of either of those states. His own choice was Richard Stockton of Princeton. Burr countered by suggesting William Paterson, but before this letter arrived, Troup had committed himself to Stockton, only to realize at once that he had made a mistake. Although a relatively young man, Stockton, as the result of harsh treatment by the British while a prisoner of war, was incurably ill. To make matters worse, Troup was unable to find living quarters in the Princeton countryside, and "I must have a retired place or none," he wrote Burr in April 1780. "To lodge in Town would be to live exposed to a world of Company and objects that would constantly draw my attention from study." In a previous letter he conceded that Stockton's "unmarried daughters" might prove a distraction to them both. Now he repented "of my Folly in acting as I . . . have done. It is therefore out of my Power to write to you [about his plans] with much certainty at present . . ."

But things sorted themselves out. During the summer Titus Hosmer died, releasing Burr from whatever arrangements he had made at Middletown. Troup, meanwhile, had extricated himself from Stockton and was studying with Paterson in Raritan, New Jersey. There, in midwinter, his friend joined him, Burr's health having taken a turn for the better, and Mrs. Prevost having been safely deposited in Connecticut.

Mild-mannered William Paterson was a demanding tutor. He insisted that his students be grounded in the fundamentals of jurisprudence and familiar with the many branches of learning that feed into it. Time was when Burr and Troup might have relished this time-consuming procedure, for in the beginning they had looked forward to their study together as a leisurely and monastic interlude, during which they would not only acquire the skills of counselor and advocate but would also drink deep of the Pierian spring. Subsequently, these dreams had given way to more practical considerations. Their determination, in late winter, to leave Paterson and find a teacher willing to qualify them for the bar as rapidly as possible rested on simple human need. Both of them were broke. Twice in recent months Troup had borrowed small sums from Aaron, and contrary to popular opinion, Aaron was not rich and never had been. His generosity to his soldiers had seriously diminished his share of his father's modest estate, and in the spring of 1780 he had further depleted his resources by investing in an expensively outfitted privateer that was chased ashore and wrecked before it could bring prizes into port and produce profits for its owners.

Not that a lack of money, or even the absence of it, ever deterred Aaron Burr from spending it. In February 1780 he endeavored to come to the rescue of a companion of his army days, a Major R. Alden, who had just received his discharge and was having a hard time financing his own studies for the bar in Fairfield. Burr suggested that the major move to Raritan and act as a tutor to Mrs. Prevost's sons, Frederick and Bartow. The boys' father had already sent them home from Jamaica or was about to do so, and Burr was planning to bring them to Raritan at "the beginning of April." If Alden wanted the job, Burr would pay him sixty pounds a year, and see to it that he had free access to Paterson's law library. Nothing came of this effort to help not only a friend in need but also Mrs. Prevost, who could not afford a tutor for her boys. In a profuse letter of thanks, Alden turned down the job. Nor were the young Prevosts brought to Raritan, for by "the beginning of April"

Burr and Troup had left Paterson and were continuing their studies under attorney Thomas Smith in Haverstraw, New York.

A respected figure in the profession, Smith had promised, for a fee, to "fit" both of them "as soon as possible for submission to the bar." At Haverstraw, Aaron went back to the regimen of his first year at Princeton—sixteen hours of concentrated reading and note-taking a day. Speed was becoming more important with every passing moment. Already under consideration was the bill that, as voted by the New York legislature in the fall, would bar Tories from practicing law in New York State until 1786, thus opening the field wide to newly created barristers. Smith had assured Burr and Troup that "with close application on your part, I should be able in a short time to introduce you to the bar, well qualified to discharge the duties of the profession, with honour to yourselves and safety to your clients." He was as good as his word. By early fall, Burr and Troup were spending much of their time in Albany, hopeful of getting their licenses during the forthcoming session of the state supreme court.

5

BUSY AND TRYING DAYS for both of them. At one point Burr wrote Theodosia that he was not sure Troup was going to make it. He need not have worried about that "master of the friendly hint and the suave suggestion." Troup would get his license; and after a satisfactory career as a lawyer and a jurist, he would become rich and fat as a land agent, a lobbyist of more than ordinary skill, an intimate of practically every contemporary figure of any importance, and a promoter of the Erie Canal. On the other hand, Burr, during the final phase of his run for the bar, found himself coping with a special difficulty. Under a ruling of the New York supreme court, dating back to colonial days, no attorney could be admitted to practice in that tribunal unless he could show at least three years of training under a qualified instructor; and Burr could claim no more than twelve months of such study at the most. In recent years, to be sure, the court had made allowances for the unavoidable interruptions of wartime, but every exception required the unanimous consent of the bench, and Burr's path was not a smooth one. As the brisk upstate-New York fall merged into the rough upstate-New York winter, he endeavored to get in touch with each of the three sitting judges.

In a letter to Chief Justice Richard Morris, he pointed out that he had begun his studies before the war, at a time when the "present rule" was nonexistent—a misstatement, as the rule was over ten years old; "surely," he added, "no rule should be intended to have such retrospect as to injure one *whose only misfortune is having sacrificed his time*, *his constitution*, *and his fortune*, *to his country*." This letter was written in Albany in late October. During the preceding month Mrs. Prevost had sent encouraging news from Sharon, where she was living in a rented cottage she once described to Burr as "à la rustique chez votre amie." A doctor friend had assured her that another of the supreme-court justices, John Sloss Hobart, was sympathetic with Aaron's situation, and confident that both he and Troup would be admitted to the bar in October.

But that month passed with no word from the court, and December was well underway, with Albany buried in "twelve or fourteen inches of snow," before Burr was able to get an interview with the third justice, Robert Yates. Of this conference he wrote Theodosia that "I really fear Yates is playing the fool with me. Still evasive . . . Tomorrow I must and will come to a positive eclaircissement." But it would be some time before he and Yates came to an understanding, for on the morrow the judge was too busy to see him.

Coming and going from Albany during these months of anxious waiting, Aaron dabbled at his legal studies and availed himself of whatever distractions were at hand. He read more of Rousseau's works and discussed them by mail with Theodosia. He struggled with the repeated attacks of what today would be called migraine that were to trouble him for the next twenty years. "A sick headache this whole day," he wrote Theodosia. "I took the true Indian cure . . . Made a light breakfast of tea, stretched myself on a blanket before the fire, fasted till evening, and then tea again. I thought through the whole day, that if you could sit by me, and stroke my head with your little hand, it would be well."

On its pine-covered bluff above the Hudson, the Albany of 1781 was still a frontier town, its streets unpaved, its steeply gabled houses separated by patches of white clover and wild strawberry, its three thousand inhabitants dependent for their water supply on the beautiful but filthy river. Still, it had its social life, and the handsome son and grandson of Presidents Burr and Edwards of Princeton was not permitted to fret in solitude. Members of the local society, male and female, sought him out and plied him with invitations. A representative of the leading family, Philip Van Rensselaer, called on him, pronounced his quarters "inelegant and inconvenient," and insisted on providing him with better ones in the home of two maiden aunts. "Obliging ladies," Burr told Theodosia, "and (incredible!) good-natured. The very paragon of neatness. Not an article of furniture, even to a teakettle, that would soil a muslin handkerchief. I have two upper rooms."

For his friend in Sharon he jotted down a running account of his comings and goings. He commanded her to do likewise. To those close to him, Burr was always a preacher. He would do well as an attorney, but the pulpit or the classroom would have been a more congenial rostrum to a man driven by a passion to direct the lives and mold the thoughts of others. He instructed Theodosia to devote a half hour of every day to writing him. Except "on special occasions," she was not to exceed the half hour by so much as a second. In issuing this order, he was thinking of her health. It is a measure of his affection for her that he already realized that, if he ever had her, he would not have her for long. "I know you to be ill," he wrote, "and dangerously so"—a reference, no doubt, to the cancer that would eventually destroy her. He was convinced that the cottage in Sharon was too "à la rustique" for the hard Connecticut winters. He insisted that she install a Franklin stove, nay, two Franklin stoves. "If you have fears about *Brat* [one of her children], I have none. He will never burn himself but once; and, by way of preventive, I would advise you to do that for him." Thus spoke the student of Rousseau, who, as the Dr. Spock of his day, had recommended this practice to parents. Burr's preachments could be harsh. "You wrote me too much . . ." he complained of one of Theodosia's letters. "You must . . . deal . . . more in ideas . . . Write me facts . . . and don't torture me with compliments, or yourself with sentiments to which I am already no stranger."

Dispatched in late December, this rude missive was that of a man worried about his woman's health and still on tenterhooks about his future as a lawyer, if any. The year had gone before the supreme court acted. Some accounts of Burr's premature admission to the bar depict him as valiantly battling every established lawyer in the state, to win for himself alone a waiver of the three-year rule. As a matter of fact, the justices had been pondering the problem for some time, and shortly after the first of the year they issued a blanket edict, stating in effect that for the next few months considerable leniency would be extended to candidates whose training had been cut short by service in the patriot cause.

On 19 January 1782, Burr was licensed as an attorney in the supreme court. This action did not bring him to the end of the line. In those days the New York bar operated under a "simulacrum" of the system in England, where lawyers fall into two classes—attorneys or solicitors, privileged to prepare cases for submission to the courts, and barristers, privileged to plead them there. As an attorney, Burr could practice in the supreme court, subject to the guidance of an experienced lawyer. Under the regulations then in effect, he was supposed to remain at this clerk-like level for two years before applying for his license as a counselor-at-law, the next and highest status. But in the early 1780's, lawyers capable of pleading before the supreme court were in short supply, and on 17 April 1782, "having on examination been found of competent ability and learning," Burr was qualified as a counselor, an action that permitted him to open an office in Albany and begin on his own the profession that would be his bread and butter for the rest of his days.

6

SOMEWHAT IN ADVANCE of these events, both so important to him, came another, equally fateful. On the next to last day of 1781, Theodosia's half sister, Catherine De Visme, was writing him from Paramus that "if you have not seen the York Gazette, the following account will be news to you: 'We hear from Jamaica that Lieutenant Col. Prevost, Major of the 60th foot, died at that place in October last.' " Very possibly it was not news to him. It stands to reason that word of the death of Theodosia's husband in mid-October 1781 had reached him before the announcement of it in the 19 December issue of the *Royal Gazette* in New York City. Strong evidence of this is found in the lack of surprise at the development on the part of those concerned. Indeed, the suspicion arises that for a year or more they had known that James Mark Prevost was not expected to live. Support for this possibility is found both in Colonel Prevost's monthly reports to his superior and in the correspondence of his American family. In one of the colonel's 1780 communications to London, he complained that most of his captains were in the battalion infirmary at Spanish Town, Jamaica. He described them as "fitter for Chelsea," the soldier's hospital in London, than for "active service." In another, he foresaw the "annihilation" of his regiment unless it were moved soon from fever-stricken Spanish Town to a healthier climate. Theodosia, in her note to Mrs. Reeve in the summer of 1780, expressed the wish to treat Sally "with the familiarity of a sister." Catherine De Visme, in the letter calling Aaron's attention to the news, identified herself as "Your Friend and Sister." Even Burr's abortive attempt to underwrite the education of the two Prevost boys can be construed as indicating that by early 1781 he had reason to believe that the day was near when their mother would be free to marry.

Now that she was free, she hesitated. She wanted time to think, to consider. He went often to see her, to press his suit. She had become the closest of friends with his sister and her husband, "the squire," as Burr called patient, good-hearted Tapping Reeve. She and Aaron met sometimes at the Reeve home in Litchfield, sometimes in Sharon, once at a medicinal spring near Albany. He was still a candidate for the bar, not yet licensed, but he repeatedly assured her of his optimism on that score, of his confidence that, once in practice, he would be able to support her. But "I wish you to study for your own sake," she wrote him, "to ensure yourself respect and independence."

Gently she put him off. She was more sensitive than he to the opinions of others. She reminded Aaron that her attentions to him had always been "pointed enough to attract the observation of those who visited the house." As a result, the two of them had been "the subject of much inquiry, conjecture, and calumny." She yearned to say yes to his proposal, if only "to suppress their malice," but there were certain things to be weighed. She made no direct reference to her illness, but a consciousness of it, as a detriment to the marriage, lay behind every word. It subjected her to spells of melancholy, and he had complained about these. "You speak of my spirits," she wrote, "as if they were at my command, or depressed only from perverseness of temper . . . Believe me, you cannot wish their return more ardently than I do."

A sick and troubled woman, she wanted to, and she feared to. "When I am sensible I can make you and myself happy," she told him, "I will readily join you . . . But till I am confident of *this*, I cannot think of our union. Till then I shall take shelter under the roof of my dear mother, where, by joining stock, we shall have sufficient to stem the torrent of adversity."

She had not spent all of her time in Connecticut since her flight there a year and a half before. She had passed the warm months of 1781 "under the roof" of her mother, and in the summer of 1782 she returned to the Hermitage, this time to help with the preparations for the approaching marriage of half sister Catherine to Dr. Joseph Browne. Burr followed, and if she had not already said yes, she did so now. On the second of July, in a double ceremony performed by the Reverend Benjamin Van Der Linde of the local Dutch Reformed Church, Catherine De Visme became Mrs. Browne, and Theodosia, Mrs. Aaron Burr. From Albany later that month Mrs. Burr was writing Sally Reeve that "the particulars of our wedding . . . may be related in a few words. It was attended by two singular circumstances, the first is that it cost us nothing. Brown and Caty had provided abundantly & we improved the opportunity. The fates led Burr on in his old coat; it was proper my gown should be of suitable gauze; ribbons, gloves, etc., were favors from Caty. The second circumstance was that the parson's fees took the only half Joe Browne was master of; we partook of the good things as long as they lasted and then set out for Albany, where the want of money is our only grievance . . . Our House is roomy but inconvenient, I have not yet been able to procure a good Servant tho' my dear Burr has taken all imaginable pains; but we have one in prospect . . ."

As the Burrs settled into their "roomy but inconvenient" house in Albany, the world around them was changing rapidly. In late 1782, King George III conceded the loss of his American colonies. By spring 1783, it was known that the British would be evacuating New York City as soon as the definitive treaty of peace was signed. To Burr it was plain that the resumption of American control there would be attended by a plethora of legal problems, making the busy seaport on the Hudson a good place for a beginning lawyer to be. In the fall he was writing Timothy Edwards of his determination to leave Albany, adding that "this resolution has cost me much anxiety, but as I have adopted it . . . from the purest motives, I trust I shall have no cause to repent it." His practice had prospered, but with Burr what he called "the want of money" was then—and thereafter—endemic. One of the purposes of the letter to his uncle was to ask that long-suffering gentleman to arrange for a payment in advance of a sum coming due on one of the young attorney's cases. The move to New York, Aaron explained, called for more funds than he was "able to command." As usual, Uncle Timothy took care of matters. By 25 November 1783, when the British left New York City and the Americans marched in, the Aaron Burrs were living at Number 3, "Wall Street, next Door but one to the City Hall."

5

The Scarlett of the American Bar

COVERING NO MORE than three hundred and fifty acres between the Battery on the south and the Fields (now City Hall Park) on the north, and with a population of about twenty thousand, the New York that greeted the Aaron Burrs was far from being Walt Whitman's "million-footed Manhattan." Already in evidence, however, were some of the qualities of the future super-city—cosmopolitanism, freedom of manner, enterprise—and in the winter of 1783–84 enterprise was in high demand, after seven years of occupation by the enemy. Some ten thousand loyalists had gone with the British, depriving the town of many of its most productive minds. Since the official cessation of hostilities in early 1783, hundreds of people had flocked in from the countryside, choking the narrow streets and further taxing already overburdened hostelries. Some came to stay, others only long enough to ascertain the condition of properties seized for use by the British during the occupation, after which they were happy to leave a city struggling with an acute shortage of goods and services, and with soaring prices—half a dollar a night for a bed, a dollar for a dinner without wine!

The British conqueror had converted the best buildings, including most of the churches, into riding halls, prisons, hospitals, and storage dumps. The prettiest edifice of all, Trinity Church at the head of Wall Street, was a spectral ruin, a victim of the first of the two fires that, engulfing the city during the war, had left seventeen hundred buildings in ashes. For months after the Burrs arrived, the newspapers were filled with references to the "burnt district," with stories of lawlessness and disorder in a region between Broad Street and the East River strewn with temporary shacks and known, because of their roofs, as Canvas Town. On evacuation day and for some time thereafter, the city was more garrison than community: streets torn up to make trenches, barricades at main intersections, forts on every hill.

Not only must these eyesores be removed, old facilities repaired and new ones built, but the operations of a municipal administration must be put underway. In an election in December, held under a charter framed long before the war, the voters selected the fourteen members of the local lawmaking body, interchangeably known as the Common Council or the Corporation. On 5 January, in accordance with the state's seven-year-old constitution, Governor George Clinton appointed the wealthy landowner and expert on Indian affairs, James Duane, as the first post-Revolutionary mayor. Meeting with the council two days later, fifty-one-year-old Duane articulated the stresses of the hour by announcing that, instead of the public entertainment customarily expected of a new chief magistrate, he was contributing twenty guineas toward the relief of the hungry and the homeless in the poorer wards. When in February the Mayor's Court opened its doors after a hiatus of many years, it was to cope with a snarl of problems: questionable property titles resulting from careless handling of the records during the long military seizure, puzzles connected with the confiscation and disposal of the holdings left behind by fleeing Tories, losses arising from the suspension of rents during the war and from the changing money values and tightening credit that came in its wake.

Troubled waters everywhere. Wonderful fishing for a capable new lawyer like Aaron Burr.

2

He was not the only neophyte to sense the opportunities in the shipping center at the foot of Manhattan and to pull up stakes elsewhere to take advantage of them. His old friend, Robert Troup, had moved down from Albany. So had Alexander Hamilton, having been admitted to the bar on the basis of a program of formal training even skimpier than Burr's. Add to these names perhaps another fifty, including those of the three Livingstons—Edward, Brockholst, and Robert R.—and you have the cream of the crop of lawyers who, beginning their careers in the aftermath of the Revolution, would dominate the bench and bar of New York for years to come. Of these practitioners, a twentieth-century lawyer has written that "in the last years of the eighteenth century and the beginning of the nineteenth, the standing of the New York bar for learning, efficiency and character has never been exceeded, and perhaps not equalled in any later period."

Even in this dazzling company, Burr stood out. "Very able," wrote Gouverneur Morris, an able practitioner himself and not a man to scatter praise indiscriminately. The surviving court minutes leave the impression that for well over a decade Burr handled at least as many and probably more of the writs coming before the benches of his city and state than any other attorney. His annual income, during this period, exceeded $10,000, a large sum for those days. It has been said that on occasion he got that much for a single case, but the often advanced assertion that his fees were uniformly exorbitant rests on a misconstruction of his remark to a fellow barrister that "I have never undertaken the management of a cause of any moment in error under £40." Alexander Hamilton's law-practice papers show that in such actions Burr did not always charge that much. There is the further fact that, although many of his causes were in error—cases carried on appeal from a lower to a higher forum—many were not. Neither were all of them of "moment," in the sense of involving important legal issues or large amounts of money. They ranged in magnitude from a suit to recover a stolen horse to such classics of the juridical arena as *People v. Levi Weeks*, the most sensational criminal trial of the era, and *Le Guen v. Gouverneur & Kemble*, a long and complicated litigation, so crucial to the development of commercial law that, since its resolution in the spring of 1800, it has been cited more than a hundred times in American tribunals.

It is the judgment of Burr's peers that he was not a scholar of the law. Neither its theory nor its philosophy interested him. He was preeminently the technician. Not the appellate courts, where logic counts heavily, but those lower courts where issues of fact are brought *de novo* to a judge and jury, were his element. Lawyers speak of these tribunals as *nisi prius* courts, and it has been said that, as "a *nisi prius* lawyer," Burr may be termed "the Scarlett of the American bar." The reference is to James Scarlett, first Baron Abinger, a nineteenth-century English barrister acclaimed for his proficiency before a jury. Eugene Didier wrote of Burr in a 1902 issue of a legal magazine: "As a lawyer who possessed all the legal weapons of offense and defense, and could use them with skill and daring, his equal has never lived."

When Burr opened his office in New York, American law was a pathless wilderness. Not so much as a single case had been reported in the thirteen states. There were no written decisions to cite, no rules or precedents to follow. To a practice begun under these challenging conditions, he brought a memory characterized by Didier as "wax to receive and marble to retain." He brought also a tireless capacity for work. "No lawyer," according to Didier, "ever appeared before our tribunals with his case better prepared for trial, his facts and legal points being marshalled for combat with all the regularity and precision of a consummate military tactician." The colonel, Didier noted, "was never surprised by his adversary, but often took his adversary by surprise." One of his causes pitted him against a group of attorneys who were upholding the distribution of an estate under a recent will. This will depended upon an older one, and when the lawyers for the estate limited themselves to a formal proof of the existence of the previous document, Burr caught them unprepared, and demolished their case, by proving the earlier will to be invalid.

The pedagogue at home was the pedagogue in the office. "Now, move slowly," he instructed his clerks. "Never negotiate in a hurry." He had his own version of the old saying, "Never put off until tomorrow what you can do today." That, in his opinion, was "a maxim for sluggards." A better reading of it, he said, was "never do today what you can do as well tomorrow, because something may occur to make you regret your premature action." "Things written remain," he cautioned his clerks and his own adherence to the ancient caveat, especially in his political correspondence, would be the despair of future historians. It was probably to his overworked assistants that he uttered his often-quoted pronouncement that "the law is whatever is boldly asserted and plausibly maintained," a statement that, had it originated with one of his more admiringly remembered colleagues, would now no doubt be somewhere engraved in marble.

He had a number of partners. The first of them, William T. Broome, was the son of the onetime president of the New York Chamber of Commerce. Probably the most talented and undeniably the most colorful was Boston-born William Coleman. Product of a poorhouse, handsome in a flushed and full-faced way, humorous and debonair, Coleman later became a political affiliate of Alexander Hamilton and the first editor of one of the latter's journalistic mouthpieces, the *New York Evening Post.* (Though in principle Coleman was opposed to dueling, his blitheness of spirit was demonstrated on one occasion when, having been drawn into a challenge and having mortally wounded his opponent, he hastened back to the *Evening Post* "and got out the paper in good style although half-hour late.")

Burr's clientele spanned the social worlds of his day. He worked for William Malcolm, his old colonel, handled properties in Maine for distant English owners, represented the De Peysters, a prominent New York family, and acted as general counsel for the even more prominent Livingstons. Among his many clients were Elias Boudinot, the well-known New Jersey statesman; James Rivington, the Tory printer; and Mrs. Maria Reynolds. An unknown when Burr obtained a divorce for her in 1793, Mrs. Reynolds would achieve notoriety as the "other woman," following Alexander Hamilton's published confession, a few years later, of an extramarital affair during his years as the Secretary of the Treasury. When Abraham Yates, a quarrelsome Albany politician, sued a couple of election inspectors for denying him the vote because of his refusal to take an oath upholding the federal constitution, he hired Burr as his counsel—a good choice, it would appear, for the inspectors apologized, the suit was withdrawn, and in the next election Yates voted sans oath. Other lawyers frequently utilized his expertise. Thomas Jefferson, for example, once solicited Burr's assistance in connection with the case of a Virginia physician who was endeavoring to recover a sum of money from Robert Morris of Philadelphia.

Most of the contemporary word portraits of Burr the lawyer focus on his abilities as a performer in the courtroom. He is reputed to have remarked that he never spoke in that setting "with pleasure to himself, or even self-satisfaction," and it has been observed that "he seemed unconscious of the effect

. . . he produced on the minds of his hearers." His personal appearance, one gathers, had much to do with the impact of his arguments. It is hard to believe that he was as noble-looking in person as he is in some of John Vanderlyn's portraits. For one thing, the nose was slightly off-center, "rather inclined to the right," in the words of a contemporary—an aberration of which the colonel, a vain man, was uncomfortably aware. Overall, however, the picture he presented to juries and spectators was a striking one.

"Under the medium height," to quote a first-hand observer, "his figure was well proportioned . . . forehead . . . high, protruding but narrowing directly over the eyes and widening immediately back. The head was well, even classically, poised upon his shoulders; his feet and hands were peculiarly small; the nose rather large, with open, expanding nostrils; and the ears so small as to be almost a deformity. But the feature which gave character and tone to all, and made his presence felt, was the eye. Perfectly round, not large, deep hazel in color, it had an expression which no one who had seen it could ever forget"—a comment echoed almost two centuries later in the statement of a gifted short-story writer that "there was a kind of dominion promised in his gentlest glance." Until late in life his hair remained long and thick, save for a pronounced receding in the front. He wore it massed on the top of his head, anchored by a small shell comb, and generously powdered. His customary dress consisted of a single-breasted jacket, usually blue, a standing collar, a buff vest, and dark trousers. On winter days he came and went in a fur cap, buckskin mittens, and long, full cape. To many observers he seemed, on the whole, a rather wispy figure, his smallness of stature accentuated by the massiveness of his head and by what an English-born observer described as "that urbanity which, while it precludes familiarity, banishes restraint."

He had overcome the tendency of his college years to speak too fast. In the courtroom he spoke deliberately, conversationally, contriving to be weighty where the substance demanded, but never ponderous; sarcastic on occasion, but never overbearing. He had a genius for brevity, for compacting a mountain of matter into a molehill of words: no pleonasms, no expletives, and few metaphors.

Much of his appeal as a speaker lay in a quality of manner often commented on by associates. Burr was a good raconteur and a good talker, but he was an even better listener. Asked wherein his excellence resided, one associate replied, "In his manner of listening. He seemed to give your thoughts so much value by his manner of receiving [them], and to find so much more meaning in your words than you had intended. No flattery was more subtle." Carried into the courtroom, this attitude did him no harm with juries.

3

No truly stenographic report of any of his courtroom speeches was ever made. Our closest look at Burr the spellbinder is furnished by a sketch of one of his arguments in James Hardie's *An Impartial Account of the Trial of Mr. Levi Weeks for the Supposed Murder of Miss* [*Gulielma*] . . . *Sands*. Hardie was a spectator at this dramatic occurrence, and his impressions, recorded on the scene, identify *People v. Levi Weeks* as the first murder mystery of consequence to find its way into an American tribunal.

The bill of indictment against Weeks, a pleasant-mannered young carpenter, alleged that on the night of Sunday 22 December 1799 he took twenty-two-year-old Gulielma Sands away from the Greenwich Street boardinghouse where both lived, "beat and abused her," and threw her into a well owned by the Manhattan Company in a northwest corner of the city known as Lispenard's Meadow. Long before the indictment was brought in on 28 March 1800, public opinion had condemned Weeks. Handbills, appearing around town, generated distrust of him by describing the nightly appearance "of ghosts and goblins at the Manhattan Well." In the dainty phrase of the day, Gulielma was described as "generous with her favors." Having enjoyed them, rumor ran, the young carpenter proposed marriage, later repented of doing so, and committed murder to avoid keeping his promise. On the first morning of the trial, according to Hardie, "the concourse of people was so great, as was never before witnessed on a similar occasion." It took place in one of the larger rooms of Federal Hall, as City Hall was renamed when it became the meeting place of the first Congress under the federal constitution. Even so, only a fourth of those wishing to attend could get in. As the proceedings began, the others could be heard in the street outside, chanting "Crucify him! Crucify him!" Opening at 10 a.m. on the last day of March, the trial continued with only one recess until the verdict was returned three days later at three o'clock in the morning.

Some seventy-five witnesses were sworn in. From three written accounts of the testimony, a synopsis of the drama emerges. About eight o'clock on the Sunday night before Christmas, young Weeks was seen holding Gulielma's coat for her as she prepared to leave the Greenwich Street boardinghouse. None of the observers of this scene was certain that Weeks departed with her, although some of them assumed as much. Testimony offered at a later point indicated that he did leave the house for a time, but not with Gulielma. On returning about 10 p.m., he asked if Miss Sands was in her room, and displayed anxiety on being told that she was still out. No sign of her that night, or the next. By Christmas Eve, all concerned were worried. One witness quoted Weeks as voicing the belief that the missing girl was "now in eternity." Asked why he thought so, he declared that "he had frequently heard her say she wished that she had never been in existence." In Gulielma's possession when she left the boardinghouse was a muff she had borrowed from a friend. On the morning after

Christmas a small boy, at play in Lispenard's Meadow, saw the muff floating on the surface of the Manhattan Well. Later that day, workmen recovered the body.

The whole burden of the case for the state was borne by Cadwallader David Colden, the assistant attorney general. Hardie's story of the trial puts no less than six lawyers on the defense team. The official account by William Coleman, as clerk of the court, lists only three: Burr, Alexander Hamilton, and Brockholst Livingston. The question naturally arises: how could a young carpenter afford this high-powered representation? The answer lies in the date of the trial, spring 1800. Coming up shortly was a crucial election, one that would determine which of the current political parties—the Federalists or the Democratic-Republicans—would control the state of New York. Conceivably, neither Hamilton, acknowledged leader of the Federalists, nor Burr and Brockholst Livingston, prime movers in the opposition, could pass up the opportunity of participating in a case that had riveted the attention of voters throughout the commonwealth.

Burr opened for the defense, and it is this address to the jury that Hardie sketched in his *Impartial Account*. He thought it "one of the most masterly speeches, both with respect to composition and oratory," he had ever heard. Burr, according to his paraphrase, began by complimenting the jury for "the great calmness" with which its members had listened to the evidence presented by the state. "He observed," Hardie wrote, "that, notwithstanding the intimacy between the prisoner and the deceased, it did not amount to courtship . . . that the deceased had manifested [as much] partiality for other persons as for Mr. Weeks; and that she was . . . in the habit of going out late at night, and . . . hence it might be fairly concluded that if [her] conduct . . . had not been irregular, it at least had been very indiscreet, and might have exposed her to danger, both with respect to her morals and person." Burr then warned the jury against paying attention to popular rumors and related the case of a man who, having been indicted for murdering a young woman, "got affrighted and, in order, as he hoped, to save himself from the agony of death upon the gibbet, got another woman to represent the person who was supposed to be missing. The fraud was discovered and this connected with other circumstances induced the jury to bring their verdict *guilty*. The man was hanged, but the woman supposed to be murdered afterwards made her appearance . . ."

Hamilton's law papers indicate that all the defense attorneys participated in the questioning that followed. Burr rose once to argue a point concerning admission of evidence, only to be "waved down" by one of the three judges. After the defense rested at 2:35 p.m., 2 April 1789, he read to the jury a brief passage on "Presumptive evidence" from Hale's *Pleas of the Crown*. Hamilton then pointed out that, as everyone present was "sinking under fatigue," the defense would waive summations and "rest the case on the recital of the facts" by the bench. Justice John Lansing of the state supreme court then gave the charge, and the jury retired—to return five minutes later with a verdict of *not guilty*.

4

FROM 1784 TO 1800, nearly every cause of consequence at the bar of New York placed Burr and Hamilton in the same courtroom. Sometimes they were on the same side, sometimes opposed. Whether they were cooperating or contending, their coming together was always a confrontation. In time their rivalry became principally political. In the beginning it was professional, but no less intense, the simple presence of the two men in the same place imparting a spark to the proceedings. Parton passes on a tale that a legal friend, who had heard it from Burr, passed on to him. In the course of an action that Burr and Hamilton were managing conjointly, the question came up as to which of them should be the last to address the jury. This was the place of honor. When there were two or more lawyers on a side, the etiquette of the bar assigned it to the most respected of them. Modesty was not one of Hamilton's attributes, and he insisted that he speak last. Burr politely acquiesced. In conferences the two of them had discussed all aspects of the case, and when his time to speak came, Burr presented not only the points he himself had worked up but also those Hamilton had developed. Hamilton, in consequence, was left with practically nothing to say, and the story goes that the question of who should speak last never arose between them again.

General Erastus Root, who as a New York lawyer often watched them at work, concluded that they were "much the two greatest men in the state, perhaps in the nation." He was struck by the difference in their styles of speaking: Hamilton "flowing and rapturous," Burr "terse and convincing." The young New York attorney, John Van Ness Yates, put his view of the contrast another way: "Hamilton addressed himself to the head only," Yates said. Burr "first enslaved the heart, and then led captive the head."

The imagination handily conjures up the picture of the two of them in the courtroom together: both small, about five foot six, both large in the legal atmosphere they understood so well; both quick to see the humor in a situation and to overlook the weaknesses of human nature; both generous, Hamilton so given to putting his talents at the disposal of the poor that colleagues had to remind him that "charity cases never yet provided a lawyer with a living" and Burr always ready, if not always able, to give a friend a handout; each carrying within himself a troubling awareness, Hamilton of the illegitimacy of his birth, Burr of the awesome impeccability of his.

Hamilton was cognizant of Burr's abilities and Burr of Hamilton's, but neither was overwrought with admiration for the other. Still, like a web that is visible in some lights and not in others, one espies a certain regard running between them, the sort of unwilling regard that can so easily burgeon into a love-hate relationship. Before political differences came along and cast them as adversaries, literally to the death, Hamilton spoke of Burr as "a man of honor, influence, and ability," and Burr gave Hamilton timely notice that a house he was renting was for sale and could be had at a bargain price. Both were fixtures in the city's best drawing rooms, and both were fond of women and above-average attractive to them. Hamilton would never be forgiven for his public confession of an illicit love affair, Burr for neither confirming affairs that were real nor denying those that lubricious gossip invented and foisted upon him.

A native of the West Indies, a child of poverty and hard work, Hamilton would spend his life nurturing the interest of "the few, the rich, and the well-born." Burr, the aristocrat, would become at least a nominal Republican, usually operating within the party of Jefferson, the party of the people—on his own terms, to be sure, and with a tolerance of opposing views that would get him into trouble in an age when Americans took their party affiliations seriously and articulated them with vehemence. To the central event of their lives, the Revolution, both had made admirable contributions, Hamilton for the most part as an aide and intimate of George Washington. During the war, each of them had broken with the stolid commander in chief, but in the case of Hamilton the breach would be healed, partly because the older man harbored no grudge, chiefly because, as the first architect of the government breathed into life by the federal constitution, he would need the younger man's penetrating mind and inventive energies. Each had been fortunate in acquiring a wife suitable to his needs and temperament. Hamilton finding in Elisabeth, second-oldest daughter of Major General Philip Schuyler, land-rich patroon of the upper Hudson River valley, the tie to wealth and gentility that as the son of a ne'er-do-well member of a noble Scottish family he felt entitled; Burr in the plain but fetching Theodosia a surrogate for the mother he had barely known.

Hamilton was the more open of the two. What he thought, he said—not infrequently to his personal detriment. Of the precise tenor of Burr's thought, no one, with the possible exception of his wife and daughter, was ever altogether certain. Hamilton's pen was as unrestrained as his tongue. He was forever putting his frequently changing beliefs and even his feelings into print. Burr preferred to keep his own counsel; it pleased him to be an enigma. In a letter to his daughter he described himself in the third person. "He," wrote Burr of Burr, "is a grave, silent, strange sort of animal, inasmuch that we know not what to make of him." Ask a question of the shade of Alexander Hamilton, and you soon get an answer. Ask one of the shade of Aaron Burr and, like a shout into an empty well, it sends back only a faint and mocking echo.

Hamilton was often feisty, Burr never. Few men admired Hamilton more than Robert Troup. Yet when the closing arguments of the celebrated case of *Le Guen v. Gouverneur & Kemble* found them on opposite sides—Hamilton for Le Guen and Troup for the defendants—Troup had occasion to notice that Hamilton spared no one when his temper was aroused. "The cause of Gouverneur & Kemble with Le Guen," Troup wrote a friend, "is beginning to excite attention. Genl Hamilton is very confident of success. I shall deem myself fortunate [if] we all get out of this cause [without] fighting . . . With my moderation of temper I hope to escape the General's pistols as well as his sword." And at a later moment in the case, to another friend: "Hamilton never appeared to have his passions so warmly engaged in any cause. He was full of acrimony against Gouverneur and Kemble and was not without asperity towards their council [sic]. I think he was guilty of an indelicacy toward me."

Hamilton, in short, let off steam as he went along. Burr

did not. As the American incarnation of Lord Chesterfield, it was a point of pride with Burr to maintain his composure. No façade, however, is proof against all weathers. The day would come when long-repressed resentments, to borrow a phrase from his mother's diary, would "belch out all at once like a cloud," and do him—and Hamilton—fatal harm.

6

Nothing but the Best

O, MY AARON, how impatient I am to welcome thy return; to anticipate thy will, and receive thy loved commands." So Mrs. Theodosia Bartow Prevost Burr was writing to her husband in the fall of 1785. "Read the Abbé Mably's little book on the Constitution of the United States," he was requesting in a letter of the same year. "This . . . will save me the trouble of reading it; and I shall receive it with much more emphasis per la bouche d'amour."

To trace Aaron Burr's life as a husband and father during the twelve years that Theodosia's steadily declining health allowed them to be together is to glimpse the man at his best. Domesticity became him. There was a family for him to care for from the beginning, and it was one of the requirements of his nature to have around him young minds to train and direct. Taking over Frederick and Bartow, Theodosia's sons by her first husband, he fathered them to a fare-thee-well. They were bright strapping fellows, Frederick about sixteen when the Burrs moved to New York City in 1783, Bartow about fourteen. Their stepfather set up clerkships for them in his office. Bartow would follow the law, occupying a succession of judicial and diplomatic posts. Frederick would find his life work in the land, becoming, with Burr's help, the owner of a large farm at Pelham in Westchester County. Of the disposition of the daughters of Mrs. Burr's previous marriage, nothing positive is known. A child variously referred to as "Lou," "Louise," and "Louisa" shows up in a few of her letters but the absence of the Prevost girls' names from her and Aaron's correspondence suggests that they were taken over by relatives.

Already on hand when the Burrs reached New York was the first child of their own marriage—a daughter, born in Albany on 21 June 1783. "Will you believe me, Reeve, when I tell you the dear little girl has the eyes of your Sally?" Mrs. Burr wrote in great joy to her brother-in-law in Litchfield. If Mrs. Burr had had her way, the little girl would have had Sally's name as well, but the colonel would not hear of it. His heart was set on perpetuating his wife's name, and at the christening on 28 July the words pronounced by the celebrant were "Theodosia Bartow." "A lovely daughter!" the mother exclaimed. No doubt the father agreed, although he could not have had the smallest inkling of all this child would mean to him in the years to come.

There was another daughter. Born on 20 June 1785, she was named after Sally Reeve. Then came two stillbirths. Reporting on the second of them, Theodosia wrote Tapping Reeve in the summer of 1788 that on the "ninth of July . . . I had a most unfortunate lying-in, in every particular resembling the one in February 87; another lovely, beautiful boy expired 7 hours before its birth." A few months later the in-laws at Litchfield were called on to share the grief of a sick woman, pushed almost to the end of her endurance by another disaster. "Variegated have been my scenes of anguish," Theodosia wrote them, "but this exceeds them all———a tender, affectionate friend just opening into life . . . and flushed with health till the sly viper stole upon her vitals, there preyed unperceived . . . till too late. All aid proved vain—she passed gently from me to the regions of bliss . . . yes, my Sally, she is . . . gone . . ." This pathetic note was written in March 1789, little Sally having died the preceding October. Of the children of the marriage, only Theodosia would live to adulthood, to become one of the most admired and accomplished women of her day, something of a legend in her lifetime and after that the subject of many legends arising from the mystery of her disappearance at sea in her thirtieth year.

2

BURR'S LEGAL WORK took him from home a great deal—to Albany for sittings of the Supreme Court of Judicature, the Court of Probate, and the Court for the Trial of Impeachments and Correction of Errors; to Chancellor Robert R. Livingston's manor of Clermont for sittings of the Court of Chancery; to a barn behind the Yelverton Inn in Chester for a series of hearings dealing with ancient boundary squabbles among the owners of a tract of Orange County land; to a stone-walled, square-towered church in what is now Mount Vernon for sessions of the circuit court, to Kingston, Bedford, Rhinebeck, Westchester, and other New York townships and boroughs. Conferences with clients and other business took him into New Jersey and occasionally to Philadelphia. Of necessity, he and Theodosia lived much of their life together on paper, and the letters flowing between them chart the ups and downs of a good marriage.

She was many things to him: companion, mistress (so she repeatedly referred to herself), seamstress, often designing clothes for him that he wore with pride, and business associate. He was forever writing her to take care of this or that aspect of his work. From Albany: "Give Johnstone the enclosed memorandum . . . ; the business is of importance, and admits of no delay." From Chester: "Tell one of the boys to send me some supreme court seals; about six. I forgot them." From Claverack: "I wish you would often step into the office, and see as many as you can of the people who come on business." His requests were scrupulously attended to. "Bartow," she wrote him, "has been to the surveyor-general; he cannot inform him of the boundaries of those lots for J.W. There is no map of them but one in Albany." It is not without significance that during Theodosia's lifetime Burr worked alone save for his clerks. William Broome, his first partner, was not admitted to the bar until two years after Mrs. Burr's death, having served a long apprenticeship in the colonel's office.

The discomforts and dangers incident to her husband's journeys were never far from Theodosia's mind. Stagecoach owners advertised their "waggons and horses" as "elegant," touted "the pains" they had taken "to establish good houses of entertainment" along the line, and bragged of their "exertions to repair the roads." In truth, the wagons were dirty and crowded; the inns dirty, crowded, and noisy; and the roads little more than paths. When the winds were erratic, the 160-mile trip from New York to Albany by Hudson River sloop required at least "a fortnight—sometimes twenty-five or thirty days," involved seven or more stops from two to three hours each, and entailed more uncertainty and adventure than the modern tourist encounters in a trip around the world.

Burr's departure for New Jersey on a stormy winter morning found Theodosia awaiting word of his safe crossing of the river. "Pensive, surrounded with gloom," she wrote him later, "thy Theo sat, bewailing thy departure . . . [until] our son was the joyful messenger of thy safe landing at Paulus Hook [Jersey City] . . . I envied the ground which bore my pilgrim . . . Love engrossed his mind; his last adieu to Bartow was the most persuasive token—'Wait till I reach the opposite shore, that you may bear the glad tidings to your trembling mother.' O, Aaron, how I thank thee! Love in all its delirium hovers about me like opium . . ."

Her letters were passionate, his tender. In the fifth year of the marriage, "Tell me, Aaron," she wrote, "why do I grow every day more tenacious of thy regard? Is it possible my affection can increase?" He wrote from Chester, "Homesick and think of nothing else. I am wholly yours." The pedagogue at home and at the office was the pedagogue in absentia. There was the matter of dancing lessons for the children: "Let T[etard] give them any new steps he pleases, but not one before the others. If anyone is behind or less apt, more pains must be taken to keep them on a par." She was not to worry because the dancing master's methods of instruction did not always conform to his. "The girls must go on with Tetard in his own way till I come, when I will set all right." The main thing, in his opinion, was that the youngsters keep busy. "To hear that . . . no time is absolutely wasted," he wrote, "is the most flattering of anything that can be told me of them . . . Endeavor to preserve regularity of hours; it conduces exceedingly to industry." The children bore up well under his oppressive supervision. He cared, and they knew he cared. "Bartow never quits the office, and is perfectly obliging," Theodosia informed him. "Your dear little daughter seeks you twenty times a day; calls you to your meals, and will not suffer your chair to be filled by any of the family."

The children were not his only pupils. He told his wife both what to read and how to read it. He was anxious for her to study Gibbon's *History of the Decline and Fall of the Roman Empire*. "Never pass a word you do not understand, or the name of a person or place of which you have not some knowledge," he wrote. "You will say that attention to such matters is too great an interruption. If so, do but note them down on paper, and devote an hour particularly to them when you have finished a chapter . . . Lempriere's Dictionary is that of which I spoke to you . . ."

The lawyer riding circuit was busy; but wherever he was, Burr found time to keep the home folks abreast of his doings and thoughts. He took a walk in the woods and wondered, Rousseau-like, "why all animated nature enjoyed its being but man? Why man alone is discontented, anxious—sacrificing the present to idle expectations? . . . Never enjoying always hoping? Answer, *tu mihi magna Apollo.*" Hearing that little Theodosia was ill, he wrote her mother from Albany: "I tell every one who asks me that both she and you are well, because I abhor the cold, uninterested inquiries, which I know would be made if I should answer otherwise."

Even when he was at home, she read and reread his letters. Knowing where his heart lay, she filled her own with chatter about the youngsters. "Little Theo," she wrote him, "grows the most engaging child you ever saw." A supercilious relative came to call. It pleased her to be able to report that none of the children took to him. "Few parents," she added, "can boast of children whose minds are so prone to virtue."

Health—his as well as hers—ran through their correspondence like a refrain. He was not yet a well man. What he called the "paroxysm of the headache" came and went. Bouts of "eye trouble" forced him to request delays in the hearings on his cases, and to seek relief at the spa in Balston, New York. This ailment appears to have run in the family. We find him on one occasion rebuking sister Sally for failing to tell him that she had been temporarily blind. It would seem that both Sally and he were victims of the Edwards legacy, which Jonathan Edwards's biographer, Ola Winslow, calls the "erratic strain"—the "over delicate, over sensitive, highly nervous organization"—that cropped up with some frequency among the descendants of the great theologian.

As for Theodosia's dread disease, brief remissions were bracketed by periods of maddening pain. She did not write of it often to Aaron, although he begged her to, and when little Theodosia become old enough, he gave her the duty of reporting on Mama's health. Mrs. Burr was more explicit about it in her letters to the Tapping Reeves, with whom she enjoyed a rapport of great depth. "I believe I have been as near a state of insanity as possible," she told them once, "indeed there are hours in which I am confident it still threatens me . . . In the morning I wake with regret. At night I lye down with the hope of never waking to the disappointments of another day."

For years Aaron clung to the illusion that a cure could be effected if only she would take proper care of herself. On this point his instructions were unending. She must use the stairs only twice a day, down in the morning, up in the evening. "I hope you persevere in the regular mode of life which I pointed out to you," he wrote. "I shall be seriously angry if you do not. I think you had best take less wine and more exercise. A walk twice round the garden, and a ride in the afternoon will do for the present . . ."

3

THE GOOD MARRIAGE had its bad moments. She could be as arrogant and as exacting as he was. Inefficient servants roiled her, and he was the target of her tirades on the subject. One of the domestics was always drunk, another was beginning to think himself "too good for some works. It will be necessary to check every rise of false pride." A defective carriage put her in a pet. "Dean," she told Aaron, "has cheated us abominably . . . All the straps have given away, there is danger in using it."

When the colonel's demands on her seemed unreasonable, she let him know. She spent a summer at her son's farm, taking care of her daughter and the children of a traveling relative. Finding that her letters from Pelham were slow in reaching him, Aaron suggested that she send them "by the bridge," a stop on the post road. "You don't recollect," she replied tartly, that "I have ten miles to send & ten to return, which is twenty miles for horse and servant; and this is the harvest season, & to take Fred's hands from their work more than I am obliged is painful." Just to make sure her husband appreciated how put-upon she was, she mentioned the many "intrusions that so large a family must necessarily make: wood, water, provisions . . . Charlotte is two thirds of her time washing and ironing."

She had numerous relatives, and Burr felt some of them visited too often and stayed too long. For years he carried on a feud with one of them, Lieutenant General John Maunsell, a gout-stricken curmudgeon of a retired British army officer. Maunsell had seen active service in the New World during the colonial period, had married one of Theodosia's beautiful aunts in 1763, and had commanded a military post in his native Ireland during the Revolutionary War. After peace came, he and his wife lived for a time in London. The news of their niece's second marriage, reaching them there, delighted the general. He wrote a kinswoman in New York that he had heard "a great character" of Burr and thought "Theo . . . lucky in meeting so good a man." Sometime after the return of the Maunsells to America in 1784, he changed his mind. Theodosia's mother had died, and the aging soldier and Burr were thrown together as co-trustees under Mrs. De Visme's will. The general plagued Burr with questions about the latter's management of the estate. Burr was appalled at the inability of the older man to cope with the finer details of the business. When the general was arrested, some members of the family held Burr responsible. No support for their suspicions, however, is found in Maunsell's revelation that "*on the day that I was arrested*" Burr placed certain sums of money at his disposal—a statement which suggests that the younger man tried to help the older one out of his scrape, whatever it was, rather than put him in it. The general was often in court in connection with land claims. In 1786 Burr obtained a judgment for him. Six years later he represented a landowner who had brought suit against the general, and the two of them were no longer on speaking terms. Maunsell told a relative he would "never more have any intercourse with Burr." Burr told Theodosia, "You have really a distressing family. I hope it has by this time diminished."

Melancholia continued to be one of the symptoms of her

illness, and Aaron continued to complain about it. Cheerfulness, in his opinion, was not an attitude a person was free to put on or off as health and feelings dictated. It was a duty every human being owed to those he loved. "Gloom, however dressed, however caused," he lectured his wife, "is incompatible with friendship. They cannot have place in the mind at the same time. It is the secret, the malignant foe of sentiment and love." In this matter, as in others, she endeavored to please him. "When Aaron smiles, shall Theo frown?" she asked. "Forbid it!"

Her illness was not the only shadow across the marriage. A strange letter, written by Burr in the summer of 1788, discloses another. He had spent a day at Fort Johnson, thirty-five miles northwest of Albany on the shores of the Mohawk River. The name notwithstanding, Fort Johnson was a private estate, acquired and improved prior to the Revolution by the late Sir William Johnson, well-known land developer and Indian agent. As Sir William's son and heir, Sir John Johnson, had remained loyal to Britain, the fine house and grounds on the Mohawk had been confiscated by the state and were now up for sale. "Oh, Theo!" Aaron wrote, "there is the most delightful grove—so darkened with weeping willows, that at noonday a *susceptible* fancy like yours would mistake it for a bewitching moonlight evening . . . This shall be yours. We will plant it with jessamines and woodbine, and call it Cyprus. It seems formed for the residence of the loves and graces, and is therefore yours by the best of titles." There is another paragraph or so in this vein before suddenly the tone of the letter changes as Burr plunges into an extended *mea culpa.* "I know that you was opposed to this journey to Fort Johnson," this section begins. "It is therefore with the greater regret that I communicate the event . . . I am indeed unhappy in possessing a singularity of taste; particularly unhappy when that taste differs in anything from yours . . . I abhor preface and preamble, and don't know why I have now used it so freely. But I am well aware that what I am going to relate needs much apology . . . Be assured . . . that whatever diminishes your happiness equally impairs mine. In short, then . . . my dear Theo, the beauty of this same Fort Johnson, the fertility of the soil, the commodiousness and elegance of the buildings, the great value of the mills, and the very inconsiderable price which was asked for the whole, have *not* induced me to purchase it . . ."

The import of this letter is clear. Aaron's extravagance, his incontinent indulgence of his "singularity of taste," had become a source of worry to his ailing spouse.

4

HE LOVED fine houses, costly furnishings, the best of wines, the best of books, the best of everything. It pleased him to travel the streets of New York in graceful curricles and coachees, and he once boasted of having "a nice, new, beautiful little chariot, very light, on an entirely new construction" that he himself had invented. His clerks noticed, and he acknowledged, that he got no pleasure out of his law practice; he regarded it simply as a way of making money. He pursued that "paltry object," he wrote his wife, only because it was "the means of gratifying those I love." It is perhaps to his credit that he never ventured this or any other rationalization to justify his passion for opulence and high living. He recognized that for what it was, a drive, a compulsion. He told his wife, "We cannot control necessity, though we often persuade ourselves that certain things are our choice, when in truth we have been unavoidably impelled to them."

From the moment the family arrived in New York in 1783, he began playing the Chesterfieldian gentleman to the hilt. Although he had been hard put to finance the hegira from Albany, the home he rented on Wall Street seems to have been one of the best in what was then the most fashionable neighborhood of the city. Burr spoke of it as "Ver Planck's house," and a listing by the appraisers gave it the largest frontage (a hundred fifteen feet) of any of the forty-six properties along Wall Street between City Hall and Queen Street. In 1784 the Burrs moved to a "more spacious" domicile at No. 10 Little Queen Street (now Maiden Lane) at the corner of Nassau Street; and by 1790 they had moved again. General Maunsell, spending a year in England at the time of this change, got the impression that Burr had leased "*Big* Symmon's house" in Wall Street. It would have been smarter of him, the old man snorted, to have "hired apartments in *Big S's* paunch, which is large enough . . . " Actually, the Burrs' third New York home was No. 4 Broadway, only a few doors below the Maunsells' No. 11. But if the testy general meant to imply that Burr was living beyond his means, he was speaking simple truth.

Burr had resisted the lures of Fort Johnson, but he could not resist those of Richmond Hill, the place of his first meeting with George Washington, when that handsome residence became available. Richmond Hill's origins went back to 1767 when Abraham Mortier, Paymaster General to the British forces in North America, acquired from Trinity Church a ninety-nine-year lease, at $269 a year, on a tract of land along the Hudson, just south of what is now the Greenwich Village section of New York. Here, on a small hill on the shores of the river, Mortier erected a sixty-by-fifty-foot wooden dwelling with "a lofty portico supported by Ionic columns, the front walls decorated with pilasters of the same order." Today the hill is gone and the triangular plot of farm land that Mortier leased—now a densely built-up area roughly outlined by Clinton Place, Varick and Charlton Streets—no longer adjoins the river.

Vice President John Adams and his wife were Richmond Hill's occupants during the opening months of George Washington's Presidency. "Grand and sublime" were Abigail's words for the house and the vista it gave of "the noble Hudson" and the "fertile country of the Jersey's" beyond. By the time she and John moved in, New York City had begun its expansion up the island, but the setting of Richmond Hill remained essentially rural. Its northern windows, according to Mrs. Adams, provided "a view of fields covered with verdure, and pastures full of cattle." On the south, she noted, "the city opens upon us, intercepted only by clumps of trees and some rising ground, which serve to heighten the beauty of the scene by appearing to conceal a part."

It was the removal of the federal government to Philadelphia in 1790 that gave Burr his chance to possess this Eden on Hudson. Apparently the transaction was complicated, for the Burrs had been living in the mansion for at least three years when on 1 May 1797 Trinity Church leased the Richmond Hill estate to the colonel for sixty-nine years. Meanwhile, the Burrs had landscaped the grounds, had dammed Minetta Creek to form an ornamental pool at the main gateway near what is now the foot of Macdougal Street, and had refurbished the house itself from "below the stairs" to "garret." An inventory of the contents listed among the drawing-room pieces a dozen mahogany chairs, two cabriole sofas, two inlaid card tables, and an "Elegant Turkey Carpet," overlaid with another "carpet of Blue Bays" and edged by a green cloth. The library fixtures included four reading tables, one on castors; a variety of mahogany chairs, two of them with rush bottoms; and a "Dutch liquor case." Hundreds of books on every subject lined the shelves, thanks to a standing order with a London dealer for anything new and important. Guests, using the front door, found themselves in "a spacious hall with a small room on each side opening to more spacious apartments beyond." At the front of the formal dining room on the second floor, wide Venetian windows overlooked the river, and a door gave access to a balcony beneath the portico.

In these grand surroundings Burr entertained grandly. The turmoil in France had sent many glittering personalities to the New World, some fleeing the Revolution, others its Napoleonic aftermath. Practically all of them appeared on Burr's guest lists: Talleyrand, Volney, Jerome Bonaparte, and Louis Philippe among them. Hamilton, Jefferson, Madison, Edward Livingston—sooner or later these prominent Americans and others dined at Burr's table and slept in the "White Room," or the "Blue Room," or the "Little Bedroom West," on the second floor of Richmond Hill. The big house on the Hudson served the family as a country seat. For stays in the city proper, Aaron purchased a town house at No. 30 Partition (now Fulton) Street at the corner of Church Street, setting aside a portion of it for his offices.

As befitted the lord of these demesnes, he became a patron of the arts. An impecunious young Englishman, John Davis, traveled to America in steerage and turned his first shilling in the New World by translating from the French a recently published account of Napoleon Bonaparte's Italian campaign. Burr read the translation, liked it, summoned the young author to Richmond Hill, bade him make free of his library and table, and wrote a number of introductions to influential Americans for him. Thus fortified, Davis toured the country, and published a fascinating travel book.

When lack of funds forced a twenty-year-old Kingston-born artist, John Vanderlyn, to abandon his studies under the great portrait painter, Gilbert Stuart, Burr got in touch with his best friend in Kingston, Peter Van Gaasbeek, a young venture merchant and politician. He asked Van Gaasbeek to apprise the student artist of his (Burr's) desire to rescue "Genius from Obscurity." Writing from Philadelphia, the colonel said that Vanderlyn was to "draw on J. B. Prevost, New York, for any sum which may be necessary . . . And on his arrival in this city, where Stewart [sic] now lives, he will find a letter . . . pointing out the channel of his future supplies, the source of which will never be known except to himself . . . I should not have communicated this even to you, had I known how otherwise to get at Mr. V.D.L. I beg you to consider it as confidential." In this instance, the patron struck talent. Vanderlyn's historical composition, the "Landing of Columbus," hangs today in the rotunda of the national Capitol, his portraits and other paintings in museums and private collections. Burr saw to it that he completed his studies under Stuart, and then sent him to Paris, where the young painter finished his training and began what was to be a long and distinguished career.

5

PLAYING THE Chesterfieldian gentleman was expensive. It cost more than Burr could manage even at the zenith of his earning power as an attorney. Throughout much of the early post-war period, the American economy was notably unstable. Speculation in local currencies was commonplace, and the value of commercial paper fluctuated wildly. For the first decade or so, hard money was scarce everywhere, and in some sections nonexistent. Burr would have had to incur a good deal of indebtedness even if he had been willing to live on a more modest scale. He never would be. The thought of easing his hardships by a pinch of economy here and there was one that never so much as crossed his mind. He preferred to spend—and borrow.

In 1785 he negotiated the first of the numerous loans that, during the next two decades, would wrap him in a tangle of debt from which he would never escape. He borrowed from friends, from relatives, from law clients. He persuaded these and other people to endorse his notes. He devoted an unconscionable amount of effort, often to the detriment of his practice, to arranging for the notes to be extended. "So hampered by money matters," he confided to a political cohort, "that I am not master of my own time." When friends, relatives, and clients balked, he turned to professional lenders. Writing to his Kingston associate, Peter Van Gaasbeek, in the mid-1790's, he described himself as "in the hand of usurers."

Van Gaasbeek had his own problems: his once prosperous

store and other businesses were languishing, victims of the prevailing financial uncertainty. Facing bankruptcy, he appealed to Aaron. The two were old friends, but at this point Aaron's ability to help was limited. In 1793 he lent a small sum to Van Gaasbeek, but after that, he could do no more. For months his letters to Kingston were filled with apologies. "In the same state of impotent distress as heretofore," he wrote Van Gaasbeek from Philadelphia. "If you could see the letters that Mr. Strong [Roger Strong, manager of his law office] writes me every day about my affairs in NYork you would think me the last man in the world to apply to for one shilling. I have been ten days endeavouring to raise the pitiful sum of 500 dolrs without success and have now a note laying over in the Bank at NY for the Want of it. I should not trouble you with these details but that it must appear very singular to you that a man of my large possessions and reputed Wealth should not have a few thousand dollars to spare for a friend." Another letter said that "on the subject of money, my prospects are at present not very flattering." Repeatedly, Burr stressed the temporary nature of his predicament. In his eyes the long pull was ever bright. He was like a gambler, always in the red, always certain that tomorrow would bring the big win. To Van Gaasbeek he spoke mysteriously of a "very great" thing that a friend, then in Paris, was trying to do for him there. If this deal succeeded, he would be as "rich as any man can reasonably hope to be" and his friend in Kingston would be the first to benefit. Somehow, the "very great" thing never came to pass, and the thought obtrudes that it was largely imaginary, a product of Burr's incorrigible optimism.

His daughter was horrified to learn one day that Frederick Prevost's farm in Westchester was up for sale. "Sure it will not be sold," she wrote Bartow, her other half brother. "It is impossible, it is his all; it would be cruel to deprive him of it." Frederick, it turned out, had supplied a $20,000 bond in connection with one of her father's debts. All Theodosia could do was hope that "Papa" would find "some means of raising the money." She need not have worried. Arrangements were already in process for taking up her brother's bond. Frederick would continue to farm his acres at Pelham for many more years.

His own overextended finances notwithstanding, Burr cheerfully went surety on a friend's debt, only to regret it. The friend defaulted, and the holder of the note brought an action against Burr as the endorser. The old records of the incident exude a certain irony. Under the verdict for the plaintiff, Burr was obliged to pay $3,823.27, including court costs. It took him six years to raise the money. As a result, the attorney for the plaintiff, Alexander Hamilton, signed the acknowledgment of satisfaction of the judgment on 25 January 1804, only a few months before he and Burr faced each other on the dueling grounds of Weehawken. In the course of the multiple hearings connected with the case of *Le Guen v. Gouverneur & Kemble*, both Hamilton and Burr borrowed heavily from Le Guen, a French citizen and trader. Burr's borrowings began in 1798. Twenty-eight years later, the balance due was in dispute and Le Guen's wife was writing plaintively from Paris to see if her New York attorney had "any hopes of recovering in Col. Burr's business."

One of the most generous of Aaron's creditors, and in the end the most damaged, was General John Lamb. About this "brave but turbulent" New York patriot, a few words. Born in New York City in 1735, Lamb was the son of a mathematical-instruments maker who had begun his American life as an indentured servant, after being shipped to the New World in punishment for his part in a London burglary. John worked at his father's trade for a time before beginning the career as a wine merchant that would gain him a fortune. Seeing a threat to his profits in the Stamp Act of 1765, he became a leader of the local Sons of Liberty, throwing himself into the opposition to British tax laws with the same ardency that would mark all his later activities, including his contributions to the fiscal delinquency of Aaron Burr.

The two men met for the first time on the Plains of Abraham, only a few days before the unsuccessful American assault on Quebec. Lamb was a captain of artillery at the time, Aaron a recently created aide-de-camp to General Montgomery. Lamb's immediate reaction was to wonder "that the General should encumber his family with the addition of . . . a mere boy." But "a more thorough scrutiny of the boy's countenance, of the fire of his eye, and his perfect coolness, and immobility, under dangerous fire," convinced the hard-bitten artillery officer that this "young volunteer was no ordinary man." Obviously, Lamb's admiration never cooled, for when the master of Richmond Hill came to him for aid, he responded lavishly—not once, but again and again. Within two years he had loaned Burr at least forty thousand dollars and was endorsing his notes with abandon. For days on end, messages passed between them—from Burr, pleas for more cash or further endorsements; from the general, mild little expressions of hope that a way could be found of ending what was fast becoming a monetary nightmare. At length, Burr proposed to settle accounts between them by selling the furnishings of Richmond Hill. The general agreed to this arrangement, and Burr did sell the furnishings—to Sir John Temple, the English Consul General in New York—but Lamb never saw a cent of the proceeds, a paltry $3,500. Meanwhile, another creditor had put in his claim, and the general, always putty in Burr's hands, wrote to say that if the money received from Temple would enable the colonel to settle, "as you say, with the holder of one of your notes, I consent to release you from your offer."

But the inevitable could not be staved off forever. Unable to get anything out of Burr, a group of creditors turned on Lamb. Burr was in Albany when he learned that a warrant had been issued for the general's arrest. He set out at once, through legal contacts in New York, to save his benefactor from the indignity of a debtor's cell. Somehow he contrived to solicit endorsements satisfactory to the irate plaintiffs, and General Lamb, still far from paid off but vastly relieved to be free, at last summoned up the courage to remove himself from the path of the colonel's financial juggernaut.

Struggling with a growing mass of obligations, Burr lunged now this way, now that. Land speculation was rife in the beginning days of the republic. The empty or almost empty reaches of the frontier beckoned to those who could afford to buy now and wait for the settlers to pour in. Burr couldn't afford to, but he bought anyhow. At one point his holdings in a single western New York county came to more than four thousand acres. He invested in land companies—with indifferent success. Often the payment on his stock subscriptions came due before the money was in hand. Much that he purchased was a case of here today and gone tomorrow. The property or the shares in a land company, or whatever it was, swiftly passed through his hands into those of his creditors or the tax collector. In 1799 he mortgaged Richmond Hill for $38,000. This encumbrance was still intact, part of the debit at his bank, when a few years later, after several futile attempts to do so, he found a purchaser willing and able to take the leasehold—and the mortgage—off his hands. In 1801 Alexander Hamilton was writing a friend in the South that "with interest" Burr's indebtedness to one of his many creditors amounted to "about 80,000 Dollars." It is not known how the colonel managed to continue living at his country seat after the sale of its furnishings in 1797 to Sir John Temple, but manage he did, albeit only occasionally and for short periods of time. His letters show that as late as the summer of 1804 he was still maintaining at Richmond Hill what he spoke of as an "establishment," complete with furnishings, carriages, and a retinue of servants.

6

BURR'S FINANCIAL MISADVENTURES may have been extreme, but in the context of his time and place they were not unique. The nation born in the fires of the Revolution began its life in a depression characterized by stringent credit conditions and a paucity of specie. In 1787 Patrick Henry was unable to attend the federal constitutional convention in Philadelphia owing to lack of cash. Two years later, land-rich George Washington had to borrow to travel to New York for his inauguration as first President under the constitution. So woebegone were the financial affairs of Peter R. Livingston, eldest son of the third and last lord of the so-called "upper Manor of Livingston" in upstate New York, that for many years "he scarcely dared leave his house for fear of his creditors." In a country with no industrial plant to speak of, speculation in Western lands struck many enterprising individuals as the quickest, if not the only, route to wealth; and the American landscape of Burr's day was littered with the casualties of this conviction. Burr was luckier than some. He never went to debtor's prison, probably because at the critical moment he got out of the country before his creditors could get to him. Others were not so agile. By 1798, unfortunate land speculations had made a prisoner of Robert Morris, the "financier of the American Revolution," and a number of other financiers, once counted among the high and mighty of the country, already had or were about to join him behind bars.

That the colonel escaped this not undeserved fate was due to no special business acumen on his part. He was remarkably able in the handling of other people's affairs as an attorney, but his management of the Richmond Hill lease indicates that he was not indulging in false modesty when he confessed to brother-in-law Tapping Reeve that he was inept at taking care of his own affairs. His acquisition of the lease put him in control of "twenty-six acres, 3 roods, and 36 perches" of readily improvable land, and this at a time when New York City was growing so rapidly that, although hundreds of new houses were rising every month, finding a rental was a frustrating experience. Shortly after obtaining the leasehold, Burr sublet four lots for sixty-six years for eight hundred pounds, plus an annual rental of one peppercorn. There is no evidence that, aside from this transaction, he made any effort to exploit the tract. Busy playing lord of the manor, he never got around to making the manor work for him.

When in 1803 he finally succeeded in selling all the Richmond Hill lease, save the mansion itself and a few adjoining acres, its new owner—John Jacob Astor—did not make the same mistake. The shrewd German-born master of the Western fur trade knew exactly what to do with the property. He filled in swamps, cut down hills, and created 456 building lots. During the remaining life of the lease, the rentals on these contributed substantially to a fortune that was estimated at thirty million dollars when Astor died in 1848. When in late 1804 Burr's creditors forced the sale of the old house, the glory and the glamour that had been Richmond Hill rapidly evaporated. To make way for razing the hill on which it stood, the old house was moved fifty-five feet to a location close to what is now the corner of Varick and Charlton Streets. Here, until the wreckers came, it first sheltered a circus, then a theater, and finally a combination bar and library, very popular, we are told, with the city's "bibulous literati."

The "wily," the "cunning" Aaron Burr—how frequently those adjectives appear in the chronicles of his time, and how misleading they are. No well-known figure of the American past was ever so consistently outsmarted, especially in financial matters, as the subject of this biography.

7

Courtesy of Hamilton

BURR MIGHT HAVE RECOVERED from his fiscal follies had he concentrated on his profitable law practice and eschewed politics, in a day when it was a rare public position that paid as much as five thousand dollars a year. But he did not eschew it. Perhaps he couldn't. If politics American-style did not exactly originate in New York State, they took shape there at an early date, providing a stage too brightly lighted for the actor in Burr to resist.

In the beginning, as a matter of fact, he did resist. He was still in Albany when he learned that he was being talked of for a post in the state government and that Justice Hobart of the supreme court was pushing him for the job. The same pride of self that had forbidden him to beg for promotion in the army now moved him to tell the judge that he wished no part in an unseemly scrabble for office. Hobart expressed admiration for the purity of his motives but warned that, as long as the young lawyer was determined "to avoid competition," he would have to endure the anonymity of "a private gentleman."

The judge need not have worried. Aaron had been in New York City only a few months when the local voters, impressed by his performance in the courtroom, the charm of his manner, and the élan of his family background, thrust office upon him.

In April 1784, at the annual election for state officials, they named him to one of the nine seats in the Assembly, the lower branch of the legislature, then allotted to the city and county of New York.

Thus began the unorthodox and often puzzling career that in much less than a decade would lift Aaron Burr to the upper rungs of the New York political ladder, and from there —courtesy of Alexander Hamilton—into the United States Senate.

2

BURR HAD NO compunction about accepting the honor. A little fame is no detriment to a beginning lawyer, provided the inconvenience is bearable. In this case, there was none. For the time being, New York City was the capital of the state. With the legislature meeting at the Exchange, a comfortable walk from his office, he could keep one eye on his thriving practice. During the first session of his one-year term, he obviously kept both. The session opened on 12 October, but there was no sign of the colonel until the fifth of the next month. During the remaining twenty-four days, he initiated no legislation, sat on no committees, and answered less than a fourth of the roll calls.

During the second session, beginning in January 1785, his presence was more tangible. He worked on a variety of committees, including one charged with revising the state laws, and sponsored a few bills. When the Assembly took under consideration a proposal for the gradual abolition of slavery, he introduced an amendment under which the slaves would have been freed instantaneously. Where this burning issue was concerned, Burr, like Hamilton and many other contemporaries, never seems to have felt any compulsion to adjust practical conduct to personal conviction. Burr inveighed frequently against slavery, and Hamilton was long active in the New

York Manumission Society, but from time to time both men owned slaves. Burr's battle for instant abolition came to naught, and although Assembly and Senate agreed upon a program for gradual abolition, neither house was able to muster the two-thirds vote needed to reverse a veto. As Governor George Clinton and his advisers well knew, the upstate landowners, big and small, were not yet ready for emancipation.

Only once during Burr's first year as a practicing politician did his actions put him at the center of a public brouhaha of the sort that would be a commonplace of his later life. This one erupted when a group of New York mechanics, in an effort to cope with the problems of the post-war depression, petitioned the legislature for a charter of incorporation. Burr, alone among the nine New York City assemblymen, opposed their request. The Journal of the Assembly neglects to list his reasons. Presumably they were identical with those accompanying the veto that killed the bill of incorporation after both houses had passed it by large majorities. The veto message argued that the requested charter would allow some of the city's artisans privileges not open to others, give birth to an organization vulnerable to political manipulation, raise labor costs in the city, and deny jobs to immigrant workers. One of Burr's biographers treats his subject's stand on this matter as an act of statesmanship. A knowledgeable student of early New York politics, on the other hand, dismisses the objections to the bill as "vague and ridiculous," and a later legislature, seemingly of the same mind, would issue papers of incorporation to the still-functioning General Society of Mechanics and Tradesmen of the City of New York.

Right or wrong, Burr for several weeks was the butt of considerable abuse. The aggrieved mechanics, taking to the press, accused him of pandering to "the mighty and powerful ones [who] . . . prey upon the weak, the poor, the helpless." Dark rumors flew. Some spoke of threats of violence to the colonel himself, others of a plan to stone his house. When friends offered to stand guard, Burr is reported to have waved them aside, saying, "Gentlemen, I will live no longer than I can protect myself."

On 27 April the Assembly adjourned sine die, and for the next three years the colonel stuck close to his law practice. In 1788, shortly before the spring election for members of the Assembly, handbills around town and advertisements in the press announced that the "sons of liberty, who are again called upon to contend with the sheltered aliens [Tories], who have, by the courtesy of our country, been permitted to remain among us, will give their support to the following ticket: — *William Denning, Melancton Smith, Marinus Willet, and Aaron Burr.*" The support given was inadequate. The ticket lost, and Burr does not appear to have exerted himself much in its behalf, other than to permit the use of his name.

By the following year, when at last he began edging into public life as though he meant it, the political atmosphere of both his state and the country had changed dramatically. Gone was the confederation, the national government installed toward the end of the war by the Articles of Confederation. In its place stood the federal constitution: written in Philadelphia in the hot and insect-noisy summer of 1787, argued over in all thirteen states, and in the course of this clamorous controversy ratified by the more than nine states required to give it effect. Now the Congress it called for was sitting at New York City's Federal Hall on Wall Street. The first President and Vice President had been elected. And the newspapers were speaking of "Federalists" and "Anti-Federalists."

Federalists? Anti-Federalists? Can we think of the factions behind those terms as political parties? Not exactly. The country's first party system would come along later, pricked into existence by issues sharper and more resistant to compromise than those responsible for the great debate of 1788 over whether the document drafted at Philadelphia should or should not be adopted as the basic law of the land. For the time being,

"Federalist" was simply a convenient name for those political leaders who wanted the constitution and fought for it. It was the Federalists who prepared the way for the convention in Philadelphia. To a significant extent, their ideas went into the document that was formulated there. And in the ensuing debate it was their spokesmen who argued and cajoled the states into accepting it. With the term "Federalists" designating the friends of the constitution, the term "Anti-Federalists" for its enemies followed as the night the day. Indeed, the Federalists are believed to have coined it, often and dismissively speaking of their opponents as the "Antis."

Why did the Federalists work so hard for the constitution? Why did the Antis oppose it? Any groping for the answers to those questions is worthwhile as an effort to comprehend the nature of the ideological cleavage along which the country's first full-fledged parties, the Federalists and the Democratic-Republicans, would later take form. The once widely honored assumption that the Founding Fathers—the Federalist constitution-makers, that is—were motivated primarily by economic considerations has received short shrift from modern historians. It is true, as Charles Beard pointed out in 1913 in his *Economic Interpretation of the Constitution*, that many of the "Fathers" were holders of government securities. Naturally, they looked forward to the establishment of a government able and willing to protect property interests and uphold the sanctity of contracts. It so happens, however, that the same statement can be made about many of their most active antagonists. "The Anti-Federalist politicians in the ratifying conventions," Gordon S. Wood notes in his *The Creation of the American Republic 1776–1787*, "often possessed wealth, including public securities, equal to that of the Federalists." Economic concerns, in other words, cut across the line that divided one faction from the other.

Self-interest can never be ruled out of any large human enterprise, but this kind of monetary self-interest is not very useful in the attempt to grasp the political realities of the argument over the constitution. On the other hand, two noneconomic factors are far more serviceable to that end.

One of these factors is probably best described as a matter of vision. At base, the Federalists and the Antis were struggling for the same thing. To borrow a pregnant phrase from Richard Buel, both were interested in "securing the Revolution," in bringing off successfully one of the few attempts by a body of people in modern times to organize their society on republican principles. The line that separated Federalists from Antis was forged by their differing views as to how this end could be accomplished. The Antis felt that the country was so large, its occupants so heterogeneous, and their interests so diverse that republicanism could endure only if the bulk of the political power was entrusted to their local governments. The Antis were as aware as the Federalists that the confederation was sick and must be strengthened. In the prescription formulated at Philadelphia, however, they saw what they took to be an over-cure, an instrument that would convert the central government from a weak creature of the states into a behemoth certain in time to make the states creatures of itself. Now that the constitution was in effect, they were clamoring for a series of amendments—the so-called Bill of Rights—that would say in so many words just where the power of the new national government ended and that of the states began. In the words of Stanley Elkins and Eric McKitrick, "Republican government that went beyond the compass of state boundaries was something they [the Antis] could not imagine." The Federalists could and did. To a marked degree, the debate over the constitution was parochialism versus cosmopolitanism, state-oriented men versus nation-oriented men. It was a theme that would sound again and again in American life, not even completely silenced by the Civil War.

Another substantial element in the great debate had to do, not with *where* the power should be lodged, but *with whom.*

On this point the Federalists may be pictured as taking the narrow and safe position, the Antis the broader and riskier one.

In the eyes of the Federalists, practically all the ills that beset the country during the confederation period were traceable to the caliber of the individuals flowing into the lawmaking assemblies of the various states. Brought to the fore by the conflict with Mother England, a new and growing spirit of egalitarianism was abroad. Wherever the Federalists turned, they saw new faces in the state legislatures, faces belonging to men whose pre-Revolution fathers—unrich and little educated —would never have dreamed of running for any public office. In the opinion of the Federalists, these new men were simply not equipped to provide the American society with the stability and order it must have if the great experiment in republicanism was to succeed. In the words and deeds of those who spoke for these new men—the Anti-Federalist leaders—the Federalists perceived a challenge to "the eighteenth-century assumption that social authority was a necessary prerequisite to the wielding of political power." The Federalists fought for the constitution because they thought they saw in that document the framework of a national government so hedged about with safeguards against the "tyranny of the majority" that it would draw into its orbit only the "Best people," only those who could be described as belonging to the country's "natural aristocracy."

The "struggle over the Constitution," Gordon Wood has written, "can be best understood as a social one." It was aristocracy versus democracy. The Federalists wanted a government of the people by the elite. Some of the Anti-Federalist leaders had as little faith in the capacities and rectitude of the people as the Federalists did. As a group, however, the Antis took the position that only the butcher, the baker, and the candlestick-maker could understand the problems of butchers, bakers, and candlestick-makers. It followed that the common people should participate actively in the forming and executing of the laws. The Antis wanted a government of the people by the people.

In nearly every state the division brought into view by the great debate over the constitution had deep historical roots. This was certainly true of Aaron Burr's state. There the debate did not so much create the division as simply make more visible a cleavage that had been a staple of the life of that region since before the Revolution. There the two factions had existed in embryo for well over a decade, and the tensions responsible for their emergence were to supply the background of Burr's political pilgrimage.

3

FOR SOME YEARS before the outbreak of the War of Independence, the true rulers of New York were not King George III and his minions but the native aristocrats, meaning chiefly the "manor lords" of the huge estates along the Hudson River and their fellow gentry among the merchants, professional men, and other well-to-do dwellers in the urban centers. The Schuylers and the Van Rensselaers, presiding over their spreading acres in Albany County; the Livingstons, overseeing hordes of tenants from two manor houses some sixty miles down river; the Philipses, the Van Cortlandts, and the Morrises, engrossing among themselves much of Westchester County; and the De Lanceys on Manhattan Island—these possessors of extravagant stretches of land and their multitudinous kin by birth or marriage stood high on the list of those whose names spelled social, economic—and political—influence in colonial New York.

Cadwallader Colden, one of the last of the royal lieutenant governors, and at intervals acting governor, was under no illusion as to who was running the colony His Majesty had appointed him to run. In a report to London in 1764, the Scottish-born physician and scientist pointed to the Assembly, the sole elective unit of the provincial government, as evidence that much of the power of New York was in the hands of those whom Alexander Hamilton and his followers would later think of as "the few, the rich and the well-born." According to Colden, approximately two-thirds of the members of the 1764 Assembly were manor lords or merchants of New York City, and most of the merchants were "strongly connected" with holders of the great estates "by family interest." Had Colden analyzed the Assembly elected five years later, he would have found that, of the twenty-eight members, twenty-one were "great landowners," wealthy merchants, or wealthy lawyers; ten belonged to the "Colony's foremost families"; two-thirds had been born of moneyed parents; and only seven had been sent to the legislature by the "common farmers."

There was nothing automatic in the exercise of control by the colonial aristocrats. To maintain their dominance, they had to get themselves or their friends appointed or elected to influential posts. This meant campaigning, and campaigning sometimes entailed bribery or economic coercion. Always it involved taking advantage of the legalized practice of those days of voting by voice rather than by written ballot—an especially useful device on the heavily tenanted estates, where the manor lord could keep an ear open at the polls and where what modern scholars have termed "the politics of deference" enjoyed some of its finest hours. That the colonial aristocrats wanted to rule and often did rule does not mean that they ruled badly. By and large they were intelligent and humane, with genuine culture and unassuming good manners—powdered, knee-breeched, and buckled gentlemen who, as public officials, took their responsibilities to their constituents at least as seriously as they took themselves.

They could not always work together. Internal divisions marked by rabid rivalries were common, and on occasion these were complicated by outbursts of rebellion among the tenants of the landed gentry. Nor did every election end in triumph for one segment of the elite or another. By no means all the "common farmers" of the province were on the tenant rolls.

In Suffolk County on Long Island, and in Orange and Ulster Counties on the western banks of the Hudson, most of the tillers of the soil were yeomen, owners of their lands in fee simple, sturdy individuals who came and went as they pleased —and thought as they pleased. Among these people, and to an even sharper degree among their social counterparts in the towns, the yeast of democracy had been working for years when in 1765 the Stamp Act crisis brought from the urban tradesmen and others a cry for a variety of reforms, ranging from the abolition of slavery to universal suffrage and an end to voting by voice. When only a little more than a decade later the break with England became official, the landed aristocrats and the mercantile gentry confronted a dilemma: how were they to retain their control over the state in the face of a swelling determination by the "middle sort of people" to participate more fully in the political process?

Some of the aristocrats sought to meet the problem by becoming loyalists—the De Lanceys, for example, along with many members of the urban mercantile and professional gentry. This did not seem to be much of a gamble at the time. The unevenness with which the colonials had fought for Mother England in the past suggested that, against her, they would last little longer than a candle burns. It stood to reason that mighty Britain would quickly crush the rebellion, making it unnecessary for the De Lanceys and their fellow Tories to share their powers with the lower orders or anyone else.

Equally quick to sense the challenge to their preeminence from a rising middle class, the patriot or Whig aristocrats, the Schuylers and the Livingstons among them, were also quick to realize that only two choices were open to them. They could meet the opposition head-on, a risky procedure given the relative fewness of their numbers. Or they could swallow their pride and work with the opposition in the hopes of salvaging at least some of their threatened power.

In the summer of 1777, Robert R. Livingston was putting

on paper his conviction of "the propriety of Swimming with a Stream which it is impossible to stem." Tall and square-built, his abundant hair tumbling in ringlets over a high forehead, his strong face dominated by the large and convex nose common to the males of his family, this Livingston at the age of thirty-one was already the de facto if not the titular head of all but a portion of his influential clan. In Pennsylvania, he noted, the refusal of that state's conservatives to temporize had reduced them to political eunuchs. To William Duer, his wealthy kinsman by marriage, Livingston wrote that he had "long ago advised" the Pennsylvania aristocrats to "yield to the torrent if they hoped to direct its course—you know nothing but well-timed delays, indefatigable industry, and minute attention to every favourable circumstance, would have prevented our being exactly in their situation."

Livingston's letter may be regarded as a blueprint of the strategy pursued by New York's aristocratic Whigs during the war. They cooperated with the middle-class or "popular" Whigs. By a concession here and a deft maneuver there, they succeeded in winning the right to help organize their newly born state, putting on the record, as they did so, an early and stunning example of the role that compromise was to play in the development of American political institutions.

Furiously active in all the councils connected with setting up the state government, they won some battles and lost others. Recent scholarship shows that the first state constitution, adopted in 1777, was not the wholly reactionary instrument it was once thought to be. Neither, thanks to the "indefatigable industry" poured into it by Livingston, John Jay, Gouverneur Morris, and other brilliant aristocrats, was it the democratic charter many of the popular Whigs would have preferred.

The suffrage clauses illustrate what a hybrid it was—"aristocratical" here, "democratical" there. In the colonial days, when the Assembly was the only elective body, a free adult male had to own property worth at least £40 (roughly $100) to vote for its members. The conservative Whigs would like to have seen this qualification retained or lifted, but although the constitution as adopted set even higher requirements for voting for various top-level posts, it more than doubled the number of adult males eligible to vote for assemblymen. It did this by cutting the property requirements in half and by extending the ballot to tenement residents paying annual rents of 40 shillings ($5) or more. "Aristocratical" notions prevailed, however, with regard to governor, lieutenant governor, and senators. The constitution stipulated that only owners of freeholds worth £100 ($250) or more could vote for these officials.

The most democratic feature of the New York constitution was that alone among the early state charters it provided for the election of the governor by the people instead of by the legislature. More conservative in thrust were those clauses that limited the elective posts to governor, lieutenant governor, state treasurer, senators, assemblymen, and certain town officials. The selection of jurists was assigned to the legislature, and all the other government functionaries, including city mayors and county sheriffs, were made appointive. Fresh in the minds of the constitution-makers were the ills inflicted on colonial New York by often stupid and sometimes venal royal governors. Hence the approval by conservative and popular Whigs alike of two novel appendages to the upper levels of the state system, both designed to discourage executive despotism. One of them, the Council of Revision, consisted of the governor, the chancellor, and the supreme court justices. Intended to diffuse the veto powers of the governor, this half-executive, half-judicial body was authorized to review all bills passed by the legislature and to accept or reject them, subject in the latter eventuality to a two-thirds override by both houses. The purpose of the other body, the Council of Appointment, was to limit the governor's control of a patronage list that was large to begin with and would fatten considerably as the state grew. Set up under Article 23, this body consisted of the governor and a specified number of senators, each from one of the great districts into which New York State was divided, and all elected annually by the Assembly. Destined to become a bone of contention in time, the Council of Appointment, collectively, rather than the governor, put names to thousands of appointive posts. The popular Whigs would like to have seen an immediate end to voting by voice, but on this issue, too, the constitution was a compromise. All elections for governor and lieutenant governor were to be by written ballot, but viva-voce voting for assemblymen and senators was to remain in force until the end of the war. After that, the lawmakers were empowered to abolish the practice whenever two-thirds of them agreed to do so, as they did in 1787.

During the first election in the late spring of 1777, the conservatives canvassed so enterprisingly for their candidate for governor, General Philip Schuyler, that they were genuinely surprised when the office went to Brigadier General George Clinton, a product of the yeomanry of Ulster County and the candidate of the popular faction. Schuyler himself put words to the shocked reaction of many members of his class. He pointed out that although Clinton was "virtuous . . . brave" and "has abilities," his "family and Connections do not Intitle him to so distinguished a predominance." But, for the conservatives, even this setback at the polls was far from total defeat. A firm and sometimes stubborn man, with a short but powerful body and a great rugged expanse of face, George Clinton was a politician of more than ordinary artistry, as witness his subsequent record: governor of New York for seven three-year terms, twice Vice President of the United States. As adept in the uses of compromise as his opponents, he himself was instrumental in seeing to it that the conservatives got their share and more of the higher positions in the new government. To mention but a few of many examples—Robert R. Livingston became the first chancellor of New York, John Jay the first chief justice of the state supreme court, and Gouverneur Morris a delegate to the Continental Congress.

Thus, during the war years, did New York's aristocrats hold their own—to become the Federalists of their state in the late 1780's, even as the popular Whigs of wartime New York became the Anti-Federalists of that period and the Democratic-Republicans of the following decade.

4

AND AARON BURR? When in the late 1780's he re-entered public life, was it as a Federalist or an Anti-Federalist? In Mark Twain's memorable phrase, the question is "interesting but tough." Burr might have fared better at the bar of history had he just once taken the trouble of reducing his political beliefs to writing. Perhaps he did. If so, the words have been lost. His available political correspondence is large, but one combs it in vain for so much as a single sentence that can be cited as pointing to a political philosophy. It deals for the most part with the tactics of vote getting, provoking the conclusion that in politics, as in law, the colonel was pre-eminently the craftsman.

From the bright start of his life as a public figure to its premature climax, his conspicuous indifference to party labels was a subject of recurrent comment. Admirers, including substantial men in both parties, regarded his independency as a constructive and moderating element in the witches' brew that was the politics of New York in his day. Critics saw in it only the machinations of a political mercenary whose "services were for sale to the highest bidder."

Some historians and biographers have echoed his admirers, and others his critics, with still others hovering between the extremes. Typical of the argument of his defenders is the statement of his able biographer, Nathan Schachner, that Burr "did not believe that political opponents were necessarily rascals. In an era when invective and diatribe were almost the sole political arguments, he was amazingly urbane and courteous. He ran neither with the hares nor with the hounds, nor suffered himself to be . . . blinded by party passions and prejudices." Typical of the contrary perception is the view of Hamilton's biographer, Broadus Mitchell, that Burr was "a capricious element, quickening and confusing . . . of both parties and of neither. Darting between them, he bred suspicions that magnified the pretensions of both sides" and "wove nettles into the political shirt." Writing in the late nineteenth century, Henry Adams contended that Burr single-handedly lowered the standard of New York politics, prompting a later historian to point out that this was to credit Burr with "something that to our more experienced generation would seem impossible."

It is among these diverging opinions that the searcher for Burr the politician must pick his way, with little to go on save the outward events of his career. His votes during his year in the Assembly are uninstructive. None of them can be tied to either of the then emerging parties with the possible exception of his opposition to a charter of incorporation for the New York mechanics, who at that time, 1785, were more or less Federalist in sympathy. Whether during the great debate of 1788 he was for or against adoption of the constitution is not a matter of reliable record. Hamilton's recollection, a few years later, was that Burr was "equivocal" on the issue, although the enemies of ratification "considered him to be with them." Given the source of this comment, the "equivocal" may be disregarded as gratuitous. The rest of the statement is borne out by Burr's willingness, during the year of the debate, to let himself be nominated for the Assembly on a ticket drafted by an Anti-Federalist group.

Clear enough. Now we see him—but only fleetingly. His conduct during the New York gubernatorial election of the following year refocuses the picture. For the fourth time in a row, George Clinton was running to succeed himself, and the opening gambit of the campaign found Burr cooperating with Alexander Hamilton in what was to be an almost, but not quite, successful struggle to unseat the seemingly eternal governor. During the debate over the constitution, no American leader had fought its adoption with more vigor than Clinton. At the state convention, held in Poughkeepsie to consider the merits of the document, the governor had lost his long battle to keep New York from ratifying by only a few votes, and largely because by the end of that hectic session enough other states had ratified to make the federal union a *fait accompli.*

Now that the experiment in strong national government was underway, the thought of leaving its most outspoken enemy in the New York governorship for another three years was more than Hamilton and his cohorts could bear. On 11 February 1789 the Federalists of New York City gathered at Bardin's tavern on Broad Street to map campaign strategy and select a candidate to run against Clinton. Burr, as one of the "numerous and respectable . . . Citizens" on hand, agreed to serve on the committee of correspondence, whose members would carry the burden of the canvass by communicating with similar groups in other parts of the state and by going into the wards of the city to give speeches and drum up votes. The candidate decided upon was Justice Robert Yates of the state supreme court. Yates had opposed the constitution, but since its adoption he had gone out of his way to urge the citizenry to support the new union. The consensus of Hamilton and company was that no out-and-out Federalist could overcome the strong anticonstitutional bias among the farmers in the northern counties. As a moderate Anti-Federalist, however, Yates could be counted on to siphon off some of Clinton's strength in those areas. The votes gained thus, plus those of the Federalist majority in New York City and vicinity, might carry the day.

Why Burr joined in this attack on Governor Clinton still floats in the airy realm of conjecture. Biographer Parton ventures the theory that his motives were exclusively personal. He was fond of Robert Yates and felt indebted to him as one of the formulators of the supreme-court ruling that had eased the colonel's admission to the bar. Parton's assumption would be more convincing if it could be said that Burr's first—and last—political partnership with Hamilton was also his last excursion into Federalism. Not only would there be other such excursions, but in the perspective provided by his subsequent career, his movements during the gubernatorial election of 1789 exhibit all the earmarks of a fishing expedition—the exploration of the political terrain by an ambitious newcomer to the field, interested in staking out a base for his own future operations. Were this Burr's objective, his look at New York conservatism from the inside must have been an enlightening one. If he was not already aware that Hamilton's leadership there was fixed in granite, he knew it now; and it is difficult to think of Aaron playing second fiddle to Alexander. But if in the opening months of 1789 there was no room for a man of Burr's independent disposition in the upper echelons of Federalism, circumstances were about to make a place for him in another part of the political forest.

5

George Clinton's retention of the governorship in 1789 was, in some respects, a Pyrrhic victory for that master politician and dyed-in-the-wool Democrat. His majority, 429 votes, was disturbingly close, coming as it did on the heels of his defeat over the issue of ratification at the Poughkeepsie convention. Although, even with Burr's help, Hamilton and company had failed to dislodge the durable chief magistrate, they had succeeded in challenging his long domination of New York politics by electing Federalist majorities to both branches of the legislature for the first time. On the threshold of his fifth term, in other words, His Excellency was in trouble. He and his administration needed new friends and new blood. When in September the post of state attorney general fell vacant and Clinton offered it to Aaron Burr, his motives were those of a beleaguered chieftain, anxious to attach the touted abilities of a sought-after lawyer to his own tribe, and hopeful of persuading a well-liked and rising young politico to give up the bad company he had been keeping.

Burr's acceptance of the job, after a brief hesitation, plunged him into a welter of laborious duties. The formation in 1789 of the government outlined by the constitution rendered his position far more important than it had been during the easy-going days of the confederation. The states and the new federal government were just beginning to learn how to live together. With no precedents to follow, Burr had to cope with the many and delicate legal issues involved in resolving where the obligations of New York State left off and those of the United States took over. Day after day, petitions growing out of the turbulence of the Revolution poured into the legislature, to be referred to the desk of the state's legal expert: soldiers demanding back wages or disability pay, longtime creditors crying for relief, sufferers from losses arising out of the depreciated post-war currency, property owners alleging damages resulting from confiscation or expropriation. Prodded by the quality and complexity of the pleas, the legislature established a commission made up of Burr and two other officials with orders to draft a basis for proper settlements. Burr was the author of the commission's report. It has been described as "a masterly and exhaustive study, codifying the groups of claims, establishing uniform rules . . . for their examination, and treating all classes of claimants with . . . impartiality." Approved by the lawmakers in 1792, it became the guide for all subsequent settlements and a monument to Burr's lifelong adherence to the work ethic of his Puritan forebears.

His position also made him ex officio one of the commissioners of the state land office. The regular members were the governor and three other officials, and during the closing months of Burr's two-year attorney generalship, their operations provided the state with its first governmental scandal. At the time, New York was the owner of seven million acres of unappropriated land. The future of the area hinged on the rapidity with which these domains could be sold and opened to settlers. More to the point, the state needed the proceeds from such sales now that the collection of duties at the port of New York, once the prerogative of the state, had been transferred to the federal government by the new constitution—a factor of no small weight in George Clinton's dislike of that document.

Sales had been slow, and to speed them up, the legislature in 1791 authorized the commissioners of the land office to dispose of any "unappropriated lands, in such parcels and on such terms and in such manner as they deemed in the public interest." It was a case of *carte blanche*, and like most bestowals of discretionary power by one segment of a government on another, it turned out to be a source of trouble.

A few statistics tell the tale. The land commissioners received their generous grant of powers from the legislature on 22 March 1791. During the remainder of the year they sold 5,542,173 acres for $1,034,483, putting the average price at nineteen cents an acre. Included in the total, however, was a single sale to the New York City merchant-speculator, Alexander Macomb, of an area larger than the state of Connecticut —3,365,200 acres in all, at eight cents an acre.

When the report of the commissioners went to the Assembly, and from thence into the newspapers, the howling began. All over the state, ugly charges moved from tongue to tongue. On the floor of the Assembly a representative from Montgomery County intimated—nay, stated—that Governor Clinton and his friends had lined their own pockets in the matter of the sale to Macomb. For months the accusations persisted, finally dying away for lack of evidence—although the speed with which the Assembly disposed of the subject suggests that few members of that body were looking for any. Formal debate on the report from the land commissioners began on 9 April 1792. On the following afternoon the lawmakers voted thirty-five to twenty in favor of a motion to exonerate them of all charges of corruption. Thus was the issue swept under the rug. But not out of mind. The charges against Clinton would dog him, off and on, for the rest of his long political career.

As for Burr—to this day his part in the scandal, like so many facets of his life, continues to be a matter of clashing interpretations. The report of the land commissioners shows that they held nineteen meetings, and that the attorney general was present at only one of them. All the meetings took place in New York City, and Burr's correspondence reveals that at the time of the crucial session—the one at which the grant to Alexander Macomb was approved—he was out of town on official or personal business. It follows, according to his apologists, that he had nothing to do with the huge and questionable grant of land to Macomb. Other historians are not so sure: one notes that, if Burr was away from his desk during all the necessarily protracted negotiations connected with the Macomb affair, he must have been neglecting his duties as attorney general; another finds it not insignificant that, when Macomb's mammoth tract went on the market, Aaron managed to buy two hundred thousand acres of it, and this at a time—1793 or 1794—when he was hard put to take up even the smallest of his overdue notes. If Aaron did derive any profits from his perhaps ill-gotten parcel of the Macomb land, it can be assumed that they clung to his hands only until his creditors got word and hied themselves to court. Incidentally, the brush that tarred Burr did not spare Alexander Hamilton. Newspaper articles in the summer of 1792 accused both Hamilton and his father-in-law, Philip Schuyler, of having "been interested" in the Macomb landgrab.

6

ONCE WHOLLY COMMITTED to politics, Burr would become a chronic office seeker, but it is worth noting that the opening phase of his public life was marked by a minimum of outward aggressiveness. His one-year term in the New York Assembly was none of his doing. It was a gift of the people. If he made any campaign speeches or shook the hands of a single voter, the record fails to reveal it. The attorney generalship sought him, not he it; and to move on to the next phase of his career—his election to the United States Senate—that event, too, owed little to his own efforts and much to a recent realignment of party loyalties in the state of New York, a sudden and dramatic development, inadvertently fomented by Alexander Hamilton and brought to fruition by Chancellor Robert R. Livingston and Governor Clinton.

The skirmishes that put Burr in the Senate in 1791 had their beginnings two years earlier when in the summer of 1789 Clinton convened a special session of the legislature at Albany for the purpose of choosing the state's first federal senators. James Parton, being more amusing than accurate, described the New York political world of the late 1780's as divided, like all Gaul, into three parts—the Clintons, the Livingstons, and the Schuylers—adding to this his often quoted statement that "the Clintons had *power*, the Livingstons had *numbers*, and the Schuylers had *Hamilton*." In 1789, New York's Gaul consisted not of three but of two parts. Ranged on one side were the Clintons and their largely Anti-Federalist followers. On the other side stood a political coalition that derived much of its strength from the willingness of the Schuylers and the Livingstons to work together under the banner of Federalism and the leadership of Hamilton.

It was the coalition that during the spring election had managed to put both houses of the legislature under Federalist control. Naturally, everyone involved in this triumph looked forward to reaping the benefits thereof. It was a foregone conclusion that both of New York's first United States senators would be Federalists. It was also taken for granted that one of the Senate seats would go to General Philip Schuyler, as the titular head of his big family, and the other to James

Duane, whose marriage to a Livingston made him an acceptable representative of that even more numerous clan. Covering this aspect of things was a gentleman's agreement. General Schuyler had promised that, in return for backing from the Livingstons for his own senatorial ambitions, he and his supporters would see to it that Duane was also elected. By the start of the special session, these neat balancing acts had been arranged, and all was in order. But almost before the echoes of the opening gavel had died away, all was disorder.

Watching the proceedings from New York City, Alexander Hamilton decided to intervene. It was an ill-considered move on the part of the Federalist czar, one that his biographer, John C. Miller, offers as a striking example of Hamilton's ignorance of the "art of holding together" a political party comprised, as New York Federalism was, of jealous and uneasily cooperating factions. Hamilton did not want Duane to go to the United States Senate. His reasoning was, to say the least, circuitous. Duane was still mayor of New York, and Hamilton was convinced that, were he to vacate that post, his successor would be "some very unfit character," whose policies would be "injurious to the city." The impetuous Federalist leader neglected to specify what "unfit characters" he had in mind. Apparently not Burr. In the summer of 1789 he and Burr were still on such good terms that Aaron, who was in Albany, was using the mails to keep Alexander informed of what was going on there.

Hamilton's choice for what had previously been thought of as the Livingston seat in the federal Senate was thirty-four-year-old Rufus King of New York City, a New Englander by birth and rearing who had only recently moved into the Empire State. One can only wonder whether Hamilton would have opted for the transplanted New Englander had he known that, behind the scenes, George Clinton was also pushing Rufus King, the wily governor understandably assuming that any outcome of the senatorial election that left the Livingstons mad at the Schuylers, or vice versa, would redound to the benefit of the Clintons.

During that erratic special session of the legislature, Burr was not the only politician making heavy use of the mails. So was Hamilton. Somehow he persuaded his stern and haughty father-in-law to break the promise to support Duane that Schuyler had given to the Livingstons. Consequently, when the legislative hassle ended on 16 July, General Schuyler had one of the New York seats in the federal Senate, Rufus King had the other, and the Livingstons had nothing!

To Robert R. Livingston, with his large and tender ego, the insult was twofold. His candidate had been passed over, and the seat Duane was supposed to have won had been bestowed on a newcomer to the state, a rank interloper who owed no allegiance to the Livingstons or to any of the other large and opulent families that constituted the warp and woof of New York Federalism. If at first the chancellor's anger could only be directed, scattershot-style, at the Federalist majorities in the legislature, it swiftly found a focus when Alexander Hamilton's decisive role in the upset became a matter of common knowledge.

Herein lay the principal reason for the chancellor's decision to strike back at Hamilton by removing the powerful Livingston clan from the Federalist fold. The break became known on 17 December when Livingston delivered one of his notably polished orations at a large Masonic gathering in New York City in honor of St. John's Day. Secretary of the Treasury Hamilton, as part of his bold effort to put the credit of the new national government on a sound basis, had fashioned and persuaded the Congress to pass the so-called assumption bill. Under this famous measure the federal government, having arranged to fund its own war debts, now undertook to pay off those of the states as well. Livingston, in his St. John's Day speech, assailed the assumption law as having opened the door to widespread stockjobbing, to the benefit of the rich and the detriment of the poor. Having made clear his objections to a key aspect of Hamilton's grand financial scheme for the country, the chancellor proceeded to lead most of the major factotums of his family out of the Federalist camp. Some of them protested loudly, to be sure. As speculators in public securities, they were already richer as a consequence of Hamilton's monetary arrangements. But, in the end, family loyalty prevailed. Like so many sheep they followed the chancellor straight into the welcoming arms of Governor Clinton. The resulting alliance, often spoken of as the Clinton–Livingston coalition, was to have a profound effect on the future of New York—and national—politics.

7

GOVERNOR CLINTON had at least as much reason as the chancellor to want to see Alexander Hamilton's wings clipped, and in the closing weeks of 1790 their newly combined forces gave them the power to attempt such a ploy, and an impending event the opportunity of carrying it out. In conformance with the constitutional requirement that a third of the seats in the first federal Senate go up for election every second year, Schuyler and King had drawn lots. As Schuyler had drawn the short term, due to expire on 4 March 1791, the legislature convening in New York City in January would be called on either to send him back for a second term or to elect someone else to his seat. Under these circumstances, the nature of the Livingston–Clinton attack on the Secretary of the Treasury was preordained. To attain their ends, the leaders of the coalition had only to defeat Hamilton's father-in-law for reelection.

Their first task was to agree on an alternative candidate, and their choice of Aaron Burr was a natural one. Burr came as close as an active politician could to having no identifiable party coloration. The memory of his collaboration with Hamilton in the gubernatorial election of 1789 rendered him inoffensive to the Federalist majorities in the legislature. His status as an official in the Clinton administration made him acceptable to the Anti-Federalists. In addition, his brilliant handling of the attorney generalship had not gone unnoticed. Neither had Philip Schuyler's less impressive behavior as a United States senator. Both in and out of the state, there was a widespread feeling that Schuyler was not his own man, that, as Senator William Maclay of Pennsylvania had noted in his pungent diary, the patroon was "the supple jack" of his son-in-law, the Secretary of the Treasury. Schuyler, moreover, had annoyed the New York lawmakers by ignoring their passage in 1790 of a ban on dual officeholding. Under this measure, Senator King and a number of other New Yorkers had been compelled to give up their seats in the state legislature. Alone among those affected, Schuyler had declined to bow to the law. In the face of repeated challenges, he had refused to resign from the Council of Appointment, regularly attending its meetings and just as regularly voting against Governor Clinton's nominations.

Last but not least, Burr was widely liked, whereas the patroon, in the words of a biographer, "was formed for unpopularity." Even so high-toned a Federalist as Nathaniel Hazard of New York City had to admit that to meet Aaron Burr but once was to be fascinated by him forever. In a long and chatty letter to Hamilton, the wealthy ironmonger wrote: "This Person (C.B.)," meaning Colonel Burr, "has an Address not resistable by common Clay . . ." Burr's always courtly but always easy manner charmed. In the case of Philip Schuyler, a big man with overlarge features and penetrating eyes, the same courtliness exuded a fortress-like quality that repelled.

It is not known at what point in their preparations for the upcoming election Livingston and Clinton approached Burr and drew him into the plot. In the opening days of 1791 Livingston was holding sessions of the Court of Chancery at his

New York town house. The attorney general, as an officer of the court, was often present. There were ample opportunities for the two men to discuss the local political situation.

In his biography of Hamilton, John C. Miller writes that the attorney general was happy to join the Clinton–Livingston attack on the Secretary of the Treasury, via his father-in-law, because Burr was "always sedulous to put himself on the winning side." Admittedly he was, but it may be fair to add that a politician is, by definition, a person "sedulous to put himself on the winning side." Certainly Clinton and Livingston were sedulous, so much so as to suggest that they were not all that sure of winning. Once having agreed on the attempt to dump Schuyler and replace him with Burr, their actions as the legislature got underway in January were those of conspirators determined to leave nothing to chance.

The ubiquitous Robert Troup found their "twistings, combinations and maneuvers . . . incredible." He wrote Hamilton that it "would take a quire of paper to do them justice." One of the first duties demanded of the newly convened Assembly was to name a Council of Appointment for the year 1791, and in the course of the give-and-take of this operation, Clinton wielded the patronage with such dexterity, according to a pro-Hamilton observer, "that many who were Federalists were sucked into his Excellency's vortex." One of the governor's more telling maneuvers was to let it be known that, whenever Burr stepped down from the attorney generalship, that post would be offered to Morgan Lewis, who like James Duane was an adherent of the Livingston faction by marriage. In the state senate the chancellor's doctor brother-in-law, Thomas Tillotson, was tagged to ride herd on the Clinton–Livingston interests. Burr was not idle. It was observed that he was wining and dining selected members of the Assembly, spending money he did not have, as usual.

In both houses the election fell on 19 January. In the Assembly the customary formula was employed. First came a motion calling for the election "of ———" to the federal Senate. Then a motion to insert Philip Schuyler's name in the blank space was defeated by a vote of thirty-two to twenty-seven, after which a motion to substitute Aaron Burr's name carried by the same figures. In the state senate the vote for Burr was fourteen to four.

8

PANIC COURSED Federalist ranks. Hamilton's supporters bombarded him with letters black with prophesies of doom. The Secretary himself was stricken. From this hour on his own letters would be filled with excoriations of Burr, with those flashes of naked hate that would light the way to Weehawken. Philip Schuyler was convinced, as he wrote Hamilton, that Burr had been the "principal" in the maneuvers that had so humiliatingly toppled the proud patroon from his high position—a declaration which indicates that Schuyler either failed to recognize, or preferred not to recognize, the pivotal part his son-in-law had played in the affair: Hamilton, by his own political ineptitude, had driven Chancellor Livingston and his followers out of the Federalist Party—and elevated Aaron Burr to a position of commanding influence on the national stage.

8

"Commence Politician"

NOW, AT LAST, Burr was ready, as his wife put it, to "commence politician" seriously—and this at a time when the country was passing through an uneasy transition. Issues and political combinations valid to the preceding decade were wearing away. New ones were forming. Burr's senatorship would see the rise of the country's first party system, and it may be helpful in following his career as a national figure to linger briefly over the genesis of that phenomenon.

At Philadelphia the Founding Fathers were not indulging in idle rhetoric when they described their labors there as an attempt "to form a more perfect union." To these heirs of the rebellion against imperial England, "union" was a glorious word. It meant stability, and the whole purpose in shifting from a weak to a strong central government was to solidify the accomplishments for which the Revolution had been fought. The Fathers realized that whatever government came out of their efforts would be a step into the unknown. It would be fragile and vulnerable. Factionalism could easily tear it apart, strangling the infant, as it were, before it had a chance to exhibit its ability to "secure the Blessings of Liberty to ourselves and our Posterity." The adherents of a formal political entity tended to put excessive value on their particular theories, forgetting, in their zeal to beat down the members of the other party, that there are few issues so intractable that they cannot be resolved by give-and-take.

In the 1780's the aversion to partisanship, so pronounced among the Founding Fathers, seems to have been shared by practically all national leaders and by the bulk of the voting citizenry. One can imagine, therefore, a great welling up of relief across the country when the first Congress to sit under the constitution framed and asked the states to ratify the first ten amendments, the Bill of Rights. Sponsored by the "father of the constitution," Congressman James Madison of Virginia, this action, as his biographer states, "smothered the dangerous fire of Anti-federalism." It provided the give-and-take, the compromise, whereby the great debate over the constitution was settled. With the adoption of the Bill of Rights, the fear that the argument over ratification would engender a party system disappeared—only to rise again when in 1790 Alexander Hamilton, as the first Secretary of the Treasury, set forth his grand financial scheme for putting the credit of the new central government on a sound basis. Hamilton's fiscal proposals plunged the country into its second great debate. Of this controversy Richard Buel has written that, like the debate over the constitution, "it raised a question more fundamental than any clash of economic interests, how to stabilize the Republic and secure revolutionary achievements." For this second great debate, however, no compromise was available. Consequently, it first divided the national leadership, then the Congress, and ultimately the people. These splits made the emergence of a party system a strong likelihood, and a subsequent and even sharper quarrel over foreign policy—about which more in its proper setting—rendered it inevitable.

To a people longing for unity and stability, the early actions of the first Congress were reassuring. Rapidly the two houses proposed the Bill of Rights. Rapidly they organized the executive and judiciary branches of the government and established a national revenue. Disagreements arose over specifics, but nowhere along the line did there arise the sort of divergence that produces political parties. For seven months a remarkable harmony prevailed. Then, toward the close of the first session of the first Congress, the lawmakers took up the question of how the holders of public securities—the new government's numerous creditors—were to be satisfied. Involving the retirement of an enormous debt, here was a problem too vexing and intricate for the tired solons to tackle on their own. They turned for help to the country's foremost expert on such matters, Secretary Hamilton.

Hamilton embodied his suggested solution to the problem in two now famous documents: his "Report on the Public Credit," submitted to the Congress on 14 January 1790, and his "Report on the National Bank," delivered nine months later. What was to become his grand financial scheme consisted of four proposals. He suggested not only that the federal government provide for its own domestic debts, totaling some $42 million, but also that it assume and provide for those of the states, estimated at $25 million. Another recommendation aimed at making this giant undertaking possible by reducing the rate of interest on the consolidated debt, originally six percent, to four percent. Still another called for the creation of a sinking fund to buy the debt at the market rate. Hamilton's fourth proposal was that the federal government establish what was to be the Bank of the United States. This would be a national institution, authorized to issue notes and with most of its capital subscribed in the funded debt of the United States. Funding, assumption, and the bank—by these catchwords has Hamilton's grand financial scheme become known.

The arguments over it erupted at once. Naturally, many of them revolved around the matter of whose pocketbooks the scheme would fatten and whose it would pinch. But, as Richard Buel points out, questions of this type are always open to compromise. What was not open to compromise—what was to help shape the future of the Republic—was the ideological issue that had given the debate over the constitution its intensity, and that this second great debate was about to set forth in high relief.

Madison brought this issue into the arena when he rose in the House of Representatives to propose a change in the Hamiltonian system that would be spoken of as the policy of discrimination. The bulk of the debt dated back to the War of Independence. To finance that mammoth struggle, both the national government and the state governments had borrowed heavily from their citizens. Large numbers of soldiers, among others, had accepted government I.O.U.'s—certificates of one sort or another—in lieu of wages or other monies due them from governments with almost no funds in their treasuries. Most of the wealthier public creditors had held on to their certificates, hoping that someday the debtor governments would be strong enough to pay them off. Desperate for cash, however, many of the poorer creditors—numerous veterans of the battlefield among them—had long since sold their certificates at a discount to speculators. Under Hamilton's proposals, only current holders of certificates were to be rewarded. It was this aspect of his scheme that Madison challenged when he proposed that, in the case of any certificate that had changed hands, the original buyer be given an appropriate portion of whatever sum was now due on it.

Hamilton's resistance to this change gave birth to the classic quarrel that would eventuate in the formation of the Democratic-Republican or, as it was then usually termed, the Republican Party, under the leadership of Madison's Virginia neighbor and philosophical ally, Thomas Jefferson. The details of the quarrel, shot through as it was with delicate questions of legality and equity, need not detain us in these pages. Behind Hamilton's determination to see his scheme in effect, exactly as proposed, lay the conviction that the new Republic could attain its proper destiny only by a marriage of the federal government to the monied interests of the country. Madison and

Jefferson, on their part, wanted a government with a broader and more popular base. They believed that Hamilton's doctrines could only point the country in the direction of monarchy. Hamilton was equally certain that the doctrines underlying their objections to his fiscal program would point it to anarchy. He won the great fiscal battle of 1790, but the ideological difference lingered on, to become one of the major issues around which American politics would evolve.

It may be assumed that Aaron Burr watched with interest the development of the quarrel. By the time of the colonel's election to the Senate in January 1791, Hamilton's funding and assumption plans had become law, and the bank was about to follow suit. If Burr had any strong inclinations, one way or the other, about funding and assumption, he never reduced them to writing. He did mention the bank in one of his frequent letters to his longtime Federalist friend, Congressman Theodore Sedgwick of Massachusetts. "The bank," he wrote that stalwart pro-Hamiltonian on 3 February 1791, ". . . is thought by our speculators and Brokers to be the most interesting object" of Hamilton's scheme. "To me," Burr added, "the promised advantages appear problematic. There are . . . some ingenious thoughts respecting the utility of banks in Humes [sic] Essays on Money, on Interest, and on the Ballance [sic] of Trade or in one of them." Burr confessed that he had not examined the essays with care. Nor had he "read with proper attention" Hamilton's published arguments for wishing to see the bank installed. Burr felt, therefore, that he could not "pass on its merits." But "because of your deeper study," he told Sedgwick, "you may discern benefits not obvious to me and adapt remedies to some inconveniences which a cursory view of the Subject had led me to apprehend."

One is struck by the blithe airiness of this comment. Obviously, the ideological implications of the controversy over Hamilton's scheme were lost on New York's new senator-to-be. Given Burr's subsequent voting record in Congress, we can describe him as a Democrat by instinct. Apparently, the man who believed that the "road to heaven was open to all alike" also believed, with Jefferson and Madison, that the road to political power was open as much to the butcher, the baker, and the candlestick-maker as to the aristocrat. But no deep thought underlay the colonel's never well-defined political leanings. He was a doer, not a thinker. To some degree, his later troubles with Jefferson can be ascribed to the temperamental gulf across which they viewed one another. To a man of Jefferson's thoughtful disposition, the colonel seemed superficial. To Burr, the Virginian often seemed lacking in vigor and daring, those attributes so dear to the heart of the doing man.

2

DURING THE NINE MONTHS between Burr's election to the Senate and the opening of the second Congress, the alarm set off by his victory continued to clang among "Hamilton's gladiators," as Senator Maclay of Pennsylvania had nicknamed the Secretary of the Treasury's army of political informants. The rich and high-living New York speculator, William Duer, wrote Hamilton: "Our political situation . . . has a most gloomy aspect." Robert Troup, "disgusted to my heart," declared himself ready to "withdraw from politics."

Troup was the Cassandra of his party. It was a rare day when "that great fat fellow," as Burr now spoke of his old friend, did not put pen to paper to say in effect to Hamilton or Rufus King or some other Federalist luminary that "We are undone." Dark suspicions flooded Troup's mind when in the summer after Burr's election Secretary of State Jefferson and Congressman Madison undertook their 920-mile "botanizing tour" of five Northern states. On the road for a month and two days, the Virginians spent most of their time in the primeval forest, studying the flora and fauna. But Robert Troup was not taken in. What registered in his mind was that they tarried a few hours in New York City and another few hours in Albany, long enough "to study *Clintonia borealis* and other hardy perennials" of those centers of political horticulture. Writing Hamilton from New York City, Troup noted that there "was every appearance of a passionate courtship between the Chancellor [Livingston], Burr, Jefferson & Madison when the two latter were in town. *Delenda est Carthago* I suppose is the maxim with respect to you. They had better be quiet, for if they succeed they will tumble the fabric of the government in ruins to the ground." Behind all that devotion to the birds and the bees, in other words, Federalism's keenest political voyeur thought he saw an effort by Jefferson and Madison to forge an alliance between the anti-Hamiltonians of Virginia and those of the Empire State, a linkage calculated to pose a severe threat to Federalist domination of the country. Troup may have been right. Future events would indicate as much.

It has been written of Burr that at the time of his election to the Senate he had "no inkling" of Hamilton's rage. One must acknowledge that the key to many of the colonel's future troubles lay in his failure to appreciate the depth and durability of the Secretary of the Treasury's anger. Burr's mind was on the whole an unsuspicious one. Little inclined to harbor malice, he was slow to spot it in others—too slow, on occasion, to protect himself against it. No one detected this quality in him more shrewdly than Andrew Jackson, or better expressed it. "Burr," the great Tennessean once remarked, "is as far from a fool as I ever saw, and yet he is as easily fooled as any man I ever knew." Too wrapped up in himself to see other men clearly, Burr lacked that touch of paranoia so essential to success in politics.

Still, even Burr, overly sanguine though he was, could not overlook the obvious. Only three days after his defeat of Schuyler, he was writing Theodore Sedgwick that "my election will be displeasing to several persons in Philadelphia—there was uncommon animosity and eagerness in the opposition."

Other than this remark, he seems to have said little about

his triumph. His restraint was matched by that of his wife. Theodosia had never reconciled herself to his many absences from home. Nor did she contemplate with relish the long stays in the Quaker City his new post would entail. Seemingly, however, she voiced no complaint on this score. Her only known expression of concern dealt with the prolonged headaches and bouts of fever and fatigue that still afflicted him. "It is, indeed, of serious consequence to you," she admonished Aaron, "to establish your health *before you commence politician:* when once you get engaged, your industry will exceed your strength; your pride cause you to forget yourself. But remember, you are not your own; there are those who have stronger claims than ambition ought to have, or the public can have."

She knew him well. Too well, no doubt, to expect him to follow such prudent advice. As he pointed out to Sedgwick, he was not looking forward to a "life of Dissipation & Ease" in Congress. No longer did he regard politics merely as a handmaiden to the law. It had become his primary vocation. He meant to make the most of it.

Having been handpicked for the Senate by Clinton and Livingston, he was ostensibly a partner in their coalition. He had not yet departed for Philadelphia, however, before another of Hamilton's watchful gladiators, Nathaniel Hazard, was discerning signs that the senator-elect was pulling away from his sponsors. Clinton had promised Burr's post as attorney general to Morgan Lewis of the Livingston clan. Presumably the governor wished to make good on his offer as soon as possible, but eight months after the election in the New York legislature, Hazard was reporting gleefully to Hamilton that "Clinton is staggered, he is afraid to turn Burr out, and Burr won't resign . . . if he can avoid it," until a new Council of Appointment was chosen.

Like Troup, Hazard was a tireless collector of political gossip. Like Troup, he sometimes overdramatized his findings. In this instance, however, the gabby New York merchant struck fact. When on 24 October 1791 the second Congress came to order, Burr was still attorney general of New York. He would remain so until the eighth of the following month.

Obviously, he was not taking his ties to the coalition too seriously. He was entering the Senate as a political freelance. He was an independent and a loner by temperament. Many of his future troubles can be attributed to a lifelong inability to function within a conventional political framework. Fresh in the memory of his countrymen was an almost unbelievable fact of history—how, with a boost from France, a handful of ill-clad and ill-armed farmers had turned back the mighty armies and navies of Great Britain. In doing so, they had not only won the right to found their own nation; they had also deprived England of approximately one half of its overseas empire. If one of the world's greatest powers could be thus cracked, how much more easily could their infant Republic be torn apart. It was a rare Federalist who was not convinced that unless the great American experiment in representative government was conducted according to his ideas, it would fail. It was a rare Republican who did not believe exactly the same thing. Caught between these understandable extremes of fear, the independent Mr. Burr was certain in time to become widely suspect in both political camps. As Gouverneur Morris pointed out to Hamilton, "It is dangerous to be impartial in politics; you, who are temperate in drinking, have never perhaps noticed the awkward situation of a man who continues sober after the company are drunk."

During his six years in the Senate, Burr used his seat there as a base from which to stage electioneering forays into his home state, some of them in an effort to snatch the governorship from Clinton, others with bigger game in his sights. In the pursuit of these ends he welcomed support from any faction. Ultimately, his efforts in New York would redound to the benefit of the democracy; and he would come to think of himself as a champion of that cause and to regard the refusal of many Republican leaders to see him in that light as rank ingratitude. Much that has been written of this phase of his life has a moralistic tinge. It leaves the impression that running for office, however acceptable in other politicians, somehow became an evil when practiced by Aaron Burr—a case of imputing wickedness where the only reasonable charge would seem to be faulty judgment.

3

WITH THE CONGRESS scheduled to open on the next to last Monday in October, Burr left home early the week before in the hopes of locating "tolerable winter quarters" before the session started. Illness detained him en route. It was Sunday before he reached Philadelphia. Four days later he was writing Theodosia that he was still at a boardinghouse, "unsettled" and "having some trouble on that head, as well because I am difficult to please, as because good accommodations are difficult to find . . ." No doubt she was relieved to learn from his next letter that he had obtained lodgings appropriate to his Chesterfieldian standards. "The house," he wrote, ". . . is inhabited by two widows. The mother about seventy, the daughter about fifty . . . The old lady is deaf, and upon my first coming . . . she with great civility requested that I would never attempt to speak to her, for fear of injuring my lungs without being able to make her hear. I shall faithfully obey this injunction."

He was no sooner settled in than he began begging Theodosia to make good on a promised visit. He assured her that his quarters were "commodious" enough for both her and "Mrs. A," a reference to Mrs. Mary Allen of Union, New York, known as Mama in the Burr household, where for years she acted first as a companion to the older Theodosia and, after her death, as an adviser on dress and deportment to the younger one. For weeks Mrs. Burr's frequently planned and frequently postponed visit was the burden of numerous letters.

Pleas on Aaron's side, excuses on hers, engendered by a fear of the effect on her always uncertain health of a long journey by stagecoach. It occurred to him that she might have "a particular aversion" to the Quaker City. If so, he would arrange for her to spend part of her visit at the home of their friend, Dr. Enoch Edwards, ten miles out of town. His first session in the Congress was almost over before she finally arrived, to discover presently that she did have an aversion.

"This is the most inhospitable region that ever was inhabited," she wrote her son Bartow. ". . . Chestnut Street excepted, one dark gloomy narrow confined straight pictures all this celebrated city." This somewhat obscure sentence means apparently that in Mrs. Burr's mind most of Philadelphia was a pattern of dull, straight streets, one exactly like the other. "The parties," she told her son, "resemble a playhouse before the curtain is drawn up. The ostentatious part is a footman with a silver breadbasket, and the Hospitality is profering a cup of cold tea to a mob."

In short, the New York snob could not abide the Philadelphia snobs. She was eager to be back in her own city, but Burr was temporarily out of town. She thought it best to wait until he returned and could travel home with her. "Preferable to dying on the road," she wrote her son, "indeed to dying anywhere." She would visit Philadelphia no more. Whenever in the future Aaron's long stretches there grew intolerable to the two of them, they would get together at some intermediate point in New Jersey.

4

BURR, MEANWHILE, had begun his senatorial chores. In Philadelphia the Congress met in the prim, two-story brick building with its high and generous windows that still huddles under the more impressive flanks of Independence Hall and is known as Congress Hall. The representatives convened on the first floor, the senators above. According to an anonymous letter writer of the day, the Senate chamber was overheated and underdecorated. The presiding officer, Vice President John Adams, a man passionately fond of the trappings of office, had to content himself with "a very plain chair, without canopy, and a small mahogany table . . . festooned at the sides and front with green silk." Amid these unpretentious surroundings, the most elaborate punctilio prevailed. Our unknown correspondent asserts that "during the debate" the thirty senators "constantly" exhibited "the most beautiful order, gravity, and personal dignity of manners."

Of the content of the debate, not much is known. When Burr took his seat, the Senate was still meeting behind closed doors, its premises barred to public and press save on specified occasions. During this period the *Annals*, the official record of the proceedings, consisted of little more than a list of motions and votes. Burr and his colleague, Rufus King, were under instructions from the New York legislature to work for an open Senate. Both were diligent to this end, but not until 1795, two years before the close of Burr's term, were visitors admitted to the Senate gallery on a regular basis. Only at this point did the *Annals* begin to carry a paraphrase of the debate.

The meagerness of the official record makes it impossible to say how effective Burr was on the floor of the Senate. It is known that during a debate on an important matter the Virginia senator and political philosopher, John Taylor of Caroline, left a note on the New Yorker's desk, urging him to carry the burden of the argument for the Republicans because "all depends on it" and "no one else can do it." On the other hand, Senator King thought his colleague's reputation as a debater overrated. King said Burr had a genius for summing up everything previously said on an issue, but that he rarely added any ideas of his own.

Although sketchy, the official record is not opaque. Its many roll calls find Burr siding with the emerging Republican Party. A twentieth-century quantitative analysis, done with the aid of a computer and covering the first four Congresses, reveals that when he left the Senate he could point to a voting record as Republican as that of any member of those Congresses. What neither the new study nor the old record brings out is that his consistently Republican voting record was accompanied by an equally consistent aversion to standing up and being counted in the party of that name or any other.

5

THE FIRST SESSION of the second Congress began in the usual way. Washington's custom was to deliver his report on the state of the Union in person. On the second day the representatives came upstairs, the President appeared, and the conjoined lawmakers drank in his words. After Washington and the congressmen had gone, the senators named a three-man committee to draft a reply to the President's address. To Burr, as the chairman of this body, fell the privilege of doing the work. On the following day his message was approved as written, and a few days later the senators went in procession to the handsome Robert Morris mansion at 190 High (now Market) Street, where Washington and his family resided. There, in a dining room cleared of tables and chairs, the stately general stood before the fireplace, his blond features rigidly composed, his powdered hair gathered into a silk bag behind, a sword with a gleaming hilt and a white sheath highlighting the somber black of his velvet suit. The visiting solons formed a semicircle around him. Vice President Adams read the brief reply Burr had prepared. The President read an even briefer reply to the reply. Then the senators returned to their working quarters.

Such were the opening formalities of a session that lasted for more than six months. A quiet session on the whole. The fireworks would come later. In or out of the Senate chamber, the gentleman from New York kept busy. The official record puts him on numerous committees. His name on a large percentage of the roll calls suggests a fairly steady attendance.

The winter months of 1792 found him spending the early part of the day reading in the archives of the Department of State. Regularly reaching this sanctuary at five in the morning, he devoted the hours until the ten o'clock opening of the Senate to searching the records. One of his purposes was to gather material for a history of the War of Independence. He would often return to this project in the future, but it never materialized. Too bad. Whatever its other qualities, his account would have had the value of being a history *sui generis*. Burr was convinced that the real heroes of the Revolution remained unsung. Those touted by posterity, he would contend to his dying breath, were in truth only secondary actors in the drama.

Another of his purposes in inspecting the State Department records was to increase his knowledge of the relations of his country with foreign powers. Having obtained Jefferson's permission to do so, he was startled one day to feel the heavy hand of authority. Suddenly there was a message from Washington ordering him to desist from his studies. Baffled, the senator penned an inquiry to the secretary. "Thomas Jefferson presents his respectful compliments to Colonel Burr," the secretary replied, "and is sorry to inform him it has been concluded to be improper to communicate the correspondence of existing ministers. He hopes this will, with Colonel Burr, be his sufficient apology."

It wasn't. Burr seethed at what he considered a "peremptory" order. Once again, by his lights, General Washington had treated him shabbily for no apparent reason.

6

HE WAS NO STRANGER to the Philadelphia of silver breadbaskets and cold cups of tea. The better drawing rooms had always been open to him. They still were. "Many invitations to dine &c," he wrote Theodosia. Presently Elizabeth

Drinker, wife of a respected Quaker leader, was noting in her diary: "Aaron Burr called . . . talk on various subjects." "Aaron Burr called . . . detained my husband from afternoon meeting." "Aaron Burr, James Ross, John Cannon, and John Cadwalader here this evening." Word of his socializing traveled to New York. We find him assuring Theodosia that the "reports of my life style are . . . much too absurd to gain belief."

Pointing to what? It has always been taken for granted that he was in every way faithful to his Theodosia during her lifetime. The evidence to the contrary is ambiguous, but suggestive. It consists of three brief notes written by Burr to his friend, Peter Van Gaasbeek. Two of them bear dates falling in the winter and spring preceding the death of Mrs. Burr. The third, undated, would seem to belong to the same period. As at the time of their writing both the author of them and Van Gaasbeek were living in Philadelphia, it can be assumed that the three missives were conveyed by messenger. What seems to be the earliest of them reads:

> I am glad to hear it. It is a proof that you was amused. Your best remedy is to dance again tomorrow if you can have the same Inducements.
>
> I am very much obliged to Mrs. Gilbert. The chariot will wait her orders in the Morning.

The other dated note:

> I am much obliged to your charming Inmate for accepting any part of my offer, & to you for your obliging Manner of communicating it. What relates to myself is so equivocal it leaves me room to believe that some more agreeable partner is at her disposal. The carriage will therefore wait her Orders at or before four.

The undated note:

> Upon a moments reflection, aided by the upsurge of interested feelings, I have doubted whether an *undue* diffidence

on my part, has not led me to decline the obliging overture of Mrs. G.

I shall come with the Chariot & we will then settle the rest.

On the surface of it, these notes point to a liaison. But the repetition of the unamorous phrase, "wait her Orders," gives pause. At the time these words were written, Burr and Van Gaasbeek were engaged in various speculative deals, and these tiny messages could be ciphers, with "Mrs. Gilbert" being the code name of a business go-between.

Much has been made of Burr's use of coded communications. Too much perhaps. In his era the regular mail was slow and uncertain. The surest way of getting a letter to its destination was to send it "by private hand," which is to say, entrusting it to someone who happened to be traveling to the vicinity of the addressee. Where confidential matter was concerned, this procedure, too, had its drawbacks. There was nothing to keep the carrier of the letter from opening and reading it en route. Many people, therefore, resorted to ciphers. Jefferson used them regularly in his correspondence with Madison. Hamilton, in a bantering reference to the code duello, wrote Gouverneur Morris that "I accept your challenge to meet you in the field of . . . *confidential communication*." Hamilton was preparing a cipher for their mutual use. He hoped to send it on soon. Meanwhile, he was enclosing a list of names of ancient Romans. By these he and Morris could refer to "official characters." Hamilton's code name for Burr was "Savius," meaning apparently Plautus Saevius, a first-century A.D. citizen of the Imperial City. Saevius's claim to fame was that he was ordered by a court to take his own life after being convicted of corrupting his son.

As always when he was away from home for long intervals, Burr showered his wife with detailed recitals of his comings and goings. She did the same for him. A recurrent subject of their correspondence was what would later be known as women's rights. An ardent feminist, Mrs. Burr was fascinated by the military and diplomatic coups of the empress of Russia. "The ladies should deify her," she wrote of Catherine the Great. "It is a diverting thought, that the mighty Emperor of the Turks should be subdued by a woman. How enviable that she alone should be the avenger of her sex's wrongs for so many ages past. She seems to have awakened Justice, who appears to be a sleepy dame in the cause of injured innocence."

Burr shared her predilections. A winter day found him relating his discovery of Mary Wollstonecraft's *A Vindication of the Rights of Woman* with the enthusiasm of a man newcome upon a priceless treasure. He wrote that he had heard this now classic pamphlet "spoken of with a coldness little calculated to excite attention; but as I read with avidity and prepossession every thing written by a lady, I made haste to procure it, and spent the last night, almost the whole of it, in reading it. Be assured that your sex has in *her* an able advocate . . . I promise myself much pleasure in reading it to you."

It was Burr's privilege, during his sojourns in Philadelphia, to have a hand in providing the country with one of its First Ladies, Dolley Payne Madison. His friendship with the buxom, Quaker-bred Dolley began whenever it was he moved into the boardinghouse run by her widowed mother, Mrs. Mary Coles Payne, at 96 North Third Street. At that time, probably early 1793, Dolley was living nearby with her lawyer husband, John Todd, and a small son. Six months later she, too, was a widow. Lawyer Todd had fallen victim to the yellow-fever epidemic of the preceding summer and fall. For at least a year after his death, Dolley was in financial straits, owing to the efforts of a brother-in-law to challenge her claims on her husband's estate. Burr did not act as her attorney, but as a "trusted friend and adviser" he was helpful with the arrangements that put the worried widow in possession of her inheritance. She was grateful. In a will signed on 13 May 1794, she named the senator from New York as the sole guardian of her son. About these matters Burr preserved a gentlemanly silence. In later years, however, he spoke often, and with pleasure, of his part in bringing the widow Todd and the future President together.

It happened on a spring day in 1794. For Dolley the day began with a note from Burr that she recognized at once as presaging a turning point in her life. Having dispatched a reply to the senator, she wrote an excited message to her Quaker friend, Eliza Collins. "Thou must come to me," she commanded. "Aaron Burr says that the great little Madison has asked to be brought to me this evening." He was duly "brought"—for a candlelit tryst, chaperoned by Miss Collins. Madison was forty-three, Dolley twenty-six, although at that time, as was her amiable wont, she claimed to be even younger. A few months later they were married.

7

DURING THE OPENING MONTHS of 1792, Burr can be described as presenting a double image. In the flesh he was in Philadelphia, attending to his duties as a United States senator. In spirit he was in his home state, running for a different office. There, with the balloting beginning toward the end of April, another of the triennial lotteries-*cum*-butchery, known as the general or gubernatorial election, was in process.

Its course was marked by confusion. Not without reason did John Adams, that exemplar of New England orderliness, characterize the leaders of New York's warring and shifting factions as "the Devil's own incomprehensibles." In this election, as in others, the party lines in the Empire State were so fluid that to picture Aaron Burr, during his run for the governorship, as darting from party to party is to suggest that he could see boundaries barely visible to anybody else.

George Clinton was hoping for a sixth term. As the campaign got underway in January 1792, however, the eyes of the fifty-three-year-old governor were not fastened exclusively on the immediate race. They were also on the Presidential election, coming up a few months hence. It was not yet known whether Washington would accept a second term. If he did, there would be no competition for the Presidency. But the Vice Presidency would be up for grabs, and if the longtime governor of New York were to have a chance at that position, he must once more demonstrate his ability to hold on to the political machinery of his own state.

To Hamilton and his Federalist followers, the race represented another chance to realize a hope deferred: the ouster of the "Old Incumbent"—Clinton, that is—and his replacement by a governor more in sympathy with the national aims of their party. Three years before, they had come close to attaining this end by backing the moderate Anti-Federalist, justice—now chief justice—of the state supreme court, Robert Yates. In 1792 their original plan was to go the same route again in the same way. But this time Yates disappointed them. To Philip Schuyler, who sounded him out in New York City in late January, the judge pleaded pecuniary considerations. He said that he could not afford the money he would lose were he to be "placed in the seat of Government." Nor was this his only reason for declining. Another, Yates revealed, was that his old friend, Aaron Burr, had asked him not to run.

Here was ample cause for apoplexy on the part of Schuyler and Hamilton. Schuyler was so taken aback that he at once made plans for a trip to Philadelphia to consult with his son-in-law. It was bad enough losing Yates, whom both men had come to regard as a winner. It was even more upsetting to learn that not only was New York's junior senator edging into the race but he was being encouraged to do so by men in both parties. For a time, even Robert Troup toyed with the idea of pushing Burr. James Watson of New York City, a stalwart Federalist and a director of the Bank of the United States, wrote Hamilton that "the cautious distance observed by this gentleman [Burr], towards all parties, however exceptionable in a politician, may be a real merit in a Governor." In Watson's opinion there were many reasons why the Federalists should make Burr their candidate. Suppose the senator won without Federalist support? Would "it not make him an enemy if he is not one now"? On the other hand, if the Federalists sponsored Burr, they stood to gain whether he won or lost. Never mind that to date the senator's political stands in Philadelphia had been those of a Republican. If the Federalists got behind him in New York, he would either have to support their policies henceforth or, by refusing to do so, would stamp himself an ingrate and "make all future opposition to him equally just and popular." Watson's final argument was that every effort should be made to remove a man of Burr's "talents, perseverance & address . . . as far from the opposition as possible."

By the time these words were written in early February, Burr was no longer working alone. Around him had gathered the little band of collaborators whom history has denominated the "Burrites." Hamilton spoke of them as "Burr's myrmidons." Burr's classically educated daughter called them the "Tenth Legion." They were never as numerous as those terms would suggest. Neither, so long as Burr himself was on the New York political scene, were they as powerful as some accounts would have us believe. Strong evidence exists that the Burrites did not come into their own as a political force until Burr had fallen from grace and the leadership of his little group had shifted to his friend Matthew L. Davis.

Over the years, the composition of the Burrites would alter frequently. Among the charter members were Melancton Smith and Marinus Willett of New York City, Van Gaasbeek of Kingston, and Dr. Isaac Ledyard of Newtown, Long Island. In the Empire State the term "Republicans" was not yet in common use. Nominally, Smith and Willett were Anti-Federalists, but dissident ones in that they had come to believe that George Clinton had been in office too long. Originally an Anti-

Federalist, Van Gaasbeek in recent years had organized the first Federalist machine, the Kingston Junto, to take form in Governor Clinton's native Ulster County.

Ledyard, too, was a Federalist, and in late January he was giving Hamilton and Schuyler food for thought—and dyspepsia. Yates's refusal to run was not yet known to the public. Hamilton and his father-in-law were trying to keep it a secret until they could get together and consider other possible candidates. Having been taken into their confidence, Ledyard proposed that, as Yates was "resigning his pretentions," they put Aaron Burr in his place. In a letter dated 1 February, directed to Hamilton and carried to Philadelphia by Schuyler, the Long Island surgeon set forth his arguments in support of this proposition.

Burr himself could not have put them better. In truth, the suspicion arises that, remotely speaking, he did put them, that the doctor was playing Trilby to the senator's Svengali. Ledyard began by quoting Schuyler as having asserted that if Clinton and Burr were the only competitors in the race, "it would be doubtful which succeeded." Ledyard felt that to defeat Burr, under such circumstances, the Federalists would have to support the Old Incumbent. That procedure, he delicately added, "might be considered a dereliction of sentiment." Were the Federalists to seek a way out of their dilemma by putting up a third candidate, then, in Ledyard's opinion, Clinton would be sure to "triumph."

Bearing these varying possibilities in mind, Ledyard "had sought repeated interviews" with Burr, during which he had procured from that gentleman an "*artless* declaration" of where the senator stood on the great issues of the day. Burr, Ledyard was happy to report, had "expressed a sincere desire for the safety and well being of the . . . [Union] . . . , an entire confidence in the wisdom & integrity of your [Hamilton's] designs, & a real personal friendship . . . which he does not seem to suppose you doubt of, or that you ever will, unless it may arise from medling Interveners." Having presented his case—and Burr's—Ledyard expressed the ardent hope that "the result" of the upcoming talk between Hamilton and his father-in-law would be "an adoption" of Burr as the gubernatorial candidate of the Federalist Party.

Hamilton replied to Ledyard, but his letter has not been found and his reaction to the doctor's arguments must be deduced from subsequent events. Burr's ultimate objective, like Clinton's, was not the governorship but the Vice Presidency; and it would be straining credulity to suppose that Hamilton did not suspect as much. Nor is it likely that he found Burr's avowal of his political positions as "artless" as Ledyard did. So the senator was for the Union. But was he for the Union according to Hamilton or according to Thomas Jefferson? Less reassuring to the Federalist leader than to Ledyard was Burr's reported expression of confidence in Hamilton's "designs." The Secretary of the Treasury was on close terms with Congressman Theodore Sedgwick. To that gentleman Burr had long since declared that he doubted the necessity for Hamilton's Bank of the United States. To be brief about it, Burr was not the fly that Hamilton and Schuyler wanted to lure into their parlor.

Their candidate was to be John Jay, the moderate Federalist. It has often been ventured that Hamilton talked Jay into running, although no evidence to that effect has been found. Whoever did was persuasive. In 1792 Jay was Chief Justice of the United States. A successful campaign for the governorship would require him to step down from the second highest station in the land. A bona-fide aristocrat, tall and slender with black hair and classic features, he combined rare abilities as a statesman with a manner so self-effacing that a newcomer to the facts of his life could be forgiven if the first thought to cross his mind were that "this fellow is too good to be true." Few New Yorkers were more widely admired. Few could point to a more impressive catalogue of public services: guiding spirit in the framing of the New York constitution, one of the peace commissioners responsible for the treaty that ended the American Revolution, Secretary for Foreign Affairs under the Articles of Confederation, first chief justice of New York and first Chief Justice of the United States—to mention only the highlights of his career.

As late as 13 February, the *Albany Gazette* was listing Jay among the several men, including Chancellor Livingston, who had turned down a Federalist bid. On the fifteenth the Clintonians convened at Corre's hotel in New York City and surprised nobody by nominating the Old Incumbent. On the following day the Federalists met in the same place and surprised everybody by naming Jay and announcing that Robert Yates had promised to support him and that the Chief Justice had agreed to run.

End of the road for Burr. If there had ever been an understanding between him and Yates, it was gone, and his failure to obtain the official backing of either party left his prospects in shambles. On the day after the Federalist nominating caucus, Dr. Ledyard informed Hamilton that Burr realized that the "circumstances of Mr. Jay's candidateship . . . is a conclusive objection to your aiding his views." Ledyard still harbored the hope that Hamilton would find it in his heart to refrain from opposing Burr openly. The senator had no illusions on that score. He knew he was beaten, but as his followers were not so sure, he remained in the race for a few weeks at their behest. By the end of March, however, he had publicly withdrawn, releasing his followers, some of whom then went over to Jay, others to Clinton.

Now Burr was through with the election. But the election was not through with him. The gubernatorial race of 1792 ended in a dispute, and an ensuing battle over the legality of the ballots in three frontier counties was to subject the senator's determination to function as an independent to an embarrassing challenge.

9

Republican at Large

In New York's 1792 election the balloting began in late April and lasted through the first of May. In those days of slow travel, time was needed for the gathering of the votes so that they could be counted by the six state representatives and six state senators whom their respective branches of the legislature had selected as a board of canvassers. Most of May had gone before the people of the state realized that they were in the midst of a crisis. By that time, two facts were in evidence. One was that in the frontier counties of Tioga, Clinton, and Otsego the officials in charge of the ballots had not handled them in strict conformance with the procedures laid down in New York's five-year-old election statute. The other was that the outcome of the election was going to depend on what was done about the Otsego votes. Unofficial estimates showed that Tioga and Clinton together had given the Old Incumbent a moderate majority. In Otsego, however, the Federalist majority appeared to be so large that if the canvassers counted the votes of that county, John Jay would be the next governor. If they did not, Clinton would be in again.

The provisions of the election statute were designed to protect the voters against corruption or coercion. Each elector was obliged to fold his paper ticket so "as to conceal the writing thereon" and put it into a locked box via a slot at one end. At the closing of the polls the inspectors had to bind the box with tape and seal it "in such manner as to prevent its being opened without discovery." A clerk then carried it to the county sheriff, who, in turn, was required to transport it to the secretary of state. That official presented it to the canvassers. Their task was to open the box, make and report the count, and destroy the ballots.

In Tioga, the sheriff gave the box to his deputy, who, taken ill on the way to New York City, handed it to a clerk, who completed the delivery. The Clinton sheriff entrusted his ballots to an individual who got them to their destination in the proper condition but who had no legal right to carry them. In Otsego, there were complicating factors. A small fraction of the ballots cast in that county did not reach the secretary of state in the single sealed box stipulated by law. They arrived in a separate packet that could have been opened, without detection, en route. More to the point was the vexed status of the county official who had put the ballot box and the packet on their way.

At the time the votes cast in Otsego were sent off, the one-year term of the sheriff of that county, Richard R. Smith, had expired, and the individual named to succeed him had not yet received his commission. Nevertheless, Smith accepted the ballots as delivered to him at the closing of the polls. He himself, however, did not take them to the secretary of state. He deputized another man for that purpose. The problem raised by these actions revolved around a section of the state constitution which read that each sheriff "shall be *annually appointed*." Did this mean that Smith could exercise his authority only during the period covered by his appointment? Or could he, in the interval between the end of his appointment and the commissioning of his successor, continue to perform his shrieval duties on a de facto basis? As later paraphrased by the board of canvassers, these questions became: "Was Richard R. Smith the sheriff of . . . Otsego when he received and forwarded the ballots by his special deputy?" and "If he was not sheriff, can the votes sent by him be legally canvassed?"

For months after these problems came to light, the New York political world, never precisely calm, was sound and fury. The major Federalist cry was that the Clintonians, knowing themselves to be beaten, were using legal technicalities to steal the election from John Jay. Lending color to this suspicion was the revelation, if Philip Schuyler's mathematics can be accepted, that at least seven of the twelve canvassers were pro-Clinton men. On the Clintonian side the main argument was that so sacred were the suffrage rights of the people that even a minor violation should be met by a resort to the letter of the law. Supportive of this view was the disclosure, during an investigation by the legislature, that in Otsego the Federalist election campaign had been shot through with the arts of "Hook and Snivery." The rough-hewn Federalist boss of that county, Judge William Cooper, had not hesitated to put pressure on voters who were either in his employ or otherwise obligated to him. Before the Federalists talked of stealing an election, the Clintonians said in effect, let them first ponder their own sins of coercion and corruption. On these matters there was a vast amount of tit for tat. Chancellor Livingston, campaigning for Clinton, revealed that the Federalist candidate for the lieutenant governorship, Stephen Van Rensselaer, had compelled the tenants on his large holdings in Albany County to use a special ballot "written on silken paper . . . so as to enable him to know with certainty whether . . . [they] had acted conformably to his wishes." Federalist James Kent countered by accusing the Livingstons of driving their tenants to the polls like "sheep to slaughter," and the chancellor himself conceded that the farmers living on his family's two manors had voted "in some measure under the influence of their landlords."

Charge and countercharge! A typical New York State election, except that this was a disputed one. In New York City the twelve canvassers met and argued, met again and argued again, and finally undertook to shift the burden of decision to Philadelphia by asking each of New York's United States senators, Rufus King and Aaron Burr, to issue an opinion as to the validity of the votes from the three erring counties.

Poor Burr! His effort to preserve "a cautious distance . . . towards all parties" was about to be thwarted by a cruel turn of the political wheel. An opinion advising the canvassers to count the disputed votes would stamp him as a Federalist; one urging them to throw them out, as a Clintonian, or, more broadly, as a Republican. Either way, he must commit his views to paper—a painful prospect for a lawyer who cautioned his clerks, "Things written remain," and who on large issues tended to shrink from the finality of the written word.

We have his own account of what happened when the request of the New York canvassers reached Philadelphia. He and his senatorial colleague at once got together. "We conferred," Burr later told Jacob De Lamater, one of his Federalist supporters in Ulster County, "and, unfortunately differed; particularly as to the questions upon the Otsego return. I therefore proposed that we should decline any opinion, being for my own part much averse to interfere in the business. Mr. King, however, determined to give his separate opinion, from what motives you may judge. This laid me under the necessity of giving mine also, which I did."

As these words indicate, King advised the canvassers to count practically all the disputed votes. Burr advocated throwing out most of them, including all those from the crucial county, Otsego. Since King in effect "voted" for his party and Burr for his, the only question of consequence would seem to be which of their opinions was more in keeping with the spirit of the New York election laws. On this score, it must be admitted that King took the highroad. He argued that since the intent of the election laws was "to render effectual the constitutional right of suffrage," no votes cast in a legal manner and clearly untampered with should be ignored simply because of technical errors in the way in which they had been handled. Burr turned to the common law of England to prove that Robert Smith "was not the sheriff of Otsego when he received and forwarded the votes" of that county. It followed that those ballots should not be canvassed. He also cited irregularities in Tioga that, in his view, ruled out the ballots of that county as well. So narrow and legalistic was his reasoning that Robert Troup churlishly predicted that Burr's opinion would "damn his reputation as a lawyer." It didn't, but it did identify him in the public mind as a Republican Party regular. For the time being, he was stuck with a label whether he wanted one or not.

Evidently he didn't. On 15 June he was trying hard to convince Jacob De Lamater—and himself—that his opinion was innocent of political bias. In a letter marked by uncharacteristic righteousness, Burr wrote that "I was obliged to give an opinion, and I have not yet learned to give any other than which my judgment directs. It would, indeed, be the extreme of weakness in me to expect friendship from Mr. Clinton. I have too many reasons to believe that he regards me with jealousy and malevolence . . . Some pretend, indeed, but none can believe, that I am prejudiced in his favour. I have not even seen or spoken to him since January last."

Apparently the predominantly pro-Clinton canvassers were happy to have Burr's advice. They acted on it promptly, voting to reject all the disputed votes and thus insuring the Old Incumbent another three years in the gubernatorial chair. At the time their ruling became known in early June, Chief Justice Jay was traveling in New England in connection with his judicial duties. He made haste to urge his wife not to fret, and assured her that he was not bitter. "The reflection that the majority of electors were for me is a pleasing one," he wrote; "that injustice has taken place does not surprise me . . . A few more years will put us all in the dust, and it will then be of more importance to me to have governed myself, than to have governed the state."

On 1 July, Governor Clinton began his sixth term in an

atmosphere rife with protests at the dubious manner in which the disputed election had been settled. On the fourth, the arrival of the Chief Justice at his New York City home touched off a large popular demonstration. Huge banners declared "Jay Governor by voice of the people." Shouted demands that Clinton resign competed with booming cannon and pealing church bells. A few months later a Connecticut Federalist detected what he took to be signs that the embarrassed followers of the Old Incumbent wanted to put him in a higher post "to give him an honorable retreat from the resentment of the majority of the people" of his state. The author of this speculation was right on one point. In Republican circles, in New York and in other states, Clinton was being talked of in connection with the Vice Presidency of the United States. So, too, was Aaron Burr.

2

BY LATE SUMMER, the country's second Presidential election was in full swing. Washington had finally let it be known that he would accept another term, and the autumn witnessed a struggle by anti-Administration leaders to stake their claim on the national government by denying John Adams a second term in the Vice Presidency and electing a Republican to that position.

As early as June, Alexander Hamilton was aware of this movement and of the groundswell for the New York governor. Not until mid-September, however, did he learn that "a greater menace—Burr" had entered the race. The Secretary at once put his reactions on paper, in a letter to a friend whose identity has been lost. It was the agitated communication of a man who had quite enough of Aaron Burr. That audacious and free-wheeling politico had put down the Secretary's father-in-law. He had helped George Clinton steal the governorship from John Jay. Now he was running for Vice President! What would Burr go after next—the leadership of the Federalist party?

In a burst of inaccuracy, Hamilton informed his unknown

confidant that he had "hitherto scrupulously refrained from interference in elections." The presence of Burr in the competition, however, struck him as "of sufficient importance to warrant . . . a departure from that rule." He intended to fight to keep Adams in the Vice Presidency. Should worse come to worst, he hoped Clinton—not Burr—became Adams's successor. A "Clinton victory," he wrote, "would not be an unadulterated evil," because the governor "is a man of property, and in private life, as far as I know, a man of probity," whereas "I fear the other gentleman [Burr] is unprincipled both as a public and a private man . . . I take it he is for or against nothing, but as it suits his interest or ambition. He is determined, as I conceive, to make his way to be the head of the popular party, and to climb, *per fas aut nefas*, to the highest honors of the State, and as much higher as circumstances may permit. Embarrassed, as I understand, in his circumstances, with an extravagant family, bold, enterprising, and intriguing, I am mistaken if it be not his object to play the game of confusion, and I feel it to be a religious duty to oppose his career."

This was not wholly the language of political contention. This was personal hate. Obviously, there was a side of Hamilton that knew it was. The day was not far off when he would be urging a Federalist governor of New York to appoint Burr to a demanding and lucrative public office on the grounds that, with the exception of himself (Hamilton), no one else had the competency to handle it.

In a "private letter" to Washington, by way of keeping him apprised of what was going on, the Secretary of the Treasury took care to refrain from personalities. "A letter from Mr. King . . . of the 17th inst," he wrote on 23 September, had "surprised" him with the "intelligence" that Burr was "being industrious in his canvass," that he had backing in Pennsylvania and that his lawyer-uncle, Pierpont Edwards, was "to make interest for him in Connecticut." Hamilton had but one comment on the development. "I am not certain," he told Washington, "that this is any thing more than a diversion in favour of Mr. Clinton."

Hamilton may have been essentially right about this, although some authorities have concluded otherwise. In the light of the known events of the campaign, it is clear that Burr would have welcomed the backing of his party for the Vice Presidency, equally clear that he understood the realities of the situation. Vis-à-vis the seasoned and powerful New York governor, his prospects were iffy. There was a good chance that in the end he might have to content himself with nothing more than the realization that he had served the cause by providing the Republicans with a standby candidate in the event Clinton decided not to run. Herein lay the crux of the matter. In the opening weeks of the fall, the Old Incumbent was playing hard to get. "Mr. Clinton," Senator King was writing a Federalist colleague in late September, "has been sounded but whether he will consent to run against Mr. Adams is at present uncertain."

While Clinton wavered, Burr worked. He spent time in Philadelphia, conferring with Republicans there. Later, having returned to New York, he dispatched Melancton Smith to the Quaker City and sent other Burrites to Virginia and elsewhere. In mid-September the tall and imposing figure of Alexander James Dallas was visible on the streets of New York City. The Philadelphia Republican leader had come north to consult with Burr, Clinton, the Livingstons, and others. At the time of his return to Philadelphia, two reports were current. One was that the Pennsylvanians were planning to uphold Burr. The other was that Clinton, apparently in one of his "I won't run" moods, was thinking of doing the same thing. Toward the end of the month John James Beckley, longtime clerk of the House of Representatives, was in New York. Beckley, it would seem, had made the journey from Philadelphia as an envoy of the Virginia Republicans, Congressman Madison and Senator James Monroe. There was concern among the Virginians lest the adherents of the cause make the mistake of dividing their allegiance between Burr and Clinton. Only by uniting behind a single candidate could they hope to attain their ends. No doubt Madison was relieved to receive Beckley's report on his findings. "Nothing particular occurred at New York," the clerk of the House wrote him, "except Colonel Burrs [sic] assurance to me that he would . . . lend every aid in his power to C[linton]'s election."

A strange development in early October indicates that by then Clinton was backing away from his reported intention of leaving the field to Burr, and was preparing to run on his own. At a meeting of the Council of Appointment the governor proposed that New York's junior United States senator be given an associate justiceship on the state supreme court. As the four legislative members of the council divided evenly, Clinton had to use his casting vote to make the nomination stick. Burr seems to have known nothing of this move when it took place. So swiftly and secretly did the governor act that to this day a published "list of the judges of the [New York] Supreme Court of Judicature" carries the entry, "Aaron Burr, Esq., puisne Judge, 2 October 1792." A footnote tells us that "Mr. Burr did not accept the appointment." Was Clinton trying to reduce Burr's power by luring him away from his influential senatorship? If so, the Old Incumbent was not performing with his usual subtlety. The bait he dangled before the colonel was attractive: a lifetime job at a salary considerably in excess of the six dollars per diem then received by a United States senator. But the fish was not biting.

In New Haven, Connecticut, Burr's lawyer-uncle, Pierpont Edwards, was doing what he could for the Republican interest in the heavily Federalist states of the Northeast. "We are not without hope from New England," he reported on 4 October to Dr. James Hutchinson, one of the most active and effective of the Republican organizers in Philadelphia. Edwards noted that the "names of Governor Clinton and Col. Burr (and of no others) are seriously mentioned. Some votes we flatter ourselves can be procured for either of them. But all that can be done here will be fruitless, if it is not done in concert with the South. Rhode Island, Vermont, New York, and New Jersey will yield, as we are led to believe, important support to either of them." However, Edwards reiterated, "our dependence is upon the States which form the Southern division of the empire. May I solicit the favor of a line from you, advising me of the arrangements which are, or shall be made, on this subject . . . Candor obliges me to observe to you, that ancient political antipathies to Governor Clinton will render his success here more precarious than Col. Burr's." Personally, in other words, the Connecticut lawyer preferred his nephew but, like Burr, he stood ready to work for Clinton if the members of the party generally opted for the governor.

They did. Madison and Monroe had already done so when on 16 October the Pennsylvania faithful met in Philadelphia and voted to support the Old Incumbent. At this point Burr desisted from all further efforts on his own behalf. On 5 December the members of the electoral college met in their respective states. Under the constitution as it then stood, they did not vote separately for President and Vice President as they do now. Each elector named two men, one of whom had to be a resident of a state other than his own. Whoever got the highest number of electoral votes, provided it was a majority, became President; whoever got the second highest number, provided it was a plurality, Vice President. As anticipated, all the electors voted for Washington. Seventy-seven named Adams, giving him the plurality he needed to remain in the Vice Presidency. Clinton got fifty votes, including all of New York's twelve. Burr got one—from South Carolina.

Again, as during the gubernatorial race, he had made a good try and missed. But there would be other gubernatorial elections and other Presidential elections. When the next ones came around, the "enterprizing" colonel would try again. Meanwhile, senatorial duties called.

3

DURING HIS REMAINING four years in the Senate he repeatedly flung aloft the banner of democracy.

There was his support in January 1794 of a proposed constitutional amendment reflecting Republicans' distaste for banks in general—"little better than houses of ill fame," one of them said—and of Hamilton's Bank of the United States in particular. Summarily repulsed by a Senate filled with Hamilton's supporters, the amendment would have forbidden membership in either branch of the Congress to any person "holding an office or stock in any institution . . . issuing or discounting bills or notes . . . under the authority of the United States."

There was his unavailing attempt, later the same year, to censor President Washington's official criticism of the appearance in Pennsylvania and elsewhere of a number of popular organizations unfriendly to Administration policies and variously known as the Democratic or Republican Societies.

There was his stand during the long argument over the right of the future Secretary of the Treasury, Albert Gallatin, to continue as a member of the Senate. A native of Geneva, Switzerland, Gallatin in his late teens migrated to the New World. Industrious, well educated, and personally attractive, he rose fast. Having settled in the Pennsylvania backwoods and entered politics, he soon achieved a more than local reputation as an opponent of strong government and one of the founders of the Republican Party. To Hamilton, not the least of Gallatin's sins was that this sharp-faced immigrant, with his good but heavily frenchified English, was one of the few men in the country with sufficient grasp of the arcana of public finance to spot the technical errors in the Secretary of the Treasury's calculations. As Hamilton bent in the winter of 1794, the controlling Federalists in the Senate inclined. On 28 February they ousted the Pennsylvanian from his seat. Their case was that at the time of his election he had not been an American citizen for the nine years required by the constitution. Throughout the preceding debate on the floor, no one had fought harder for him than Burr. This fact Gallatin would not forget. He would be of immense political help to the colonel in the years ahead.

And there was his vigorous opposition to Jay's Treaty, an action that put the junior senator from New York at the center of the foreign policy debate of the mid-1790's, the controversy that completed the process initiated by the fight over Hamilton's fiscal policies by drawing athwart the country an ideological crevice that all could see. As the dust of this battle slowly lifted, two distinct parties would stand revealed—on one side of the crevice, the Federalists; and on the other, the Democrats, or, as they then more often spoke of themselves, the Republicans.

Like most of the diplomatic moves of the Washington Administration, the negotiation of Jay's Treaty in 1794 was a by-product of the turmoil in the Old World that began with the outbreak of the French Revolution in 1789, reached one critical point two years later with the abolition of the Bourbon monarchy and the establishment of the first French Republic, and another in 1793 when the monarchies of Europe ganged up in an effort to crush the Republic and restore the Bourbons. The many ramifications of the American quarrel over these occurrences belong to the general history of the country. For the purposes of this biography, only a few aspects of them need be mentioned.

In the beginning, most Americans welcomed the upheaval in France as a sequel to their own Revolution. Subsequent events, however, wrought a division of opinion and feeling more intense than anything the country had yet experienced. The violence surrounding the proclamation of the French Republic, the execution of the King, the Reign of Terror under Robespierre and its counterrevolutionary aftermath—these spectacular developments convinced American Federalists that France was not heading toward liberty but toward those extremes of social disorder that invite the intervention of a despot. Rapidly, Federalism took on a strong anti-French and pro-British orientation. Rapidly, adherents of the emerging democracy moved in the opposite direction, fearful that if the crowned heads of Europe succeeded in destroying France's new Republic they would at once try to do the same thing to America's only slightly older one. As America's age of political innocence ended and the first party system hove into view, Federalism versus Republicanism was to a marked degree pro-England versus pro-France. Federalist newspapers began speaking of Thomas Jefferson and his followers as "Jacobins," the name of one of the more radical groups among the French revolutionaries. Republican newspapers began calling all Federalists "monarchists" and hinting of a dark plot by Hamilton and others to replace George Washington with George III.

Such was the political alignment in the United States when in April 1793 the news that France and England were at war reached Philadelphia, and confronted the Washington Administration with a dilemma. Gratefully remembered by the American people were the contributions that French money and French arms had made to the winning of their Revolution. Officially the two nations were still allied, with the United States pledged by treaty to defend France's possessions in the West Indies in the event of war. On the other hand, commercial dealings with Great Britain constituted the backbone of the American economy. That nine-tenths of the country's imports were coming from England was a crucial point with Alexander Hamilton, whose grand financial scheme depended to a large degree on the revenues collectible as a result of this vast trade with the one-time mother country.

The Administration's first effort to cope with the problem took the form of Washington's proclamation of neutrality on 22 April 1793—a signal by the new nation of its intent to stand aloof from the wars of the Old World. To the relief of the President and his Cabinet, France registered no protests, made no demands. The British authorities, however, took an ominous tack. They let it be known that they would recognize no neutral rights that might interfere with their war on France. They would regard any goods carried by a neutral vessel to that country or its possessions as contraband of war and subject to seizure. By way of implementing this denial of freedom of the seas, they promulgated a number of orders in council. Acting on these decrees, the British navy began the impressment of American sailors that, as later resumed, would help bring on the War of 1812. A British fleet, cruising in the waters of the Caribbean in the early spring of 1794 seized approximately three hundred American vessels found trading with the French islands in that region.

Word of these depredations sent a wave of anti-British feeling across America. It created a crisis in Philadelphia. In the House of Representatives, the Republicans succeeded in passing trade and navigation bills so inimical to the interest of Great Britain that war might have ensued had these measures not died in a Senate still dominated by Federalists. Simultaneously, Washington decided to send an envoy extraordinary to London with instructions to seek a treaty of amity, commerce, and navigation with Britain that would tranquilize relations with the island kingdom.

The President's choice for the job, John Jay, was an understandable one. Jay's many negotiations with foreign potentates had long since marked him as an able diplomat. Too able, in the opinion of the Republican leaders in Congress, who saw nothing in the proposed mission save a slap at France. Having caucused at length, they hit upon the scheme of trying to persuade the President to entrust the mission to someone other than Jay, preferably to a man who, through incompetence or disinterest, could be counted on to bungle the job. Burr may have been the author of this stratagem. It was he who rose in the Senate to argue that there was no need to send the Chief Justice of the United States on an errand that a man already in London—the American Minister to the Court of St. James's, Thomas Pinckney of South Carolina—could handle just as well. Perhaps this maneuver was too transparent. After only one day in executive session, the Senate concurred in the nomination of the Chief Justice. Burr was the only member from east of the Potomac to vote against it.

Jay reached England in June 1794. Of the controversial document that he brought home a few months later, a great diplomatic historian has written that "Jay's Treaty . . . saved American nationality in an hour of crisis." However true this may seem today, the generality of Americans did not see it thus at the time. When the terms of the treaty became public, there was an outcry that Washington likened to "that against a mad dog." Jay was heard to say that on the darkest night he could have made his way across the country by the light of the burning effigies of himself. Chalked large on the walls of a building not far from his New York City home was the legend, "Damn John Jay. Damn everyone that won't damn John Jay. Damn everyone that won't put up lights in the windows and sit up all night damning John Jay." When at a gathering in Wall Street Hamilton attempted to speak in defense of the treaty, a furious crowd stoned him into humiliating flight. Nowhere in the document procured by Jay was there a single word that so much as nodded in the direction of freedom of the seas. On the contrary, the President was asked to sign and the Senate to "advise and consent to" what amounted to a proposition that the seas belonged to any navy that could command them. Granted that in return for American obeisance to this doctrine, England agreed to rectify some long-standing violations of the treaty that had ended the American Revolution in 1783. British soldiers still occupied a number of forts standing on American soil in the far Northwest. These England promised to surrender on a stipulated date. Also included was a mechanism for recompensing American property owners for damage resulting from the burning of towns and other wanton acts by the British during the war.

One section of the treaty, Article 12, was so shot through with commercial concessions to England that even the pro-

British Federalists of the Senate could not stomach it. When in the early summer of 1795 that body convened in special session to consider the treaty as approved by President Washington, its first action was to excise Article 12. It was at this point that Burr went into action. Parton found in the press of the day mentions of a "great speech" against the treaty. Unfortunately, no inkling of what he said remains. All the record shows is that he offered, and bolstered with brief arguments, a motion that would have removed from the treaty not only Article 12 but also all or parts of nine other articles. Had Burr's proposals carried, there would have been little treaty for the Senate to consent to. They didn't. By a bare two-thirds vote, the senators bowed to the President's wishes, and Jay's Treaty became the law of the land.

4

THE SENATOR'S OUSTER from the archives of the State Department was not his last rebuff at the hands of George Washington. Another occurred in the spring of 1794 when France asked the President to recall Gouverneur Morris as America's minister to that government. Burr wanted the job, and a congressional committee headed by Madison and Monroe called on the President to recommend him. Washington said no, giving as his reason that he never appointed to high office "any person . . . in whose integrity he had not confidence." Twice more, the committeemen called on the President. On the third occasion he refused to see them, and on 27 May he named Monroe to the French embassy.

Although most observers thought they saw Hamilton's hand behind the President's attitude toward Burr, some Federalists heard different overtones. Theodore Sedgwick was convinced that from the beginning the congressional Republicans meant Monroe to have the job and that their advocacy of the senator from New York was more lip service than substance. "Respecting Mr. Burr," Sedgwick wrote to his, and Burr's, good friend, Jonathan Dayton of New Jersey, "no man better than yourself knows the estimation in which I hold him. But . . . the party with which he has generally acted, altho' they covet the aid of his character & talents, have not the smallest confidence in his hearty union to their cause. Indeed it is my firm belief that their views and his are not only distant but opposite. Their want of confidence in him was incontrovertibly demonstrated in the support which the party gave to the appointment of Monroe.

"You remember how anxious you was that Burr should be gratified by that office, and how complete the evidence was to both our minds, that he was defeated by the insidious machinations of that party. And wherefore was it that they preferred Monroe to him? Had they more confidence in Monroe's talents? They are not so stupid. In his integrity? no. But they knew the one would & the other would not condescend to Act as their tool. They doubtless respect Burr's talents, but they dread his independence of *them*. They know, in short, he is not one of them, and of course they will never support but always effect to support him."

The truth of history lurks in its incongruities. Both those who blamed Hamilton for the President's rejection of Burr and those who blamed the "machinations" of the Republican party may have been right. Whatever the role of the Secretary of the Treasury in the affair, he soon had reason to wish that his hated rival was tucked away in France, far from the madding compaign trails of New York State. By the end of the year, another gubernatorial contest was shaping up there, and Burr was running.

5

A PECULIARITY of New York's 1795 election was that for the first time in almost twenty years George Clinton was not in it. The governor's political liabilities had become conspicuous. People still remembered the scandal connected with the sale of the public lands. Even fresher in their minds was the disputed election. Realizing that to run again would be to court defeat, the Old Incumbent took himself out of the competition in late January, citing "bad health" as his excuse. With Clinton's withdrawal, the electioneering began in earnest.

It was more orderly than had been the case three years before. The state's Republicans were beginning to act like an organized party, and fewer Federalists were interested in supporting Burr, as a "Correspondent" to the *Albany Gazette* put it, "not because I know him to belong to either one faction or another, but because I believe him to belong to none." Again, as in 1792, Burr had the aid of his little band of Burrites, augmented by a number of newcomers, including Matthew L. Davis, John Swartwout, Ebenezer Foote, John Addison, Thomas Witbeck, and William Root. Again he solicited the support of both parties, and again neither responded favorably. In early February, two Federalist caucuses nominated John Jay. The Chief Justice of the United States was still treaty-making in England, but it was known that he would be home in time for the actual balloting. Later in the same month the Republican leaders assembled. Their choice was Robert Yates. Again, as in 1792, Burr continued as a candidate for a few weeks to please his followers, and again he released them a month or so before the campaign ended. In the April voting Jay was an easy victor, and in July he resigned from the Supreme Court to begin the first of what were to be two consecutive terms as governor of New York.

Burr and his supporters were undaunted, plainly taking the view that the gubernatorial race was no more than a preliminary to the larger event of the coming year. As early as the summer of 1795, rumors were abroad that Washington would not accept a third term. A little more than a year later his Farewell Address was in the columns of a Philadelphia newspaper, and the country was caught up in the first national election to eventuate in a change of Presidents.

6

THE PRESIDENTIAL ELECTION of 1796 was marked by firsts. It was the first contest of its kind to be fought along clearly Federalist-vs.-Republican lines; the first to find Hamilton and Jefferson operating outside the Cabinet (both had resigned); the first to signal the emergence of Jefferson as the leader of the democracy; and the first to yield tangible evidence that qualms about the independence of Aaron Burr were abroad in the Republican strongholds of the South and especially in the Old Dominion.

In the Federalist camp, no official nominations were necessary. John Adams was generally accepted as the party's Presidential candidate and Thomas Pinckney of South Carolina as its Vice Presidential standard-bearer. Hamilton, to be sure, had other ideas. Regarding Adams as personally overbearing and politically suspect, he carried on a subterranean campaign aimed at persuading the Federalist electors to put Pinckney on top. But in 1796 Hamilton's dedicated effort to destroy the party he himself had helped create was premature. Its fruition would have to await a later date and another set of political and economic circumstances.

Jefferson had retired to Monticello. He was "struggling to get his walls up" and a roof over his head when in the autumn of 1795 one of his guests was Aaron Burr. As neither man penned a record of the occasion and as no other "political characters" were present, what the two of them discussed remains unknown. Ignorance of the facts, however, did not prevent the Federalist press from capitalizing on the visit for political purposes. Newspapers pictured Burr and Jefferson as plotting anti-Administration moves for a forthcoming session of the Congress and as scheming together to overthrow the government—this last, incidentally, being the favorite and almost only occupation of all Republicans, according to the propagandists of the opposition. What they meant, in plain English, was that the Republicans were trying to put one of their own in the Presidency or, failing that, in the Vice Presidency.

Republican plans took form slowly. As early as spring 1795, Jefferson was aware of the growing interest in himself as the Presidential candidate, but reluctant to accede to it. In his opinion, the fittest person to head the party ticket was his longtime friend and neighbor. "There is not another person in the United States," he wrote Madison on 27 April, "Who, being placed at the helm of our affairs, my mind would be so completely at rest for the future of our political bark."

A year later four other Republicans were being widely mentioned as either Presidential or Vice Presidential possibilities: Burr, Chancellor Livingston, John Langdon of New Hampshire, and Pierce Butler of South Carolina. It was the impression of Federalist William L. Smith of South Carolina that Livingston was a favorite with the Virginians because of his recent newspaper attacks on Jay's Treaty. According to this source, each of the others was viewed by Republican leaders as having a serious flaw. Butler was a Southerner and would have to be ruled out if Jefferson agreed to run; Langdon had "no influence"; and "Burr, they think unsettled in his politics and are afraid he will go over to the other side."

As always, Burr was "industrious in his canvass." His letters for the summer and fall of 1796 put him all over the map, pushing his candidacy in New Hampshire, Massachusetts, New York, Pennsylvania, and Virginia. Writing a senatorial colleague from Richmond, Virginia, he revealed that his exertions had taken such a toll of his still erratic health that he was "totally unfit for Society." So time-consuming were his electioneering chores that when a close friend, Dr. William Eustis of Boston, came down to New York, the two men barely saw one another, and Burr was presently trying to patch things up with an apology. "No incident for many years," he wrote Eustis, "has given me more real pain and regret than your visit here . . . I prevailed on you to make it. I counted on it with the most lively satisfaction. Yet I ran off and left you in solitude . . . You was wrong not to make my house your home. But let it rest. We cannot explain on paper."

By the fall of 1796 the Republican ticket had crystallized. Jefferson had "consented to serve if elected." Partly through correspondence, partly as the result of a summer caucus in Philadelphia, he and Burr had been selected as the nominees of their party.

On the first Tuesday in November the Federalist-controlled legislature of New York met to name the twelve men who would gather at Hudson on the first Wednesday of the next month and cast the electoral vote for their state. The common knowledge that all of them were pledged to vote for Adams and Pinckney did not discourage the Burrites. Exchanging information and plans by means of coded letters, they labored to persuade some of the electors to switch to Burr. Toward the end of November, Van Gaasbeek was able to give the colonel an account of an almost night-long "interview" with "H," code name for Johannes Miller, one of the twelve electors. Miller had spoken "highly" of Burr's "Talents," and Van Gaasbeek was hopeful. Only a few days before the balloting at Hudson, the Kingston merchant was the recipient of two letters, both suggesting last-minute actions to be undertaken in Burr's interest.

Neither letter was signed, but one of them could have been written by Burr himself. Two facts underscore the possibility. One is the inclusion in it of a little lecture on how the electoral college worked in those days, the sort of lecture so often found in the correspondence of that compulsive educator. The other was the presence in the code drafted by the Burrites of an instruction to "Speak of yourself in the third person when you wish it to be concealed that you are the Person in question."

Endorsed "Private Instructions" by Van Gaasbeek, the letter read in part:

> From the Returns in Pennsylvania it is certain that Adams cannot be elected. The President and vice Prest. must therefore be taken from Jefferson [,] Pinkney [sic] and Burr. Six or Seven votes for Burr, in this State will make him Prest. whether intended for him as Prest. or vice Prest. . . . You know how important and critical the thing is, and must therefore spare no Pains.
>
> It will be surprising indeed if you . . . and others cannot Influence Miller and Cantine [Peter Cantine, Jr., another elector] so far as to induce them to do what is right. Burr must be spoken of however only as Vice Prest. for the Present. This Caution must not be neglected for cogent Reasons which will in due time be communicated. Somebody must confer with Miller & Cantine Personally and without delay.

Shrewd strategy lay behind this letter, whoever wrote it. As would come out after the election, Burr had extracted from some of the Republican electors below the Potomac a promise that they would give him as many votes as they gave Jefferson. To win the Presidency in 1796, a candidate had to have at least seventy electoral votes. *If* Burr had got as many votes as Jefferson did—sixty-eight—and *if* he had been able to pick up two more votes in New York at Adams's expense, he would have been the next President.

But the Southern electors did not keep their promises. Those in North Carolina gave him six votes as against eleven for Jefferson; the Virginians shut him out with only one vote as against twenty for Jefferson; and he got only thirty votes in all. Adams, with seventy-one, was elected President, and Jefferson's sixty-eight were more than enough to give him the Vice Presidency. As for why the Southern electors rejected Burr, Oliver Wolcott, Hamilton's successor as Secretary of the Treasury, was privy to a statement by a Virginia politician that may explain it.

"I have watched the movements of Mr. Burr with attention," Wolcott quoted the unnamed Virginian as saying, "and have discovered traits of character which sooner or later will give us much trouble. He has an unequalled talent for attaching men to his views, and forming combinations of which he is always the centre. He is determined to play a first part; he acts strenuously with us in public, but it is remarkable that in all private conversations he more frequently agrees with us in principle than in the mode of giving them effect . . . I shall not be surprised if Mr. Burr is found in a few years, the leader of a popular party in the northern states; and if this event ever happens, this party will subvert the influence of the southern states."

Jonathan Edwards (1703–1758), grandfather of Aaron Burr, painted around 1740 by Joseph Badger

Sarah Pierrepont Edwards (1710–1758), grandmother of Aaron Burr, in a portrait also painted by Joseph Badger around 1740

Reverend Aaron Burr (1716–1758), father of Aaron Burr and the second president of Princeton

Esther Edwards Burr (1732–1758), mother of Aaron Burr

Aaron Burr, around age thirty-six, painted by Gilbert Stuart
Courtesy the New Jersey Historical Society

A nineteenth-century photograph of "The Hermitage," the New Jersey residence of Mrs. Aaron Burr, the former Theodosia Bartow Prevost

Burr's daughter, Theodosia, painted at age twelve by Gilbert Stuart (*see page 196*)

Theodosia Burr Alston in 1802, painted by John Vanderlyn

Theodosia, in a later portrait by John Vanderlyn

A late-eighteenth-century drawing of "Richmond Hill," Burr's residence in New York City

Thomas Jefferson, in 1805, by Rembrandt Peale

The duel between Burr and Hamilton at Weehawken, New Jersey, as imagined by an early illustrator

Alexander Hamilton, after 1804, by John Trumbull

The bust of Vice President Burr by Jacques Jouvenal in the U.S. Senate gallery

10

The Theodosias

"IT WAS A KNOWLEDGE of your mind," Burr wrote his wife one winter, "which first inspired me with a respect for that of your sex . . . I confess that the ideas which you have often heard me express in favour of female intellectual powers are founded on what I have imagined, more than what I have seen, except in you. I have endeavoured to trace the causes of this *rare* display of genius in women, and find them in the errors of education, of prejudice, and of habit . . . Boys and girls are generally educated much in the same way till they are eight or nine years of age, and it is admitted that girls make at least equal progress with boys . . . Why, then, has it never been thought worth the attempt to discover, by fair experiment, the particular age at which the male superiority becomes so evident?"

Long before 1793, when these thoughts were conveyed, Burr had begun his own "fair experiment" with his daughter. The younger Theodosia, he resolved, was not to be reared in that state of near-illiteracy then generally considered both appropriate and attractive in women. She was to receive every sort of training—mental, physical, social, moral—that would have been her lot had she been born a gentleman's son instead of a gentleman's daughter.

In 1793 the object of his ambitious design was in her tenth

year, a plump and rosy little girl with auburn hair and pert features, an active child who laughed easily and often, told outrageous fibs with a straight face, doted on her big half brothers—Bartow and Frederick—and displayed toward her father an "attachment" that her mother described as "not of a common nature." At home she was "Miss Prissy." In letters to her father it tickled her to refer to herself by grand-sounding appellations, such as "Augusta Louisa Matilda Theodosia Van Horne." As she moved swiftly from girl to woman, she mirrored enough of Burr's traits to make her story integral to his own, as revealing of the parent as of the child.

She inherited his stoicism. She would know great pleasure and great sorrow, and handle the one as graciously as the other. Burr once remarked that if "Theo" were to become "a *mere* fashionable woman, with all the attendant frivolity and vacuity of mind, adorned with whatever grace and allurement, I would earnestly pray God to take her forthwith hence." A properly Chesterfieldian sentiment, but it can be taken for granted that he would have been mortified had she turned out to be an unfashionable woman. She didn't. One of her first charges to the man she later married was that he learn to speak French because she was "averse" to any language "understood by all the canaille." The delivery of inferior cabinets to a home she occupied after marriage brought a prompt decision to remove them because their remaining in the house would be "too great an impeachment of my taste."

Her attachments, like those of her father, tended to be deep and durable. Brother Bartow was a great favorite. As the passing years put them more and more apart, she entered into a long correspondence, first with him alone and then with his wife as well, that she once spoke of as an "intercourse of the heart." When Bartow's work took him from home, "thinking of my dear brother," she wrote, "is my greatest pleasure next to seeing and speaking to him." She viewed her affection for him as permitting her to chide him for his "giddiness" and his failure on occasion to appreciate what others did for him. She ran errands for him gladly. "The greatest sacrifice," she assured him, "would become [a pleasure] . . . if to please my dear Bartow." When he took a job with political overtones, she asked, "Will the office you hold prevent the other party's giving you business?" If so, her advice to him was to "Keep that, but in every other form resign politics; they will do you no good, perhaps they may do you harm." She was delighted, in early 1799, with the news of his approaching marriage to Frances Ann Smith, daughter of Samuel Stanhope Smith, president of Princeton. "I really feel that I can love her too," Theodosia wrote. So it was to be. During the ensuing years, she often discussed with Bartow's wife intimate problems she kept from others.

She shared her father's whimsy and his pleasure in the fads and foibles of the world. "Have you seen a few verses on female fashions?" she wrote Bartow, enclosing a copy of them. Patterned after a popular jingle of the day, "Shepherds, I have lost my love," the verses read:

> Shepherds, I have lost my waist
> Have you seen my body?
> Sacrificed to modern taste,
> I have become a dotty toddy.
>
> Never will you see me more
> Till common sense returning,
> My body to my legs restored,
> To gladness turn my mourning.
>
> For fashion's sake I have forsook
> What sages call the belly,
> And fashion has not left a nook
> For cheese cakes, tarts or jelly.

Like her father, she was at home wherever she went. Her mother had disliked Philadelphia. The daughter, when it came her turn to spend time there with Papa, enjoyed it. This was especially true when she and Papa moved into City Tavern after being ousted from private lodgings following a "disagreement" with their landlady. Of the Tavern she wrote Bartow, "I declare it is an easy place to live in. You have only to put your hand in your pocket and hall out some money and every thing is at your service. We pay thirty dollars a week." She shared her father's hunger for excitement and his dread of ennui. Aaron often relieved the tedium of senatorial debate by penning letters to his Theodosias. His daughter, finding a long trip going much too smoothly, entertained herself with dreams of the carriage "oversetting two or three times"—a common occurrence on the rough roads of those days—and of "other amiable casualties." The melee accompanying a thievery observed in Philadelphia put her in ecstasy. "Oh, how I love a riot," she wrote brother Bartow.

2

"The ideal college," James A. Garfield declared many years later, "is Mark Hopkins on one end of a log and a student on the other." When Burr set out to play Hopkins to his daughter, he extracted his guiding principles from Chesterfield, Rousseau, and Wollstonecraft. His objective was not an ornamental woman, but a thinking one. He took to heart Wollstonecraft's statement that "the grand source of female folly and vice has ever appeared to me to arise from narrowness of mind; and the very constitution of civil governments had put almost insuperable obstacles in the way to prevent the cultivation of female understanding:—yet virtue can be built on no other foundation." He asserted that through his daughter he hoped "to convince the world what neither sex appear to believe—that women have souls!"

Classics, the languages, and mathematics constituted the core of his curriculum, with Juvenal's *mens sana in corpore sano* hovering in the background. So that Theodosia might improve her French, he took into his home an attractive young refugee from France, Nathalie De Lage, treated her as one of the family, and spoke of her in a letter to Dr. Eustis as "my adopted daughter." A descendant of French aristocrats, Nathalie would become the wife of Thomas Sumter, Jr., of South Carolina, son of the General Sumter of Revolutionary War fame, and pass the bulk of her adult life in her husband's state.

At the age of ten the younger Theodosia was reading Terence and Horace in the original Latin, studying Greek grammar, perusing Gibbon, playing the harp and the piano, taking lessons in ballet, and learning to skate. As Burr was seldom home, he did most of his tutoring by mail. He ordered her to keep a daily journal and send it to him page by page. He used the journal and her letters to make his points. "You write *acurate* for *accurate*," he wrote her; "*laudnam* for *laudanum; intirely* for *entirely;* . . . use all these words in your next letter, that I may see that you know the true spelling. And tell me what is laudanum? Where and how made? And what are its effects?" When two of the more tricky English verbs gave her trouble, he wrote: "When you *sit* down to write to me, or when you *set* about it, be it sitting or standing, peruse all my letters and leave nothing unanswered." He utilized a sentence from one of hers—"Ma begs you will omit the thoughts of leaving Congress"—for a lesson in diction. ". . . 'omit,' " he pointed out, "is improperly used here. You mean '*abandon*, *relinquish*, *renounce*, or *abjure*' . . ." He added that the "last of these words would have been too strong for the occasion," and advised more use of the dictionary. He reminded her repeatedly that learning was of no value unless accompanied by consideration for others. "I am . . . very sorry," he wrote, "that you are obliged to submit to some reproof. Indeed, I fear that your want of attention and politeness, and your awkward postures require it . . . I have often seen Madame [Madame Senat, founder and keeper of Theo's school] . . . pay you the utmost attention; offer you twenty civilities, while you appeared scarcely sensible that she was speaking to you . . . A moment's reflection will convince you that this conduct will be naturally construed into arrogance; as if you thought that all attention was *due* to you, and as if you felt above showing the least to anybody . . . Observe how Nathalie replies to the smallest civility which is offered her."

Theo was in her twelfth year when Gilbert Stuart did his portrait of her. It "is really like you," Burr allowed; "still, it does not quite please me. It has a pensive, sentimental air, that of a love-sick maid. Stuart has probably meant to anticipate what you may be at sixteen; but even in that I think he has missed it." Stuart had given him a young beauty, a belle of the ball. Burr was hoping for something more. "And do you regret that you are not also a woman?" he asked her. "That you are not numbered in that galaxy of beauty which adorns an assembly room, coquetting for admiration and attracting flattery? No. I answer with confidence. You feel that you are maturing for solid friendships. The friends you gain you will never lose; and no one, I think, will dare to insult your understanding by such compliments as are most graciously received by too many of your sex . . ."

Stern the instructor, willing and apt the pupil. In her seventeenth year he presented her, in effect, with her diploma. "You reflect," he rejoiced, "and that is a security for your conduct. Our most humilitating errors proceed usually from inattention, and from that mental dissipation which we call heedlessness . . . Many are surprised that I could repose in you so great a trust as that of yourself; but I knew that you were equal to it, and I am not deceived . . . At your age to prefer duty to pleasure when they are in collision, is a degree of firmness rarely exhibited, and therefore, the more calculated to inspire respect."

3

BURR'S MOST FREQUENT complaint in his letters to his daughter was that she gave him too little news of Mama. How was the older Theodosia's health? Was she obeying her physicians?

Wherever his travels took him, he consulted the local doctors—in Boston, his friend William Eustis; in Philadelphia, the great Benjamin Rush. Their prescriptions did Theodosia no good. Her last years were a torture. So that he might spend more time with her, Aaron offered to resign from the Senate. She would not hear of it. He was in Philadelphia when she died on 28 May 1794.

4

HER DEATH could not have come as a total surprise to him. Almost from the beginning of his marriage, he had known that he was living with an unwell woman—known it, and dreaded the inevitable. Some years after her death, he would describe his wife in a letter to his son-in-law as "the woman whose life brought me more happiness than all my success, and whose death has dealt me more pain than all sorrows combined."

There would be a great many other women in Burr's life. What little we know of these relationships, however, suggests that never again did he commit himself emotionally to any woman, save his daughter. On the second Theodosia, as long as she lived, Burr spent whatever love was left in him.

Off and on he toyed with the idea of remarriage—only to pull back, alacritously, at the slightest sign of hesitancy or rejection. He regaled Theodosia with a running description of one of these courtships. There was no need to use the lady's name. Theodosia knew her well. He spoke of her as "Céleste," a Philadelphian, obviously wealthy and of good family. The two of them enjoyed numerous tête-à-têtes, in the course of which he essayed to point out from time to time that the single life was not without its compensations. Finally he nerved himself to speak to "le père," who was more than willing that he speak to Céleste herself, which he did. For Theodosia's eyes he recounted this "duette" in detail. "Céleste was profoundly occupied in tearing up some roses which she held in her hand, and Reubon [Burr] was equally industrious in twirling his hat and pinching some new corners and angles in the brim." He heard her utter what he took to be no, and turned to leave. She asked him to stay a moment. A few more words, abstract in nature, and he was gone.

Theodosia was not fooled. "As to Céleste, *voilà mon* opinion," she wrote. "She meant from the beginning, to say that awful word—*yes;* but not choosing to say it immediately, she told you that you *had* furnished her with arguments against matrimony, which in French means, Please, sir, to persuade me out of them again. But you took it as a plump refusal, and walked off. She called you back. What more could she do? I would have seen you to Japan before I should have done so much."

In his old age he would undergo a brief second marriage with a worldly widow well endowed with worldly goods. In the long interval between his only real marriage and this geriatric digression, he distracted himself with many women, and committed himself to none.

11

Affairs of State

In 1797, Burr's senatorship ended. With John Jay in the New York governor's chair and Federalists in command of both branches of the New York legislature, a second term was out of the question. In January, the legislature not only named Schuyler to Burr's seat in the United States Senate but did so by a close to unanimous vote. It was a moment of triumph for the patroon and his son-in-law, although in a sense an empty one, as illness shortly forced Schuyler to resign.

In March, Burr returned to New York City and his law practice, although with no intention of settling for the possibly nutritious but to him dull pudding of private life. Never, perhaps, will it be possible to dispel all the shadows that cloak this affable, exasperating, often self-defeating but indestructible and somehow likable man. But it throws a small beam of light into the mass to bear in mind that to the end of his days Aaron Burr was driven by a terrible need to keep himself entertained. The year before, seeing the end of his senatorship in sight, he had allowed a group of Republicans to nominate him for the upper house of the New York legislature and to declare that, if "selected Senator of this state," he would resign from "the Senate of the United States." Nothing came of this effort, but in April 1797 he encountered little difficulty in getting himself elected to the lower branch of the legislature.

Robert Troup found this development baffling. What did his old friend want of a job so "beneath his talents"? In a long letter to Rufus King, Troup essayed several possible answers to his own question. Confronting the New York lawmakers were a number of bills aimed at liberalizing the state's bankruptcy and land-purchasing rules. Troup was correct in believing that Burr would be interested in these measures, but his ordinarily sharp eyes missed another factor. As Burr made ready for the transfer to Albany, now the capital of the state, his thoughts were on the next Presidential election—the election of 1800. A humble seat in the Assembly could be a satisfactory center from which to cultivate the Republican interest in that event.

To note that Burr was thinking along these lines is not to suggest that at last he had become a party regular. He was still a Burrite first and a Republican second. Left standing by itself, that statement could be faulted as unfair to him, for the same thing could be said of the Clintons and the Livingstons. Probably in no other state was the democracy less cohesive than in New York. Just as Federalism there had once been a loose coalition of uneasily cooperating factions, so now Republicanism there was clearly demarked into the Burrites, the Clintons, and the Livingstons—and not infrequently each of these groups showed itself at least as attentive to its own narrow interests as to those of the party as a whole. Granted that more than once in the past Burr had strayed beyond even the New York democracy's indifferently staked-out borders, knocking on the portals of Federalism, only to find them unyielding, well guarded by the dragon, Alexander. By 1797 he needed no special intelligence to see on which side his bread was buttered—that for the foreseeable future he must conduct his own political affairs within the Republican ambience.

2

THOMAS JEFFERSON saw the potentialities of Burr's new post. At the time of Burr's election to the Assembly, the Republican leader was scanning the political panorama from Philadelphia, where his recently assumed duties as Vice President of the United States were to hold him until well into the warmer months. Jefferson was fifty-four that summer, a tall and slender man, long-limbed and loose-jointed, with blue eyes in a sandy-complexioned face. He wore his hair loosely over his forehead and lightly queued in back. As one historian has put it, no doubt exists as to its color because Jefferson took care to preserve a letter whose writer greeted him as "You red-headed son of a bitch." He was not the democracy's founding father, considerable wordage to the contrary notwithstanding. The paternal honors would seem to belong largely to his close friend, Madison, and to the cunning first clerk of the House of Representatives, John Beckley. Only reluctantly had Jefferson accepted the leadership that these men and others thrust upon him, but having grasped the nettle, he would soon show himself the possessor of political instincts of an extraordinary fineness.

As the second man of the government in 1797, his position was touchy—*of* the Adams Administration but not *in* it—and it may be offered as a demonstration of his ability to work effectively behind the scenes that it was during his four years in the Vice Presidency that he pieced together the political machine that in 1800 would bring the Federalists down for good and all. As the human symbol of a party associated in the public consciousness with revolutionary France, he had weighty worries. Jay's Treaty had accomplished its main objective. It had averted a war with Britain. Now France was the enemy. French privateers and men-of-war were preying on American shipping. During the next three years French damage to American commerce would come to almost $13 million in court-adjudicated claims alone. In other words, the infant Republic stood on the brink of a quasi- or a cold war with France. Anger at the changing governments of that nation was widespread. Even in Republican Virginia, it was playing havoc with party loyalty. No longer could democracy hope to survive as an almost exclusively Southern phenomenon. It must have help from the outside, an opening into the Federalist North. It was with this awareness that the Vice President inaugurated by mail the alliance between himself and Aaron Burr that was to have such memorable consequences for both of them.

Jefferson's 17 June communication to Burr was an attempt to pour oil on troubled waters. The Vice President recognized that the New Yorker had reason to be chagrined at the short shrift he had received, the year before, from the Presidential electors in Jefferson's own state. An angry Burr could be a bull in the Republican china shop. On the other hand, a mollified one could be helpful. Accordingly, Jefferson wrote in a pleasant and chatty manner. He opened with a rundown of his views on the state of the Union. Not good from where he sat. The Federalist leadership had interpreted Jay's Treaty in a way that had antagonized France. Hence the present difficulties with that government. It seemed to Jefferson that the Federalists in Congress were making things worse by talking endlessly of new fortifications and new frigates for the navy. He considered the "future character of our republic as in the air; indeed its future fortune will be in the air if war is made on us by France . . ." He expressed the hope that Burr would find these comments "not . . . unacceptable," if only because the sending of them provided him with the "opportunity of recalling myself to your memory, and of evidencing my esteem for you."

The election that was sending Burr to Albany had registered a few Republican gains. Jefferson described himself as "much pleased to see a dawn of change in the spirit of your state." Having struck this cheery note, he at once plunged into gloom. He did not come right out and ask Burr's assistance in swinging New York into the Republican column. He described Federalism's hold on the Northeast as strong beyond the ability of the most skillful manipulator of men's minds to break. No doubt Jefferson reckoned that a man of the colonel's mettle would find a challenge of this magnitude irresistible. What "with the English influence in the lower, and the Patroon influence in the upper part of your state," he wrote, "I presume little is to be hoped. If a prospect could be once opened upon us of a penetration of truth into the eastern States; if the people there, who are unquestionably republicans, could discover that they have been duped into the support of measures calculated to sap the very foundations of republicanism, we might still hope for salvation, and that it would come, as of old, from the east. But will that region ever awake to the true state of things? Can the middle, Southern and Western states hold on till they awake? These are painful . . . questions; and if, in assuring me of your health, you can give me a comfortable solution of them, it will relieve a mind devoted to the preservation of our republican government."

This letter makes interesting reading against the background of Jefferson's subsequent appraisal of Burr. It would be the Virginian's recollection, as recorded years later, that his disapproval of the New Yorker went back to the very genesis of their acquaintanceship in the early 1790's. "His conduct," Jefferson wrote, ". . . soon inspired me with distrust. I habitually cautioned Mr. Madison against trusting him too much. I saw afterwards that under General Washington's and Mr. Adams's administrations, whenever a great military appointment or a diplomatic one was to be made, he came post to Philadelphia to show himself, and in fact that he was always at market . . ." These words were written in 1804. By that time Jefferson was President and had long since concluded that the ambitious and freebooting Burr was a threat to his own political plans—plans that already envisioned the Virginia Dynasty, the force that for a quarter of a century would dominate the democracy and monopolize the Presidency. What Jefferson actually felt about Burr back in 1797 is an unanswerable question. To forge the politically necessary Virginia–New York axis, he could have written to George Clinton, out of office for the time being but by no means out of sight, politically speaking; or to Chancellor Livingston, who with his large and ramified family constituted another powerful segment of New York's faction-ridden democracy. That he chose instead to get in touch with Burr indicates that he then regarded the colonel as the key Republican leader of his state and thought well enough of his talents to want to use them.

Burr's answer to Jefferson's letter was prompt and friendly. He wrote that, generally speaking, his views and those of the Vice President were similar. He added, however, that it "would not be easy neither would it be discreet, to answer your inquiries or to communicate to you my ideas with satisfaction to either of us, in the compass of a letter. I will endeavor to do it in person." He was as good as his word. Toward the end of the month he was in Philadelphia. Monroe, recently recalled from his ministry to France, was in town. So, too, was Albert Gallatin, and the problems of party strategy kept the four Republican leaders—Monroe, Gallatin, Burr, and Jefferson—closeted in animated conference for at least a couple of hours. These matters taken care of, Burr returned to New York City to await the opening of the legislature and to play a not unimportant role in that mysterious episode in the life of Alexander Hamilton known as the Reynolds affair.

3

THE REYNOLDS AFFAIR entered its final phase in the early summer of 1797 when in a series of pamphlets, later reissued in book form, the Scottish-born journalist James Thomson Callender asserted that Hamilton, while Secretary of the Treasury, had joined with a financial schemer named James Reynolds in a number of improper and probably illegal speculative ventures. Two months after the appearance of Callender's accusations, Hamilton answered them in a hastily assembled book entitled *Observations on Certain Documents Contained in No. V and VI of "The History of the United States for the Year 1796," In which the Charge of Speculation Against Alexander Hamilton, Late Secretary of the Treasury, is Fully Refuted. Written by Himself.* "The charge against me," Hamilton wrote, "is a connection with one James Reynolds for purposes of improper pecuniary speculation. My real crime is an amorous connection with his wife for a considerable time with his privity and connivance, if not originally brought on by a combination between the husband and wife with the design to extort money from me." Having set forth the nub of his defense, Hamilton elaborated on it. He described his affair with Maria Reynolds, along with her husband's blackmailing activities, and appended to his book the copies of some twenty love letters that he said Maria had written to him.

No sooner was Hamilton's defense in view than Callender asked permission to examine the original letters. When Hamilton ignored this request—endorsing Callender's letter "Impudent Experiment NO NOTICE"—the journalist published another book. In this he pointed out that Hamilton could have written the love letters himself, the implication being that they were forgeries and the Secretary's tale of adultery and blackmail a fabrication designed to distract public attention from his official peculations. According to Callender, Hamilton's biggest crime was not that he had kissed and told but that he hadn't kissed and said he had.

The battle of words thus launched in 1797 was an outgrowth of recurrent attempts by the Republicans in Congress, in the opening half of the decade, to uncover proof for their conviction that during his secretaryship Hamilton had used his inside knowledge of the government's fiscal plans to enrich himself and his speculator friends. In the late autumn of 1792, Representative Frederick A. C. Muhlenberg of Pennsylvania came into possession of data that he believed constituted the sort of evidence for which Hamilton's critics were looking. The source of this information was Jacob Clingman, who for a period had worked as a clerk in one of Muhlenberg's mercantile establishments.

Earlier in the fall, the government had brought two suits against Clingman and his then business partner, James Reynolds. The specific charge was that, having somehow got a Treasury Department employee to supply them with a list of creditors of the United States, the two men had persuaded an acquaintance to perjure himself so that they could pose as executors of the estate of one of the individuals on the list. Both were arrested in mid-November. Clingman at once obtained his release on bail, but Reynolds was still in the Philadelphia jail when his partner made the first of several visits to Muhlenberg to solicit the congressman's help in what would eventually be a successful effort to get a dismissal of the government's cases. According to Muhlenberg, "Clingman, unasked, frequently dropped hints to me, that Reynolds had it in his power, very materially to injure the Secretary of the Treasury, and that Reynolds knew several very improper transactions of his." To the Pennsylvania congressman, these insinuations pointed only one way. The Secretary had engaged in illegal speculations, using Reynolds as his agent.

Muhlenberg was himself a moderate Federalist, but he was justly renowned for his honesty and not a man to suppress facts for partisan reasons. On 12 December he shared his suspicions with two Republican members of the Virginia delegation in Congress, Senator Monroe and Representative Abraham B. Venable. Monroe and Venable immediately visited Reynolds in his prison cell. He confirmed Clingman's statements, and that evening Monroe and Muhlenberg called at Reynolds's home, where they talked with his wife. Not much is known of Mrs. Reynolds, then in her twenty-fourth year, other than that she was born Maria Lewis in New York State, could claim what were then spoken of as "respectable family connections," had wed Reynolds in 1783, was the mother of a seven-year-old daughter, would obtain a divorce in 1795 to marry Clingman and live with him in Virginia, and be last heard of, historically speaking, as having moved to England with her second husband.

To the distinguished visitors to her Philadelphia home on that winter night in 1792 she was helpful. Not only did she corroborate Reynolds's and Clingman's charges; she also provided her guests with a few unsigned notes which she believed Hamilton had written to her husband and some of which her husband had so endorsed.

On the morning of 15 December, Muhlenberg, Monroe, and Venable called on Hamilton himself. They showed him the "incriminating" documents, as they had come to think of the items Mrs. Reynolds had given them, and demanded an explanation. What they got was an invitation from Hamilton to meet with him at his home that evening, along with a promise that he would there supply them with proof that he had in no way abused his trust as a public functionary. That evening he showed them the love letters from Maria Reynolds and related the story behind them. The three visitors then pronounced themselves disabused of all suspicions of official wrongdoing on his part, and on the following morning they signed a memorandum to that effect. There the matter rested, save for a veiled rumor in a Philadelphia newspaper, until publication of James Callender's accusations in the summer of 1797.

To Hamilton the appearance of these charges raised painful questions. Had Muhlenberg or Venable or Monroe, or perhaps all three of them, retreated from their asserted belief in his official probity? Who had shown Callender the written documents connected with the Reynolds affair—documents to which the journalist had obviously had access? Hamilton lost no time in getting in touch with the three statesmen. The replies of Muhlenberg and Venable were thoroughly satisfactory to him. That of Monroe was just as thoroughly disturbing, and the revelation that only Monroe had held on to the pertinent written documents swiftly strengthened Hamilton's not unjustified supposition that the Virginian was not, and never had been, certain of Hamilton's innocence of underhanded doing while Secretary of the Treasury.

As Aaron Burr would discover and deplore seven years later, Hamilton had a genius for obfuscation when he took to the written word. On 22 July he sent Monroe what seemed to be a challenge, and on the last day of the month Monroe, although not sure whether Hamilton had challenged or not, accepted.

It was during the period of these exchanges that Colonel Burr came into the picture. Acting as one of Monroe's seconds and his chief counselor, he played the peacemaker. There would be a good deal more correspondence between Monroe and Hamilton, but there would be no duel. Exactly how much the colonel's labors contributed to this happy ending is not clear. Obviously, he brought to the dispute a spirit of compromise and common sense woefully lacking in either of its principals. On one occasion he contrived to withhold from Hamilton a belligerent letter that Monroe had written and had sent to Burr for comment and transmission. Indeed, it is difficult to quarrel with the observation of Hamilton's biographer, John C. Miller, that "No doubt, it was within Burr's power to have precipitated a duel at this time and thus, perhaps, to have relieved himself of the necessity of killing Hamilton a few years later."

Popular reaction to Hamilton's public confession of private immorality was about what he should have expected. His friends were appalled, his foes overjoyed. "Humiliating in the extreme," Federalist Henry Knox wrote Judge David Cobb of Massachusetts. Cobb was less perturbed. "Hamilton is fallen for the present," he observed, "but if he fornicates with every female in the cities of New York and Philadelphia, he will rise again, for purity of character, after a period of political existence is not necessary for public patronage." Republicans continued, as in the past, to regard Hamilton as guilty of having used his position as Secretary of the Treasury for pecuniary gain. Most of them continued to think so, that is. Not Burr. Always fiercely protective of his own private life, he probably looked on Hamilton's exposure of his as sheer madness. But, as for Hamilton's public life, "If you . . . believe, as I do," he wrote Monroe, "that H. is innocent of the charge of any concern in speculation with Reynolds, it is my opinion that it would be an act of magnanimity and justice to say so in a . . . certificate."

4

ON 2 JANUARY 1798, Burr was in Albany, to begin the first of what were to be two consecutive terms in the Assembly. During both sessions, as duly noted by Robert Troup, he fought for reforms in the state's bankruptcy and land-purchase laws. He was understandably attentive to a bill designed to discontinue imprisonment for debt, but not all his activities were directed by self-interest. Working through one of his followers, he initiated the proceedings that put human bondage on its way to extinction in New York State. This time he made no effort, as he had years before, to end slavery at once. Realizing that the lawmakers would not endorse that drastic a change, he concentrated instead on a partly successful endeavor to safeguard the welfare of New York's blacks during the long hiatus between the adoption of gradual abolition in 1799 and the arrival of total abolition twenty-eight years later.

During the second of his two consecutive terms, his position as a minority leader was bolstered by the presence in the Assembly of his stepson, Bartow Prevost, and of a striking blond giant named John Swartwout. Born in Dutchess County,

Swartwout and his younger brothers—Robert, Samuel, and Henry—migrated to New York City after the Revolution. There, except for Henry, who died young, they prospered, first as merchants and importers, later as the owners and converters to useful purposes of large sections of the New Jersey badlands. A man of boundless energy and rarely relinquished geniality, John Swartwout in 1796 tied his political fortunes to Burr, to remain for the rest of his life one of the colonel's warmest supporters. With his help and Prevost's, Burr undertook a variety of maneuvers in the Assembly aimed at strengthening the Republican Party in New York against the coming of the Presidential election of 1800. One consisted of an attempt to shift the right of naming the state's Presidential electors from the legislature to the voters, on the assumption that in 1800 both houses of the legislature would still be under Federalist control. In the lower house, Burr inveigled a favorable vote for this bill, only to see it fail in the Senate, where his beguiling ways were less appreciated.

Great success crowned another of his efforts on behalf of the Republican cause. The majority in the Assembly had its soft spots, men who although elected to the legislature as Federalists were known to harbor democratic inclinations. Most of these doubtful Federalists were from New York's so-called Western District, embracing the recently occupied frontier counties brought into being by the forced sale of the public lands during Burr's attorney generalship. The traditional conservatives of the Assembly spoke of them contemptuously as "trimmers," but this would seem to have been too harsh a term for men whose political ambivalence was a natural outgrowth of recent history.

Originally the liberal elements of the state had assumed that, once opened to settlement, the Western District would become a haven for the underprivileged and as such a bastion of democracy. Matters, however, had not turned out thus, for a variety of reasons. For one thing, many of the settlers came from strongly Federalist New England. For another, one of their greatest needs as pioneers was for defense against the nearby Indians, and on this score both the state and national policies of the Federalists were more reassuring than those of the anti-militaristic Republicans. Finally, there was an economic factor. The underprivileged did not pour into the Western country for the simple reason that they couldn't afford to. The acquisition and improvement of a parcel of frontier land required more than strong backs and willing hands. As Gouverneur Morris would one day remark, it was "absurd to suppose a person with scarce a second shirt to his back can go two or three hundred miles to look out a farm, have it surveyed, travel back again to the office for a patent, etc., clear the land, cut a road, make a settlement, and build a house and barn . . ." Although seldom rich, the majority of the successful settlers of the New York west enjoyed sufficient resources to consider their interests identical with those of the big landlords and merchant princes of the east. Once settled in, however, the conditions around them tended to dilute their Federalism. Aping the aristocrats of the east, a settler might build himself a manor house in the wilderness, but in a country where every man was bent on being his own proprietor, servants and field hands were so hard to come by that the males of the family had no choice but to toil outside from dawn to dusk, while their womenfolk did likewise within. In this kind of world, democratic manners were admired, and the pioneer's desperate need for the help and protection of his neighbors induced a profound devotion to egalitarianism. More often than not, to sum up, the inhabitant of the frontier was a Federalist at the polls but a Republican at heart.

One of the Federalists from the frontier among Burr's Assembly mates was Jedidiah Peck of Otsego County. A Connecticut Yankee by birth, Peck began his adult life as a self-educated bookkeeper, fought in the Revolution, and in 1790 moved to Cooperstown, county seat of Otsego, where he worked as a surveyor, a millwright, a farmer, and a sometime Baptist preacher. Not an effective preacher, it would appear, for although well versed in the Bible, Peck delivered his sermons in "a drawling nasal . . . twang" that, according to a contemporary, rendered his words "almost unintelligible." He was in his mid-forties when in 1798 Otsego sent him to the Assembly, a small and insignificant-looking figure with features bordering on the "disgusting," always "in shabby clothing, and with a gait ungainly." It is easy to imagine the effect of this apparition out of the west on the cultured and polished old-line Federalists of the east. From the beginning, their attitude toward him was one of condescension at best, of indifference at worst.

Burr was quick to take in the situation and to exploit it. He courted the unprepossessing but by no means unthinking representative from Otsego. When time came for the colonel to launch his attempt to change New York's method of choosing its Presidential electors, he entrusted the introduction of the original motion to his vigorous sidekick, John Swartwout. As this motion also proposed a change in the method for electing the state's senators, Burr contrived to have Jedidiah Peck present a second motion, dividing the original one into two parts and calling for the appointment of committees to draft the appropriate bills and bring them before the House. For the "almost unintelligible" Otsego surveyor-preacher, it was a sudden and happy moment in the limelight and one that made him more persona non grata than ever in the eyes of the Federalist majority. Burr knew what he was doing. Jedidiah Peck would no longer be a Federalist when he left the Assembly.

Nor was he the only westerner to change his spots because of the ministrations of the courtly colonel. For this we have the word of Jabez D. Hammond, the first chronicler of the early political wars of New York and himself a participant in some of the events he recounts with care and grace. According to Hammond, Burr lavished attention on "some eight or ten" of the lawmakers from the frontier country. At least one other among them, Obadiah German of Chenango County, having entered the legislature a doubting Federalist, departed therefrom a confirmed Republican. It is Hammond's opinion that the creation of these converts to democracy was Burr's first and probably his most important contribution to the Republican seizure of the New York government—and the Presidency of the United States—in 1800, for while the colonel was winning over the eastern half of the Empire State that year, these recruits to the party of the people were winning the equally crucial west. Referring to subsequently published attacks on Burr by a New York City pamphleteer, Hammond wrote that their author was "wrong in alleging that Col. Burr, while a member of the assembly in 1798–9, did not act efficiently in support of the republican interests. He probably effected more than any other individual."

5

BUT THERE WERE LIMITS to what he could accomplish, for in the late 1790's the cold war with France was warming up and disapproval of the pro-French leanings of Jefferson and other leaders of the democracy was on the rise. In the summer of 1797 President Adams sent three ministers plenipotentiary to France in the hopes of negotiating a gallicized Jay's Treaty—something on paper that would stop France's piecemeal destruction of America's oceangoing commerce. In Paris, for a period, the President's representatives cooled their heels in the anterooms of the five-man Directory that was then the ruling body of France. At this time the French Minister of Foreign Affairs was that scheming embodiment of human greed, Charles Maurice de Talleyrand. When the plenipotentiaries finally reached the conference table, they found themselves facing, not Talleyrand, but three of his agents, whom the Americans in their subsequently published dispatches referred to as Messrs. X, Y, and Z. From these gentlemen came two demands—that the United States lend France several million dollars, along with a bribe of $250,000 to be split between Talleyrand and his associates.

The envoys were not overwhelmingly shocked. Then as later, such arrangements were a commonplace of diplomacy. But they were not prepared to turn over such sums. More to the point, there was no assurance that the requested gratuities (for the loan, of course, was not intended to be repaid) would buy them anything more than a formal chat with Monsieur de Talleyrand. One of the Americans, Charles Cotesworth Pinckney of South Carolina, shouted, "No. No. Not a sixpence!," never dreaming that a short time later his interjection would be translated into the rousing "Millions for defense, but not one cent for tribute!"

President Adams's release to Congress of the "XYZ Papers" —the envoys' report of their Parisian junket—and their appearance in the American press sent popular anger at France to fever pitch. Hitherto, the Federalists in Congress had talked of forts and frigates, as Jefferson had complained to Burr. Now there was action, Republicans and Federalist congressmen closing ranks to put the country on a war footing. Swiftly enacted laws installed a new post in the Cabinet to be known as the Secretary of the Navy, authorized enough frigates to bring the country's tiny navy up to at least the point of visibility, and created a 10,000-man army. George Washington agreed to come out of retirement to lead it, on two conditions. One was that Hamilton be his second in command. The other was that he, Washington, would play an active role only in the event of actual hostilities. Both provisos horrified Adams, who was just beginning to realize what had long been no secret to many others—that at least three members of his Cabinet were taking their orders from the quondam Treasury head. But even the President of the United States dared not brook the Father of His Country, and for the remainder of the undeclared war with

France, Hamilton would be the de facto commander and main shaper of his country's enlarged military apparatus, with the rank of major general and the title of Inspector General.

To the always militarily minded Burr, news of the enlargement of the army was as a flower to a bee. By the summer of 1798 it was common knowledge that the top commissions—the major generalships—were going to Hamilton, Charles Cotesworth Pinckney, and Henry Knox. But several brigadier generalships remained to be filled, and Burr was eager to have one. Most of our knowledge of what came of this ambition is contained in a letter penned by John Adams many years after the incidents it describes. "I proposed to General Washington, in a conference between him and me," the former President wrote his Boston friend, James Lloyd, in 1815, "and through him to the triumvirate [Hamilton, Pinckney and Knox], to nominate Colonel Burr for a brigadier-general. Washington's answer to me was, 'By all that I have known and heard, Colonel Burr is a brave and able officer; but the question is, whether he has not equal talents at intrigue.' How shall I describe to you my sensations and reflections at that moment? He had compelled me to promote over the heads of Lincoln, Gates, Clinton, Knox, and others, and even over Pinckney, one of . . . the most restless, impatient, artful, indefatigable and unprincipled intriguers in the United States, if not in the world, to be second in command under himself, and now dreaded an intriguer in a poor brigadier! He did, however, propose it to the triumvirate, at least to Hamilton. But I was not permitted to nominate Burr. If I had been, what would have been the consequence? Shall I say, that Hamilton would have been now alive, and Hamilton and Burr now the head of our affairs? What then? If I had nominated Burr without the consent of the triumvirate, a negative in Senate was certain. Burr to this day knows nothing of this."

If it was the intent of Adams to imply that "one of the most unprincipled intriguers in the United States" was at the root of Burr's failure to get a brigadier generalship, he was in error. When in June 1798 Hamilton, then in New York, learned that Burr was heading for Philadelphia to apply for a commission, he wrote his successor in the Cabinet, Secretary of the Treasury Wolcott, that he had "some reasons for wishing that the administration may manifest a cordiality to him. It is not impossible he may be found a useful cooperator. I am aware there are different judges but the case is worth the experiment."

Kind words for Burr from this source? They would not be the last such sentiments to glide from Alexander Hamilton's pen. In that summer of anti-French hysteria and rabid preparations for war, he and Burr were serving together on a military committee set up by the citizens of New York City to expedite the strengthening of the harbor defenses with funds coming in part from the city and state, in part from the federal government. So amicable were their relations that Robert Troup, out of his mind with wonderment, reported to a friend that with his own eyes he had seen Aaron being polite to Alexander and vice versa. The two men talked over Burr's desire for a commission. Hamilton put the important question bluntly: was Burr ready to serve the commander in chief loyally and without reservations? Burr so far forgot himself as to reply in kind. He said "he despised Washington as a Man of No Talents, and one who could not spell a sentence of common English." When Burr repeated this remark to Adams, the President scolded him, asserting that "his Prejudice made him very unreasonable," for to Adams's "certain knowledge, Washington was not so illiterate."

Perhaps Burr's sally reached Washington's ear. Perhaps not. In any event, the rejection of his application was not Hamilton's doing. Washington's distrust of Burr went back to the early days of the Revolution, antedated his intimacy with Hamilton, and needed no prodding from that quarter.

Hamilton's note to Wolcott, expressing his willingness to

see Burr become a brigadier general, was not his only effort to assist his great rival. "Dear Sir," he wrote Governor John Jay on 12 February 1799:

> After a plan for fortifying our port shall have been settled, the execution of it with energy and dispatch will demand a very great portion of the time and attention of a competent character as Superintendent. This task I cannot undertake consistently with my other occupations. Col. Burr will be very equal to it and will I believe undertake it, if an *adequate compensation* be annexed. He would likewise be useful in the formation of a plan. I know not what collateral objections may have arisen from recent conduct of that gentleman [a reference to Burr's attempt to change the method for selecting Presidential electors]; but independent of these I should favour his agency in the business . . . . Dr Sr Yr obed ser
>
> A. Hamilton

Jay did not honor this request. The Federalist governor of New York had his own thoughts and was never noticeably influenced by those of the leader of his party. Still, Hamilton's letter to him poses a question: if Hamilton really believed, as he monotonously averred in private correspondence, that Burr was an "embryo-Caesar" and the "Catiline of America," why did he recommend him to a position whose very nature called for the services of a man of unquestioned devotion to the welfare of his state and country?

6

TO TURN AGAIN to Burr's performance in the New York legislature, it is worth noting that on at least one occasion his status as an upholder of democracy in that Federalist-ruled body endured a slight jolt as a result of the eclectic character of his own political past. Each January the members of the lower house named four members of the upper house, one from each of the state's large senatorial districts, to serve with the governor on the powerful Council of Appointment. On the eve of this election in 1799 it was apparent that the contention for one of the council seats lay between a Republican senator, John Addison of Ulster County, and a Federalist senator, Ebenezer Foote of Delaware County. For Burr, the situation spelled trouble. Both men were, or had been, Burrites. If he voted for Republican Addison, he offended an old Federalist crony who had supported him for governor in 1792 and in 1795. If he voted for Federalist Foote, he lost caste as a minority leader. The Journal of the Assembly records his solution of the problem. He absented himself from the chamber during the balloting. Foote won by a close vote, 49 to 47, and it would be claimed later that the Republican members of the Assembly held Burr responsible for the defeat of their candidate.

7

At no time, to be sure, was Assemblyman Burr in a position to give his undivided attention to the well-being of his party. Long-standing personal problems remained with him. He was still mired in debt, and when an opportunity arose to alleviate his pecuniary pains to some extent, he did not hesitate to avail himself of it.

His benefactor in this instance was a conglomeration of Dutch banks, banded together to invest in virgin American soil and known as the Holland Land Company. Over a period of years Théophile Cazenove, the conglomerate's American-based agent, had purchased for his principals close to five million acres in Pennsylvania and New York. As the potential purchasers of these acres were Europeans, New York presented Cazenove with a difficulty. Under the laws of that state, no alien could hold direct title to land, and two attempts to change the law had failed, when in early 1796 or thereabouts Cazenove employed the services of Alexander Hamilton. So strong was the Federalist leader's standing with the legislature that a bill authorizing aliens to hold land in fee simple for seven years became law on 11 April of that year.

Helpful? Not to the Holland Company proprietors, straining to unload a million and a half acres of New York land at a nice profit. At Cazenove's bidding, Hamilton tried again, this time with the assistance of his father-in-law, Philip Schuyler. The patroon was now president of the Western Inland Lock Navigation Company, recently incorporated by the state for the purpose of improving the waterways in central and western New York and commonly referred to as the canal company. The canal company was hungry for cash, and the combined efforts of the patroon and his son-in-law had the effect, on 17 March 1797, of producing a measure that can be best described as a financial deal masquerading as a law. The gist of this remarkable legislation was that the land tenure allowable to aliens would be increased from seven to sixteen years, provided the Holland Land Company lent the canal company $250,000 or purchased shares in it to that amount. When the proprietors of the Dutch company decided to pass up this golden opportunity, Cazenove turned for help to Aaron Burr.

He and the colonel were already doing business. "In December, 1795 or 1796," to quote Burr's own account of some of their transactions, the colonel had "entered into a covenant with the Holland Company for the purchase of one hundred thousand acres . . . payable by installments." According to Burr, the "covenant contained a penalty of twenty thousand dollars" in the event of his failure to fulfill its terms. As security for this penalty, he mortgaged to Cazenove twenty thousand acres previously bought from a domestic land company and assigned to him "Thomas L. Witbeck's bond, payable to me, for the twenty thousand dollars . . ." Later, unable to take up this instrument when pressed by Witbeck to do so, Burr arranged to replace it with the bond of his farmer-stepson, Frederick Prevost.

When Cazenove asked Burr to take over where Hamilton

and Schuyler had left off, the colonel concluded at once that the Holland Company could get what it wanted by the simple device of distributing some five thousand dollars among selected members of the legislature and the state government. Cazenove offered no objections, writing his superiors in Holland that Burr's scheme would probably get them more and certainly cost them less than the proposed $250,000 investment in Schuyler's canal company. Thus matters were worked out, and on 2 April 1798 a law permitting aliens to acquire unrestricted ownership of New York land went on the books. For services to this end, the attorney general of the state, Josiah Ogden Hoffman, got $3,000. For steering the bill through the upper house of the legislature, Senator Thomas Morris got a thousand dollars, and a gentleman identified as "Mr. L———" got another thousand dollars. On the books of the Holland Company, these items appeared as legal fees. As for Burr, his known receipts, amounting to at least $5,500, went on the company records as a loan—never repaid. In addition, his failure to meet the terms covering his attempted purchase of one hundred thousand acres of Holland Company land was settled, after protracted negotiations, by an arrangement under which the land—now valued at twenty shillings an acre as against the twelve shillings Burr had promised to pay—went back to the company, along with the twenty thousand acres he had previously acquired from another firm, the $20,000 penalty called for in the covenant was forgiven, and the bond provided by Burr's stepson was taken up.

Any comment on these procedures can only labor the obvious. The efforts of Schuyler and Hamilton to fatten the coffers of the older man's canal company with the help of the state may be cited as a prime example of political logrolling. Burr's use of his seat in the Assembly to further the interests of a private firm was not precisely cricket. And the "legal fees" to Hoffman, Morris and Mr. L———, to say nothing of the favors to Burr, are the sort of payments sometimes spoken of by the irreverent as bribes.

Indeed, the word "bribes" was much noised about in the more knowing political circles of Albany and New York. Among those spreading the inevitable rumors was John Barker Church, Hamilton's close friend and business associate and his wife's brother-in-law. When Church loudly and openly attached the word "bribes" to Burr, the latter called him out, and the two men confronted one another one autumn morning on the dueling grounds of Hoboken, New Jersey. The surmise arises that Burr's reputation as a man of deadly eye on the field of honor did not take form until after his encounter with Hamilton at Weehawken. At Hoboken, challenged and challenger fired their pistols once. Church put a ball through Burr's jacket. Burr hit nothing at all. At this point, Church stepped forward to apologize, and the seconds declared the interview honorably concluded. Old or new, scandals never die, but if the furor over the Holland Company affair faded rather precipitately, it was probably because, on the heels of it, Burr provided the public with an even juicier escapade—a spate of maneuvers whereby he gave his party a useful financial institution known in its beginning days as the Manhattan Company Bank.

8

In the spring of 1799, Burr persuaded New York's preponderantly Federalist lawmakers to charter what was ostensibly a badly needed water-supply company for New York City, only to discover after the bill had become law that they had brought into being not only a water company but also a bank, and a Republican-controlled bank at that. How Burr accomplished this legislative coup is literally a twice-told tale. For well over a century, the more or less accepted story of the chartering of the Manhattan Bank pictured Burr as single-handedly hoodwinking both the legislative and executive divisions of the state government to achieve his partisan ends. Then, in 1957, in the columns of the *Political Science Quarterly*, Beatrice G. Reubens unveiled a new and more plausible version of the old tale. Although her brilliant and meticulously documented study did not divest the Manhattan Bank episode of all the conjectures surrounding it, it did make certain things abundantly clear. Burr does seem to have fooled some of the legislators all of the time or all of them some of the time, but he was not the episode's only hero, or its only villain, depending on whether you wish to applaud him as the possessor of unique legal skills and political acumen or condemn him as an underhanded schemer. Reubens's main revelation is that Burr could not have brought off his triumphant coup without the help of several prominent Federalists and most notably that of Alexander Hamilton.

As the modern phrase goes, it figures. Hamilton seems always to turn up in the shadow behind Burr. Perhaps "shadow" is the wrong word for either man, for each of them shed a glow of sorts as he moved through life. Coming from opposite ends of the social spectrum, they were seemingly ordained to meet and mingle in a curious symbiosis. Nor would this situation end at Weehawken, for thereafter, wherever Burr happened to be, the ghost of the other hovered.

To review, then, the highlights of the Manhattan Bank affair: prior to 1799, New York City, hive of commerce though it was, had only two banks. One was the Bank of New York, organized by Hamilton and others in 1784 and chartered by the state legislature in 1791. The other, also Hamilton's brainchild, was the local branch of the Bank of the United States. Both were Federalist. To paraphrase the older version of the tale, as recounted by Gustavus Myers in his history of Tammany Hall, their directors were always ready to make loans to personal or party friends, often for questionable purposes. On the other hand, if a merchant was known to be a Republican, his paper was likely to be rejected just when he most needed cash.

Somewhere along the line, it came to Burr that the remedy for this problem was to create a Republican-controlled bank. There were more ways than one of skinning this cat. Banking was still a common law occupation, and Burr and his friends could have set up a private bank were they so minded. That Burr was not so minded is indicated by a letter to his Boston friend, Dr. Eustis, in December 1796, in which the colonel wrote that "I have for a month past been striving without success to get a Copy of the Charter of your Union Bank—will you have the goodness to send it to me." Presumably the colonel reasoned that, for full effectiveness as a political instrument, the institution he had in mind should have the sanction of the state. Incorporated by the legislature, such a bank could lure merchants, who were wavering Federalists, into the Republican camp. It could enfranchise any number of propertyless democrats by enabling them to acquire enough real estate to vote for certain offices. Not that party considerations occupied the whole of Burr's thoughts. The idea of a new source of credit had a natural appeal to a man of his extravagant tastes and borrowing ways.

To dream up such a bank was one thing. To get the legislature to charter it another. At the slightest hint that Burr was behind the idea, the Federalist lawmakers would smell a rat. As for the Republicans, many of them would be hesitant to say "aye" in view of the belief among the rank and file of their party that all banks should be eschewed as centers of "monopoly power, speculative profit seeking and moneyed influence." Obviously, Burr was going to have to propose some worthy cause to the lawmakers—a bill of such virtuous intent that it would sail through the legislature like an arrow with the authority for a bank buried in its lily-white feathers.

But what virtuous intent would serve his purpose? Burr found the answer to that question in the disreputable condition of the drinking water available to the citizens of his home town. In this respect, New York had been a disaster area for almost as long as anyone could remember. Thirty years before the Revolution, the Swedish naturalist, Peter Kalm, noted that the well water in the city was so bad that the horses balked at drinking it. By 1782 the only reservoir of consequence, Fresh Water Pond, had become a stinkhole, and the only source of potable liquid was the Tea Water Pump next door to the Old Punch House at No. 25 Chatham Street. Gathering at this facility in the early hours of the morning, cartmen filled casks with the precious fluid and hawked it through the streets. By 1785 the Tea Water Pump had become contaminated, and in 1798 the situation reached crisis proportions when a yellow-fever epidemic struck New York and some of the local medicos concluded that the main cause of the disease lay in the refuse rotting in the city's unwashed streets and in the flow from its polluted wells. Subsequent events show that, long in advance of the debacle, Burr had matured his plans. He would try to get the legislature to charter a private company to supply New York City with "pure and wholesome water," slip into the bill a clause permitting the company to invest its surplus funds as it saw fit, and hope that no one noticed—or if he did, be ashamed to protest—so trifling an addition to so worthy a proposition.

A master stroke, if he could pull it off. But the course of even the most respectable legislation rarely runs smooth, and Burr was to encounter more than one obstacle. For years New York City's legislative arm, the Common Council, had been talking about the water problem. Not until February 1796, however, did it go so far as to appoint a committee to look into "the subject of supplying this City with fresh water." Although the committee received numerous proposals from various individuals, the council took no further action until the yellow-fever epidemic of 1798 forced it to do so. Among those submitting plans was Dr. Joseph Browne, Burr's brother-in-law. In December 1796, and again in July 1798, Browne suggested that the council ask the state legislature to incorporate a private company to provide the city with water from the Bronx River. Were Aaron's fingerprints on his brother-in-law's proposals? Very likely. Certainly the doctor's prescription was just what the colonel would have ordered. But on 17 December 1798, when the Common Council endorsed Browne's plan "with some variations," it at the same time rejected his request for a private company. Instead, it ordered the preparation for submission to the legislature of a bill under which the city would be empowered to establish and operate a municipal water-supply system. Here was a severe check to Burr's scheme, for his dream of a new bank was wholly dependent on his ability to get the legislature to authorize not a public but a private company.

Burr was no stranger to difficulties. His talents were more than equal to this one. In Albany, on 16 February 1799, the Assembly "*Ordered*, that Mr. Burr have leave of absence for ten days," whereupon the colonel hied himself to New York as fast as the difficult travel conditions of those times permitted. On reaching the city, he at once persuaded five of the community's most respected and representative men to serve with him on a committee whose mission would be to convince the Common Council of the superior merits of a private company in contrast to those of a bureaucratic organization. Burr, as he would demonstrate even more vividly during the Presidential election of 1800, knew the value of putting big names behind big projects. Beatrice Reubens describes his committee of six as "a masterpiece of political influence, which was little diminished by the claim that the men appeared as private citizens." It consisted of three Republicans and three Federalists. The Republicans were Burr, the only legislator among the six; John Broome, president of an insurance corporation and war hero; and Peter H. Wendover, president of the Mechanics Society. The Federalists were John Murray, president of the Chamber of Commerce; Gulian Verplanck, president of the Bank of New York; and Alexander Hamilton. Only a man of Burr's impeccable social background could have put together such an aggregation of untouchables.

If one wishes to speculate on Hamilton's willingness to serve on it, he must begin with the admission that the Federalist chieftain was a public-spirited soul. He realized that a private institution could finance a water system by selling stock in the enterprise. On the other hand, were the city to install and run the system, it might have to seek additional tax revenue, and this at a time when New York was hard pressed to underwrite the enlargement of its harbor defenses. One must also concede the justice of Reubens's suggestion that a "personal factor . . . influenced Hamilton's decision to help Burr form a private water company." The investment possibilities of such an organization were exceedingly attractive to Hamilton's speculator brother-in-law, John B. Church. In the past Hamilton had acted as Church's attorney and business adviser, continuing in these roles even during his term as Secretary of the Treasury, when his "purchases of United States securities on his relative's behalf" helped convince the Republicans in Congress that the Treasury head was using his high position for improper purposes. Church would sit on the Manhattan Company's first board of directors, and Reubens's guess is that originally Burr offered this post to Hamilton, who then recommended his brother-in-law. Whatever Hamilton's motives, no member of the committee of six worked harder to make possible Aaron Burr's upcoming triumph in the New York legislature.

On 22 February 1799 the colonel ushered his blue-ribbon committee into the presence of Mayor Richard Varick. Having listened attentively to his visitors' remarks—how otherwise could a Federalist mayor treat such eminent gentlemen?—Varick asked them to put their views in writing. They did so. More exactly, Hamilton did. His was the only signature on the memorandum presented to the Common Council, and he, apparently, was its sole author. His arguments in favor of a private company were numerous and cogent. The Common Council considered them for one day only and then announced that it would not ask the legislature to set up a municipal water works but would suggest the creation of a privately conducted one instead.

One can almost hear Aaron Burr sighing with relief. Had the Federalist Common Council asked for a public company, the Federalist legislature would have been hard put to refuse. Now Burr was free to seek a private company—thanks to Hamilton.

9

Back in Albany, Burr pursued his ends with the deliberation of a man wedded to the doctrine of never doing today what a little further time and thought might enable him to do better tomorrow. Along the line, he encountered other threats to his as yet unrevealed intent of burying the authority for a bank in his bill to charter a company "for supplying the city of New-York with pure and wholesome water"—threats that the colonel somehow contrived to brush from his path.

Originally the twenty-second session of the legislature was scheduled to adjourn on 28 March 1799, but the pressure of unfinished matters forced a postponement of the closing date to 3 April. Burr waited to the end to have his bill introduced, reasoning perhaps that the little change he was planning for it would be overlooked by lawmakers occupied with a rush of business and eager to get away. He presided over the committee charged with framing the measure, and at the last minute—apparently, just before the bill was brought to the floor of the Assembly for action—he inserted toward the end of it a passage reading: "*And be it further enacted*, That it shall and may be lawful for the said company to employ all such surplus capital as may belong or accrue to the said company in the purchase of public or other stock, or in any other monied transactions or operations not inconsistent with the constitution and laws of this state or of the United States, for the sole benefit of the company."

Such was the "surplus capital" clause, or "bank clause," as it would come to be known. Assigning to the Manhattan

Company privileges unprecedented in the prior history of incorporations, it said in effect that the proposed water works, capitalized at $2 million, could use its free funds "to operate a bank, insurance office, real estate business, trading company, or all of them simultaneously." Reubens believes that Burr anticipated a fight over this sweeping proviso and was surprised when none materialized. By the time the Manhattan Company bill reached the Assembly on the afternoon of 27 March, its progenitor had arranged for twelve eminent New Yorkers, three of them Federalists, to act as the company's directors, taking care to provide all the factions of the state democracy—the Livingstons, the Clintons, and the Burrites—with three representatives apiece. It is not known whether he did or did not call the attention of the Federalist directors to his seventy-word bank clause. On 28 March the bill that included it passed the Assembly in a voice vote. Two days later it passed the Senate in the same manner. If so much as a peep about the bank clause was heard in either chamber, it failed to find its way into any of the now available records. It would be said later that during the last week of the twenty-second session of the legislature many of the members had already gone home. Unless all the absentees were Federalists, leaving only Republicans on the floor—and sleepy or illiterate ones at that—we would seem bound to assume that Burr indited the bank clause in invisible ink.

If so, the words had emerged enough to be read by the members of the Council of Revision. Let it be recalled that under New York State's original constitution no bill became law until it had passed inspection by this body. If the council approved, the governor had no choice but to sign the bill, even if, as a member of the council, he had voted against it. If the council disapproved, the bill went back to the legislature, where a two-thirds vote was needed to override the veto.

In addition to the governor, the Council of Revision consisted of the chancellor of the state and the justices of the state supreme court. When the Manhattan bill came before this group, only one member, Chief Justice John Lansing, protested the bank clause. Lansing's objections were many, tellingly stated—and ignored. No other member spoke out on his side. In recent months Chancellor Livingston's appearance at sessions of the council had been infrequent. He was on hand for this session, however, and one shares the pain with which his sympathetic biographer, George Dangerfield, notes that at this point the chancellor's option on two thousand shares of the stock of the Manhattan Company made him one of its largest potential stockholders. But if the position of the Republican chancellor was at least understandable, what is to be said of that of the Federalist governor, John Jay? He is supposed to have agreed with Lansing, but he is known to have said nothing. Apparently he also did nothing, and the explanation bruited about later was that he "had no vote," although, as Dangerfield observes, "according to the constitution of 1777, a vote was what he had." On 2 April, Jay signed the Manhattan bill into law.

The water company came into being at once, and when its bank opened to the public in September 1799, it did so under the aforementioned twelve directors, of whom nine, including Aaron Burr, were Republicans. Hamilton repented at leisure of his part in the affair, later pointing out to a Federalist colleague that the Manhattan Company was "a perfect monster in its principles," but conceding that it was "a very convenient instrument of profit and influence." Certainly, Burr found it so. His debit on the books of the company stood at $64,903.63—much of it built up by getting friends to borrow for him—when in December 1802 he stepped down from the board of directors to form another bank with the assistance of John Swartwout. One of the Manhattan Company's first decisions was not to use the Bronx River as the source of "pure and wholesome water" for its parched customers. Instead, it built its works around a complex of wells—the one in Lispenard's Meadow would figure in the murder trial of Levi Weeks—wooden pipes and steam-driven pumps. Never adequate, the company's water system went out of business in 1840. Its financial arm, however, "continued, prospered and exists today as the Chase Manhattan Bank."

10

In the spring of 1799, Burr ran again for the Assembly and was trounced. A factor in his defeat was the issuance of the Manhattan Company charter, large segments of the electorate choosing to view his role in that matter as at least faintly scandalous. Another was that throughout the state the year 1799 was a bad one for the democracy and a good one for Federalism. Never again would this condition obtain. Already in the making were the events that would lay the groundwork for the great political reversal of 1800.

12

President-Maker

A CONVENIENT POINT from which to date the start of the great political reversal of 1800 is the summer of 1798, when a Federalist Congress and President, emboldened by the prevailing anti-French hysteria, wrote into law the Alien and Sedition Acts of that year. The Alien Act authorized President John Adams to deport without trial émigrés from France suspected of being spies for their native country—a power that he never used. Destined to become the center of the ensuing hue and cry, the Sedition Act made it a criminal offense for anyone to utter, write, or publish what was spoken of as "seditious libel," meaning any "false, scandalous and malicious" statement about the Congress or the President. What aroused the ire of Republican leaders at this law was neither its endorsement of the dubious concept of seditious libel—most of them went along with that—nor its cavalier disregard of the free-speech and free-press provisions of the first amendment to the constitution. What hit them were its political implications. With the next Presidential election fast approaching, Jefferson, Madison, and others saw in the Sedition Act a brazen attempt by the Federalists to keep themselves in power by making it dangerous, if not impossible, for the Republicans to criticize the policies of the Adams Administration.

Unwittingly, the Federalists had furnished their opponents with an appealing issue—and this at a moment when the Republicans badly needed something to counteract the advantages accruing to the Federalists by reason of their status as the bulwark against an anticipated attack from France. Jefferson and Madison made the most of what the opposition had given them. By late fall they had drafted their responses to the Alien and Sedition Acts—the memorable Virginia and Kentucky Resolutions. In the Virginia Resolutions, as adopted by the Virginia legislature, Madison declared the two federal statutes unconstitutional and argued that the people of the states collectively had the power to take corrective measures. In the Kentucky Resolutions, so named because of their adoption by the legislature of Kentucky, Jefferson asserted that the legislature of each state had the right to take such measures. He was delighted when on 16 November the governor of Kentucky proclaimed the Alien and Sedition Acts of no effect in that state and urged the other states to do likewise.

It is worthy of mention that the Virginia and Kentucky Resolutions were essentially propaganda. They cannot be cited as accurate reflections of Republican doctrine at the time or even as mirroring the true thinking of their authors. As Jefferson would demonstrate during his Presidency, his personal position on seditious libel was that, although the prosecution of such libel was forbidden to the federal government by the constitution, action against it was one of the rights reserved to the states by that same document. Where freedom of speech and press was concerned, Jefferson, as Professor Leonard W. Levy has brought out, was not always a Jeffersonian. Merely a great man—not a superman—he sometimes preached one thing in this field and did another, one of the more common human failings, and one of the few that cannot be attributed to Aaron Burr, who remains unique among the Founding Fathers in that he never preached anything at all.

From the legislative halls of Kentucky and Virginia the

resolves authored by Madison and Jefferson went to the legislatures of the other states, to be approved, condemned, or ignored. In early February, Burr wrote Jefferson that Governor Jay had laid the two documents before the New York lawmakers. No action had yet been taken, and Burr's guess was that if it were, the resolutions would be roundly disapproved. "Under circumstances so inauspicious," he explained, "I have not thought it discreet to urge a determination in either house." In New York's heavily Federalist lawmaking body, the colonel would like to have avoided a test of the strength of his party over so touchy a question as whether a state or the people thereof had the right to nullify federal law. When the test was forced upon him, he did what he could. The proposal placed before the Assembly called for a resolution stating that only the federal judiciary could pass on the constitutionality of a federal statute. For two days Burr and two of his closest friends, John Swartwout and Erastus Root, took turns introducing motions designed to soften this statement by inserting words to the effect that a state legislature did have the right to protest a federal law. The sterner resolution passed with ease, and Burr took off for New York to plow the more productive furrow leading to the chartering of the Manhattan Company.

Six other states endorsed statements similar to that of New York, three went on record as opposed to the Virginia and Kentucky Resolutions in principle, and the remaining four—Delaware, North Carolina, South Carolina, and Tennessee—preserved what might be termed a pregnant silence. None of these results vitiated the value of the resolutions as political instruments. The publicity attendant on their tour of the legislatures called attention to the partisan nature of the Alien and Sedition Acts and to the extent to which they encapsulated Federalist disdain for the liberties and judgment of the people.

Numerous arrests of defiant newspaper editors and others added to the hullabaloo. The central figure of one of the most celebrated of these instances was Burr's recently acquired political supporter, Jedidiah Peck, who by the spring of 1800 had become the holder of a minor judgeship in Cooperstown, New York. When the judge circulated a petition for the repeal of the Alien and Sedition Acts, the local United States marshal arrested him and carried him two hundred miles to New York City to stand trial. A Republican newspaper described the judge as "taken from his bed at midnight, manacled, and dragged from his home," prompting Jabez Hammond to write later that a "hundred missionaries in the cause of democracy, stationed between New York and Cooperstown, could not have done so much for the republican cause as this [five-day] journey of Judge Peck, as a prisoner . . . It was nothing less than the public exhibition of a suffering martyr for the freedom of speech and the press, and the right of petitioning." Did Burr engineer this spectacle? Two of his biographers say as much, asserting that the offending petition was written in the colonel's law office and sent up to Cooperstown for the judge to sign.

A Federalist Congress having supplied the Republicans with a viable issue by passing the Alien and Sedition Acts, it remained for a Federalist President to relieve them of the onus of unpatriotic attachment to France by terminating the cold war with that nation. An oft-told tale, this, and one that does John Adams great credit. In 1797, on learning of the French government's insulting handling of America's peace commissioners, Adams announced that never again would he send envoys to Paris without solemn assurance that they would be treated with respect. Two years later, word reached him that the French foreign minister, Talleyrand, had undergone a change of mind—that if another American commission came to see him, something might be accomplished. Although there were no direct assurances from Talleyrand, Adams acted on this hint at once. Across the sea went a second commission to what was now Napoleonic France. In and out of Congress the war hawks among the Federalists cried foul. As the chief architect of the country's new army, Inspector General Hamilton was beside himself. Secretly, he had fought Adams's election in 1796, and was already planning to fight his reelection in 1800. He had long regarded the eccentric New Englander as egotistic, touchy, ill-tempered, and stubborn (meaning that he would not take orders from Hamilton), and now was appalled to discover that he was also a peacemonger. Nothing daunted, Adams went ahead with his plans, and long before his envoys returned from Paris it was common knowledge that they were bringing home with them the treaty that would end French harassment of American shipping and pacify relations between the two countries.

In the impending demise of the cold war and in a growing popular indignation at the Alien and Sedition Acts, the Republicans saw cause for optimism. But it was a cautious optimism. The Federalists had run the country for almost a dozen years. They were entering the contest of 1800 panoplied with the I.O.U.'s of the numerous benefactors of a large and interlocking state and national patronage system. Their dying war had been galling to the Republicans but good for business. The shipbuilding and oceangoing North was booming, and, then as now, prosperity was a hard thing to campaign against. By the close of 1799, every Republican leader had become a mathematician. Assuming that most of the Southern states went Republican, as in 1796, how many electoral votes could their candidate count on in 1800? Sixty-one was the widely accepted figure. But they needed seventy to win. Were the other nine available, and, if so, where? The New England states, impenetrably conservative save for Rhode Island, were out of the question. That left only the middle states, notably New Jersey, Pennsylvania and New York. New Jersey? The prospects there were generally rated as ranging from dim to nonexistent. Pennsylvania? Better, but probably not better enough. New York? As the election got underway in the spring, a consensus was arrived at. New York was the pivotal state. It had twelve electoral votes. If those could be pushed into the Republicans' column, their Presidential candidate would be in. If not, Federalism would reign on.

But Federalism was doomed, and for many years to come, students of the period would ponder the whys and wherefores of its fall, most of them concluding that the party was brought low by its lack of faith in the people—with a strong assist from Aaron Burr.

2

To APPRECIATE the colonel's contribution to the acquisition of the Presidency for his party in 1800 calls for a glance at the election machinery of that time. Each state, as is still the case, had as many members in the electoral college as it had senators and representatives in Congress. In 1800 there were sixteen states, the total number of electors was 138, and a federal law obliged them to assemble in their respective states on the first Wednesday in December and cast their ballots for President and Vice President, or more exactly—since they made no distinction between the two offices—for the two individuals they wished to see elected to those offices.

In New York the crucial moment in the Presidential election of 1800 was not when its twelve electors gathered at the little riverside town of Hudson to make their choices. It came during the preceding spring, when for three days, beginning on 29 April, the voters of the city and county of New York went to the polls to choose the thirteen representatives allotted to their region in the lower house of the state legislature.

What made this so was that the people of the state did not vote directly for their electors. That privilege rested with the legislature. Nor was New York alone in this respect. Ten other states followed the same procedure. In some the two branches of the legislature voted separately, and in those states the electoral slate was sometimes politically split. In New York it tended to be all or nothing, because the law required the legislature to vote as a unit. First each house selected a slate of twelve names. Then the two houses met together. Whether the winning slate was Federalist or Republican depended on which party could muster a majority on this joint ballot.

In 1800 the outcome of the general elections in much of New York was predictable. With Federalist sentiment fading in the frontier counties, it was a certainty that rural New York would divide pretty evenly, with the Republicans enjoying a slight edge. The balance of power lay along the lower Hudson, in New York City and its outlying farm areas. Traditionally this was Federalist country. In the current legislature, due to expire on 1 July, all of its assemblymen were members of that party. As the recognized strategist for the local Republicans, Burr's mission was clear. He must reverse this situation. If he succeeded, his party would dominate the upcoming state legislature, the one authorized by law to choose the electors. In all likelihood, as a result, the next President of the United States would be a Republican. As one modern chronicler of the tumultuous election of 1800 has written, the "April contest" in the city and county of New York "was in fact a popular presidential election."

3

To THE WINNING of it Burr brought a dazzling array of techniques. Some of them were new, old as they may seem to readers familiar with the tactics of modern campaign bosses walking in the colonel's footsteps. All of them were worthy of inclusion in a textbook on the art of influencing suffrages and making Presidents.

His first action was a flying trip to Philadelphia in January 1800 to talk with Jefferson. Although formal handling of such matters would come later in the campaign, it was already fully understood that the race for the Presidency would be between the incumbent, John Adams, for the Federalists, and Jefferson for the Republicans. Not that all was sweetness and light within the Federalist camp. Hamilton's dislike of Adams was no longer a secret to anyone, including Adams. Nor was the former Secretary alone in this respect. Sedgwick and other prominent members of the party shared his antipathy. In the closing month of the preceding year Gouverneur Morris had begged George Washington to make himself available again, arguing that Adams was "unfit for the office he now holds." Washington probably never saw this letter. It was written on 9 December. Ten days later the Father of His Country was dead, and the Federalists would have no choice but to nominate Adams and assign the second slot on their ticket to the South Carolinian, Charles Cotesworth Pinckney, then thought of as the hero of the XYZ affair because of his inadvertent origination of the war-cry, "Millions for defense, but not one cent for tribute."

In Philadelphia, Burr outlined for Jefferson his plans for New York. The Republican leader did little more than nod in agreement, although somewhat shocked at the directness of the New Yorker's methods, being himself inclined to a more dignified, which is to say, a more roundabout approach to such things.

Back in New York, Burr began at once to build a vote-getting organization that, in the words of Jabez Hammond, "would do credit to the management of the latter-day chiefs of Tammany." The phrasing used by this authoritative historian—"do credit to the latter-day chiefs of Tammany"—deserves attention. Still making the rounds is the story of how Burr won New York City for his party by converting the Society of St. Tammany or Columbian Order from a philanthropic and fraternal organization into a political machine subservient to his bidding. As a matter of fact the politicization of the Tammany Society came at a later date. In Burr's heyday it remained what it had been from its beginnings, a group of convivial souls, ranging in social status from mechanics to bankers, who enjoyed gathering at Martling's Tavern—known to the faithful as "the Wigwam" and to the city's aristocrats as "the pig sty"—to smoke, quaff porter, swap anecdotes, and indulge in culinary orgies. Not infrequently, the members passed resolutions or offered toasts by way of expressing their views on political issues. From 1795 on, these views were increasingly Republican, but politically the society's local deity was not Aaron Burr but George Clinton. At its three biggest get-togethers in 1800 Burr's name was not so much as sounded once in the fusillade of toasts that characterized these hilarious occasions. To quote a recent study of the early days of the Wigwam, "a careful examination of the minutes of the Society indicates that Tammany did not participate as an organization in the campaign of 1800."

The organization Burr led was the General Republican Committee, which he subdivided into lesser units representative of the various wards. At the nucleus of this aggregation was his little band of personal followers, the Burrites—such men as Matthew L. Davis, John Swartwout and his brothers, William Peter Van Ness and his brothers, Theodorus Bailey, David Gelston, and Burr's stepson, Bartow Prevost. These men would do anything for the colonel, and everything was what he had them do.

He had them prepare a roster of every voter in the city. It was not a short list. Latter-day investigations show that in early New York the property qualifications stipulated in the state constitution did not bar as many individuals from the polls as was once thought to be the case. In the rural regions land was cheap, and in New York City many low-income citizens occupied rental quarters of sufficient value to entitle them to vote at least for assemblymen. From time to time, both parties lengthened the eligibility table by a device known as the tontine. Banding together, a number of men would purchase property under a legal arrangement that enabled each of them to claim the whole on election day. In 1800, approximately two-thirds of the city's free adult males, including its free blacks, could vote.

What made Burr's roster unique, however, was not its length but the little dossiers attached to every name. Based on data gathered by the colonel's aides, each of these annotations described the voter's political preferences, the degree of his zeal in their pursuit, his temperament, his willingness to serve the cause as a volunteer, his financial standing, etc.

Campaigns run on money. Burr sent groups of canvassers from door to door, soliciting funds. The members of his little band drafted a list of wealthy Republicans, indicating after the name of each man the amount to be requested of him. Burr examined this list carefully. He knew every man on it. "Ask nothing of this one," he would say. "If we demand money he'll be offended and refuse to work for us." Of another: "Double this man's assessment. He'll contribute generously if he doesn't have to work."

To the citizens of the city the drama of the election lay in the extent to which it pitted their best-known political figures one against the other. From beginning to end, it was Burr versus Hamilton. Burr's single most effective maneuver was the manner in which he handled the ticklish business of choosing and getting party support for the Republican slate of candidates for the Assembly. One of his earliest decisions was to keep his slate a secret until such time as Hamilton had selected and announced his.

Where this important operation was concerned, the Federalist leader was at a disadvantage. Most of the prominent members of his party were owners of profitable businesses. A man of this ilk was not inclined to look kindly on service in a state legislature where the salary came to less than $250 per session. Better to stay home, close to his counting room. By early spring, eleven of the thirteen Federalists then representing the city and its environs in the Assembly had made known that they would not run for reelection.

Hamilton was hard pressed to assemble a slate of known or even able men. He began his search in March. No sooner was his list chosen than its contents were known to Burr. The story goes that when Burr's aides brought him Hamilton's slate, the colonel "read it over, with great gravity folded it up, put it in his pocket, and . . . said, 'Now I have him all hollow' . . ."

He did, indeed. With one or two exceptions, Hamilton's tally was a parade of nonentities. It included a banker, a ship chandler, a potter, a grocer, a shoemaker, a mason, two booksellers, some lawyers, and a bankrupt. A Federalist was heard to complain that "gentlemen are not worth their salt in a political struggle . . . They are in kid gloves and cannot shake hands with an honest man who is poor." Obviously Hamilton had been shaking hands with many such men. His slate would have done justice to the party of the people, whereas the one that Democrat Burr was already in the process of creating would read like a page from the record book of the local peerage.

Burr's Assembly ticket was headed by George Clinton, six times governor of the state. It included John Broome, president of the New York Insurance Company; Brockholst Livingston, eminent lawyer and member of a powerful clan; Samuel Osgood, ex-Postmaster General of the United States; and Horatio Gates, "the hero of Saratoga," the general whose capture of a British army had helped turn the tide during the Revolutionary War. Gates was in his seventies and unwell. These days he spent much of his time taking the waters at Ballston Spa. He was not in politics, never had been, and after the election Burr would find it advisable to send the old man a letter gently reminding him to be sure to reach Albany in time to participate in the choosing of the state's electors.

Politically, Burr's ticket was neatly balanced. Significantly absent in the spring of 1800 was the Republican infighting so common to New York elections. Neither the Livingstons nor the Clintons made any effort to share Burr's leadership of the campaign or to interfere with his activities in any way. It was as if the heads of these jealous factions had heard and heeded the same small voice, saying to them, "Let Burr do it. If he fails, the onus will not be on you. If he succeeds, you stand to gain as much as he—maybe more, depending on who contrives to reap the largest share of the spoils of victory." Burr well understood the makeup of the New York democracy. That the Livingstons and the Clintons had temporarily waived their rights did not mean they were any less conscious of them. In drafting his ticket, he arranged for all three factions to be represented—Brockholst Livingston for his wing, George Clinton for his, John Swartwout for the Burrites. The colonel did not put his own name on the ticket, having decided to run for the Assembly from Orange County. There he could count on his Burrite friend, Peter Townsend, to pull the necessary strings and the preponderantly Republican electorate of that county would not regard his connection with the chartering of the Manhattan Company as a matter of much consequence and be happy to elect him by a substantial majority.

When his star-studded Assembly slate for New York City and county was made public, many informed observers declared that only a man of Burr's charm and enterprise could have brought it off. Doing so was not easy. Almost every man on the slate was already so highly placed that the prospect of spending months in the relatively undistinguished environs of the state Assembly was not alluring. At first, three of them balked—Clinton, Livingston, and General Gates. Three days of argument went into Burr's struggle to bring the former governor around. Clinton offered a variety of objections. He pointed to his advanced age. He said his political days were over, a statement no one took seriously, including probably the old man himself. Finally he didn't think well of Thomas Jefferson. If a Burrite version of his remarks can be trusted, he regarded the national leader of his party as a "trimmer who would change with the times and bend to circumstances for purposes of personal promotion." Unspoken but obvious was the real reason for Clinton's reluctance to cooperate with Burr, his jealousy of the younger man's burgeoning political importance. Only after much hemming and hawing did he bow to the plea that his party had need of him at this hour. But with conditions. He agreed to lend his name to the ticket but said he would take no part in the campaign. Neither would he hesitate, in private conversation, to declare his disinterest in being elected to the state assembly.

Once the Old Incumbent came aboard, Livingston and Gates did likewise, and Burr's ticket was complete. At a meeting in the Tontine City Hotel on the evening of 15 April, the Federalists endorsed and made known their Assembly slate. At a private home in William Street two nights later, the Republicans did the same. In their release to the press the leaders of the Republican caucus did not limit themselves to a listing of their candidates. Appended to their report, as published in the *Commercial Advertiser* on 26 April, was a resolution passed by the William Street meeting. "Whereas in the last election in this city," it read,

> such were the abominable practices by certain persons styling themselves as Federal Republicans [Federalists], by threats and otherwise to influence electors to vote for their candidates,
>
> Resolved, unanimously, That the general committee appointed by the Republicans of this city . . . be and hereby are directed to offer a suitable reward to all persons who will give information of threats, bribery or corruption, exercised and practiced by the said Federal Republicans . . . to influence the vote of any man at the approaching election, so that persons guilty of such nefarious practices may be prosecuted agreeably to the law . . .

Caught off-guard by this reference to a "nefarious" practice, actually common to both parties, the Federalists promptly met again and issued a counter-resolution, branding the charges of the opposition as false and accusing "certain persons pretending to be Republicans" with "meditating Revolution."

4

As THE ELECTION NEARED, and especially after the balloting began on 29 April, the city was treated to a whirl of political activity such as it had never seen before. "Col. Burr," to quote from the diary of a New York City merchant, "kept open house for nearly two months, and Committees were in session day and night during that whole time at his house. Refreshments were always on the table and mattresses for temporary repose in the rooms. Reports were hourly received from sub-committees, and in short, no means left unemployed." Taking note of Burr's movements about the city, the Federalist *Daily Advertiser* wondered how a "would be Vice President could stoop so low as to visit every corner in search of voters." It was left to a Republican newspaper to reveal that Alexander Hamilton was engaging in the same unseemly exercises. "Hamilton harangues the astonished group," reported the *General Advertiser*, "every day he is seen in the street hurrying this way, and darting that; here he buttons a heavy hearted fed, and preaches up courage, there he meets a group, and he simpers in unanimity, again to the heavy headed and hearted, he talks of perseverance, and (God bless the mark) of virtue!" Robert Troup jogged at his chief's side, puffing considerably with all that weight. "I have been night and day employed in the business of the election," he wrote a friend. "Never have I witnessed such exertions on either side before. I have not eaten dinner for three days and have been constantly upon my legs from 7 in the morning till 7 in the afternoon . . ."

Even the weather seemed to be aware of the prevailing tension. As the election days drew near, a "storm of rain" fell upon the city. It was accompanied by "lightning and thunder, and the extraordinary appearance of sulphur on the waters which fell." When it was over, people noticed a peculiar sheen on the earth. On examination, the streets proved to be covered with a substance "resembling brimstone," a discovery that no doubt struck Federalist leaders as ominous, inclined as they were to regard all Republicans as coming from—or on their way to—the nether regions.

On one of the election days Chancellor Livingston got out his "elegant chariot" to carry an elderly black voter to the polls in the seventh ward only to discover later that the old man had voted Federalist. Burr was a cornucopia of vote-getting devices. When the balloting began, a flotilla of "carriages, chairs and waggons" suddenly appeared on the streets, making it easier for known Democrats to get to the polls. Into the heavily German seventh ward poured a phalanx of Republican spellbinders capable of speaking to the residents in their native tongue. Burr was everywhere, spending ten consecutive hours in one ward alone, flying from ward to ward, and making speeches wherever he landed. The minute the polls closed, he posted guards at every voting place with instructions to make certain the inspectors committed no inadvertent errors while counting the ballots and making their returns. Simultaneously, arrangements were made for keeping a constant and cautious watch for a time on "every movement" of the "leading Federal gentlemen" of the city.

The polls closed at sunset on 1 May. By midnight, the results were known. All thirteen Republican candidates had been elected to the Assembly by a majority that averaged out to two hundred and fifty votes apiece. A Federalist newspaper underscored the import of what had happened. The *Daily Advertiser* noted that Thomas Jefferson was the acknowledged leader of the democracy. It followed that the Virginian "will . . . in this state have 12 votes for President at the ensuing election." Many Republican leaders found their smashing victory hard to believe. Recalling that only a year earlier the Federalists had carried the city and county by nine hundred votes, one of them attributed the outcome of the 1800 election to "the Intervention of a Supreame Power and our friend Burr the agent." Burr modestly declined deification. "So . . . you Democrats have beat us in the election," an aristocrat is reported to have said to him. "Yes," replied the colonel, "we have beat you by superior *Management*."

News of the results sped to Philadelphia. On its arrival there the Senate, suddenly unable to do business, adjourned so that its Federalist members could mill about the lobby, talking wildly of plans to protect their wives and children from the revolutionary horrors certain to descend upon the country if Jefferson became President. In New York City, Robert Troup peered into the future and saw nothing there but "shadows, fiends and darkness." Hamilton was flabbergasted. So much so that he came down with an attack of democracy, an ailment to which he was not ordinarily susceptible and from which he would recover rapidly. With this frenzy upon him, he wrote an astounding letter to Governor Jay. The terms of the members of the present dominantly Federalist New York legislature extended through June. Hamilton proposed that Jay summon this lame-duck body into special session and ask it to pass a law transferring the power of choosing electors from the legislature to the people. By this device, the Federalist chieftain reasoned, his—and Jay's—party could count on winning at least a few Presidential electors. Shades of Burr's attempt, a year and a half before, to do precisely the same thing for his party by legitimate means. Hamilton conceded that the maneuver he was suggesting was not legitimate, but "in times like this in which we live," he contended, "it will not do to be overscrupulous. It is easy to sacrifice the substantial interests of society by a strict adherence to ordinary rules." He reminded Jay that if the choice of the electors was left to the upcoming legislature, Jefferson would very likely be the next President. He argued that "scruples of delicacy and propriety . . . ought not to hinder the taking of a *legal* and constitutional step to prevent an *atheist* in Religion and a *fanatic* in politics from getting possession of the helm of state."

During the election campaign Burr's followers had become adept in the arts of espionage. On the day after Hamilton's letter was dispatched, a Republican paper published a copy of it—one that a Federalist editor promptly castigated as a "fraud," implying that it had been made up out of whole cloth by the opposition. But the letter was real. The original can be read today in Jay's papers, bearing across it, in the honest governor's handwriting, an endorsement reading, "Proposing a measure for party purposes, which I think it would not become me to adopt."

5

In the wake of the critical New York election, the two parties proceeded to name their candidates. In the early days of the Republic this was an informal, almost catch-as-catch-can process. In the spring of 1800, it was taken care of in Philadelphia by congressional caucuses meeting on the second floor of Congress Hall.

Both parties acted in early May. The results of the Federalist gathering had been anticipated for months: for President, the incumbent, John Adams; for Vice President, the popular South Carolina general and diplomat, Charles Cotesworth Pinckney.

Jefferson was the unanimous choice of the Republicans for the top of their ticket, but the secondary slot presented a ticklish problem. Because of their party's triumph in New York, it was agreed that the Vice Presidential candidacy should go to someone in that state. But to whom? The directors of the caucus in Philadelphia were aware of the presence within the Empire State democracy of three distinct groups. Obviously, the candidacy must be bestowed on the leader of one of them—on George Clinton or Chancellor Livingston or Burr. Simple expediency dictated the decision of the caucus managers to let the New Yorkers themselves choose—thus perhaps ensuring the nomination of a man acceptable to all three factions. With this end in mind, they solicited the services of the brilliant Pennsylvanian, Albert Gallatin, a member of the caucus by reason of his election to the House of Representatives almost immediately after his ouster from the Senate in 1794.

Gallatin was in a good position to find out which of the three possibilities—Clinton, Livingston, or Burr—the New York democracy would prefer. Hannah Gallatin, his wife, was one of the daughters of the prominent and colorful New York City Republican, James Nicholson, a retired naval hero whose friends fondly—and inaccurately—addressed him as the "Commodore," and who was on intimate terms with everyone of consequence in the local party.

Presumably the members of the Republican caucus were aware that Gallatin himself would not be unhappy if the choice of Vice Presidential nominee fell on Burr. He liked Burr and no doubt remembered with gratitude the futile but earnest efforts of the latter in 1794 to prevent Gallatin's dismissal from the Senate. Speaking once of the contending chieftains of the three factions comprising the New York State democracy, the Swiss-born financial genius is reported to have said that he considered Burr "the least selfish" of the lot. When in the late winter of 1800 the Pennsylvania congressman was seized with curiosity about the impending New York election, he chose to address his questions to Matthew L. Davis, Burr's closest political crony and friend. Davis, in his response, outlined the colonel's plans for the campaign in the open manner of a man conscious that he was writing for understanding eyes. "If we carry this election," he added in the same between-us-friends spirit, "it may be ascribed principally to Colo. Burr's management and perseverance."

When the election was carried, Davis wrote again to Gallatin. It was his understanding that only three "characters" were being "contemplated for the vice-presidential candidacy": Governor Clinton, Chancellor Livingston, and Colonel Burr. Clinton, Davis wrote, "seems averse to public life, and desirous of retiring from all its cares and toils . . . To Mr. Livingston there are objections more weighty: The family attachment and connection; the prejudices which exist . . . throughout the United States, against the name; but above all, the doubts which are entertained of his firmness and decision in trying periods. You are . . . acquainted with certain circumstances that occurred on the important question of carrying the British [Jay's] Treaty into effect. On that occasion Mr. L. exhibited a timidity that never can be forgotten. Colo. Burr is therefore the most eligible character . . . Whether he would consent to stand I am totally ignorant; and indeed, I pretend not to judge of the policy farther than it respects this state. If he is elected to the office of V.P., it would awaken so much of the zeal . . . of our friends in this State, as to secure us a Republican Governor at this next election (April 1801). If he is not nominated, many of us will experience much chagrin and disappointment."

Davis's comments on the three possible candidates seem to have made an impression on Gallatin, for in his own subsequent communications on the matter he took the position that the choice lay between Clinton and Burr, apparently accepting Davis's "weighty" objections to Livingston. When Gallatin began his exploration of the situation in the Empire State, his wife was in New York City, staying with her parents in their fine house on fashionable William Street. It would appear that he wrote first to his father-in-law, a letter that has not been found. What is available is an urgent message to his wife, dated 6 May and seemingly sent off because he had not yet heard from the Commodore, who was unwell. Gallatin knew, of course, that Hannah would show his letter to her father. He wrote that "the New York election has engrossed the whole attention of all of us, meaning by us Congress and the whole city. Exultation on our side is high; the other party are in low spirits." Now the big question was, "Who is to be our Vice-President, Clinton or Burr? This is a serious question which I am delegated to make, and to which I must have an answer by Friday next. Remember this is important, and I have been engaged to procure correct information of the wishes of the New York Republicans." Gallatin did not expect his wife to carry out this errand. That was a job for her father, and the testy old Commodore attended to it as soon as he was well enough to do so.

Two versions exist of how the old man handled the matter. One of them is summed up in two of his letters to Gallatin. In the first of these, written on 6 May, Commodore Nicholson apologized for his delay in sounding out Clinton and Burr about the Vice Presidency, mentioning his health as the reason for it. At this point the old man was still bubbling with excitement over the New York election. Burr, he said, had done everything. "His Generalship, perseverance, Industry and Execution," he exuded, "exceeds all description, so that I think I can say He deserves any thing and every thing of His country, but He has done it at the Risque of his life. This I will explain to you when I have the pleasure of seeing you . . . I shall conclude by recommending him as . . . far superior to your Hambletons [sic] as a man is to a boy." To these effusions the Commodore added that he was planning to call on Clinton later in the day.

On the following day the old man was ready to pronounce on the question of whom the Republicans in Philadelphia should nominate for the Vice Presidency. "I have conversed with the two Gentlemen mentioned in your letters," he wrote Gallatin.

> George Clinton, with whom I first spoke, declined. His age, his infirmities and his . . . attachment to retired life, in his opinion, exempt him from an active life. Governor Clinton thinks Colo. Burr is the most suitable person and perhaps the only Man. Such is also the opinion of all the Republicans in this quarter that I have conversed with. Their confidence

> in A.B. is universal and unbounded. Mr. Burr, however, appeared averse to be the Candidate. He seemed to think that no arrangement could be made which would be observed to the southward, alluding as I understand to the last Election, in which He was certainly ill used by Virginia and No. Carolina.
>
> I believe he may be induced to stand if assurances can be given that the Southern states will act fairly . . . but his name must not be played the fool with. I confidently hope you will be able to smooth over the business of the last Election . . .

On the same day these words were written, Mrs. Gallatin, in a separate letter to her husband, also mentioned Burr's annoyance at the failure of the Virginia and North Carolina electors to support him for the Vice Presidency in 1796 after having promised to do so. "Burr," Mrs. Gallatin wrote, "says he has no confidence in the Virginians; they once deceived him and are not to be trusted."

So much for one version of how Burr became his party's Vice Presidential candidate in 1800—an account that has the merit of resting on words written at the time of the happenings they cover. The other version rests on two documents drafted three years later. Both were private communications. Neither saw the light of day during its author's lifetime, although some of the events that the two documents describe found their way into print during the so-called Pamphlet War of 1802–4.

The gist of the earlier of these communications—a letter dated 13 December 1803 and written by George Clinton to his nephew, DeWitt Clinton—was that the older Clinton would have had the Republican Vice Presidential nomination in 1800 had not Burr euchred him out of it. "I believe it can be ascertained beyond a doubt," George Clinton wrote, "that our republican Friends in Congress were . . . in my favour in case I would consent to be held up as the Candidate . . . and that it was only on my declension that Chancellor Livingston and

Mr. Burr were to be proposed. To this effect Mr. Gallatin . . . wrote to his father in law, Commodore Nicholson"—Clinton's reference was to the letter from Gallatin to the Commodore that has not been found—"who shewed me this Letter and importuned me very earnestly to authorize him to express to Mr. Gallatin my consent." Clinton's recollection was that when Nicholson came to see him he at first declined. When the Commodore continued to press him, however, "I finally agreed that in answering Mr. Gallatin's Letter he might mention that I was averse to engage in public life yet rather than that any danger should occur in the Election of President . . . I would so far consent that my name might be used without Contradiction on my part. It being understood, however, that if elected I would be at liberty to resign without giving umbrage to our Friends, and he agreed to draught a Letter to Mr. Gallatin & shew it to me."

Apparently Nicholson offered no objections to Clinton's curious proposition—his declaration that he would take no active part in the campaign and that, if elected, he would probably resign! The remainder of Clinton's story is that the Commodore drafted a letter to his son-in-law recommending that the Republican caucus nominate Clinton and brought it around on the following day. Clinton read and approved it, but when the Commodore "left my house," he wrote, "he went to Mr. Burr's where Mr. Swarthoudt [sic] and some others of Burr's Friends were. He disclosed to them the Business he had been on and shewed the Letter. On reading of it, Mr. Burr was much agitated, declared that he would have nothing more to do with the Business, That he could be Governor of the State whenever he pleased to be. This conduct alarmed Mr. Nicholson and to appeaze Mr. Burr and his Party he consented to alter the letter to Mr. Gallatin to an unqualified declension on my part and by this means Mr. Burr's nomination was effected."

Two weeks after this letter was written, Nicholson drew up a deposition in which he dotted Clinton's i's and crossed his t's.

In this account of what happened at Burr's house—a story shot through with the most exasperating vagueness—the Commodore pictured himself as showing Burr the drafts of two letters to Gallatin. Although he failed to identify the contents of either draft, the implication was that in one of them he recommended Clinton and in the other he recommended Burr. Nicholson described Burr, on reading the two drafts, as charging out of the room in anger, shouting as he did so "that he would not give up the certainty of being elected Govr. to the uncertainty of being chosen V.P." For some seconds Nicholson was left alone, pacing the floor in bewilderment. Then Burr sent in two of his friends, one of whom—to quote the Commodore's statement further—"declared with a determined voice that Colo. Burr should accept and that he was obliged to do so on principle." These two men then left the room, only to return at once with Burr, who "with apparent reluctance consented."

Although these belatedly documented stories are markedly different from the earlier version, they cannot be dismissed as contradictory. George Clinton's account of his conversations with Nicholson and of what the Commodore did about them is probably as accurate a reconstruction of three-year-old events as that faulty instrument, the human memory, could contrive. Obviously the old man wanted the nomination in 1800, sincerely believed that Burr had tricked him out of it, and never intended to forgive him for doing so. Just as obviously, it never penetrated Clinton's able but not notably subtle mind that the bosses of the Republican caucus in Philadelphia might not have looked kindly on the incredible conditions he attached to his willingness to stand for the Vice Presidency. As for the Commodore's statement, so at odds with his enthusiastic endorsement of Burr three years before, that muddy thesis must be judged in the light of the political changes that had occurred in the interval. In New York State at the time the statement was written, the Clintons were riding high and the Burrites were in trouble. In the new national capital on the banks of the Potomac it was no secret that President Jefferson wished for the time being to have no truck with Vice President Burr. And on the very eve of his drafting of the deposition, Commodore Nicholson had been named to a federal office by the President, on the recommendation of the Clintons.

None of these behind-the-scenes events had any bearing on what happened in Philadelphia when Albert Gallatin received the eagerly awaited report on the wishes of the New York Republicans that he had asked his father-in-law to obtain. Gallatin had no way of knowing that the suggestible old man had spent the better part of two days laboring over two letters, one recommending Clinton, and the other, Burr. All Gallatin had before him was his father-in-law's letter, dated 7 May 1800, in which the Commodore declared that all the major party figures in New York, including George Clinton, favored Burr. Before him was not only this letter but one from his wife, making it clear that Burr would not run unless given assurances that this year the Southern electors would not "play the fool" with his name as they had in 1796. From what happened next, it is plain that, having read both communications carefully, the conscientious Gallatin proceeded to carry out the instructions in them to the letter.

On the evening of 11 May the Republicans met in caucus in Congress Hall. They nominated Jefferson for the Presidency, Burr for the Vice Presidency. In addition, they endorsed a compact, pledging all Republican electors to vote equally for Jefferson and Burr. The members of the caucus realized that if this pledge was honored, the actual choice of a President would have to be made in the House of Representatives. Better to take the risks involved in that eventuality, they reasoned, than to lose the election as the result of some electors' trying to insure the elevation of Jefferson over Burr, or vice versa, by throwing away their second votes. Caucusing at an earlier date, the Federalists had adopted the same pledge for the same reason. During the remaining six months of the campaign, the extent to which the Federalists abided by their pledge would turn out to be a matter of no significance. On the other hand, the extent to which the Republicans honored theirs was to have a pronounced effect on the country—and on the political career of Aaron Burr.

6

WITH THE CANDIDATES now proclaimed, the Presidential campaign proper got underway. Neither Burr nor Hamilton broke stride. Both continued the fight begun with the New York election. During the summer months and well into the fall, Hamilton was frantically busy, charting a course so erratic and so harmful to his cause as to raise the likelihood that not Clio, with her scroll, but Puck with his "What fools we mortals be!" should be regarded as the Muse of history.

The New York Federalist chieftain seems to have been instrumental in the decision of his party's caucus in Philadelphia to demand that all Federalist electors vote alike for the party's nominees. Even as the Federalists of the Senate and House prepared to go into conclave, Hamilton wrote his friend, Speaker of the House Sedgwick, that to "support *Adams* and *Pinckney equally* is the only thing that can save us from the fangs of Jefferson. It is therefore essential that the Feds should not separate without coming to a distinct and solemn concert to pursue this course *bona fide*." For the remainder of the campaign, Hamilton would give lip service to this policy, simultaneously waging a struggle to manipulate the electoral college so as to give the top prize to Pinckney rather than to Adams.

In his 7 May letter to Governor Jay, proposing a scheme to change the state's method of choosing electors, Hamilton, it will be recalled, castigated Jefferson as an "atheist" and a "fanatic," adding that the election of the Virginian would subject the country to "a Revolution after the manner of Buonaparte." One is tempted to believe that the great financial genius's invaluable contribution to his country would now be more fondly remembered had he given less latitude to his unparalleled talents for name calling and billingsgate. Only three days after the dispatch of his harsh note to Jay, he was writing Sedgwick that, where Adams was concerned, "my mind is made up. I will never more be responsible for him by direct support, even though the consequences should be the election of *Jefferson*."

It is not altogether clear how conscious Adams had been of Hamilton's furtive opposition to him in 1796. There is reason to believe that rumors of it reached the crusty New Englander but that he refused to take them seriously. In 1800 he knew exactly what Hamilton was up to. Shortly after the New York election he purged his Cabinet of two of its pro-Hamilton members, Secretary of State Timothy Pickering and Secretary of War James McHenry. By so doing, he threw down the gauntlet to Hamilton, and the New Yorker snatched it up. He began at once gathering data for a pamphlet that would expose Adams's human failings and political faux pas to public scorn.

As a matter of fact, he did not intend all of the public to see his projected masterpiece. His plan was to print only a few copies and distribute them among selected Federalist leaders. South Carolina loomed large in his mind. The different states chose their electors at different times. South Carolina would be the last to act, naming its slate on 2 December, only two days before the members of the electoral college were obliged to cast their ballots for President and Vice President in accordance with federal statute. The Palmetto State's eleventh-hour election could have a surprising effect on the outcome. In 1796, its eight electors had voted Federalist. In 1800, things were likely to be different. Hamilton's prayer was that this time the South Carolinians would cast eight votes for Pinckney, their native son, and bestow their other eight votes on Jefferson, or, at any rate, not on Adams. With the idea of inducing such a result, he was thinking of sending copies of his upcoming pamphlet into

South Carolina just before the lawmakers there chose their electors. It is a clue to the madness that had come upon him that he really believed he could limit the readership of his pamphlet in a country, as Hammond wrote later, where you could as easily "confine the light of the sun" as keep people from reading anything once it got into print.

With the help of the one remaining Hamiltonian in the Cabinet, Treasury Secretary Wolcott, Hamilton had no trouble rounding up instances of the President's ill temper, fits of jealousy, and general cussedness, the mote in Hamilton's eye having the effect of sharpening his perception of the beam in Adams's. "We fight Adams on very unequal grounds," Hamilton said to close friends, "because we do not declare the motives of our dislike." To make those motives abundantly clear was the avowed purpose of his *Letter from Alexander Hamilton Concerning the Public Conduct and Character of John Adams*. For three months he toiled over its composition. At length, in October 1800, it was ready to be printed, for distribution to a carefully picked few among the party elders. But no sooner was the *Letter* off the press than a copy of it was in the possession of Aaron Burr.

How did he get it? There was a saying about in those days that if the colonel "did not know everything in 'Heaven and Earth,' he at least knew everything material that was passing in New York." Exactly how he learned of Hamilton's pamphlet and obtained a copy of it remains an unbroken secret to this day. One of several unsubstantiated tales attributes his procurement of the copy to the good offices of an agreeable young woman well known to both him and Hamilton. According to another, the colonel, an early riser, was out walking one morning when he saw a boy heading for Hamilton's house carrying a basket with a cloth over its contents. "What's in the basket, son?" Burr is represented as inquiring. "Only papers, sir," was the reply. Burr asked to have a look, and a second later a copy of Hamilton's *Letter*-contra-Adams was in his hand. However he got it, he knew what to do with it. He released extracts to the press. Presently the readers of the *Bee* in New London, Connecticut, and of the *Aurora* in Philadelphia were being edified by Hamilton's contentions that the President of the United States was a man of "disgusting egotism . . . liable to paroxysms of anger, which deprive him of self command and produce very outrageous behavior." Having banged away at the chief magistrate for several thousand words, Hamilton concluded his philippic, feebly enough, by repeating his hope that the Federalist electors would hold to their promise to vote equally for Adams and Pinckney. Not that anyone was fooled by this pious afterthought, for the obvious intention of his diatribe as a whole was to persuade those same electors to support Pinckney and abandon Adams.

They didn't. No Federalist elector would desert Adams. On the other hand, as Burr had no doubt assumed would be the case, the spectacle of a Federalist leader viciously attacking the Federalist President and Presidential nominee angered many prominent members of Hamilton's party, drove one of them to defect to the Republicans, prompted some of Adams's followers to a short-lived attempt to form a third party (called the Constitutionalists), and probably contributed, at least in a small way, to the downfall of Federalism. The President took Hamilton's printed attack on him in stride. In the old New Englander's mind, the author of the intemperate *Letter* was no longer worthy of being thought of as a member of the party of the few, the rich, and the wellborn. Adams told friends that he would rather see Jefferson in the Presidency than owe his reelection to that post to such as Hamilton. Jefferson, in his view, was the better man by far, and were the Virginian elected, Adams stood ready to serve him as his Vice President or even in some more modest office. Hamilton would be dead for some years when Adams, recalling his controversy with that "bastard brat of a Scotch pedlar," concluded that the latter's strange ways and elaborate schemes issued from "a superabundance of excretions which he [Hamilton] could not find whores enough to draw off."

7

WHILE HAMILTON STROVE to improve the lot of his party by tearing it apart, Burr attended to a variety of matters, mostly but not entirely political. During the summer months he was bothered by "a kind of suppurative tumors, resembling the itch," treated the ailment with warm salt water, and contemplated a visit to Ballston Spa to see what the baths there could do for him. He read Albert Gallatin's newly published *Observations on the finances of the United States*, and arranged to send copies of it to friends in New England. A young lady, apparently met during a stay in Philadelphia, caught his eye, and another halfhearted courtship with faint matrimonial overtones ensued. "If you should not have foresworn all Virtuous Women," he wrote his Boston friend, Dr. Eustis, "I beg you will take the trouble to find out and make some acquaintance with Miss Binney of Boston, lately returned from Philada to the Vicinity of your City—and tell me what you think of her." For several months the virtuous Miss Binney flickered across the pages of his correspondence, only to fade from his life as heaven only knows how many other women had and would.

In late August he began a two-week political junket to Rhode Island and Connecticut, accompanied by his daughter and for at least a part of the trip by a dark, thickset young newcomer to the political lists named Joseph Alston. Rhode Island was one of the few states where the people, rather than the legislature, selected the electors. On the basis of conversations with its Republican governor, Arthur Fenner, Burr concluded that, although hitherto Rhode Island's four electors had voted Federalist, this time at least some of them would opt for Jefferson. By late September he was ready to pronounce it a "moral certainty" that Jefferson would get "all" of Rhode Island votes. "I think," he wrote Chancellor Livingston, "he [Jefferson] may count on them with as much certainty as on those of Virginia. Adams has declared that he will serve as v.p. if elected and such will from present appearance be the result." To these remarks Burr appended a couple of comments. "The matter of V.P.," he told the chancellor, "is of very little comparative consequence—and any sacrifice [however difficult] ought to be made to obtain a single [extra] vote for J—. It is supposed that the votes of R.I. [will] be for J & Adams." A couple of weeks later Burr was writing to James Madison and repeating what he had told the chancellor, that Jefferson would "have all the votes of R. Island."

He was wrong. In 1800 Rhode Island would give all its electoral votes to Federalism; and one of the more stinging charges hurled at Burr during the Pamphlet War of later years was that he knew he was mistaken and that he deliberately falsified the Rhode Island situation in the hopes that the Republican electors in the South, under the impression that extra votes for Jefferson were coming up in New England, would be more likely to honor their agreement to vote evenly for Jefferson and him. No evidence for this accusation has ever been adduced, but the logic of it is hard to ignore. Burr's fingers were crossed with regard to the assurances he had received that the Southern electors would support him and Jefferson alike. When James Madison learned of Burr's uneasiness on this score, he at once took up the problem with his fellow Virginians, Monroe and Jefferson. To Monroe he wrote that David Gelston, a member of the colonel's little band, had described himself as "uneasy lest the Southern States should not be true to their duty." Madison's comment on Gelston's concern was that "It seems important that all proper measures should emanate from Richmond for guarding against a division of the Republican votes, by which one of the Republican Candidates may be lost. It would be superfluous to suggest to you the mischief resulting from the least ground of reproach, and particularly to Virginia, on this head." To Jefferson he wrote that

Gelston "expresses much anxiety . . . with respect to the *integrity* of the Southern States in keeping [Burr] in view for the secondary station. I hope the event will skreen all parties, particularly Virginia, from an imputation on this subject; though I am not without fears that the requisite concert may not sufficiently pervade the several states."

Such were Burr's fears that the electors in the South would let him down this time, as they had in 1796, that he was tireless in his efforts to protect his interests in that region. Another of the charges thrown at him during the Pamphlet War was that in 1800 he spent a small fortune, sending emissaries into the Southern states and elsewhere. For this statement there is at least a scintilla of evidence, namely a letter from Burr to his New York City supporter, Marinus Willett, dated 11 September, and reading: "Mr. Gale handed me your letter. I have let him have about 300 Dolrs and in few days I shall do something more. Mr. Gelston shewed me the letter which you wrote in answer to mine, which is very satisfactory. I am persuaded that you may do much good. Herewith goes Mr. Green. He will confer with you & travel with you. He is I think well known to you. If not, you may confide in him entirely on political subjects. I refer you to him for the State of things in Jersey & more Southward." The Green mentioned in this communication was Timothy Green, a New York City attorney who, like Gelston, was an adherent of the Burrites. Traveling south on business in the fall of 1800, Green was to spend the remainder of that year and much of the next at Columbia, the capital of South Carolina. As the Presidential campaign moved into its closing phase, Burr would rely heavily on Green and on the well-known South Carolina Republican, Wade Hampton, to keep him informed of developments in that crucial state.

8

EARLY NOVEMBER found Burr in Albany for the first meeting of the twenty-fourth legislature, a special session called by Governor Jay so that the lawmakers could select New York's electors. The outcome of this process was foreordained. On the afternoon of the sixth, with a twenty-two-vote majority on joint ballot, twelve Republicans were assigned to the electoral college that a month later would choose the next President and Vice President of the United States. Although the handling of this duty was the only announced purpose of the meeting, the legislature remained in session two more days so that the members of the Assembly could name the next Council of Appointment. And in the course of the voting on this critical matter Burr committed a political blunder of the first water.

9

LET IT BE REMEMBERED that the Council of Appointment consisted of the governor and four state senators, one from each of New York's large voting districts; and that the selection of the senatorial members, an annual event, was the exclusive privilege of the Assembly. Officially the next council would not exercise its functions until 1801. But in November 1800 the Republicans had been out of power in New York for five years. Now that they were in again, they were understandably eager to determine the makeup of a body whose pleasant task it would be to fill thousands of public positions, ranging in stature from county sheriff to mayor of New York City. Little or no excitement accompanied the selection of the electors on the sixth, but there was tension and anticipation in the air when shortly after noon on the following day the Republican majority in the Assembly was asked to endorse a slate of four senators, headed by DeWitt Clinton, George Clinton's tall and handsome nephew.

DeWitt Clinton was thirty-two that year. Physically he was not unlike his famous uncle, although a much larger man, over six feet, with a strong, broad face, rather on the fleshy side; a high forehead under a cap of thick brown curls; and large, steady, dark eyes. They were the brooding eyes of a scholar, for by temperament and inclination he was as much scientist as politician. Not that he was deficient in whatever qualities political success demanded in those days. Quite the contrary, as his subsequent seizure and long control of the Republican machine in New York would certify.

After a distinguished career as the first student to matriculate in Columbia College, when old King's College reopened under that name after the Revolution, DeWitt served for several years as private secretary to Governor Clinton. It was a good political apprenticeship, although there were those who would say later that, had the young man started his climb to power on a more workaday level, he might have learned to repress a quick and violent temper and a tendency to hold himself aloof from the common herd. The reserve, to be sure, was a family trait. Uncle George, popular though he was, had not moved up by slapping backs and kissing babies; and nephew DeWitt probably would have disdained the rewards rather than trod that vulgar route.

When in 1795 Governor Clinton retired temporarily from public life, DeWitt practiced law for a couple of years, courted and wed a wealthy Quaker, and devoted his spare hours to the study of the natural sciences. His first elected office came in 1797 when he accompanied Burr into the lower house of the state legislature. A year later the Southern District elected him to a four-year term in the state senate. Such was his conduct there that by 1800 it was apparent to knowledgeable New Yorkers that, although Uncle George remained the symbol and rallying point of the Clinton wing of the state democracy, his young kinsman had become its actual leader.

In other words, when on 7 November of that year Aaron Burr reluctantly helped elect DeWitt Clinton to the Council of Appointment he, in effect, elevated the de facto head of the Clintons to a position in which DeWitt, who well understood the uses of power, would find it easy to begin the process that in the near future would read Burr straight out of the Republican Party.

It is certainly worth asking why. Why on that animated afternoon in the chamber of the New York Assembly did Burr make no effort to keep the leader of a rival faction from being named to New York's powerful patronage-dispensing body? At that hour the attractive leader of the Burrites stood at the zenith of his political life. He was easily the most popular Republican in New York State, probably in the country as a whole. The éclat and skill with which he had humbled the Federalists in the New York City election—these were everywhere a subject of talk and admiration. Some of the most devoted members of his little band sat around him in the Assembly chamber. It stands to reason that, had Burr let it be known that he was not supporting DeWitt Clinton, that enterprising young man would never have been named to the Council of Appointment. At the very least, such an announcement would have served notice on the Clintons that the colonel knew what was going on and had no intention of letting them get away with it.

One has to agree with biographer Schachner that Burr's political demise was engineered for the most part by the Clintons, with the assistance of Thomas Jefferson. But, in his understandable liking for his subject, Schachner overlooked, or more precisely minimized, the colonel's own contributions to his downfall. As England's Edmund Burke once remarked, "All men that are ruined are ruined on the side of their natural propensities."

Recalling the election of DeWitt Clinton to the council long after it took place, one of Burr's most intimate friends, William Peter Van Ness, wrote that Clinton was well aware of the "impending passage of power to the Republicans" and for that reason "spared no pains to secure" his election to the council. According to Van Ness, Clinton and one of the other candidates buttonholed every member of the Assembly. Burr "was not left unharrassed for a moment, until fatigued with importunities he incautiously assented . . ."

By the time these words were written in 1803, Burr had long since realized the error he had committed three years earlier. It is proposed, however, that his mistake was not caused by lack of caution but by that "heedlessness" which he himself once defined as "mental dissipation." His vision blocked by self-absorption, he failed to spot the swords flashing about him. Not long after the election in New York City, Robert Troup noticed that Burr was "in very high glee. He entertains much company and with Elegance." Troup's comment suggests that the Republican triumph at the polls had left the colonel in a state of euphoria. Perhaps he was still in that state when the legislature convened in November. That was Burr. He liked to savor his victories, to celebrate them by entertaining his friends, courting the ladies, and generally preening himself. For his own sake, he should have come down from the clouds as quickly as possible and ascertained the whereabouts of his enemies. Burr was a first-class campaign manager, and every subsequent machine politician has had reason to bow reverently in his direction. But when it came to the nitty-gritty of the business, to the unavoidable infighting, his singularly complacent nature caused him considerable trouble.

10

When the special session of the New York legislature adjourned on 8 December, the day set for the electoral college to cast its ballots was less than a month away—but the outcome of the election remained as much a mystery as ever. The slow communications of the era made it difficult even for Burr, watchful as he was, to ascertain what was happening in the various states. Not until the middle of November did he realize that he had been wrong about Rhode Island. He wrote his uncle, Pierpont Edwards, that the "rumors" from that state "tend to alarm us something." The rumors were that Rhode Island was going Federalist. Earlier, Burr had thought the Republicans might pick up a few electors in the normally Federalist states of Connecticut and New Jersey, but it was now believed that the opposition would win both. In Pennsylvania the Federalist upper house of the legislature and the Republican lower house, after a protracted quarrel, had compromised by naming eight Republican and seven Federalist electors—giving the Republicans a one-vote majority there. They had hoped to win big in that key state. With their failure to do so, it became evident that the election was going to be decided by the eight electors of South Carolina.

In New York City, Burr kept a close eye on his mail box, daily hoping for news from Timothy Green and his other friends in that state. On 4 December, when the electoral college voted, he was still in the dark. On 7 December he was writing Eustis that "a letter from Charleston of the 21st [November] said that J[efferson] will have every [South Carolina] vote, and there are fears that P[inckney] will also, but . . . this latter point will be contested inch by inch." On 9 December he was writing his Boston friend that, according to a letter from Timothy Green, there was a good chance that the South Carolina electors had given eight votes to Jefferson and eight to Burr. On the tenth he was writing a close friend in Philadelphia that "Our accounts from South Carolina assure us of all the votes for Jefferson—if so, he is President."

Almost no informed politician expected either the Federalist or the Republican electors to abide by the request of their leaderships that they support their candidates evenly. Strictly speaking, the electors were not bound by the pledges that their party caucuses had issued on this point. They were free to vote as they pleased. When in late December, at long last, the results of the electoral-college balloting became generally known, there was cause for shock in both camps.

On the Federalist side, sixty-five electors had voted for Adams and sixty-four for Pinckney. Only one elector, a Rhode Islander, had reneged on the party pledge, throwing away his second vote in an obvious desire to put John Adams at the top of the list. If the conduct of the Federalist electors can be called surprising, that of the Republicans can only be described as phenomenal. Not one Republican elector disregarded the party pledge. As a result, Jefferson had seventy-three electoral votes and Burr had seventy-three; the choice of a President was thrown into the House of Representatives—and a Federalist-dominated House at that; and the country was thrown into a constitutional crisis, a development that one witty Federalist cited as a glaring example of the trouble politicians get themselves into when they keep their promises.

13

Dilemma: The Tie for President

FEW PHASES of Burr's life have generated as much conjecture and argument as his conduct during the tie election of 1800–1. Constitutionally he had as much right to the Presidency as any eligible American. In point of fact, however, the leaders of his party and most of its rank-and-file members intended that post to go to Jefferson.

For a couple of weeks after the electoral college acted in early December, the outcome of the election remained in doubt, owing to the slowness of the mails. Not until mid-December was it generally recognized that a tie was in the offing—a prospect that threw the country into turmoil because of the electoral procedures then in effect. The results would not become official until 11 February 1801, when, in accordance with federal statute, the ballots cast by the electors would be opened and counted in the Senate. At that moment, in the event of a tie, the choice of a President would devolve upon the House of Representatives. There, in such elections, the voting was not by individual but by state. Each of the sixteen states could cast one vote, with nine votes required to name a President. Although the Federalists had a numerical majority in the House, their distribution was such that they controlled only six states. The Republicans controlled eight states, and neither party could count on the remaining two. Vermont's delegation consisted of one Federalist and one Republican. If one voted for Jefferson and his colleague for Burr, Vermont would register no vote at all. Maryland had five Federalist and three Republican representatives, but one of the Federalists, George Dent, was known to be a Jeffersonian. For all practical purposes, that state, too, was evenly divided and belonged to neither party.

These mathematics presented the Federalists with two possible maneuvers. They could block the election of either candidate and then arrange by law for the Presidency to fall on a member of their own party. Off and on, there was talk of doing this—a scheme that had it been attempted would have angered the electorate and perhaps thrown the country into civil war. The aging governor of Pennsylvania, Thomas McKean, let it be known that if the Federalists tried to usurp the Presidency the militia of his state would march at once for the national capital. Time would show that probably less than twenty congressmen looked favorably on usurpation, but for many weeks the likelihood of such an attempt by the opposition hung like a cloud over Republican minds.

Far more operative in Federalist thinking was a dread of Jefferson. Many members of the party believed that Jefferson the agriculturalist would wreck the country's trade by phasing out Alexander Hamilton's financial arrangements, that Jefferson the pacifist would endanger its defenses by reducing a still inadequate navy. So "radical" and "doctrinaire" was the Virginian in the eyes of some citizens that they suspected him of having introduced the Hessian fly into the country. Housewives buried family Bibles on the assumption that he was an atheist and would confiscate them if elected. Against this widely accepted caricature of the statesman from below the Potomac, Burr looked good. He came from a commercial state, understood the importance of trade. In the view of most Federalist leaders, he had no visible principles. He was interested only in money and power, "normal" ambitions, they said, that would induce him to leave things much as they were. When

Hamilton, alarmed at this reasoning, pointed out that Burr was "*selfish* to a degree which excludes all social affections," his friend, Theodore Sedgwick, responded that the Republic would be safer under Burr's selfishness than under Jefferson's "pernicious theories." By the turn of the year, it was common knowledge that many Federalist congressmen were giving thought to an attempt to keep Jefferson out of the Presidency by the simple device of putting Burr into it.

2

As THE RUMORS of a tie reached flood proportions, Burr realized that he was in trouble. Only yesterday he had been in line for the Vice Presidency. Now he appeared to be tied with the acknowledged leader of his party for the top post. Here was a dilemma that, for obvious political reasons, he could not ignore. Hence his decision to convey his personal views on the situation to a longtime friend, Republican Congressman Samuel Smith of Maryland, commonly addressed as General Smith by reason of his rank in the state militia.

At forty-two, Sam Smith was just beginning the forty years in public life that would include a brief spell as acting Secretary of the Navy, nine terms in the House of Representatives, and two in the Senate. Part owner of a prosperous mercantile firm in Baltimore—tall and handsome, with a vigorous intellect and an imperious manner—Smith occupied a political position in Maryland not unlike that of Burr in New York. He was the regional Republican boss. He, too, operated through a small band of devoted followers, known to the Federalist press as the Republican townies. The general has been described as "given to cabals and intrigues." He was definitely a busybody, with a flair for double-talk. In the course of the tie election, he made a point of assuring Burr that no Republican leader credited recurrent charges that the colonel was working with the Federalists against Jefferson. A few years later he would be writing that, although unaware of any proof that Burr "had connected himself with the Federal party" to secure the Presidency, neither was he aware of "any fact that would exonerate [him] . . . from such a charge." Smith was one of Jefferson's closest friends. At the time of the tie they were living in the same Washington boardinghouse, were often in each other's company. It has been suggested that Burr might have suffered less at the hands of the Jeffersonians in the years ahead had he chosen someone other than Sam Smith to be his confidant during the tie election.

On 16 December 1800 Burr wrote the general:

> It is highly improbable that I shall have an equal number of votes with Mr. Jefferson; but if such should be the result, every man who knows me ought to know that I would utterly disclaim all competition. Be assured that the federal party can entertain no wish for such an exchange. As to my friends, they would dishonour my views and insult my feelings by a suspicion that I would submit to be instrumental in counteracting the wishes and expectations of the United States. And I now constitute you my proxy to declare these sentiments if the occasion should require.

This letter of disclaimer remains central to the still lively effort to comprehend Burr's behavior during this time. In the event of a tie, the colonel was not going to compete with Jefferson for the top post. Neither was he going to participate in any Federalist attempt to exploit the situation. Clear enough. Learning shortly that Smith was away from Washington temporarily, Burr wrote again, this time to the general's home in Baltimore. He enclosed a copy of his disclaimer letter and further fortified its sentiments by asserting that "I could hardly forgive any democrat who would for a moment doubt about the line of conduct I shall pursue."

Thomas Jefferson, too, was thinking about the problem. On 15 December he wrote Burr from Washington, sending the letter northward by private hand because of his distrust of "the postoffice at this prying season." Startling news had reached the federal city that day. Heretofore, the report had been that in South Carolina two or more of the electors had thrown away their second votes so as to put Jefferson on top. Now the actual tally was available: eight for Jefferson and eight for Burr, a fact that the Republicans in Washington interpreted as meaning that a tie could now be regarded as of "the highest probability." If Jefferson knew of this development, he gave no inkling of it in his message to Burr. He wrote instead as if he were already the President-elect and Burr the Vice President-elect.

"From South Carolina," he wrote, "we have not even heard the actual votes, but we have learned who were appointed electors, and with sufficient certainty how they would vote. It is said they would withdraw from yourself one vote. It has also been said that a General Smith of Tennessee had declared that he would give his second vote to Mr. Gallatin . . . It is also surmised that the vote of Georgia will not be entire. Yet nobody pretends to know these things of a certainty [but] . . . we know enough to be certain that [you have] four or five votes at least above Mr. Adams. However, it was badly managed not to have arranged with certainty what seems to have been left to hazard. It was the more material because I understand several high-flying federalists have expressed their hope that the two republican tickets may be equal, and their determination in that case to prevent a choice by the House of Representatives (which they are strong enough to do), and let the government devolve on a president of the Senate. Decency required that I should be so entirely passive during the late contest that I never once asked whether arrangements had been made to prevent so many from dropping votes intentionally as might frustrate half the Republican wish . . ."

One wonders if Jefferson realized what he was admitting to Burr by this reference to the "Republican wish." During the preceding autumn, both Madison and Monroe had called his attention to the importance of making certain that the Southern electors obeyed the party request that they give each of the Republican nominees the same number of votes. Obviously, Jefferson had made no efforts to that end.

"While I must congratulate you, my dear sir," he wrote Burr in his 15 December letter, "on the issue of this contest, because it [the Vice Presidency] is more honourable, and doubtless more grateful to you than any station within the competency of the chief magistrate, yet, for myself, I feel most sensibly the loss we sustain of your aid in our new administration. It leaves a chasm in my arrangements which cannot be adequately filled up. I had endeavored to compose an administration whose talents, integrity, names, and dispositions would at once inspire unbounded confidence in the public mind, and ensure a perfect harmony in the conduct of public business. I lose you from the list and am not sure of all the others . . ."

This letter reached New York on 22 December. Answering it the following day, Burr signified his willingness to fill the "chasm." He assured Jefferson that there "is in fact no such dearth of talents or patriotism as ought to inspire a doubt of your being able to fill every office in a manner that will command public confidence . . . As to myself, I will cheerfully abandon the office of V.P., if it shall be thought that I can be more useful in any active station. In truth my whole time and attention shall be unceasingly employed to render your administration grateful and honorable to our country. To this I am impelled, as well by the highest sense of duty as by the most devoted personal attachment."

Was Burr sincere? It is plain that Jefferson was not. He was not interested in giving Burr an "active station" in the government, only in wringing from him an avowal of disinterest in the Presidency. Not having been frank with the colonel, it probably never occurred to the Virginian that the colonel could be frank with him. Jefferson never so much as acknowledged Burr's letter offering to give up the Vice Presidency for some lesser post. By the time Jefferson saw this offer, the tie was no longer a matter of guesswork. It was known to exist. "My dear Colonel," Federalist Congressman Robert Goodloe Harper of South Carolina was writing Burr on the day before Christmas, "The votes of Tennessee are come in and divide the tie." Had Jefferson promptly accepted the New Yorker's offer, Burr would have had to do one of two things—renege on the offer, or go a step beyond his disclaimer letter to Smith by announcing publicly that he had no aspirations for the Presidency.

On Christmas, Burr was en route to Trenton on business. From there, four days later, he dispatched another letter to General Smith. The colonel was angry. At the moment of his departure from New York, he had "received a great number of letters on the subject of the election." He had perceived in them "a degree of Jealousy and distrust and irritation by no means pleasing or flattering." He told Smith that "the letters are . . . generally answered by those which I have written you; but one [Republican] Gentleman . . . has asked me whether if I were chosen president, I would engage to resign. The question was unnecessary, unreasonable and impertinent, and I therefore made no reply. If I had made any, I should have told, that, as at present advised, I should not. What do you think of such a question? I was made a Candidate against my advice and against my will; God knows, never contemplating or wishing the result which has appeared. And now I am insulted by those who use my name for having suffered it to be used . . ."

One modern student of the tie election has found in this outburst from the proud grandson of Jonathan Edwards an indication that, now that the tie was known, Burr was beginning to regret the sentiments he had expressed in his earlier letter to the general. In truth, it is difficult to detect any change in his attitudes. His disclaimer of competition with Jefferson in the 16 December letter was not tantamount to an agreement to resign if elected to the Presidency. His 29 December letter simply expressed an additional sentiment; namely, that he would regard any questioning of his ability to perform the duties of the Presidency as "unnecessary, unreasonable and impertinent."

Even before Burr vented this cry of wounded dignity, General Smith had released his disclaimer letter of 16 December to the press. On 30 December it appeared in the journalistic mouthpiece of the Adams Administration, the *Washington Federalist*. Many Republicans took it to mean that the elevation of Jefferson to the chair of state was now assured without further ado. Caesar A. Rodney of Delaware thought "Col. Burr deserves immortal honor for the noble part he has acted on this occasion." Senator Stevens T. Mason of Virginia read into the disclaimer conclusive indications that the colonel would "cordially cooperate with us."

On the other hand, a large number of Federalists were less struck by what the letter said than by what it did not say. James McHenry of Baltimore noted that Burr had not "committed himself, not to accept the office of President, if elected by the House of Representatives." Reflecting the popular misconception of the New Yorker as the shrewdest politician in the country, Senator Uriah Tracy of Connecticut told McHenry that if the "cunning" Burr "cannot outwit all the Jeffersonians I do not know the man." Commenting at length on the disclaimer letter, the *Washington Federalist* described its "patriotic" declarations as evidence of the New Yorker's "fitness to fill the Presidency." The editor wrote that Burr "would *of choice* decline competition . . . But if the vigorous construction of the term 'competition' shall prevail so as to embrace even *involuntary* competition, it substantially operates a destruction of what Colonel Burr clings to as a principle—to wit, that he will never be instrumental in counteracting the wishes of the United States. For how otherwise . . . could Mr. Burr [counteract] . . . the wishes of the United States, than by refusing, after the people at large have acted upon the occasion, to acquiesce in an election which Congress, or rather the *United States* in Congress assembled, shall think proper to make?"

No one had to be told what these rationalizations portended. The Federalists were going to fight for Burr. Already Congressman Harper had written the colonel saying that the "language of the democrats is that you will yield your pretensions to their favourite; and it is whispered that overtures to this end are to be, or are made to you. I advise you to take no step whatever, by which the choice of the house of representatives can be impeded or embarrassed. Keep the game perfectly in your hands, but do not answer this letter, or any other that may be written to you by a federal man, nor write any of that party." Later on, Harper would take the position that adherents of the federal party in the House should vote for Burr without even ascertaining what sort of administration he would run. Most of Harper's colleagues, however, were not that lenient. They were hopeful that in some way the New Yorker, never famous as a down-the-line party man, would signal his willingness to pursue a conservative line if elected.

3

IT WAS A TUG-OF-WAR, the Federalists trying to pull the colonel their way, the Jeffersonians struggling to bring him to an understanding that would clear the way for their man. Twice Burr had offered to meet with General Smith in Philadelphia so that they could discuss the matter face to face. During the first week of the new year, accordingly, they got together in the Quaker City. It may be stated categorically that Smith was there as Jefferson's agent, that he looked forward to being able to carry back to Washington the glad tidings that at last the colonel had seen the light and was ready to announce that, if elected President, he would not serve. The general was in for a disappointment.

Burr left no record of the Philadelphia get-together. Our knowledge of it rests on three documents: a letter written to

Jefferson at the time by Benjamin Hitchborn; a letter written two years later by Gabriel Christie of Maryland, one of Smith's political associates and a member of the House in 1801; and an 1804 entry in Jefferson's diary, or more precisely in that collection of confidential jottings that he spoke of as his *Anas*.

Burr was late in reaching Philadelphia on the day appointed. The conversation took place in the evening. Hitchborn was present. He and Smith dwelt at length on their fears concerning the upcoming House election. The Federalists did not have enough states to name a President without Republican help. They did have enough to bar both Burr and Jefferson from the office. What were the colonel's thoughts on those grim hypotheses? The colonel, in Gabriel Christie's words, thought "the House could and ought to make a choice, meaning that if they could not get Mr. Jefferson they could take him." At breakfast next morning, according to the entry in Jefferson's *Anas*, Burr was even more explicit. "We cannot be without a president, our friends must join the federal vote," he is quoted as telling Hitchborn. When Hitchborn remarked that "we shall then be without a vice-President; who is to be our Vice-President," Burr answered, "Mr. Jefferson."

On the basis of these second-hand but reasonably trustworthy reports—along with Burr's angry letter to Smith—one of the questions hovering over this argument-plagued battle would seem to be answered. Burr had no intention of shrinking from the burdens of the Presidency if the House of Representatives saw fit to impose them upon him. But a willingness to accept an office is one thing; going after it, another. And the remaining events of the tie yield no evidence that Burr went after it—and strong evidence that he did not.

4

FROM PHILADELPHIA, Burr returned to New York City to wind up his affairs there quickly enough to enjoy a sojourn at Ballston Spa and still be in Albany in time for the opening of the next meeting of the legislature at the end of January. General Smith returned to a Washington awash with speculation. Republican Congressman Edward Livingston of New York, the much younger brother of the chancellor, was on close terms with Burr. It was said that the younger Livingston planned to vote for Jefferson but that if the Virginian did not win on the first ballot, Edward would switch—a move that might throw his state into the Burr column. An identical rumor circulated with regard to a New Jersey Democrat, Representative James Linn. Smith himself, a few years later, would be said to have entertained similar leanings, a charge that the general would deny with indignation.

Whatever Smith's inclinations in January 1801, he was no sooner back in the national capital than he again tried to persuade Burr to declare himself out of the Presidential race. He wrote the colonel that on his return to the federal city he had found "a stand taken by the Democrats, from which be assured that nothing can drive them, the Eight states will continue to the End of the Session to vote for Mr. Jefferson . . . *believe me*, those states are immovable. Maryland has four Members that must continue with them. In my opinion, *& I have good reasons*, Maryland will make the ninth State." Parts of Smith's long letter dealt with the recent appearance in Washington of Alexander Hamilton's law partner, David A. Ogden. That stalwart Federalist, Smith wrote, "has been here in my absence, & has undertaken to say . . . that he came to Trenton with you, that you had conversed freely with him on the subject of the Tie, from which he meant I presume to insinuate that he had your confidence." It was Smith's understanding that Ogden had urged some of the New York congressmen to back Burr for the Presidency, that they had rebuffed him "with derision," and that the feeling among the Republicans in Washington was that the visiting attorney's conduct was only "one of many attempts practicing by his party to disunite [us]." He warned Burr against being taken in by such maneuvers.

Smith's words suggest that he was now convinced that Burr was cooperating with the Federalists. But David Ogden's version of his visit to Washington, as later released to the press, shows that this was not the case. Ogden described his trip as "purely on private business and without any understanding or concert with Col. Burr." The New York attorney recalled meeting Burr at the stage office "on his way to Trenton." In the course of their journey, "no political conversation took place but of a general nature, and in the presence of passengers." During Ogden's stay in the national capital, some Federalist congressmen asked him to sound out Burr, to see if he was willing to "enter into Terms" in exchange for their support. Back in New York, Ogden did just that. Burr said he was not interested, whereupon Ogden wrote a Federalist friend in the Congress to forget the colonel and vote for Jefferson "as the less dangerous man of the two."

Burr's comment on Smith's story of Ogden's visit has not been located. According to Smith, it consisted of a brief note in which the colonel stated that "he had not written or said a word contravening" the sentiments expressed in his disclaimer letter.

The Congress had recessed over Christmas. In early January the members were dribbling back to Washington. In those days no one hurried to the national capital. With 10,266 white citizens, 738 free blacks, and 3,244 slaves, the federal city, 1801 vintage, was no city at all. On the eighty-eight-foot hill at the eastern end of town, a few drab structures, mostly boardinghouses, huddled around the original Capitol, that part of today's imposing edifice that links the Rotunda to the Senate wing. A mile and a half to the west, a larger group of buildings, mostly homes and business establishments, stood in the vicinity of the still unfinished Executive Mansion on the banks of the Potomac. Aware that he would soon be living in this largely alfresco setting, Burr had asked General Smith to "give me the history of an evening's amusement in Washington." Smith had replied, "Evening Amusement,—there is no such thing."

On 2 January, Federalist James Asheton Bayard of Delaware arrived and took his seat in the small chamber then assigned to the House of Representatives. A heavyset man "poised and impressive" and always fastidiously dressed, Bayard occupied a unique position. He was the sole representative from his state. As such, he was widely regarded as holding the upcoming election in his hands. Were he to support Jefferson, a single ballot would put him in the Presidency. If not, none could guess how long the House election would last or how it would end. Looking about him, Bayard noted that the "Demo's" were "more uneasy at the prospect of Burr's election than they even were at that of Adams." He wrote his father-in-law, Governor Richard Bassett of Delaware, that "they would rather see the union dissolved for want of a head than give up Jefferson." Bayard's own plan for the time being was to "remain inflexibly silent." But he disapproved of Jefferson, and it was a foregone conclusion that when the time came he would go along with his fellow Federalists and vote for Burr.

On 12 January, Albert Gallatin reached Washington. Jefferson was distressed by the lateness of his arrival. As the leader of the minority in the House, Gallatin's task was to keep the Jeffersonian forces there in line. As the time neared for the representatives to select a President, rumors about the activities of the Federalists and Burr abounded. Jefferson recorded some of them in his *Anas*. Apparently he believed them all. He was told that members of the opposition had promised General Smith any appointment he might wish if he would vote for Burr, that they had offered "the government of New Jersey" to James Linn on the same condition. "General Armstrong tells me," Jefferson wrote, "that Gouverneur Morris, in conversation with him . . . expressed himself thus. 'How comes it,' says he, 'that Burr who is four hundred miles off (Albany) has agents here at work with great activity, while Jefferson, who is on the spot, does nothing.' " Jefferson put no names to Burr's "agents." Among those frequently mentioned in the gossip of the hour was Edward Livingston, who at a later date would deny having done anything for Burr or having been asked by the colonel to do so. Early in December, before the existence of the tie was known, Jefferson had offered Chancellor Livingston a Cabinet post that the latter had declined with thanks. It would be contended later that this move by Jefferson was instrumental in keeping the chancellor's brother true to the Jeffersonian cause.

5

In New York City, Alexander Hamilton was in the midst of an extensive letter-writing campaign. Weeks before, he had ventured a sly proposition. It might be "well," he told Oliver Wolcott, for the movers and shakers of their party "to throw out a lure" for Burr. Let them pretend that they wanted him for the Presidency and then drop him when he "started for the plate"—a maneuver certain to "lay the foundation of dissension" between him and Jefferson. The ink was barely dry on this proposal when its author realized that the Federalists in the House were not interested in playing at cloak and dagger. They favored Burr over Jefferson and meant to act accordingly. From this point on, in a spate of letters to men in and out of the Congress, the New York Federalist chieftain pushed his notable powers of vituperation to the breaking point.

He conceded that Jefferson was "not . . . very mindful of truth, and . . . a contemptible hypocrite." Nevertheless, he was to be preferred to Burr. The Virginian had some principles, according to Hamilton; Burr had none. In Hamilton's fulsome lexicon, the colonel was "the most unfit and dangerous man in the community," a "profligate," a "voluptuary," a "bankrupt," a "Grecian horse" who must at all costs be kept out of the "Federal Troy." To Congressman John Rutledge, Jr., of South Carolina he wrote that the "expectation I know is that if Mr. Burr shall owe his elevation to the Federal party, he will judge it his interest to adhere to that party. But it ought to be recollected that he will owe it in the first instance to the Antifederal party, that among these . . . a numerous class prefers him to Mr. Jefferson as best adapted by the boldness and cunning of his temper to fulfill their mischievous views, and it will be to the interest of his Ambitions to preserve and cultivate these friends."

It would be enlightening to know what "mischievous views" Hamilton had in mind. Burr himself had never so much as dropped a hint as to the policies he would pursue if elected President. It would also be interesting to know what "friends" Hamilton had in mind. Perhaps the Burrites, although they were hardly a "numerous class." Perhaps the New York Republican congressmen, Edward Livingston and Theodorus Bailey, both of whom were known to think well of the colonel. Perhaps Governor McKean of Pennsylvania. Fearful that the House, because of its peculiar political makeup, would not be able to elect a President, McKean suggested to Jefferson that he and Burr simply get together and determine between themselves which was to serve in that office. The naïveté of this notion to one side, it would appear that the chief magistrate of Pennsylvania did not care much whether the name of the next President was Jefferson or Burr, just so long as it belonged to a Republican.

It is a safe guess that a fair number of other Republicans shared Governor McKean's indifference. In 1801, Burr was still a popular and respected figure. He was not yet the monster he would become in the eyes of many Americans after his conspiracy and trial on a charge of treason. "Who is Colonel Burr?" asked the *Aurora*, the leading Republican newspaper in Philadelphia in one of its January issues. Editor William Duane replied that Burr was a man of "ardent devotion to the principles of liberty . . . with a mind vast, liberal and comprehensive . . . With an energy and decision of character, peculiar to himself, while other men are debating, he resolves, and while they resolve, he acts. His manners are amiable, his reputation fair and unblemished . . ." He was also well known, probably as well known as Jefferson. Burr was an inveterate traveler. Much of his travel had been in the Southern states, those bastions of the democracy. In South Carolina, where in the end the Republican victory was effected, his well-wishers included Wade Hampton, one of the electors, and members of the Alston family, preeminent among the rice planters of that region.

Hamilton's essays in detraction may have had some effect on men outside of the House of Representatives. They had very little on the Federalists within it. Perhaps they remembered the overwrought rhetoric of Hamilton's published attack on John Adams. Hamilton had cried "wolf!" once too often. Many men who had once jumped at his every order were no longer heeding his wishes.

While the former Treasury head wrote letters in New York City and Jefferson collected rumors in Washington, what was Burr, the object of their concern, doing in Albany? Burr was attending to his duties in the Assembly and overseeing the preparations for the marriage of his daughter, now a handsome young woman of eighteen, to Joseph Alston, the twenty-two-year-old scion of the wealthy South Carolina family of that name.

6

BEHIND THIS FESTIVE EVENT lay a six-month courtship, marked on her part by hesitancy and on his by quiet persistence.

Prepared for college by private tutors, young Alston had entered the junior class at Princeton in 1795. A year later he left without graduating. Subsequently he read law in the office of Edward Rutledge in Charleston. In this field, too, his interest turned out to be marginal. It would appear that he was admitted to the bar but never practiced. The year 1799 found him toying with the idea of the political career that during the next decade and a half would carry him into the lower house of the South Carolina legislature and from thence into the governorship. Not that he was especially aggressive. A little stubborn, yes—enough so at times to resist Aaron Burr's unremitting efforts to mold his mind and direct his career; but as a kinsman once remarked, Uncle Joseph was "not an ambitious man, although . . . Burr instilled into him some of that with which he, himself, was somewhat overstocked."

A New Englander who saw much of Alston during his legislative days described him as "short and rather thick in stature." He had a swarthy complexion, heavy black hair, and "a formidable pair of whiskers that covered a great part of his face and nearly met at the chin." When not in the legislative chamber, he might be "seen, as often as anywhere, about the stables, looking at fine horses, dressed in a short jockey like a surtout or frock, and laced and tasseled boots, with a cigar in his mouth, and with much more of the gig and tandem levity than of the austere virtues of a senatorial leader." The New England observer may or may not have realized that he was looking at a diamond in the rough. Behind Joseph's "buckish demeanor" lay a good mind, a feeling heart, and a way with words. He wrote essays and poems. Burr, who was confessedly without skill in matters "sublime and poetical," found them admirable. More than once, he would complain that his son-in-law devoted too much time to his big rice fields along the Waccamaw River, too little to the development of what the older man regarded as a true literary talent.

The young man's father, William Alston, was a close friend of Jefferson and an active Republican. It may have been at his urging that in 1799 Joseph set out on a leisurely political tour of the country. The summer of 1800 brought him to New York City. Very likely he was a guest at Richmond Hill. In any event, he was at once drawn to its lively minded hostess.

When he expressed a desire to meet some of the politicos in New England, Burr furnished him with a letter of introduction to Dr. Eustis. Burr was even then preparing for his own tour of the New England states. In the note to his Boston friend, he asked Eustis to give young Alston "particular" attention; "analyze and anatomize him Soul & heart & body," he implored, "so that you may answer me all questions which I may put to you on that head when we meet in Providence . . . This injunction has become interesting to me from reasons you will be at no loss to conjecture."

Obviously the young man had revealed his feelings for Theodosia to the parent. He had also spoken to the daughter. "Mr. A is with us," Theodosia wrote sister-in-law Frances Prevost from Providence, "but your prophecy is not likely to be verified; notwithstanding your usual accuracy on all subjects." She had not said yes, neither had she said no, when in October the young man headed homeward, stopping en route at Richmond to see Madison and at Monticello to pay his respects to Jefferson.

For the next few months the courtship went on by mail. She objected to matrimony on the grounds of age. No less an authority than Aristotle had warned against early marriages. Always fearful of ennui, she repeated the statements of friends that life could be pretty dull in an elegant two-story mansion on the banks of the Waccamaw. He wrote her an essay of several thousand words, pointing out that Aristotle was not infallible and extolling the pleasures of plantation life in the low country of South Carolina. His letters traveled by water. Adverse winds created delays. Matters came to a head when Burr noticed that his daughter fretted when a day passed with no mail from South Carolina, and mildly suggested that she was in love. At last, on 13 January 1801, she sent the answer Joseph was waiting for. "We leave this [place: Ballston Spa] for Albany on the 26th Inst," she wrote her faraway lover, "and shall remain there till the 19th Feby. My movements will after that depend upon my father & *you*. I had intended not to marry this twelvemonth . . . but to your solicitations I yield my judgment."

He was in Albany by the end of the month. On the evening of Monday, 2 February, they were married by the Reverend John Johnson of the Dutch Reformed Church. Tuesday morning they left to spend their honeymoon at Richmond Hill. The plan was that, as inauguration day approached, Aaron would join them and they would travel to Washington together. It would be March before Theodosia saw Oaks, her plantation home. She would know much happiness there and much sorrow. And some ennui, especially when certain members of the Alston tribe came to visit. "Pray teach me," she wrote her father during a journey in the company of two members of that big family, "how to write two *A's* without producing something like an *Ass*."

7

NOW IT WAS BACK to the routine of the Assembly for Burr, and to the turbulence of the tie election. He heard from Jefferson. A Mr. Munford claimed to have seen a letter from Jefferson to John Breckinridge of Kentucky in which Jefferson had expressed unflattering opinions of the colonel. In his anxiety to set the record straight, Jefferson forgot that he had been corresponding with Breckinridge off and on for years. He told Burr he had written the Kentucky statesman only one letter. He had said nothing in it about Burr, unflattering or otherwise. It followed that the letter Munford had read was a forgery.

The reply that Burr penned to this communication was, in effect, a rebuke. He knew that Jefferson was willingly, nay eagerly, listening to every rumor floating on the ill winds of the tie election. General Smith had told him as much in a recent letter. "It was so obvious that the most malignant spirit of slander and intrigue would be busy," the colonel wrote Jefferson, "that, without any enquiry, I set down as calumny every tale calculated to disturb our harmony. My friends are often more irritable and more credulous; fortunately I am the depository of all their cares and anxieties, and Invariably pronounce to be a lie every thing which ought not to be true . . . Munford never told me what you relate & if he had, it would have made no impression on me . . ."

To Albany, toward the middle of February, came a disturbing suggestion from Albert Gallatin. Dated 3 February, this communication from the leader of the Jeffersonian forces in Washington has never been found. It probably never will be. Burr is thought to have destroyed it. Perhaps Gallatin asked him to do so. It was taken for granted that, whether Jefferson or Burr became the next President, Gallatin would be his Secretary of the Treasury. Had his 3 February letter to Burr come to light in 1801, the Swiss-born financial wizard would never have received that or any other appointment at the hands of Thomas Jefferson.

For a century and a half, it was generally assumed that the missing letter was prompted by the gossip in Washington that the Federalists were seeking an understanding with Burr, and that Gallatin wrote to see if Burr "countenanced such talk." But the journal of Benjamin Betterton Howell, unearthed in the 1960's, puts a different complexion on the Pennsylvanian's intentions. Howell was a New York City merchant in Burr's day. According to the pertinent passage in his journal, when in 1801 "The election by the House was about to come on," Burr sent for two of his closest supporters in the Assembly, Peter Townsend and John Swartwout. On their arrival at his quarters, he "laid before them a letter from *Albert Gallatin*, informing Burr, what was going on—telling him that the election was in the hands of Genl Smith of Maryland—Lynn [Linn] of N Jersey & Edward Livingston of NY—who held the balance of those three states, that they were friendly to Burr—*but to secure them he must be on the spot himself*, and urging him by all means to hasten to Washington without an instants delay."

The rest of Howell's account of the incident, as related to the New York merchant by Townsend, was that Burr showed his friends Gallatin's letter and asked them what he should do. "They replied—get into the first conveyance you can procure—lose not a moment—hasten to Washington and secure the prize—*He agreed to do so*—they left him—went to the legislature—Burr did not come—they supposed he was preparing—After the House adjourned, they called at his lodgings—found his luggage packed and he ready—*but* at *the critical moment his heart failed him*—he remained at Albany and *wrote letters* . . ."

It is not known on what date Burr saw Gallatin's 3 February letter. He answered it on the twelfth. The contents of his reply indicate that Gallatin had expressed concern at the persistent rumor that the Federalists planned to keep the government in their own hands by denying the "prize" to either Republican candidate. Apparently Gallatin believed that only the presence of Burr in Washington could avoid this distressing eventuality. On more than one occasion, Burr had asserted that a successful Federalist coup should be met by "a resort to the sword." He began his answer to Gallatin by saying that for "ten days past" his correspondence had convinced him that "all was settled, & that . . . J[efferson] would have 10 or 11 votes on the first trial. I am therefore utterly surprised by the contents of yours of the 3d." He added that in "case of usurpation . . . my opinion is definitely made up and it is known to S[amuel] S[mith] and E[dward] L[ivingston]. On that opinion I shall act in defiance of all timid temporizing projects."

It is interesting that Burr should have given such prominence to the words "timid" and "temporizing." Was he referring to some project known to him and Gallatin—a readiness on the part of certain Republicans, perhaps, to go along with a Federalist seizure of power? Or was he unknowingly externalizing his own timidity, his failure to act when a quick trip to Washington might have secured him the "prize"?

8

WASHINGTON, on the eve of the House election, was a frenzy of activity, of jockeying for position. The Federalists of the House caucused often. The outstanding figure of these conclaves was James Bayard of Delaware. Bayard's preeminence was not due exclusively to his status as the only representative from his small state. There was that about the portly lawyer from Wilmington which commanded respect and inclined others to rely on his judgment. William Plumer of New Hampshire, who would know Bayard later as a fellow senator, considered him the most resourceful man in Congress—"a man with great talents, prompt and ready on every question . . . a host."

It was probably fortunate for the country that the role of Federalist strategist should have gravitated to Bayard in that hectic winter of 1801. He was a moderate. He had no sympathy with the desire of some of the extremists of his party to deadlock the House election in an attempt to keep the government in Federalist hands. In later years he would say that he was never confident Burr could be elected President. But letters to members of his family show that those were not his feelings during the weeks prior to the House election. Like Gallatin, he was aware that Burr had good friends among the Republican congressmen from New York, New Jersey, and Maryland. Add those three states to the six states under Federalist control and the New Yorker would be in. Such must have been the thinking behind Bayard's statement in late January to his cousin, Andrew Bayard, that although Jefferson was expected to have eight votes "upon the first ballot," it was "certainly within the compass of possibility that Burr may ultimately obtain nine . . ." There was no need for the Delaware congressman to tell his kinsman that much would depend on whether or not Burr saw fit to cooperate with the Federalists by putting pressure on his Republican friends.

9

On Wednesday 11 February, the day set for the counting of the electoral votes, a heavy snow was filling up the magnificent open spaces of the federal city. Sometime that morning Republican Joseph H. Nicholson had himself carried into what the local Republican newspaper, the *National Intelligencer*, called the "anti-chamber" of the chamber of the House of Representatives. The thirty-year-old congressman from the Eastern Shore of Maryland was dangerously ill. He realized, however, that without his presence at the House election his evenly divided state would go to Burr. During the long hours of the election he would lie on a cot in the drafty antechamber, his wife seated beside him. Every time a vote was taken in the adjoining room, the Maryland tellers would bring the ballot box to his sickbed. "I would not thus expose myself," a Federalist remarked, "for any President on earth."

At noon the members of both houses collected in the Senate chamber to hear Vice President Jefferson announce the well-known results of the electoral-college vote and confirm the tie. The members of the House then filed into their own chamber, closed the doors, and began the House election. For the next six and a half days they would operate under two recently passed resolutions. One forbade them to adjourn until a President was chosen. Until this end was accomplished, under the second rule, they were to take care of no other business except under rigidly specified conditions. Even messages from President Adams would be ignored.

A hundred and four representatives, all but one of those then sitting, were on hand for the first ballot. Although the Federalists, at their last caucus, had agreed to back Burr, the breakdown of the individual voting on this ballot showed fifty-five for Jefferson and forty-nine for Burr—figures which indicate that at least five Federalists refused to follow the party line. Enough did, however, to give Burr all six of the Federalist-controlled states. Jefferson got eight states. The two states whose delegations were evenly divided, Maryland and Vermont, registered no votes at all. As nine states were needed to name a President, the representatives had to take a second ballot . . . and a third . . . and a fourth . . . On and on the session went for twenty unbroken hours. At nine o'clock the next morning, the exhausted solons resorted to a tactic they would use repeatedly during the next several days. They got around the no-adjournment ruling and gave themselves time away from their seats by voting to postpone the next ballot until noon. At this point they had voted twenty-seven times. Individuals had changed sides, some deserting Jefferson for Burr, some vice versa. But in every case the official outcome had been the same—eight states for Jefferson, six for Burr, two blank.

The twenty-eighth ballot, Thursday noon, gave the same results. So did two ballots on the following day. Shortly after the thirtieth vote was cast, there was a motion, properly seconded, to postpone the next ballot until the very eve of inauguration day, to 3 March. The motion fell overwhelmingly, every state voting against it. The election droned on. Saturday witnessed three more ballots, with no difference in the results. At their conclusion, a motion carried providing for a rest on Sunday and for the taking of the thirty-fourth vote on Monday.

That day—16 February—was a busy one for James Bayard. At a party caucus that at times became a shouting match, the Delaware statesman took the position that the time had come to name a President, so as "to run no risk of the constitution." He announced his intention of changing his vote to Jefferson. There were loud protests, cries of "Deserter!" Some members of the party, principally those from New England, expressed a willingness to go to the extreme—to elect no President at all. Bayard stuck to his guns, and calmer voices prevailed. In the end, a consensus was achieved. Before capitulating, the Federalists would try to get a quid pro quo. It was abundantly clear that Burr had offered no terms and would offer none. Perhaps Jefferson would be willing to do so.

Bayard undertook the necessary negotiations. He spoke first to Congressman John Nicholas of Virginia, "a particular friend of Mr. Jefferson." The Federalists, Bayard explained, were worried about three matters. If elected President, would Jefferson preserve the Hamiltonian financial system? Would he respect the integrity of the navy? Where subordinate government jobs were concerned, as distinct from confidential ones on the Cabinet- or foreign-ministry level, would he refrain from dismissing Federalist occupants on the grounds of politics alone? On two of these points, the fiscal system and the patronage problem, Nicholas claimed to know Jefferson's mind. He said that on those matters Bayard and his Federalist friends need not worry. Bayard said he wanted more than Nicholas's opinion. He wanted a direct word from Jefferson. Would Nicholas be willing to see what Jefferson himself had to say?

When Nicholas said no to this proposition, Bayard got in touch with General Smith. The Maryland Republican boss was even more positive than Nicholas had been. He described himself as convinced that in his conduct of the Presidency Jefferson would satisfy the Federalists on all three points. Again Bayard stressed his desire for direct assurances. Was Smith game to sound out his friend? The general said he would talk with Jefferson and report back.

Late that Monday night, Bayard wrote what has become the most quoted of his extant letters. He told his father-in-law that at an evening caucus he and his cohorts had agreed "upon a mode of surrendering." They had not "yet made" a President, he reported, "but tomorrow we shall give up the contest.

Burr has acted a miserable paltry part. The election was in his power, but he was determined to come in as a Democrat, and in that event would have been the most dangerous man in the community. We have been counteracted in the whole business by letters he has written to this place."

On the following morning, Bayard and General Smith had another talk. Smith had spoken with Jefferson. He now pronounced himself more certain than ever that, on the points discussed the day before, the Federalists had no cause for uneasiness. Bayard was relentless. Was Smith making these renewed declarations on his own, or had he been authorized to make them by Jefferson?

How Smith answered that question remains a subject of dispute to this day. Bayard would go to his grave insisting that Smith told him there was a deal, that Jefferson had authorized the Marylander to speak as he did. The general would go to his protesting that he had carefully identified his declarations as personal opinions only. Of this old dispute only one statement can be made with confidence. By 1 p.m. that Tuesday, 17 February, the Federalists in Congress thought they had a deal. On the thirty-sixth ballot, accordingly, they put into operation the "mode of surrender" on which they had agreed the night before.

James Bayard did not have to vote for Jefferson, an action he would have found exceedingly distasteful. Under the prearranged "mode," he simply cast a blank. The members of the South Carolina delegation, all Federalists, did the same. The tie was broken and Jefferson's election to the Presidency insured in the Maryland and Vermont delegations. The four Marylanders who had supported Burr through thirty-five ballots abstained from voting. This action permitted the other four Marylanders to give their state to Jefferson. The Vermont Federalist, Lewis R. Morris, absented himself from the proceedings, thus allowing his Republican colleague, Matthew Lyon, to put that state in the Jefferson column. The result of the thirty-sixth ballot: ten states for Jefferson, four for Burr, two blank. Jefferson was now President-elect, Burr Vice President-elect.

10

THE BITTER CONTEST was over. Morally speaking, Burr's conduct during the crisis appears to have been above reproach. In the smug light of hindsight, however, it is easy to see that he erred by doing nothing in a situation where doing something could have advanced his personal interests. Had he announced prior to the House election that he would not accept the Presidency, he would have silenced forever the charge that he had intrigued against Jefferson—a charge that would resurface more than once in the future. Had he harkened to the advice of his friends, hied himself to Washington and fought—who can say what would have happened? Success would have brought the complaint that he had stolen the Presidency. But *audentes fortuna iuvat*. Success has a way of palliating all accusations, and he could have claimed that he had saved the country from the horrors of usurpation.

On the third day of the House election, after thirty ballots, Federalist Congressman William Cooper declared that "Had Burr done anything for himself he would long ere this have been president." In a letter to Hamilton, Bayard said that the "means existed of electing Burr, but this required his co-operation. By deceiving one man (a great blockhead), and tempting two (not incorruptible), he might have secured the majority of the States. He will never have another chance of being President of the United States; and the little use he has made of this one . . . gives me but an humble opinion of the talents of an unprincipled man."

A cynical summation of the issue, to be sure, but not an inaccurate one. Too proud to renounce his Presidential pretensions, lest that action be construed as an admission of inadequacy; too timid or gentlemanly, or both, to exploit the situation, Burr had sat out the tie election. Because he neither ran with the Republican hares nor hunted with the Federalist hounds, he would go into the Vice Presidency an object of considerable disapproval in both political camps.

Compounding his error was one of the more noticeable characteristics of the political struggle on the national stage in his day. It is difficult to argue with the contention of historian Richard Buel that, although the architects of the first political parties were avid for posthumous fame, they tended to regard as "counterproductive" any pursuit of fame that was not subordinated "to the larger end of fulfilling the promise of the Revolution." Burr's refusal to break the electoral-college deadlock of 1800 aroused in the leaders of his own party the suspicion that he did not share their feelings on this point—a suspicion that in the near future would have an unhappy impact on his political fortunes.

14

Vice President Burr

WHEN WORD of Jefferson's election reached Albany, only two weeks remained until inauguration day. Burr left town almost at once, on 19 February to be exact, on the first lap of his journey to Washington. Awaiting him in New York were communications from Albert Gallatin, including the Pennsylvanian's personal record of the balloting in the House election. During a stopover in Philadelphia, the Vice President-elect wrote to thank him for "your very amusing history" and to report that the "feds boast aloud that they have compromised with Jefferson, particularly as to the retaining certain persons in office." Burr's comment on this development was that "without the assurance contained in your letter, this would gain no manner of credit with me," a statement which indicates that the future Secretary of the Treasury shared the belief of the opposition that Jefferson had stooped to a deal.

Theodosia and her husband were in Baltimore. Burr picked them up there. They were among the some three hundred persons who on the morning of Wednesday 4 March crowded into the chamber of the Senate to witness the first Presidential inauguration in the national Capitol. They found themselves in a semicircular room of gracious design and modest dimensions, eighty-six feet one way, forty-six the other, forty high. Located in the northeast corner of the building, it utilized both the basement and first floor of the only completed wing of the Capitol as then projected. Surrounding the senators' seats on the ground level, an arcade supported a graceful gallery, fronted by a "colonade of ancient Ionic columns, sixteen in number, surmounted by an appropriate classical entablature."

The ceremonies began at ten o'clock. Burr's part in them was minimal. No speech, only the taking of his oath of office, administered by the retiring president pro tempore of the Senate, James Hillhouse of Connecticut. The new Vice President then took the chair from whence, during the next four years, he would preside over the proceedings of the upper house. The high moment of the occasion began shortly after noon with the arrival of Jefferson, accompanied by the members of President Adams's Cabinet. Already on hand, seated next to Burr, was Jefferson's fellow Virginian and distant kinsman, John Marshall, whom Adams only recently had named Chief Justice of the United States. Rising with the others, as Jefferson entered, Burr motioned the President-elect to the chair he himself had been occupying. Most members of the audience in the Senate chamber that day would live long enough to have reason to recall with feeling the tableau that now presented itself: Jefferson seated at the center of the platform, flanked on his right by a man he would one day accuse of treason; on his left by the stubborn jurist who would frustrate all efforts to convict the accused. For a second the incoming President remained as he was. Then he rose to read his inaugural address, whose most frequently quoted passage would be that classic of wishful thinking, "We have called by different names brethren of the same principle. We are all Republicans; we are all Federalists."

Of Burr at this hour of his life, Parton wrote: "We behold our hero now upon the summit of his career . . . ten years after becoming known in national politics, he stands one step below the highest place to which by politics a man can rise." Burr was in his forty-fifth year, still youthfully spare and strikingly handsome, always the gentleman in manner, always militarily erect: a man at the prime of his powers, buoyed no doubt by the hope that to him, as to Jefferson and Adams before him, the Vice Presidency would prove a stepping-stone to the slot above it. In his thank-you note to Gallatin, the one written in Philadelphia, he had ventured the cheerful thought that, with the tie election finally resolved, "the infamous slanders which have been so industriously circulated . . . are now of little consequence." In truth, like disease germs before the symptoms appear, they were still much at work.

2

SMALL BUT TELLING was the earliest sign that Burr's "summit" was shaky, and that the twilight of a political god was at hand. One of Jefferson's first tasks was to fill the five posts in his Cabinet with men on whom he could rely. Not once during this always painful process of selection did he consult with his Vice President, an oversight the colonel was quick to notice. When the process ended, there would be two first-class men in the top positions: Madison at State and Gallatin at Treasury; and three moderately competent ones in the other posts: Levi Lincoln as Attorney General, Henry Dearborn as Secretary of War, and Robert Smith, the brother of the Maryland general, as Secretary of the Navy.

For many months, the even more ticklish question of what should be done about the Federalist occupants of subordinate government posts was a major concern of the new Administration. Jefferson may or may not have come to an understanding on this matter with the congressional leaders of the opposition. If he did, he—and they—must have known that such promises can never be fully kept. The Republicans had triumphed at the polls. They had not only put their man in the President's house, they had also acquired a large majority in the House of Representatives and a slight one in the Senate. Now the time had come for the distribution of the spoils, and the cry coming up from the democratic multitude was "throw the rascals out, and put us in."

Burr understood the necessity of appeasing this hunger as rapidly and as widely as possible. Jefferson understood it, too, although he endeavored with some success to limit the removal of Federalist officeholders to those known to be dishonest, immoral, or maladroit. Burr realized, also, that where the federal patronage was concerned, his political future—which is to say, his chance at the Presidency—depended on the extent to which he was permitted to act as the spokesman of the Administration in his home state. Jefferson understood that, too. All too well, as the Vice President would in time discover.

On the heels of the inauguration, Burr handed to Jefferson a list of five Federalist officeholders in New York City that he and the Republican members of his state delegation in Congress had agreed should be removed and replaced by members of the party in power. The replacements named and the posts to which they were recommended were Edward Livingston for district attorney, John Swartwout for marshal, David Gelston for collector of the port, Theodorus Bailey for supervisor of the city, and Matthew L. Davis for naval officer of the custom house.

Jefferson did not simply ignore this list, as has often been stated. By the end of March, Livingston was district attorney and Swartwout was marshal. Later, much later, Gelston would be named to the post to which Burr and his fellow New Yorkers had recommended him. Neither Davis nor Bailey would receive a federal appointment of any sort—and Davis would become the pivotal figure in the rapidly developing strain between the Vice President and his superior.

Jefferson spent much of the spring in Monticello. Burr was in New York City, where he would remain for the most part—dividing his time between Richmond Hill and a town house on Broadway—until shortly after the opening of the first regular meeting of the seventh Congress, toward the close of 1801. In the absence of any word from Jefferson concerning the names on the New York patronage list not yet acted upon, he could only wait and hope for the best. By the end of April the President was back in Washington. Still no word. Burr continued to wait, but less and less patiently with each passing day.

His special concern was Matt Davis. Few men were personally closer to him or more devoted to his political welfare. He wrote Gallatin that "Strange reports are here in circulation respecting Jesuit machinations against Davis . . . The character of Mr. D is in some measure at stake . . . He has already waived a very lucrative employment in expectation of this appointment [as naval officer] . . . his talents for that office are superior to those of any other person who can be thought of." In a postscript he asked Gallatin to let Jefferson see this message. He also wrote General Smith, who was in Washington. He told Smith that Richard Rogers, the Federalist incumbent of the office for which Davis had been proposed, had "called on me . . . I told him, that if asked, I would say that I had heard that he executed the duties of his office with punctuality. Yet every candid man, of whatever party, who is also acquainted with Davis, must allow him to be very, very far superior to R. in every point of fitness for that or any other office . . ." Burr supposed that this message, too, would be shown to Jefferson.

No doubt it was, but it changed nothing, and in September Davis decided to carry his case in person to the President, who was again at Monticello. En route south, he stopped at Washington to see Gallatin and deliver a letter from Burr, explaining that "Mr. D has been goaded into this Journey by the instances of an hundred friends of whom I am not one. Yet I have not opposed it and am rather gratified that he undertakes it." Gallatin was not gratified. He regarded with distaste the speed with which the New York Council of Appointment, dominated by DeWitt Clinton, was emptying state offices of Federalists and filling them with Republicans. This action, he thought, exhibited a "spirit of persecution which . . . disgraces our cause and sinks us on a level with our predecessors." He was not eager to see the incumbent of the naval office or any other Federalist thrown out for exclusively political reasons. Gallatin made his feelings on these matters perfectly clear in a letter that he gave to Davis to deliver to the President at Monticello. "However," he wrote at the end of this public missive, "if Rogers [the incumbent] shall be removed, I have no hesitation in saying that I do not know a man whom I would prefer to Mr. Davis for that office."

No sooner was Davis on his way than Gallatin wrote the President again—a long and private letter which shows that, although its author was not privy to all that Jefferson was thinking, he already sensed on the part of the President an inclination to cut Aaron Burr out of his political will. In this private communication Gallatin warned Jefferson that Burr would regard a rejection of Davis's application as a declaration of war. The Secretary of the Treasury wrote that there were "two points . . . on which I wish the Republicans throughout the Union would make up their mind. Do they eventually mean not to support Burr as your successor when you shall think fit to retire? Do they mean not to support him at next election for Vice-President?"

Had Jefferson chosen to answer these blunt queries, he would have had to say yes to both of them. If he had his wish, the party would not support Burr as his successor. Madison was the man he had in mind for that honor. He had not brought his longtime Virginia friend and neighbor into the Cabinet with the idea that Madison should end his political career at that level. One crown prince was enough. Two was a crowd. Aaron Burr must be got out of the road. To support him for a second term in the Vice Presidency would be a mistake. The colonel was too vigorous, too ambitious, too influential in too many parts of the country. Better that the next Vice President be someone like aging George Clinton—a man too wholly oriented to the interests of his own state, too near the close of his own career, to be a threat to the Virginia Dynasty.

But Jefferson knew better than to confide hopes of this sort to writing. He ignored the Secretary of the Treasury's private communication. Replying to Gallatin's other letter, the one carried to Monticello by Davis, he wrote, on 18 September, that "Mr. Davis is now with me. He has not opened himself. When he does, I shall inform him that nothing is decided, nor can be, till we get together in Washington." And there the matter of Matt Davis may be said to have ended. Federalist Rogers would remain in the naval office of New York until May 1803. At that time he would be replaced, not by Davis, but by Samuel Osgood, a Clintonian who had long since ingratiated himself with the President.

Twice during the journey of Matt Davis to the South and back in September 1801, Burr had written on his behalf to Jefferson. In early November he wrote again. Not until the eighteenth of that month did Jefferson reply. "Your favor of the 10th has been received," he wrote, "as have been those of Sept. 4 and 23 . . . These letters all relating to office, fall within a general rule . . . of not answering letters on office specifically, but leaving the answer to be found in what is done or not done on them." Burr, as he would later point out to his son-in-law, knew what this icy note meant: he was already odd man out in the Jefferson Administration. What he did not know was that six months earlier Jefferson had taken the one step best calculated to reduce his Vice President to the status of an outcast.

3

FOR IF JEFFERSON were paying little heed to the requests of his Vice President, he was paying a great deal to those coming from other sources. The Administration was not yet two months old when Madison was in receipt of a confidential letter, dated 24 April 1801 and written by the Samuel Osgood previously mentioned. Its subject: Burr. Osgood was convinced that during the tie election Burr had tried to get the Presidency for himself. "We have strong evidence," he revealed, that the individuals Jefferson had named to office in New York City "are entirely devoted to the Vice President; and had it been in their Power we have reason to believe Mr. Jefferson would not have been President."

The existence of suspicions that Burr had schemed against him was obviously not news to Jefferson. His *Anas* already contained a choice collection of rumors to that effect. It is impossible to say how much credit Jefferson gave these unproved and unprovable allegations. It is plain that he wanted to believe them. He was aware of Burr's contributions to the Republican victory. He once spoke of the colonel's "exertions and successes" in the winning of New York State as "extraordinary." No doubt it was comforting to him to be able to assume, at an early date, that Burr had tried to snatch the Presidency from his hands. It relieved him of the burden of gratitude. Perhaps he had already determined to act on Samuel Osgood's suggestion that George Clinton be consulted on federal appointments in New York. To no one's surprise, the April elections there had brought the Old Incumbent back into the governorship. He was about to begin his seventh and last term in that position when he received a long and friendly letter from the President.

Jefferson mentioned the three men on the New York patronage list on whom he had not yet acted: Gelston, Bailey, and Davis. He revealed that he had received letters questioning the competence of Bailey and Davis for the positions to which they had been recommended. "Unacquainted myself with these and the other characters in the state which might be proper for those offices," Jefferson explained to Governor Clinton, "and forced to decide on the opinions of others, there is no one whose opinion would command with me greater respect than yours if you would be so good as to advise me, which of these characters and what others would be fittest for these offices."

Thus did Jefferson render Aaron Burr naked to his enemies at home. In the years to come, they would make the most of the opportunity. At any rate, DeWitt Clinton would. "The meekness of Quakerism will do in religion, but not in politics," the master of the craft is said to have remarked.

4

ENSCONCED in the powerful position Burr had helped him to attain, the imperious nephew of the Old Incumbent had made the Council of Appointment of 1801 one that would never be forgotten and had attracted to himself the title of "father of the spoils system." Strictly speaking, DeWitt Clinton had no right to the title. The spoils system had been integral to Empire State politics for longer than any living person could remember. On taking over the governorship from the Republicans in 1796, John Jay had seen to it that most of the state's some seven thousand appointive jobs went to Federalists. When in 1801 the Republicans returned to power, the younger Clinton let it be understood that he had no intention of breaking with so hallowed a tradition. Working side by side with him was his fellow council member, Ambrose Spencer, a once influential Federalist now turned influential Republican. Beginning with the first meeting of the 1801 council in January, Clinton and his friend were indefatigable in their efforts to redistribute the patronage of New York State.

Their only roadblock was Governor Jay, whose term had not yet expired. At a meeting of the council in February, Clinton hurled a challenge at Jay by claiming the right as a member to nominate candidates for appointive posts. Heretofore, save for a brief period, the governor alone had exercised this right, the members of the body limiting themselves to the approval or disapproval of his proposals.

Clinton rested his claim on Article 23, that section of the state constitution under which the council operated. He told Jay that, according to his reading of the article, members had a concurrent right with the governor to make nominations. This was a case of bearing coals to Newcastle. Jay himself had written Article 23. He was not about to let some Johnny-come-lately tell him how to interpret his own words. His response to Clinton's challenge was to refuse to call any more meetings of the Council of Appointment during the remaining four months of his term.

Clinton and Spencer turned to the legislature. They encountered no difficulty in obtaining the passage of a resolution calling for a constitutional convention whose delegates would be empowered to change the wording of Article 23 so as to make clear the right of council members to offer nominations. This step accomplished, DeWitt Clinton had only to bide his time until July, when Jay retired to his Westchester farm and Uncle George, taking his place, set 8 August for a meeting of the council at which the prodigious work of throwing out thousands of Federalists and putting thousands of Republicans into their niches would be started.

Three weeks before this meeting, Burr had written Governor Clinton that "I have not taken the liberty to recommend to you any person for any office . . . and I am not now about to depart from the rule which I have prescribed to myself on this subject; yet a few hints by way of information may not be unacceptable and cannot add to your perplexities." Burr then recommended eight men, including his son-in-law, Bartow Prevost; his close friend and political henchman, William Peter Van Ness; and a man named John Stagg, who had served with him during the Revolutionary War. One studies this communication in vain for a glimpse of the wily, the cunning, the power-greedy Aaron Burr. Against the thousands of jobs at the disposal of the council, his shopping list—the only one he ever submitted to the council—was amazingly modest, a mere squeak amid the howls and yammers for places at the public trough then resounding throughout the state democracy. It was as though Burr realized the fragility of his political position in New York. His power base there was small, a few devoted followers unsupported by any shared political philosophy and held together by little more than the personal magnetism of their leader.

It has been written repeatedly that the Clintons paid no attention to Burr's recommendations. The record shows otherwise. Five of the eight men mentioned in his letter to the governor received appointments: Prevost, for example, as recorder of New York City; Van Ness as a public notary, and Stagg as sheriff of New York County—all valuable posts. The Clintons were seldom clumsy in these matters. The old man, particularly, had a firm grasp on those two useful tools of the politician—a sense of what could be and could not be done, and a sense of when. Burr was still a popular figure in the state. At this time a sweeping interdiction of his followers would have brought protests from highly placed individuals.

Not that the Clintons meant to leave the leadership of the New York democracy in the colonel's hands. During the Presidential election they had stood aside, happy to let Burr break the long stranglehold of the Federalists on the Empire State. Now that it was broken, now that Federalism was no longer a threat, they were determined to gather the reins of power unto themselves. But not all at once, for all at once rarely works in politics; but step by step, subtly.

Already underway was a process that would have the effect of reading Burr out of the Republican Party. If during the remaining months of 1801 the Clinton-led patronage dispensers were less than generous to the Burrites, they were overgenerous to the Livingstons. Jefferson had already taken care of the leader of that far-flung clan. He had sent Robert

R. Livingston to the American embassy in Paris, thus enabling the chancellor to pass the bulk of his final years in a station that would put him in the history books as the chief negotiator of the Louisiana Purchase. Back home, his followers fared well, the Clintons seeing to it that they received a disproportionate share of the more lucrative state positions. The motives behind this strategy are readily guessed. Years before, George Clinton and the chancellor, by pooling their forces, had seriously discomfited the Schuyler–Hamilton faction of New York Federalism. Burr had been a beneficiary of that coalition. It had sent him to the United States Senate. Of this new Clinton-Livingston coalition he was to be the victim.

So far as can be determined, he was still unconscious of the elements marshaling against him when on 13 October the duly elected delegates gathered at Albany to amend the state constitution. Burr, present as a delegate from Orange County, was elected president of the convention. DeWitt Clinton, also a delegate, did not even bother to attend. He had laid his plans well. The reworking of Article 23, to permit members of the Council of Appointment to make nominations, went through with scarcely a dissenting voice. Burr's only recorded comment on the event was that the delegates took "fifteen days" to accomplish what could have been done in "six hours." One can only wonder why he did not use his influence as president of the gathering and Vice President of the United States to try to prevent a change in the New York constitution that enhanced the powers and resources of his enemies. Once more, his unsuspicious nature had led him into error.

5

BY THE TURN of the year, Burr's inferior position on the totem pole of the Jefferson Administration had become a matter of common knowledge. One Federalist wrote another that the Vice President was "completely an insulated man in

Washington; wholly without personal influence." DeWitt Clinton, taking the seat in the United States Senate to which he had been appointed to fill a vacancy caused by resignation, relished the stories that came to his ears. "I find on my arrival here," he wrote a friend back home, "that our opinion of a certain character as formed in N. York is confirmed . . . Little or no consequence is attached to him in the general estimation . . ."

By February, when these letters were written, the seventh Congress had been in session for almost three months. Burr was late in arriving. When on 15 January 1802 he appeared in the Senate and assumed his duties as its president and presiding officer, that body was in the throes of a virulent debate. Only three weeks before the close of the preceding session, the sixth Congress had rushed into law the Judiciary Act of 1801. Designed to effect long-overdue reforms in the national court system, this memorable measure reorganized the federal judiciary and created a number of additional judges and other officers of the court. It was under the aegis of the Judiciary Act that President John Adams spent his last night in office signing the commissions of the so-called "midnight judges."

The virtues of the Judiciary Act were lost on the Republicans, whose leaders had eyes only for the political animus behind its eleventh-hour passage by the last Congress to have a Federalist majority. Thomas Jefferson came into the Presidency convinced that the enlargement of the judiciary represented an attempt by the outgoing Administration to install within *his* Administration a "stronghold" and "battery" of conservatism, from which "all of the works of republicanism are to be beaten down and erased."

In his first message to the national lawmakers he expressed the conviction that the "judiciary system . . . and especially that portion of it recently enacted, will . . . present itself to the contemplation of the Congress." It did, fast. The leaders of his party in the Senate knew an order from the executive when they heard one. On 6 January, Senator John Breckinridge of Kentucky introduced a motion calling for the repeal of the Judiciary Act of 1801. Two days later the historic debate began.

Burr followed its opening salvos in the press. After his arrival in Washington, he listened carefully from the Senate chair. So sparse is our direct knowledge of his political thinking that even second-hand reports on it must be welcomed. James Asheton Bayard purported to have heard the Vice President say openly that he was opposed to most of the projects that Jefferson had outlined in his first message to the Congress, and especially to the President's request for the abolition of all of the internal taxes enacted under preceding Federalist Administrations. On the matter of repealing the Judiciary Act of 1801, he was of two minds. Soon after his arrival in Washington, he called on New York's Federalist senator, Gouverneur Morris. Morris's diary reports Burr as saying that he was tempted to go along with the Federalists on the repealing bill. On the other hand, he could not bring himself to an open break with his party. An honest statement, certainly, assuming Morris's record of it is correct. Always Burr appears to have been as much a Federalist as a Republican in his thinking. Always his natural nonpartisanship, however admirable in theory, rendered him fearful of commitment where the sharper issues dividing the parties were concerned.

Discussing the repealing bill in a letter to son-in-law Joseph Alston, he described himself as "hesitant." Of the "constitutionality of repealing the law I have no doubt," he told Alston. Then, echoing a Federalist argument, he added: "But the equity and expedience of depriving the twenty-six judges of office and pay is not quite so obvious. Read the Constitution and . . . write me how you view the thing." What worried Burr was that the Judiciary Act was now law. Some if not all of the new judges it called for had been appointed. Under these circumstances, was it rightful to rescind the measure in the light of the clause in the constitution that entitled federal judges to "hold their Offices during good behavior," and forbade any diminution of their salaries during "Continuance in office"? Burr sought an opinion on this also from Barnabas Bidwell, a Massachusetts attorney, respected for his grasp of constitutional law. "The *power*. . . to deprive judges of their offices and salaries must . . . be admitted," he conceded in this letter, "but whether it would be *constitutionally moral*, if I may use the expression, and, if so, whether it would be *politic* and expedient, are questions on which I would wish to be further advised."

Such was Burr's frame of mind when in the little chamber of the Senate the motion came to move the bill repealing the Judiciary Act to its second reading. Even when all the senators were in attendance, the majority enjoyed by the Republicans was thin. On this day, 26 January, there were absentees among them. As a result, the vote on the motion was a tie—fifteen to fifteen, a situation the presiding officer had to resolve by giving his casting vote. At stake was an Administration bill, with the prestige of the President riding on it. Of the brief, tense interval before Burr said *Yea*, thus keeping the bill alive, Gouverneur Morris wrote that "there was a moment when the Vice-President might have arrested the measure by his vote, and that vote would, I believe, have made him President at the next election; but there is a tide in the affairs of men which he suffered to go by." Certain it is that if Burr had voted *Nay* that day, the Federalists would have taken him to their hearts, the objections of Alexander Hamilton notwithstanding.

On the following day, 27 January, Jonathan Dayton moved that the "Bill be referred to a select committee, with instructions to consider and report the alterations which may be proper in the Judiciary system of the United States." The New Jersey Federalist called his proposal "conciliatory" in that it would enable both parties to "unite their labors with a view to revise and amend the whole . . . system." The only Republican who had been arguing against repeal, John Ewing Colhoun of South Carolina, endorsed Dayton's remarks. "[I]f the report made by the committee should prove agreeable," Colhoun pointed out, "there would be time enough [in the present session] to bring in another bill. This attempt to harmonize all parties can do no injury, while on the other hand, a system might be framed that gentlemen may be better pleased with than even a repeal of the act."

But the Republicans were not interested in correcting longstanding defects in the national court system, only in pushing the Federalist-sponsored Judiciary Act off the books. When Dayton's motion came on for vote, the Senate divided evenly, as on the preceding day. Again, Burr had to break the tie. Again he voted *Yea*, thus recommitting the repeal bill for appraisal and amendments. "He felt disposed," the record paraphrases his explanation for this decision, "to accommodate the gentlemen in the expression of their wishes . . . to ameliorate the provisions of the bill, that it might be rendered more acceptable to the Senate. He did this under the impression that their object was sincere. He would, however, discountenance, by his vote, any attempt . . . that might, in an indirect way, go to defeat the bill."

It is hard to see how Burr could have spoken more clearly. Hard, indeed, to see how he could have voted other than he did, given his obligation as presiding officer of the Senate to deal as fairly as possible with both sides. From out over the country a few Republican leaders wrote to congratulate him on the evenhandedness with which he had handled matters. But in the upper echelons of the democracy—which is to say, among the reigning Jeffersonians—Burr's actions were not seen in this light. At once the word coursing these elevated demesnes was that by voting to recommit the repeal bill the Vice President had tried to scuttle a crucial Administration measure—an astounding deduction, since, only the day before, he had rescued it from sudden death.

Burr, in short, had done it again. During the tie election his neutral behavior had displeased both parties. Now his vote on Tuesday to save the repealing bill had annoyed the Federalists, and his vote on Wednesday to refer it to a committee, the Republicans. To give a new turn to the old saying that nice guys finish last, it may be argued that fairness was in the process of doing the Vice President in. As John Quincy Adams noted in his memoirs, "The country is so totally given up to the spirit of party, that not to follow blindfold the one or the other is an inexpiable offence."

Recommitting the bill put no obstacles in the path of the Republican repealers. On the contrary, its sojourn in the select committee gave them the time they needed to recoup their decimated forces in the Senate. On 2 February, with one Federalist absent and a previously absent Republican in his seat, Breckinridge had no trouble obtaining passage of a motion that brought the bill onto the floor again. A rapid series of ballots cleansed it of amendments. On 3 February the bill passed the Senate and went on to the House, where a month later the large Republican majority there sent it to the President for his signature.

Thus fell the Judiciary Act of 1801, and Aaron Burr's conduct during the memorable debate over it may now be pointed to as his last attempt to function as a Republican. In the absence of any written clue to his thinking, we can only speculate as to the reasons for his decision at this point to identify himself as an independent. Very likely he was moved by the determination of the Jeffersonians to stigmatize him as having tried to kill the repealing bill, when as a matter of fact he had kept it alive at a critical juncture. It may have occurred to him that loyalty is a two-way street, that since Jefferson had abandoned him, why should he cling to Jefferson. In any event, by the end of February he had decided to leave the party whose ruling faction had long since left him.

Late that month the Federalist members of the Congress

gathered at Stelle's Hotel near the Capitol to celebrate the birthday of George Washington. Gouverneur Morris presided over these "Bachanalian orgies," as a Democratic newspaper described them. Seated with him at the main table, James Asheton Bayard acted as his assistant. The dining was over and the wining well advanced when, in the words of the same Democratic journal, "some *gentle taps* were heard at the door" and a waiter opened it. "Now pause, reader," the newspaper continued, "and imagine, if thou canst, who it was who was thus *supplicating* entrance into this high federal company . . . It was the Vice-President of the United States!"

The organizers of the affair, without informing the rank and file, had asked him to attend. Bayard, in a letter to Hamilton, explained their motives. "We knew," he wrote, "the impression which the coincidence of circumstances would make on a certain great personage; how readily that impression would be communicated to the proud and aspiring lords of the Ancient Dominion; and we have not been mistaken as to the jealousy we expected it would excite through the party."

It has been contended that by accepting this invitation Burr walked into a trap. But it is hard to believe that he had not weighed the risks. When he entered that noisy room in Stelle's Hotel, it was because he had decided that this Federalist celebration was a good platform from which to throw down the gauntlet to the Administration. Noting the expressions of consternation and surprise on the faces before him, he apologized for intruding. Then he asked permission to propose a toast. Permission granted, he lifted his glass to "An *union* of all *honest* men!"

Most of the men who heard Burr that afternoon were puzzled by his words. In the country as a whole, when the incident became known a few weeks later, there was bewilderment. But Thomas Jefferson was not bewildered. He knew what had happened. Burr had offered his leadership, as an independent, not only to the Federalists but also to any Republicans who, like himself, did not believe that all wisdom and goodness resided within the Virginia Dynasty. DeWitt Clinton understood, and the day was near when, with Jefferson's silent blessing and the aid of a New York journalist skilled in the arts of innuendo, he would set out to demolish what remained of the Vice President's crumbling political power. Ahead lay the charge and countercharge of the Pamphlet War of 1802–4.

6

BURR'S CALL for an union of all honest men still lay in the future when toward the end of 1801 John Wood, a Scottish-born mapmaker and journalist, delivered to his printers in New York a five-hundred-page pamphlet entitled *The History of the Administration of John Adams, Late President of the United States*. Aware that the work had been prepared in the Republican interest, Burr obtained a pre-publication copy. Young Wood's *History*, he found, was a pastiche. It consisted for the most part of attacks on Adams and his friends, culled from the Republican press and interspersed with other matter, including "thirty pages of high eulogium" on Burr himself. Sensing that these "low scurrilities" would do the Republican cause more harm than good, Burr advised the publishers, Barlas and Ward, that the book was loaded with libel, some of it actionable. He went further. He proposed to suppress the publication by buying the entire edition, 1,250 copies. Divergent accounts exist as to what came of this maneuver. One has it that Burr kept his part of the agreement but that a couple of Republican editors spirited away one or more copies and printed a new edition from them. By far the weight of evidence indicates that Burr and the publishers quarreled over the amount of the purchase price and that in the end Burr failed to pay. In June, therefore, a bookstore in Maiden Lane offered for sale what seem to have been copies from the original edition. The shop proprietors excised the name of the publisher from the title page and sought to whet public interest in the *History* by advertising it as the work "said to have been suppressed by the Vice-President."

It was this effort to bury an offensive book that triggered the Pamphlet War. It did so by giving another New York journalist, James Cheetham, an excuse for launching a protracted attack on the Vice President that Cheetham had been planning for many months. Like John Wood, Cheetham was a recent immigrant from the British Isles. Of his pre-American career little is known other than that he began his adult life as a hatter in Manchester, England, that he was active in one of the dissident organizations engendered by the emergence of the Industrial Revolution, that he was once jailed on a charge of conspiring to overthrow the government, only to be released for lack of evidence, and that in 1798 an outburst of rioting in Manchester persuaded him to move to America.

Tradition says it was Burr who discovered in the newcomer a way with words and put his pen to work for the Republican cause. Presumably it was with Burr's aid that Cheetham soon after his arrival in New York managed to buy a half interest in a newspaper called the *Argus*. Not quite two years later he merged this journal with another, to become—in partnership with David Denniston, a cousin of DeWitt Clinton—part owner and editor of the *American Citizen*.

During the Presidential election he worked with Burr. When it was over, however, he was quick to sense the shift in the local political winds and to shift with them. By the summer of 1801, New Yorkers were speaking of the *American Citizen* as "Clinton's journal," and it was a common assumption that the relationship of editor Cheetham to DeWitt Clinton was that of a dummy to its ventriloquist.

In December 1801, Cheetham provided Jefferson with a sheaf of notes, headed "some account of the plans and views of aggrandizement of a faction in the City of New York" and listing in outline form most of the denunciations of Burr that the editor of the *Citizen* would begin putting in print six months later. Toward the end of the month, Cheetham was writing to inform the President of Burr's attempt to suppress John Wood's *History*. Thanking the New Yorker for this information in January, Jefferson described the development as "pregnant with considerations," expressed a longing to see a copy of the *History*, and wound up a friendly note with the assertion that "a certain description of persons are so industrious in misconstruing . . . every word from my pen, that I must pray you, after reading this to destroy it." A couple of months thereafter, the President was in touch with Cheetham again, this time to say that "I shall be glad hereafter to receive your daily paper by post as usual . . . I shall not frank this to avoid post office curiosity, but pray you to add the postage to your bill." One gets the impression that Jefferson knew that a scriptorial blast at Burr was in the offing. If so, he was not disappointed. The Vice President was in South Carolina, visiting his daughter, when on 26 May 1802 Cheetham declared in the *American Citizen* that the colonel's attempted suppression of John Wood's attack on Adams was a bid for Federalist support. This charge was not new. The Philadelphia *Aurora* had aired it weeks before. But Cheetham at once followed his short editorial with a long pamphlet called *The Narrative of the Suppression of Colonel Burr of the History of the Administration of John Adams*. In this verbal discharge he claimed that Burr and the Federalists were even now laboring hand in hand to dislodge Jefferson at the next Presidential election.

Over the next two years, Cheetham issued four more anti-Burr pamphlets, simultaneously maintaining a running fire on the Vice President from the columns of his newspaper. His *pièce de résistance* appeared on 22 June 1802, a bludgeoning philippic entitled *A View of the Political Conduct of Aaron Burr, Esq., Vice-President of the United States*. "I have endeavored to represent the character of Mr. Burr in its true light," he announced in the introductory passages of the *View*. "In doing this I have been actuated only by those considerations for the public welfare which every good citizen must feel . . . I have warned the people of an evil of great magnitude: it is for *them* to apply the remedy." His theme sounded, he proceeded to make public for the first time an often privately circulated allegation. "The moment he [Burr] was nominated," Cheetham wrote, "he put into operation a most extensive, complicated, and wicked scheme of intrigue to place himself in the presidential chair. He spent at least one year's salary on *expresses* he sent hither and yon, and he seems to have carried on a *secret* correspondence with the federalists from the period of his nomination."

It is doubtful if a more effective hit-and-run journalist than Cheetham ever spilled ink on paper. He had a genius for the irresistible inference. He reminded his readers that during the election Burr had "spent some weeks in Connecticut" and that his brother-in-law, Tapping Reeve, was one of that state's electors. As Mr. Burr was not a man to "pass his time idly," it was obvious—to Cheetham—that his sortie into the Nutmeg State was for the purpose of persuading Judge Reeve to drop one of the Federalist nominees and give that vote to Burr. On the basis of Burr's known friendship with Anthony Lispenard, one of the New York State electors, he erected a similar story: how arrangements were made for Lispenard and "some other" of the New York electors to "Drop Mr. Jefferson" so as to throw the Presidency to Burr; and how DeWitt Clinton scotched this scheme by letting the electors know that he was aware of their plans, whereupon they all agreed to follow the party command to vote evenly for the two Republican candidates. Cheetham reminded his readers that Burr's stepson, Bartow Prevost, was married to the daughter of Samuel Stanhope Smith, the president of Princeton. In the arithmetic of the incorrigible pamphleteer, these unassailable facts added up to the darkest plot of all. It ran thus: arrangements were made—Cheetham did not say exactly by whom—that if Pennsylvania chose only Republican electors, thus insuring the Presidency to that party, Dr. Smith and one or more of New Jersey's other Federalist electors, knowing their nominees could not win, would vote for Burr. Such were the methods by which Cheetham strove to prove that during the tie election Burr had tried to raise "himself to an eminence to which he was not destined by the voice of the union . . ."

Champions of Burr's cause arose in sundry quarters. John Wood published *A Correct Statement of the Various Sources from Which the History of the Administration of John Adams Was Compiled and the Motives for its Suppression by Col. Burr*. The gist of this pamphlet was that Cheetham's story of the how and why of the attempted suppression was pure fiction. Wood made much of the failure of the author of the *View* to mention that it was he—Cheetham—who had called Burr's attention to the *History* and had intimated that it ought not to see the light of day. Cheetham had charged that the adulatory biographical sketch of Burr in Wood's book rested on data that the colonel himself had supplied. Not so, said Wood. He had indeed called on the colonel, but in vain. That gentleman had refused to talk, and Wood had obtained his information elsewhere. Much of it, he said, came from William Duane, editor of the pro-Jefferson *Aurora* in Philadelphia—a fact, if fact it was, that had not prevented Duane from reprinting from the *Citizen* practically all of Cheetham's animadversions on the Vice President.

Some of the kindest words for Burr appeared in the columns of the *Evening Post*. Strange provenance for them. The *Post* was Hamilton's mouthpiece in New York City, and editor William Coleman cheerfully admitted that he took counsel with the general on all matters of importance. But Coleman had once been Burr's law partner. Sheer personal indignation at the reckless detractions printed in Cheetham's *Citizen* and repeated in Duane's *Aurora* ran through a series of letters signed "Fair Play" and penned by the *Evening Post* editor. "Lie on Duane, lie on for pay," Coleman versified, "And Cheetham, lie thou too;/More against truth you can not say/Than Truth can say against you."

As the Pamphlet War intensified, words often proved insufficient. Deadlier weapons took over. Robert Swartwout, Burrite, fought a duel with Richard Riker, Livingstonian. Coleman, stung by an attack on himself in the *Citizen*, challenged its editor. Cheetham hastened to patch things up by promising to refrain from such attacks in future. A Captain Thompson, harbor master of New York, told people that it was not Cheetham but Coleman who had backed off. Thereupon Coleman called out the harbor master, who was mortally wounded in the ensuing encounter. John Swartwout did not care who heard him say that the real author of Cheetham's effusions was DeWitt Clinton. DeWitt, hearing, pronounced Swartwout "a liar, a scoundrel, and a villain." Swartwout challenged, and the two hotheads repaired to the dueling grounds of Weehawken, where Swartwout suffered two painful wounds in a leg. At the conclusion of the fifth exchange, Clinton refused to fire again and left the field. His parting words, according to subsequent gossip, were: "I don't want to hurt him [Swartwout], but I wish I had the *principal* here."

The "principal"—Burr—was slow to respond to Cheetham's abuses. Too slow. Had he quickly gathered and got into print the persuasive refutations of Cheetham's charges that came to light later, he might have saved a deteriorating political career. But in the beginning the Chesterfieldian gentleman was reluctant to tilt lances with a guttersnipe. Burr knew that Cheetham was a hired pen and an outrageous liar, and naïvely assumed that everyone else knew it too. When his son-in-law insisted on taking to the Southern press on Burr's behalf, the older man tried to discourage him. "As to the publications of Cheetham," he wrote Alston, ". . . it is not worth while to write anything by way of comment or explanation. It will in due time be known what they are, and what is DeWitt Clinton, their . . . instigator. These things will do no harm to me personally." Such was Burr's feeling in July, but by late autumn he was beginning to realize that impressionable minds were falling before Cheetham's pounding sentences like wheat before the scythe. The influential *Albany Register* and other Republican journals, previously skeptical of Cheetham's views, were now endorsing them. Belatedly, Burr saw that he must take steps to protect himself.

On 25 November he presented New York City with another daily newspaper, the *Chronicle Express*, soon to be supplemented by a weekly edition, the *Morning Chronicle*. As the editor for this enterprise he employed Peter Irving, a scholarly young man of such dainty manners that New Yorkers spoke of him as "Miss Irving." A graceful and polished writer, Peter Irving took up his duties with vigor. He obtained and printed letters from David A. Ogden and Edward Livingston in which they denied Cheetham's statements that they had acted as "agents" for Burr in Washington during the House election. He published the only direct rebuttal to Cheetham's maledictions that their target ever brought himself to give to the world. Addressing himself to Governor Joseph Bloomfield of New Jersey, Burr wrote:

> You are at liberty to declare for me, that all those charges and insinuations which aver to intimate that I advised or countenanced the opposition made to Mr. Jefferson pending the late election and balloting for President; that I proposed or agreed to any terms with the federal party, that I assented to be held up in opposition to him or attempted to withdraw from him the Vote or Support of any Man whether in or out of Congress; that all such assertions and intimations are false and groundless.

In this public denial, the only such letter other than his disclaimer letter to General Smith that Burr ever wrote, he did not mention James Cheetham by name. Nor did he mention DeWitt Clinton. Burr had his faults, but character assassination was not among them.

Today Peter Irving's articles in defense of Burr, with their flicks of humor and sarcasm, make convincing reading. But like his younger brother, Washington Irving, the editor of the *Chronicle Express* was a literary man, not a pamphleteer. His low-voiced protestations of Burr's innocence must have seemed thin gruel to readers gorged on the red meat of Cheetham's spectacular condemnations. Not until 1803 did there arise within Burr's camp, and no doubt with his sanction and cooperation, a penman capable of meeting James Cheetham on his own level.

The last month of that year saw the publication of a polemical essay fated to be more widely purchased and more avidly read than any pamphlet issued in America since the appearance of Tom Paine's *Common Sense* on the eve of the Revolution. Its title: *An Examination of the Various Charges Exhibited Against Aaron Burr . . . And A Development of the Characters and Views of his Political Opponents.* Its author, or rather the pen name of its author: "Aristides," after the statesman of ancient Athens whom contemporaries surnamed "The Just." Not until the exchange of insults that was the Pamphlet War had spent itself did the public learn that Aristides was William Peter Van Ness, New York City attorney, federal jurist-to-be, ablest member of Burr's little band, and the man who would serve as his second in the duel with Hamilton. A far better writer than the editor of the *Citizen*, Van Ness brushed off Cheetham's censures of the Vice President as though they were so many dead flies. Hammond, that fair-minded historian, was inclined to believe Cheetham's claim that President Smith of Princeton and other New Jersey electors had agreed to support Burr if Pennsylvania went Republican. But Hammond's grounds for accepting this plot were that Van Ness did not contradict it. As a matter of fact, he did, buttressing his denial of the scheme by publishing a letter from the Princeton head indignantly asserting that neither Burr nor his friends had ever tried to influence Smith or any other Jersey elector.

Van Ness did not limit himself to answering Cheetham's indictments. He named Burr's enemies and laced them up one side and down the other. Although the contents of his vial of venom fell on many, on none did it pour more copiously than DeWitt Clinton. To the mind of that politician Van Ness traced the origin of every mean word minted by James Cheetham. On Clinton he fastened a stunning array of epithets, ranging from "cruel by nature" and "dissolute and desperate" to "an adept in moral turpitude, skilled in all the combinations of treachery and fraud, with a mind matured by the practice of iniquity, and unalloyed with any virtuous principle."

A few months after the appearance of these pronouncements, Burr commenced a suit for libel against Cheetham. For the editor of the *Citizen* there was no novelty in this development. During his short journalistic career—Cheetham was only thirty-eight at the time of his death in 1810—he was the subject of at least fourteen such actions and compelled to pay damages in the vicinity of $4,000. Burr asked no damages. His only purpose in going to court was to obtain depositions from individuals able to testify to the falsity of Cheetham's allegations. James A. Bayard supplied a statement in which he repeated his conviction that Jefferson had won the tie election by entering into terms with the Federalists. Samuel Smith exonerated Burr of the charge of intriguing for the Presidency, but accused him of trying to tamper with the general's statement to that effect. Having gathered these and other depositions, Burr for some reason did nothing with them. Two years later another libel action against Cheetham, a so-called wager suit, brought by some of Burr's friends, ran an identical gamut. Again, the same depositions were gathered from the same people. Again, nothing happened. None of the contents of the various depositions would become public until 1830, by which time Burr would be living in the obscurity of disgrace, his reputation shredded beyond the ability of any legal document to repair.

Van Ness's impressive defense of him did not go unanswered. Cheetham struck back, and the publication in which he did so, *A Reply to Aristides*, brought the Pamphlet War to its conclusion in the opening months of 1804. Van Ness had the satisfaction of having written a best seller and of having earned the reputation of being the "Junius" of his day. But James Cheetham had won the war. Vicious and concentrated as was his attack on Burr, it was no new phenomenon. Thomas Jefferson had been the object of similar outpourings. So had John Adams. But in the coming decades practically all historians would dismiss the invectives against Jefferson and Adams as the exaggerations of a grossly partisan press staffed by men unschooled in the techniques of gathering and sifting evidence. The allegations bestowed on Burr have not enjoyed a like tolerance. To this day, the charge that he intrigued against Jefferson during the tie election crops up repeatedly in accounts of his time and place.

7

INWARDLY, BURR SEETHED at Cheetham's vituperations and at the suffocating limitations of his role in the Jefferson Administration. Outwardly, he remained the unruffled Chesterfieldian he was always at such pains to appear. Commenting on his life in Washington, a Philadelphia newspaper noted that instead of "lodging and boarding . . . at an Inn," as Jefferson had when Vice President, Burr occupied a "handsome suit of rooms" and followed the routines of "a perfect gentleman." If the Jeffersonians saw fit to ignore him, he could ignore them back. "All invitations to drink Toddy and play cards . . . with the Virginians . . . have been declined," the newspaper reported, "and he is not upon terms of familiarity with any one of them." To his son-in-law he wrote that he dined with the President "about once a fortnight" and that "now and then" he saw members of the Cabinet "in the street." He got the impression that they were "all very busy."

His "handsome" lodgings were near the Capitol, and in February 1802 he wrote his daughter that, thanks to congenial neighbors, he hoped to "get through the winter without ennui." His friends, the Laws, lived practically next door. So did Dr. Eustis, come down from Boston to begin his political career as a member of the House of Representatives. Dolley Madison lived but "a mile distant." He saw much of her and of Anna Payne, her sister, whom he described as "a great belle." He entertained often and lavishly. He was diligent in the exercise of his duties as president of the Senate. His only known remark on these chores was that he and the Senate were "content with each other, and move on with courtesy." In truth, Burr reformed the manners of that body. Heretofore, its members had moved about as they pleased, slouched in their seats, and consumed food on the premises. The new Vice President put an end to these schoolboy practices. "Burr presides . . . with great ease and dignity," Federalist Plumer of New Hampshire observed. "He always understands the subject before the Senate, states the question clearly, and confines the speakers to the point. He despises the littleness and meanness of the administration, but does not distinctly oppose them or aid us."

His daughter was now twenty days away from him, but she was never out of his mind. "You know," he wrote her, "that you and your concerns are the highest, the dearest interest I have in this world; one in comparison with which all others are insignificant." She was not fond of politics, so he wrote to her husband of those matters and to her of the comings and goings of old friends in New York, of who was getting married, who having a child; of a "Madame G," a rich widow who had set her cap for him in vain; of a "lady of rank and consequence" who, having traveled to Washington for the express purpose of looking at the Vice President, concluded that "he was the very ugliest man she had ever seen in her life." "How I have labored for three months, working and writing to please a certain lady," he reported to his daughter; "nothing comes but inanity and torpor. I provoke her, and behold the effusions of spirit and genius. Be assured that I shall not speedily relapse into the same error. Indeed I knew all this before; but I thought it was only one's mistress that was to be thus managed—it is sex."

Companionable neighbors notwithstanding, his isolated status in the Administration left him with time on his hands, a maddening situation to a man who hungered for activity. "My life has no variety, and, of course, no incident," he confessed to Theodosia; "to my feelings your letters are the most important occurrences." He scolded when her scrawl was "illegible" or "slovenly." Or when she asked when the Congress was going to "ajourn." Or when she sealed a message on the writing. Surely her rich husband could afford a sheet of paper in which to wrap the letter and avoid this "vulgarism." He was still her teacher. He would remain so as long as she lived.

It was during the restless years of his Vice Presidency that he began to acquire the reputation of being a ladies' man. Numerous women flitted across the pages of his correspondence. Some were matrimonial prospects: Céleste, for one; the virtuous Miss Binney, for another; the wealthy Madame G, for still another. Some were mistresses. In the handling of these delicate affairs, it was the custom of the gentlemen of his day to run errands for one another. When Uncle Pierpont Edwards discovered that one of his women needed a retreat for a second pregnancy, he called on his nephew to take care of matters. Burr, desiring to enroll a protégé in a Boston school, relied on Dr. Eustis to make the arrangements. "The object," he explained, "is to give her the kind of education that may enable her to gain a livelihood, if that should depend on her exertions.

Economy is desirable—but nothing which is done by the patron must be done meanly." Writing from Boston, Eustis kept the Vice President informed of the doings of a Mrs. Werring and of a "reported daughter of B———," couching his communications in such cryptic language as to make it difficult to say whether the women referred to were his responsibility or Burr's. From New Haven, a Mrs. Hayt wrote to remind the Vice President that she was "in a state of pregnancy and In want . . . only think what a small sum you gave me, a gentleman of your connections. I don't wish to crowd you tou hard Because I know your short of money by your small complyments to me. Neither do I wish to expose you. But I would thank you if you would Be so kind as to send me a little money . . ."

Burr had a compulsive desire to see his friends and relatives move on to bigger and better things. No sooner was Dr. Eustis embarked on a political course than the Vice President was plotting a glorious future for him. Hearing that Jefferson was sending Charles Pinckney of South Carolina to the American ministry in Madrid, the colonel wrote posthaste to Boston, urging Eustis to move South and run for Pinckney's seat in the Senate. Even without his medical practice, Burr argued, the doctor could do well financially. He listed the figures for him: "*income* independent of your profession 350 [dollars]; Six months in Congress 1080; allowance for Travelling 270," giving a total of "$1700 which will or ought to support any Batchelor in the United States. During the Six months residence in Washington, you will not, without the aid of gambling, be able to expend more than $600." Very likely the affable Boston physician appreciated Burr's ambitions for him, but he would remain where he was, hold a variety of high public offices, and die while serving in the governorship of Massachusetts. To Burr he was always a good friend and confidant. "Shall A.B. practice law as usual?" the Vice President asked him shortly after inauguration day. "He is simply a citizen when out of the Senate and may do as he listeth, say some. But may he go into the

Courts with the Weight and influence of office and thus Retail out of there? What think you?" Eustis's feelings about this problem were quickly conveyed and quickly acted upon. "You are right about the law," Burr wrote him on 28 April 1801. "It is renounced." It would be many years before the Scarlett of the American bar practiced again.

8

AT THE END OF 1801 he was mailing copies of Jefferson's inaugural address to his son-in-law and calling the younger man's attention to the President's request that the "energies of the men" of the country be "principally employed in the multiplication of the human race." Two months later he was writing to congratulate Alston on the "successful 'exertion of your energies.' " Theodosia was expecting. Burr's mind danced at the prospect of a grandchild. Impatiently he waited for the Congress to rise. Impatiently he headed south when it did. Arriving on a Saturday evening at Clifton on the Waccamaw Peninsula, he discovered that the parents-to-be were not at Oaks, their plantation home. They had gone to their town house in Charleston. In an effort to cover the remaining fifty miles in a day, Burr offered "to engage the whole stage," only to find that it "was full—not even a seat vacant for the vice-president." He rushed a letter to Theodosia by a servant, explaining that "my horses not having arrived, Mr. Alston [the other father-in-law] will . . . set out with me in his curricle." The word from the elder Alston, he added, is that "you are *well*, and your husband *ill*. That is exactly wrong unless he means to take the whole trouble off your hands." Wednesday morning the expectant fathers-in-law were on their way, reaching Charleston in ample time for the birth in mid-May 1802 of the boy who would carry the name Aaron Burr and share with Theodosia the center of his namesake's heart.

The birth of the child left Theodosia unwell, permanently

so, as time would reveal. During the preceding year she and Joseph had escaped the malaria-stricken South Carolina summer by touring the North, stopping at Niagara Falls and at the Canadian home of Joseph Brant, famed chief of the Mohawks and long-standing friend of Theodosia's father. This summer her husband was campaigning for the legislature and unable to travel. He agreed heartily with his father-in-law, however, that Theodosia and the baby should spend what remained of the warmer months up North. On 16 June, accordingly, the Vice President, his daughter and grandson, and Maria, Lady Nisbett, oldest of Joseph Alston's sisters, embarked at Charleston on the brig *Comet*, bound for New York City.

To Theodosia the sparkling countryside at Richmond Hill was soothing, but not curative. Alarmed at her ailing health, Burr arranged for her, the baby, and Lady Nisbett to spend time in the vicinity of the mineral springs at Ballston Spa. And from there Theodosia wrote in desperation to Frances Prevost in New York—a letter that comes as a shock, measuring as it does the dangerous modesty about certain ills of the body then expected of women, even of one as advanced and worldly as Theodosia Burr Alston. "It is unfortunate, Chere Soeur," Theodosia wrote, "that in this wicked world goodness should ever be taxed yet . . . I am . . . going to lay a very heavy tax on your's. You know the disagreeable disorder with which I am tormented." Samuel Bard, her physician in New York, had recommended "partial cold bathing" but "after making use of this prescription for a day or two I was troubled by violent pains beginning sometimes at my back or side and going through me . . . A horrible sensation like a spike running up me worried me all day yesterday . . . Will you, my dear Frances, on pretence of visiting Mrs. Johnston, who has just lain in at her father's . . . see Dr. B and speak to him . . . you need only tell him the effect of his prescription and ask what I must now do . . . I know I am asking you to do a very unpleasant thing, but where can I apply, what can I do . . . ?"

Frances was equal to the burden, obtaining from Dr. Bard an "application" that was temporarily relieving and that brought from the patient a moving note of thanks. "Never, never, my best friend," Theodosia wrote, "shall I forget this mark of your affection. How few women are there who could have risen superior to all that false delicacy in which our sex in general rather pride themselves . . ." In early August, when these words were written, Theodosia and party were en route back to Richmond Hill, where they would remain through November. To Burr it was a joy to have the baby boy around long enough to hear his first lisping attempts at communication. "Gamp" or "Gampy" was as close as the infant could come to saying "Grandpa," and in the years ahead, "Gamp" or some variation of it would be the family's nickname for both of the Aaron Burrs. When in the fall Burr's visitors left him, he gave Theodosia to understand that until they came together again he must have a faithful account of his grandson's every mood and action. He would never tire of hearing about Gamp; nor would he ever be able to restrain himself from reciting the boy's marvelous words and deeds to anyone polite enough to listen. Abigail Adams, encountering him here and there, complained to her sister, Mary Cranch, that on the subject of the addition to his family the otherwise engaging Vice President was a living bore. "You would think to hear him," she wrote Mrs. Cranch, "that no man in the world had ever been a grandfather before."

Watching Gamp grow and flourish was a consolation to a Vice President stricken with a severe case of political falling sickness. Along the way, to be sure, there were other consolations—or, more accurately, distractions. In 1803 his alma mater, Princeton, in the person of Governor Bloomfield of New Jersey, conferred on him the degree of Doctor of Laws, and accepted with gratitude his offer to the college of a portrait of his father—its father, too, for all practical purposes. When shortly thereafter fire swept Nassau Hall, Dr. Burr contributed generously to the rebuilding fund. And so the troubled Vice Presidential years drifted by. But the fires of ambition in him were not dead, only banked; and the sparks began to fly again, from him and between him and his followers, as the year 1804 approached, bringing with it another Presidential election and, in New York State, another gubernatorial election.

15

Tragedy at Weehawken

IN THE OPENING WEEKS of 1804 there was no question in the minds of Republican leaders about the man they wanted at the top of their ticket in the Presidential election of that year. Jefferson's skillful conduct of the affairs of the nation, both at home and abroad, had delighted his supporters. It had also brought a sense of relief to many of his enemies, for the Jacobinic upheaval so dreaded by the Federalists in 1800 had failed to materialize. The peace-loving commander in chief had not hesitated to deploy the navy in the war with Tripoli, the new Republic's first armed encounter with a foreign power. No profane hands had fallen upon the Hamiltonian financial system. On the contrary, Jefferson's Secretary of the Treasury, Albert Gallatin, had turned out to be, if anything, more of a fiscal conservative than the architect of that noble edifice. Never a doctrinaire, the strict-constructionist President had swallowed his principles to authorize the purchase of the Louisiana Territory, an acquisition that, deriving no warrant from the constitution, more than doubled the size of the country and insured to the farmers of trans-montane America the untrammeled use of the Mississippi River. While at Albany, New York, in the famous action for libel against editor Harry Croswell, Alexander Hamilton fought the good fight for a free press, the apostle of civil liberties in the executive mansion in Washington exhibited a marked disinclination to discourage the state courts from prosecuting those who criticized him in print. As one more or less resigned Federalist put it, Jefferson had brought off the Republican revolution in the only way it could be brought off—by leaving largely intact the policies and procedures of Federalism. Under the states-rights Virginian, neither the executive nor the legislative branch of the federal establishment suffered the slightest diminishment. Only where the judiciary was concerned did the President call for a narrow interpretation of assigned powers, vigorously contesting the right of that branch to pronounce on the constitutionality of legislation and dangling over the heads of its luminaries, from Chief Justice Marshall on down, the Damoclean sword of impeachment.

So entrenched was the first democratic President in the hearts and minds of the Republicans in Congress that at caucuses called in early 1804 to plot campaign strategy he was regarded as the given candidate, for whom an official nomination would be an act of supererogation. Only when it came to selecting a Vice Presidential candidate did the Republican lawmakers deem it necessary to convene a formal conclave, complete with nominations and the casting of ballots. Even this process was accompanied by no surprises. In the fall of 1803 Jefferson had learned that George Clinton, serving his seventh term as governor of New York, would not seek another term. Subsequently, the Old Incumbent had found discreet ways of notifying the national leadership that he was both available and willing. It was common knowledge that he looked on the Vice Presidency as nothing more than a "respectable retirement." This attitude made him no threat to the Virginia Dynasty, and at the formal nominating caucus in late February he won out handily over a field of six. Shortly before that meeting, the Congress had passed and Secretary Madison had submitted to the states what in the fall of 1804 would become the twelfth amendment to the constitution, empowering the members of the electoral college to vote separately for President and Vice President. Determined to avoid another tie election and not yet certain when the amendment would be ratified, the Republican nominating caucus created a special committee and charged its members to see to it that Governor Clinton received proper support for the second post but that, when the electors met at the end of the year, Jefferson got a clear majority for the Presidency.

In these developments Aaron Burr had no part. There were no votes for him at the nominating caucus. The Clinton–Livingston coalition and the Jeffersonians had done their work well. The Vice President realized that unless he bestirred himself the end of his term would be the end of his political career. What to do? Where should he turn in an effort to effect a comeback? Months before, he had spoken to Theodosia of a plan to spend a summer touring the "Western Country." He offered no reasons for this interest. Perhaps it was inspired by the belief of friends that were he to settle in one of the frontier states admirers there would send him back to Washington as a representative or senator. Perhaps the outlines of his subsequent filibuster into the Southwest were already taking form at the back of his mind. In any case, by the opening of the Presidential-election year, he had shelved his Western plans. He was eyeing his home state, weighing the pros and cons of running for governor in the April elections, a prospect that took on feasibility when the word leaked out that popular George Clinton would not be a candidate to succeed himself. At home, Burr's followers were buttonholing prominent Federalists, drumming up support for their leader, and on 17 January the Vice President informed the Senate that in the near future he would be spending two or three weeks in New York. During the remainder of that month, however, his actions were those of a man not yet fully committed to the gamble of a gubernatorial race. Before heading north, he solicited a private interview with Jefferson in a last attempt to come to terms with that gentleman. A futile effort, of course; so patently futile that the fact that the colonel made it can be taken as a measure of how desperate he knew his political situation to be.

2

HE HIMSELF LEFT no record of the interview at the executive mansion on the evening of 26 January. We must accept the President's word as to what took place. According to one of the longest entries in Jefferson's *Anas*, Burr recapitulated his life in New York, beginning with his arrival there, "a stranger," and his discovery that the state was "in possession of two rich families (the Livingstons and Clintons); that his pursuits were not political, and he meddled not" until the crisis of 1800 when the ruling families, finding "their influence worn out . . . solicited his aid with the people." That "he lent it without any views of promotion. That his being named as a candidate for Vice-President was unexpected by him," that he had accepted only "with a view to promote my [Jefferson's] fame and advancement, and from a desire to be with me, whose company and conversation had always been fascinating to him." That recently the Clintons and Livingstons, becoming hostile to him, had "excited the calumnies" that had been pouring from the press since the onset of the Pamphlet War. That Burr "believed it would be for the interest of the republican cause for him to retire," but that he shrank from doing so under a cloud, and wanted from Jefferson "some mark of favor . . . which would declare to the world that he retired with my confidence."

The Vice President had laid it on a bit thick. Now it was the President's turn to do likewise. No stranger to the arts of befuddlement, Jefferson was well up to it. He assumed that Burr was fishing for an appointment. Indeed, the colonel had gone back to the months of the tie election to remind Jefferson of the latter's letter expressing regret that Burr's elevation to the Vice Presidency would bar him from a more active station in the Administration. Evidently Burr failed to mention that he had offered to resign the Vice Presidency for such a post. Or perhaps Jefferson preferred to keep that fact off the record. He stressed the impropriety of giving his Vice President an appointment entailing substantial duties, lest the impression go abroad that he was "buying off" the person who, in case of his death, was provided by the constitution to take his place. As for those attacks on Burr in the press, Jefferson said he had noticed them "but as the passing wind." He conceded that he "had seen complaints that Cheetham, employed in publishing the laws, should be permitted to eat the public bread and abuse its second officer; that as to this, the publishers of the laws were appointed by the Secretary of the State, without any reference to me [Jefferson]; that to make the notice general, it was often given to one republican and one federal printer at the same time; that these federal printers did not in the least intermit their abuse of me, though receiving emoluments from the governments, and that I had never thought it proper to interfere for myself, and consequently not in the case of the Vice-President." Running out of rationalizations, Jefferson agreed to take the colonel's request for a "favor" under advisement, and turned the conversation to "indifferent subjects." He then bade his visitor good night and hurried to his desk to record an interview he himself had enjoyed immensely, noting that he was not taken in by Burr's flatteries and that his distrust of the man went back to the very start of their acquaintance.

If before this exchange Burr was in some doubt as to how to proceed, he was now in none. A few days later, with eight inches of snow on the ground and runners replacing the wheels on his coachee, he headed for his home state and the gubernatorial battleground. Reaching New York City on 8 February, he stayed long enough to start his campaign. He then returned to Washington for the rest of a congressional session that would end well ahead of the balloting in New York in late April.

3

HIS PLAN WAS to run as an independent. No other course was open to him. The state Republican machine was in the hands of the Clinton–Livingston coalition. DeWitt Clinton was no longer in Washington. The federal city was too far from the state whose affairs he and his adherents were determined to direct. DeWitt had resigned his seat in the United States Senate to become mayor of New York City, a convenient post for a man bent on turning back Burr's attempt to recoup his political fortunes by seizing the reins of the Empire State.

As their candidate for the governorship the managers of the coalition had picked John Lansing, the able and studious legal light who had succeeded Robert R. Livingston as chancellor of the state. But, a few days after accepting the call, Lansing abruptly withdrew. His announced reason for this action was that he had taken the nomination solely in the interests of bringing together all the factions of New York Republicanism but that "subsequent events have induced me to believe that my hopes on this subject were too sanguine." Later it would come out that the Clintons had given the chancellor to understand that, were he elected, they and not he would continue to run the state—a prospect that had no appeal to independent-minded John Lansing. When he withdrew, the coalition bosses replaced him with mild-mannered Morgan Lewis, member by marriage of the Livingston clan and a man whose political career to date had been that of a time server, always ready to bow to the wishes of the faction in power.

On the evening of 16 February the Federalist leaders of the state gathered in the banquet hall of Lewis's City Tavern in Albany. The lively session that followed was supposed to be a secret, but two Burrites had hidden themselves in an adjoining bedroom. Next day's edition of the *Morning Chronicle* in New York would carry a full report of the proceedings. A knotty problem occupied the minds of the assembled party leaders. So poorly had the Federalists fared in recent New York elections that no prominent figure among them wanted to offer himself as a gubernatorial candidate. They came together now to decide a burning question. Should they persuade one of their own to run, or should they tie their fortunes to Colonel Burr?

Hamilton was there. Everyone present knew that when his time came to talk he would rehash his old charges against Burr. Presumably they also knew that this meeting was a critical one to the man who had once been termed the colossus of the Federalists but who was their colossus no longer. Hamilton's published attack on John Adams in 1800 had split the party and in so doing had reduced his status in it to that of a venerated but impotent elder statesman. The present gubernatorial election had the same significance for him that it had for Burr. He, too, was struggling to come back, to regain the unquestioned leadership that had once been his. The man who had first drawn public attention to himself by an impromptu speech in the "fields" or commons of New York City came to the February 1804 conference in Albany with his remarks carefully written out. They were not all of a piece. Consistency was no hobgoblin to that brilliant mind. On the one hand, he accused Burr of having no principles, political or moral. On the other hand, he warned that were the colonel elected governor he would "endeavor to rise to power on the ladder of Jacobin principles."

Hamilton was already aware of a subterranean attempt by New England Federalists to escape the Jeffersonian yoke by separating the Northeastern states from the rest of the country. He was aware, too, that the fomenters of this movement had made overtures to Burr. Putting these two facts together—the secession plot and Burr's knowledge of it—some historians have pictured Hamilton's harangue at Albany as a valiant attempt to preserve the Union by preventing the return to power of a man intent on tearing it apart. But this interpretation of Hamilton's remarks would seem to be at odds with his avowed objection to secession as enunciated in the next-to-last letter he ever wrote. "Dismemberment of an Empire," he told Theodore Sedgwick in that remarkable document, "will be a dear sacrifice of great positive advantages, without any counterbalancing good; administering no relief to our real Disease; which is *Democracy*, the poison of which by subdivision will only be the more concentered in each part, and consequently the more virulent." The speech that Hamilton read in Albany yields no statement that can be tortured into a determination on his part to save the Union. It was a plea to save Federalism. Not yet aware that John Lansing had withdrawn from the race, Hamilton called on his auditors to support the chancellor in preference to Burr. "Lansing's personal character," he said, "affords some security against pernicious extremes, and at the same time, renders it certain that his party, already much divided and weakened, will disintegrate more and more, until in a recasting of parties the Federalists may gain a great accession of force." What frightened him about Aaron Burr was not the latter's sins but his strengths. "At any rate," Hamilton declared, "it is wiser to foster schism among Democrats, than to give them a chief better able than any they have yet had, to unite and direct them." Having paid Mr. Burr this compliment, the general desisted. Later he would come out as boldly for Morgan Lewis. As Burr pointed out to his daughter, Hamilton was "for any candidate who can have a chance of success against A.B."

The members of Hamilton's audience in Albany listened to him with all the respect due to a fallen leader. They had heard his strictures on A.B. too often. His song of hate had become a jangle to their ears. The consensus, when they broke up, was that in this election Aaron Burr was their man. Let the word be spread. One of their number, a member of Congress from Herkimer County, undertook to spread it in a letter to the press. Only by the election of Burr, the congressman argued, could the stranglehold of the democracy on New York State be broken. As for General Hamilton's objections, the letter writer urged his fellow Federalists to ignore them as a case of "personal resentment."

On the evening of 18 February, "a numerous . . . meeting of Republicans . . . at the Tontine Coffee-House" in Albany nominated Burr. Two days later, at Mechanics Hall in New York City, another group endorsed him, and during the ensuing weeks similar actions occurred in almost every county of the state. Watching these activities from Washington, New Hampshire's Senator Plumer, originally convinced that the Vice President was on a wild-goose chase, changed his mind. He decided Burr would have the votes of most of New York's Federalists and of a respectable portion of its Republicans. With this backing, he might win. Hamilton, in a cry of despair to Rufus King, pointed out that, with George Clinton lost to the Vice Presidency, the colonel's chances were good. DeWitt Clinton voiced similar fears to his uncle and continued to voice them in the face of the older man's assurances that Burr would be roundly defeated.

DeWitt would have been even more worried had he known that from outside the state Burr's candidacy was being pushed by influential Federalists. Behind this development lay that secret and short-lived conspiracy, the New England secessionist movement. In the early 1790's, Senator William Maclay of backwoods Pennsylvania had predicted that once the government was established on the shores of the Potomac it would come under new influences and that the New Englanders would then turn "refractory" and try to "unhinge" it. Maclay's understanding of the mind and temperament of New England led him to believe that the Federalists of that region would "endeavor to subvert" any government they could not manage.

A prescient prophecy. In 1804 some of the Federalist

leaders in New Hampshire and Connecticut were doing precisely that. Other members of their party might take comfort in the essential conservatism of the Jefferson Administration. Not they. What haunted their dreams and left them no peace was the emergence of the Old Dominion as the dominant state in the Union. Add to this their conviction that the acquisition of the Louisiana Territory forecast a shift of power from the industrial East to the agricultural South and West, a movement certain in their opinion to fasten the incubus of Virginia on their backs for years to come. Seeing no legitimate way around the problem, they resolved among themselves to try to separate New England from the rest of the Union. But the states of that area were small and few. Maintenance of the Federalist confederacy they envisioned might prove impossible unless New York, with its identical commercial leanings, could be persuaded to join.

Hence their interest in seeing Burr in the governor's chair. No man in the country had suffered more from the Jeffersonians. None, they reasoned, had a better cause for sympathizing with disunionist aims. They sounded him out, half a dozen or more of them dining with him in Washington during the opening weeks of 1804. On hand at this meeting was Senator Timothy Pickering of New Hampshire, generally regarded as the father of the secession scheme. Among the others were Senators James Hillhouse and Uriah Tracy of Connecticut, Representative Roger Griswold of that state, and Pickering's colleague, Senator Plumer, who two decades later, having meanwhile turned Democrat, would describe his adherence to the secession plot of 1804 as the greatest political mistake of his life. At the dinner meeting in Washington, Hillhouse told the Vice President that the United States "would soon form two distinct & separate governments." Some of the others said the same. All listened carefully to Burr's comments, and Senator Plumer left the meeting under the delighted impression that the Vice President "not only thought *such an event would take place—but that it was necessary it should.*" But in the quiet of his own quarters Plumer suffered a change of mind. Thinking back over the colonel's contributions to the conversation, he was compelled to conclude that "nothing that he said . . . necessarily implied his approbation of Mr. Hillhouse's observations," and that "perhaps no man's language was ever more apparently explicit, & at the same time so covert & indefinite."

Apparently, Plumer's fellow conspirators were equally uncertain as to whether the Vice President was with them or not. Roger Griswold took the issue up with the colonel again. Describing this conversation to Oliver Wolcott, the Connecticut congressman said that Burr spoke "in the most bitter terms of the Virginia faction, and of the necessity of a union at the northward to resist it; but what the ultimate objects are which he would propose, I do not know." Griswold added that he still harbored hopes of smoking the colonel out. "I have engaged to call on the Vice-President as I pass through New York," he told Wolcott. "He said he wished very much to see me, and to converse, but his situation in this place [Washington] did not admit of it, and he begged me to call on him at New York . . . I do not see how he can avoid a full explanation with Federal men. His prospects must depend on the union of the Federalists with his friends, and it is certain that his views must extend much beyond the office of Governor of New York. He has the spirit of ambition and revenge to gratify, and can do but little with his 'little band' alone."

In New York, Griswold talked with Burr at the latter's house on 4 April. Griswold pressed hard in the hopes of getting from the Vice President a commitment to the secession movement. But all the Connecticut congressman got was Burr's assertion that "he must go on democratically to obtain the [state] government; that, if he succeeded, he would administer it in a manner that would be satisfactory to the Federalists. In respect to the affairs of the nation, Burr said that the Northern

States must be governed by Virginia or govern Virginia, and that there was no middle course."

Obviously New York's independent gubernatorial candidate was buttering up the Federalists at every opportunity. After all, he was fighting for his political life. But his saying that either Virginia must rule or the Northern states must rule and that "there was no middle course" strongly suggests that he did not look on secession as a feasible procedure. What other "middle course" could he have had in mind? The New England disunity movement had few supporters. Hamilton had spurned the idea. So had Rufus King, already quietly emerging as Federalism's national leader. So had those high-flying Federalists of Massachusetts, collectively spoken of as the Essex Junto. It is hard to believe that had Aaron Burr been elected governor of New York he would have risked the loss of his newly retrieved political stature by going along with a movement sanctioned by a handful of men in two Northeastern states.

In any event, his views on the matter were never to be put to the test. Congress rose on 27 March, and on the next day Burr was writing Theodosia from New York that "They are very busy here about an election between Morgan Lewis and A. Burr. The former supported by the Livingstons and Clintons, the latter per se." The give-and-take of the battle was tumultuous. Not that any principles were aired. A stranger chancing upon the mayhem would have been hard put to say what the regular Republicans believed as distinct from the Burrites. No issues of any substance were permitted to spoil the fun. Pro-Burr broadsides hailed the Vice President as a man unburdened by family dependents, simultaneously listing the sundry state offices held by the Livingstons and the Clintons and declaring the combined salaries from these to be stupendous. Anti-Burr broadsides dwelt at length on the colonel's affairs with women, the implication seeming to be that mistresses, too, can be expensive. Both sides claimed to have the blessing of President Jefferson, although neither could point to any public statements to that effect. In the *American Citizen*, Cheetham surpassed himself. One of his charges was that Burr had seduced a buxom wench during a "nigger ball" hosted by a black servant at Richmond Hill. Hamilton's newspaper, the *Evening Post*, supported Burr. Curious but understandable. Its editor, Coleman, still admired the Vice President, and Hamilton, vigorously defending the right of another editor to criticize a President, was hardly in a position to dictate to his own.

Coming and going from Burr's headquarters in John Street, New York, the members of his little coterie sought backers wherever they could find them. William Peter Van Ness, the talented Aristides of the Pamphlet War, dispatched a fervent letter to Kinderhook in upstate New York in the hopes of winning an endorsement from his fellow lawyer and onetime law clerk, Martin Van Buren. At the age of twenty-two, Van Buren was already exhibiting the finesse that in time would make him President of the United States and prompt disgruntled opponents to circulate the whisper that he was the natural son of Aaron Burr. "You know," Van Ness wrote this engaging young man, "that Mr. Burr is the intended victim of . . . persecution against which it is the duty of every friend of freedom to sustain him . . . I wish you to reflect maturely before you take a side." But Kinderhook's sagacious young politico had already given the matter "the most mature passionate reflection" and, although not wishing "to be understood as . . . embracing the truth or falsity of the Charges" against Burr, had concluded that support for him "would not under existing circumstances be proper." So much for filial gratitude, if any were due.

Burr was not optimistic about the outcome. As the balloting got underway, he wrote Theodosia from his New York City headquarters that "there never was, in my opinion, an election the result of which so little judgment could be formed." The polls opened on 24 April and closed on the twenty-sixth. Five days later the results were known: 30,829 for Lewis; 22,139 for Burr, giving the regular Republican an almost 9,000-vote margin and Burr the heaviest defeat suffered as of that date by a New York gubernatorial candidate. Hamilton, it would appear, had wrought better than the cool response to his remarks at the Federalist conclave in Albany had indicated. A comparison of the returns with those for state senators the year before shows that, for every Republican who voted for Burr, a Federalist, influenced by Hamilton, voted for Lewis. As for Burr, his political career was over, and it remained for John Randolph of Roanoke to pronounce the epitaph. "The storm in New York," observed that brilliant and eccentric Virginian, "is thoroughly allayed, never to rise again from the same quarters, or rather from the same men."

4

BUT THE STORM within Aaron Burr was not allayed. He wrote Theodosia that the "election is lost by a great majority: *tant mieux*," but the blitheness that continued to invest his correspondence and behavior was skin deep. Underneath was a growing anger at those he held responsible for his downfall —and a growing desire to get back at them. But how was he to accomplish that? The result of the April elections had deprived him of his last chance of overpowering his enemies in the political arena. His only legal recourse, his libel suit against Cheetham, gave him no satisfaction. In his mind Cheetham was unimportant, a hired hand, a mere creature of the powerful forces at whom Burr yearned to strike. Only one route lay open to him: a resort to what was interchangeably thought of as the gentleman's code or the code duello.

As a prologue to the tragedy about to take the stage, a few words concerning the nature and extent of this ancient practice in nineteenth-century America: in the New World, so far as can be determined, no written rules governed the "private combat seul à seul." Presumably the twenty-six commandments of the Irish code duello of 1777 prevailed, with local variations. Choice of weapons fell to the individual challenged, although a change could be effected if the challenger protested a lack of skill with the weapon proposed. Each party to the ordeal selected a second, whose tasks were to make the arrangements, see that the duel itself was conducted fairly, and take the place of his principal if unavoidable circumstances prevented that individual from reporting to the field of honor at the appointed hour. Custom required the presence of at least one physician, who stationed himself within calling distance but far enough away to be able to testify in court that he had not witnessed the engagement.

Although public opinion was already stirring mightily against what Jefferson termed "the most barbarous of appeals," dueling was widespread—and durable. Even the hue and cry over the death of Hamilton would not put a stop to it. In the 1820's, devotion to the code would lead Andrew Jackson into a number of duels. As late as 1928, members of the town council of Vienna, Virginia, women as well as men, would still be required to sign an oath prescribed by the state constitution, asserting that "I have not, while a citizen of this state . . . fought a duel with a deadly weapon, or sent or accepted a challenge." Burr had called out John Barker Church. Hamilton had stood second in one duel, had come close to being the principal in two others, and had lost a son in one of the many fatal encounters at Weehawken. New York State law made dueling a crime, but a variety of devices existed for getting around the edict. If the affair called for preliminaries in writing, it was referred to as the "interview." As both the giving and the taking of a challenge were illegal, those actions were referred to as the delivery and the reception of the "message." For the actual combat, most New Yorkers betook themselves to the New Jersey side of the Hudson River. Some, however, did not bother to leave the state. William Coleman and his adversary, for example, simply repaired to a little-traveled lane on the outskirts of New York City, trusting to popular disregard of the law to shield them from its wrath. When Brockholst Livingston mortally wounded his adversary, one Jemes Jones, a coroner's jury pronounced him guilty under the law, but the records show no further action against him. According to a Livingston-family genealogist, "the Federalist newspapers held Mr. Jones up as a martyr to their cause, while denouncing his opponent as a murderer. But in those days duels were of constant occurrence and no man was considered to have suffered in reputation because he had 'killed his man.' "

None, that is, except Aaron Burr. But as Senator Plumer observed, the colonel was "a very extraordinary man, & . . . an exception to all rules." Two or three months before the gubernatorial election he had told his friend, Charles Biddle of Philadelphia, that he was determined to call out "the first man of any respectability concerned in the infamous publications concerning him." When these words were spoken, what respectable man did Burr have in mind? Jefferson? DeWitt Clinton? Hamilton? A challenge to Jefferson or Clinton, as the main authors of his problems, would have been logical. As for Hamilton, Jefferson's report of his talk with Burr at the Executive Mansion in January 1804 quoted the Vice President as saying flatly that Hamilton had "written some of the pieces" that had been published "against him." Whether this were true or not cannot be said. The colonel thought it was, and earlier that month the ineffable Cheetham, in his newspaper, had asked: "Is the Vice-President sunk so low as to submit to be insulted by General Hamilton?" Whoever Burr had in mind when he talked with Biddle, a few intemperate utterances by the general during the ensuing election campaign, to say nothing of the "divinity that shapes our ends," decreed the course of events.

5

HAMILTON'S REMARKS were made at a dinner party at the home of Judge John Tayler of Albany. One of the guests was Tayler's son-in-law, Dr. Charles D. Cooper, who in two subsequent letters described the conversation. The first of the doctor's letters, dated 12 April 1804, was to Andrew Brown, an Albany merchant residing at the nearby town of Berne; the second, dated 23 April, to Hamilton's father-in-law, Philip Schuyler. Both found their way into the columns of the *Albany Register*. Burr may or may not have seen the first letter. He definitely saw the published version of the second one, a letter in which Dr. Cooper wrote that "Gen. HAMILTON and Judge KENT have declared, in substance, that they looked upon Mr. Burr to be a dangerous man," and that "I could detail to you a still more despicable opinion which General HAMILTON has expressed of Mr. BURR."

We have Burr's own account of what went through his mind when his eyes fell on that word "despicable." It is contained in a letter to Charles Biddle, written after the duel, a letter that answers the often-raised question of how aware the colonel was of Hamilton's private attacks on him over a fifteen-year period. Hamilton, Burr pointed out to his Philadelphia friend, "had a peculiar habit of saying things improper and offensive in such a manner as could not well be taken hold of. On two different occasions, however, having reason to apprehend that he had gone so far as to afford me fair occasion for calling on him, he anticipated me by coming forward voluntarily and making apologies and concessions. From delicacy to him and from a sincere desire for peace, I have never mentioned these circumstances, always hoping that the generosity of my conduct would have had some influence on him. In this I have been constantly deceived . . ." Twice in the past, in other words, Burr had considered challenging the general. Twice he had forborne. But when his eyes fell on the newspaper clipping of Dr. Cooper's second letter, "it became impossible that I could consistently with self-respect again forbear."

On 18 June he initiated the procedures that would take him and Hamilton to Weehawken. During the next several days a series of communications, some written and some oral, passed between them. William Peter Van Ness acted as Burr's messenger and second. Another New York attorney, Nathaniel Pendleton, performed these services for Hamilton. Accompanied by the newspaper clipping of Dr. Cooper's letter, Burr's opening communication was brief and pointed. Asserting that Cooper's letter, "though apparently published some time ago," had only recently come to his attention, he requested an "acknowledgment or denial" of the "still more despicable opinion" of himself that it attributed to Hamilton.

Hamilton's reply, penned two days later, was long and argumentative. He took the position that Burr was asking the impossible. How could he admit or deny "a still more despicable opinion" without knowing what it was, "to whom" it was said, and "when, or where?" He stood ready, he wrote, "to avow or disavow promptly and explicitly any precise or definite opinion, which I may be charged with having declared . . . More than this cannot fitly be expected from me; and especially it cannot reasonably be expected, that I shall enter into an explanation upon a basis so vague as that which you have adopted. I trust, on more reflection, you will see the matter in the same light with me. If not, I can only regret the circumstances, and must abide the consequences."

Burr found this answer evasive. He was particularly incensed at the presence in it of a dissertation on the meaning of the word "despicable." There was no question in his mind as to what that term signified. Responding promptly to Hamilton's letter, he pointed out that political opposition did not "absolve Gentlemen from the Necessity of a rigid adherence to the laws of honor and the rules of decorum," and that the "Common sense of Mankind" affixed to the word "despicable" "the idea of dishonor." The point, he added, was that the word "has been publicly applied to me under the sanction of your Name. The question is not whether he [Cooper] has understood the Meaning of the word or has used it according to syntax and with grammatical accuracy, but whether you have authorised its application directly or by uttering expressions or opinions derogatory to my honor . . . Your letter has furnished me with new reasons for requiring a definite reply."

On 22 June, Van Ness carried this communication to Hamilton, who read it in his visitor's presence. His comment on it, as paraphrased by Van Ness, was that Hamilton "had hoped that the answer he had returned to Col Burr's first letter would have given a different direction to the controversy, that he thought Mr Burr would have perceived that there was a difficulty in his making a more specific reply, & would have desired him [Hamilton] to state what had fallen from him that might have given rise to the inference of Doctor Cooper. He would have done this frankly, & he believed it would not have been found to exceed the limits justifiable among political opponents. If Mr. Burr should upon the suggestion of these ideas be disposed to give a different complexion to the discussion, he was willing to consider [Burr's] . . . last letter not delivered; but if that communication was not withdrawn he could make no reply and Mr. Burr must pursue such course as he would deem most proper."

Urged by Hamilton to address himself to the matter at hand, Van Ness, to continue with his account of the conversation, replied that "I would detail these ideas to Col Burr; but added that if in his first letter" Hamilton had "introduced the idea (if it was a correct one) that he could recollect the use of no terms that would justify the construction made by Dr. Cooper it would in my opinion have opened a door for accomodation. General Hamilton then repeated the same objections to this measure which were stated in substance in his first letter to Col Burr."

Thus, for the duration of a brief conversation, did the possibility of an "accomodation" flicker—and go out. Had Hamilton at this point denied maligning Burr's honor in the presence of Dr. Cooper, the duel might have been averted. By electing to stand on his first letter to Burr, he let the opportunity slip.

Informed of this fact, orally by Van Ness and in writing by Hamilton, Burr could only assume that the refusal of the latter to deny having uttered a "despicable opinion" of him at the Albany dinner party meant that he had done so. Angered by what he deemed "a sort of defiance" on Hamilton's part, Burr broadened the scope of the controversy. On 25 June, through Van Ness, he demanded "a General disavowal of any intention on the part of Genl Hamilton in his various conversations to convey impressions derogatory to the honor of Mr Burr."

At this point Hamilton was hoist on his own petard. In scores of letters to close friends he had heaped "depredations" on Burr's "fame and character." Were he now to comply with the colonel's request for a blanket disavowal of these slanders, he would have become the laughingstock of the very men whose respect he must have were he to regain his onetime status as their political mentor. He had no choice but to refuse to make such a disclaimer, but he now expressed a willingness to take advantage of Burr's original offer. To Pendleton, for perusal by Burr, he dictated a statement saying that "In answer to a letter properly adapted to obtain . . . a declaration Whether he had charged Col. B. with any particular instance of dishonorable conduct . . . He would be able to answer consistently with . . . the truth in substance, That the conversation to which Doctor Cooper alluded, turned wholly on political topics." This declaration came too late, the loophole that Burr had once given to Hamilton was no longer available. The Vice President stuck to his insistence on a comprehensive disclaimer, and on 27 June the negotiations arrived at their inescapable conclusion. Burr challenged and Hamilton accepted, requesting only that the encounter be postponed until such time as he could take care of certain legal and personal matters. Subsequently, the two seconds set the date for 11 July, chose Weehawken as the place, and drafted a few rules for the conduct of the duel.

6

DURING THE NEGOTIATIONS and during the interval between the acceptance of the message and the interview, the two principals and their seconds went about their lives as usual. So far as is known, no whisper of the impending encounter went abroad.* Meeting occasionally on the streets of New York, Burr and Hamilton maintained their wonted courtesy. When Theodosia's birthday, 23 June, came around, the fact that she was hundreds of miles away did not prevent her father from celebrating it at Richmond Hill. He invited friends in. Together they "laughed an hour and danced an hour, and drank to her health." He was a member and Hamilton was president of the elite organization set up in the post-war era by one of the officers of the Revolution, the Society of the Cincinnati. Both were present for the Fourth of July banquet. Hamilton, in high spirits, leaped onto the table and sang a song. Burr had little to say, and departed early.

On the day before the duel, Burr wrote at some length to his daughter. "Having . . . given my private letters and papers in charge to you," he began, "I have no other directions to give you on the subject but to request you to burn all such as, if by accident made public, would injure any person. This is more particularly applicable to the letters of my female correspondents." He had little or nothing to leave anyone. "My estate will just about pay my debts and no more," he explained. "I mean, if I should die this year. If I live a few years,

* In a genealogy published in 1910, a descendant of some of Burr's kin by marriage recounted a strange tale. He wrote that, during the "prolonged interval" prior to the meeting at Weehawken, one of his ancestors, Samuel Bradhurst, learned of the impending combat and in an effort to protect his friend Hamilton provoked a duel with Burr, in the course of which Bradhurst suffered "a sword-wound . . . in the arm or shoulder." No corroboration for this family tradition has ever been unearthed. See A. Maunsell Bradhurst, *My Forefathers: Their History from Records and Traditions*, 64–65.

it is probable things may be better." He asked her to distribute certain personal items to Nathalie, his adopted daughter, to Dr. Eustis and others; and to see to it that a "small lot . . . worth about two hundred and fifty dollars" be conveyed to one of his slaves. As for the "seal of the late George Washington," good friends had presented that to him and "You may keep it for your son, or give it to whom you please." To the addressee of this letter went these earnest words: "I am indebted to you, my dearest Theodosia, for a very great portion of the happiness which I have enjoyed in this life. You have completely satisfied all that my heart and affections had hoped or even wished. With a little more perseverance, determination, and industry, you will obtain all that my ambition or vanity had fondly imagined. Let your son have occasion to be proud that he had a mother. Adieu. Adieu."

Writing to his son-in-law on the same day, Burr was more circumstantial. "I have called out General Hamilton, and . . . Van Ness will give you the particulars," he apprised Alston in a letter containing instructions for the handling of his property and debts. "If it should be my lot to fall . . . yet I shall live in you and your son. I commit to you all that is most dear to me—my reputation and my daughter." Even in this moment of crisis and uncertainty, Burr remained the educator. He entreated his son-in-law to "aid Theodosia in the cultivation of her mind." Let her "presently acquire a critical knowledge of Latin, English, and all branches of natural philosophy." In time, he advised Alston, "all this would be poured into your son. If you should differ with me as to the importance of this measure, suffer me to ask it of you as a last favour."

Hamilton, too, put his affairs in order. He drew up his will and a statement of his holdings and obligations. He wrote a letter to be opened by his wife in the event of his death. He drafted a series of "Remarks" on the impending interview. It was in this paper that he enunciated his *mea culpa*, pointing out that "it is not to be denied, that my animadversions on the political principles, character and views of Col. Burr have been extremely severe, and on several occasions I, in common with many others, have made very unfavourable criticisms on particular instances of the private conduct of this gentlemen." It was in this paper, too, that he recorded his determination to withhold his fire during the opening rounds of the encounter. "My religious and moral principles," he asserted, "are strongly opposed to the practice of Duelling . . . As well because it is possible that I have injured Col. Burr . . . as from my general principles and temper . . . I have resolved . . . to *reserve* and *throw away* my first fire, and *I have thoughts* even of *reserving* my second fire—and thus give a double opportunity to Col. Burr to pause and reflect." How much happier our memories of Hamilton would be had he either acted on his principles by rejecting Burr's challenge or kept these thoughts to himself.

7

THE DAY OF THE DUEL, a Wednesday, dawned hot and muggy. Burr was still sleeping when John Swartwout and other friends arrived at Richmond Hill at an early hour to see him off and await his return. Only Van Ness and a hired oarsman accompanied him across the river to a narrow ledge in the heights of Weehawken on the Jersey shore. By prearrangement, he and his second were the first to set foot on the field of honor. They were clearing sticks and stones from the ground when Hamilton and Pendleton arrived, David Hosack, the New York physician who had come with them, placing himself at a discreet distance.

At approximately seven o'clock the seconds initiated the ceremonies they had formulated for the occasion. They counted off the ten paces agreed upon, and cast lots to see which principal would have the choice of position and which second give the commands. They loaded the pistols in the presence of one another. Hamilton had brought these. He had borrowed them from his brother-in-law, John B. Church, who had purchased them in England. "Of admirable workmanship and bearing the name, Wogden," they had nine-inch barrels, concealed hairsprings or single-set triggers, weighted bronze fore-ends, adjustable front and rear sights, and .54 caliber bores. According to a modern gun expert, none of these features belonged "on a proper set of dueling pistols." Even so, Church had used them for that purpose in England. It is believed that they also had seen use in two earlier American duels, the one between Church and Burr in 1799 and the one in which Hamilton's son, Philip, lost his life in 1801.

As the principals at Weehawken were in the act of receiving their weapons from the seconds, Pendleton asked Hamilton "if he would have the hair spring set?" Later Pendleton would cite his friend's answer, "*Not this time*," as one of several indications that Hamilton had held to his resolve to refrain from firing on the first round. But, during the few seconds after the command to fire sounded, both pistols went off. The ball from Burr's weapon hit Hamilton in the abdomen. That from Hamilton's gun went wide of his opponent and snapped the limb of a tree twelve feet up.* After the duel, the exact sequence of events would be the subject of much controversy. Van Ness and Burr insisted that Hamilton fired first and *at* his opponent. Pendleton disagreed. He contended that Hamilton's pistol discharged accidentally, probably as the result of "an involuntary exertion of the muscles" when Burr's bullet struck him. Time has stripped the old quarrel of its sharpness. All that merits emphasis at this late date is that Aaron Burr went to Weehawken in good faith. He comported himself there in accordance with the rules of the code duello. He had no way of knowing, as Pendleton did, that Hamilton had expressed an intention

* For the speculation of an authority on guns that the hair trigger on Hamilton's pistol *was* set, and that it was the use of this tricky mechanism that made his shot go wild, see Merrill Lindsay, "Pistols Shed Light on Famed Duel," *Smithsonian*, VII (Nov. 1976), 94–97.

of reserving his first fire, and when that fact became public, he was appalled. "Contemptible disclosure, if true," he told Charles Biddle.

When Hamilton fell, mortally wounded, Burr started toward him "with a manner and gesture that appeared" to Pendleton to be "expressive of regret." But Van Ness, "with a view to prevent his being recognized by the Surgeon and Bargemen who were then approaching," at once seized his principal and hustled him down the stony path to the boat which would bear them back to Richmond Hill. There, surrounded by friends, Burr waited for news. Learning that Hamilton had been brought across river and was at the home of his merchant friend, William Bayard, in Greenwich Village, he sent a message to the surgeon. "Mr. Burr's respectful Compliments," it read. "He requests Dr. Hosack to inform him of the present state of Genl. H. and of the hopes which are entertained of his recovery. Mr. Burr begs to know at what hours of the [day] the Dr. may most probably be found at home, that he may repeat his inquiries. He would take it very kind if the Dr. would take the trouble of calling on him as he returns from Mr. Bayard's."

This note was written on the day following the duel. At two o'clock that afternoon, 12 July 1804, Hamilton died.

8

A TORRENT of mourning set in. Thousands gathered to hear the funeral oration by Gouverneur Morris and to witness the interment, with military honors supplied by the Society of the Cincinnati and expenses defrayed by the corporation of the City of New York. In that town and in Philadelphia, flags were lowered, bells muffled, and entire editions of newspapers devoted to the substantial accomplishments of the fallen general. There were processions and mass meetings in his honor. Overnight, Hamilton became once again a colossus in the minds of his countrymen; and just as speedily Aaron Burr became his cold-blooded murderer in many of those same minds. To this end, weird tales were circulated: that for days before the duel Burr had practiced target shooting; that Hamilton had gone manfully to the field of honor and bared his breast to the foe, whereas Burr had wrapped his in bombazine, knowing that silk deflected lead; that while Hamilton lay dying in Greenwich Village the colonel and his cronies had caroused and gloated at Richmond Hill.

Burr was stunned by the outcry. "You will remark," he told Charles Biddle, "that all our intemperate and emancipated Jacobins who have been for years invoking Hamilton as a disgrace to the country and a menace to society, are now the most vehement in his praise and you will readily perceive that their motive is not respect to him but malice to me." Presumably he was referring to the sudden outpouring of affection for Hamilton from DeWitt Clinton and his followers, who no doubt saw an opportunity in the tragedy—the possibility that, with Burr thoroughly discredited, his small but able faction would fall into their hands.

Both the mourning for Hamilton and the execrations of Burr were heaviest in the Northern and Middle states. Different sentiments tended to surface in the South and West. In those regions Hamilton was little admired and many citizens regarded the circumstances of his death as nothing more than another duel and a seemingly justified one at that. When the pre-duel letters between Burr and Hamilton were published, Randolph of Roanoke read them thoughtfully and commented on them perceptively. "How visible," he wrote, "is his [Burr's] ascendancy over him [Hamilton] and how sensible does the latter appear of it! There is an apparent consciousness of *some* inferiority to his enemy displayed by Hamilton throughout the transaction, and from a previous sight of their letters I could have inferred the issue of the contest. On one side there is labored obscurity, much equivocation, and many attempts at evasion, not unmixed with a little blustering; on the other, an unshaken adherence to his object and an undeviating pursuit of it, not to be eluded or baffled. It reminded me of a sinking fox pressed by a vigorous old hound, where no shift is permitted to avail him."

For eleven days Burr lingered at Richmond Hill, hoping the tumult would subside. It didn't. John Burger, coroner for the city and county of New York, and fifteen jurors were looking into the death of Hamilton. Lawyer Burr labeled their investigation "unexampled," since the shot responsible for the death had been fired on the soil of another state. Their objective, he wrote Alston, "is to obtain an inquest of murder. Upon this a warrant will issue to apprehend me, and, if I should be taken no bail would probably be allowed. You know enough of the temper and principles of the generality of the officers of our state government to form a judgment of my position . . . I am waiting the report of this jury; when that is known, you shall be advised of my movements." But three days later he decided against waiting for the coroner's jury to complete its work. At 10 a.m., 21 July, he stepped into a waiting barge in the Hudson. He went first to Perth Amboy. John Swartwout accompanied him thus far and then hastened back to New York to keep an eye on the coroner's jury. Burr spent the night at the New Jersey seaport as a guest of his old friend, Thomas Truxton. On the following morning, Truxton's carriage bore him the twenty miles to Cranberry, where he obtained another vehicle for the rest of the trip to Philadelphia. There he lodged with Charles Biddle and came and went as he pleased. He got in touch with Céleste and went through some of the closing motions of that doomed matrimonial dance. He wrote Theodosia that "If any male friend of yours should be dying of ennui, recommend him to engage in a duel and a courtship at the same time."

By fast messengers, Bartow Prevost and John Swartwout kept him informed of what was going on in New York. On 2 August the coroner's jury handed down a presentment of murder, but a grand jury, recognizing the illegality of the charge, quickly replaced it with an indictment for misdemeanor, specifically for having uttered and sent a challenge. Matt Davis, summoned to testify, had refused, and was in jail. Van Ness and Swartwout, to escape similar services, had gone into hiding. Governor Morgan Lewis described the proceedings against Burr as "disgraceful, illiberal, and ungentlemanly," but strong pressure was being put on him to ask the governor of Pennsylvania for Burr's extradition. Coming post-haste to Philadelphia, the youngest of the Swartwout brothers, twenty-one-year-old Samuel, implored Burr to leave the state at once to avoid arrest.

On 11 August he informed Theodosia that he was heading south. His destination was the plantation home of his friend, Pierce Butler, on the little island of St. Simons off the coast of Georgia. One of his slaves, Peter Yates, and Sam Swartwout were to go with him, the latter as his "companion, secretary, and aid-de-camp." Not for the first time, he assured his daughter that her fears for his safety were exaggerated. His indictment for misdemeanor in New York had alarmed her. Even more alarming to her was the knowledge that a grand jury had been called in New Jersey and that there was going to be an indictment for murder in that state. Burr promised her that all would turn out well. He would hide out for a time, visit certain regions he had long wished to explore, and then, when the clamor against him had spent itself, return north. Meanwhile, she was to read a thousand books or so, and see to it that little Gamp got his lessons and did not gorge himself on peaches. As for mail, she was to address her letters to "Mr. R. King," the incognito under which he would be traveling. The Vice President of the United States had become a fugitive from justice.

9

He had also become a man whose mind was already busy with the plans that would eventuate in the Burr Conspiracy. He had chosen St. Simons not only because of its remoteness from New York and New Jersey but because of its nearness to that still Spanish-owned slab of the southland known as the Floridas. Two years earlier, Burr had called the attention of his son-in-law to the persistent rumor that Spain had ceded both the Floridas and Louisiana to France. He did not have to explain to Alston that Spain was weak but the presence of the aggressive France of Napoleon on the fringes of the American Republic could be troublesome. "How do you account for the apathy of the public on this subject?" he asked Alston in that letter of 2 February 1802. "To me the arrangement appears to be pregnant with evil to the United States. I wish you to think of it, and endeavour to excite attention to it through the newspapers."

Much had changed since the penning of these thoughts. The vast, unmeasured reaches of Louisiana had become American soil. But the Floridas were still in the hands of Spain, and beyond them lay Spanish-owned Mexico. Soon after the New York election, Burr had conferred at Richmond Hill with James Wilkinson, friend since the days of the Revolutionary War and now commanding general of the army of the United States. Few Americans were more knowledgeable about the peripheries of the Republic than the portly and flamboyant general. What he and Burr discussed during their meeting on a spring night in 1804 is not known, but later events suggest that their conversation dealt with possible enterprises in the South and West, projects not unconnected with the Spanish holdings in the New World. At any rate, no sooner had St. Simons Island recovered from a devastating storm in early September than Burr was on his way to the Floridas. There, giving himself out to be a London merchant, he spent some eleven days, gathering data on the lay of the land and the sentiments of its inhabitants.

Letters awaiting him on his return to St. Simons revealed that the hubbub against him in New York had died down.

At once he began preparations for the long trip—four hundred miles of it by canoe along the coastal waterways—that would carry him back home. The first of October found him in Savannah, where a crowd of citizens, aware that R. King was A. Burr, turned out to celebrate his arrival. In that city, apparently, the killer of Hamilton was regarded as something of a hero. Nor were the Georgians the last to treat the colonel in this manner. At other places, as he forged northward by slow stages, his passage took on some of the trappings of a triumphal procession.

He had no intention of leaving the South without looking in on the Alstons and their small son, his namesake. Having spent some time with them, he pushed on, through North Carolina and Virginia. Originally he had planned to go as far as New York and wait there for the opening of the next session of the Senate in early November. Somewhere along the road, however, word reached him that for the first time in history—and the last to date, it can be said now—a Vice President of the United States had been indicted for murder. In short, the New Jersey grand jury had acted. Burr wrote his daughter that now the "subject in dispute is which" state, New Jersey or New York, "shall have the honour of hanging the vice president." Meanwhile, he had concluded that, rather than risk arrest by crossing New Jersey, it would be better to terminate his wanderings at Washington.

From Petersburg, Virginia, he wrote Alston that "I came here on the . . . 29th [October], intending to stay two hours. The hospitalities of the place have detained me three days." From Richmond, he wrote Theodosia that the homeland of the Jeffersonians was the last place in the world in which he had expected to enjoy such "open marks of hospitality and respect." He could regale her with a story of a thousand pleasant things, but it "cannot now be told, because you know it must be reserved for 'The travels of A. Gamp, Esq., A.M., LL.D., V.P.U.S.' etc., etc., etc., which will appear in due time."

In the United States Senate on the morning of 5 November, William Plumer, he of the short-lived secession conspiracy, having taken his seat, looked up to behold a spectacle he found hard to believe. "The man," he wrote, "whom the Grand jury in the County of Bergen, New Jersey, have recently indicted for the murder of the incomparable Hamilton, appeared yesterday and today at the head of the Senate! This is, I believe, the first time that ever a Vice President appeared in the Senate the first day of a session. It certainly is the first time and God grant it may be the last, that ever a man, so justly charged with such an infamous crime, presided in the American Senate. We are, indeed, fallen on evil times."

10

BURR FASCINATED the New Hampshire solon, whose *Memorandum of the Proceedings of the United States Senate* is notable for its vignettes of the colonel during the closing months of his Vice Presidency. Plumer, at this time, detected a marked change in Burr. "He appears to have lost those easy graceful manners that beguiled the hours away the last session," he recorded. "He is now uneasy, discontented, and hurried." In Plumer's purview, there could be but one explanation. "So true it is," he observed: " 'Great guilt never knew great joy at heart.' " It is proposed that on this point the New Englander's often reliable perceptions halted short of the truth. The cracks that were beginning to appear in Burr's once composed exterior were the products of a still accumulating wrath. And a wrathful man is a reckless one, as his future conduct would disclose. Too long had his superlative abilities been denied any outlet other than what to him was the child's play of running the Senate. At a much later date an American playwright would put the case well. "When Pan was forbidden the light and warmth of the sun," Eugene O'Neill would write, "he grew sensitive and self-conscious and proud and revengeful —and became Prince of Darkness."

Another senator, Dr. Samuel Latham Mitchill of New

York, also found the handsome presiding officer an irresistible study. Mitchill had begun his political career in 1790 while still serving as professor of chemistry, natural history, and agriculture at Columbia College. Later he would hold the professional chair of chemistry, botany, and materia medica in the New York College of Physicians and Surgeons. He was a congenial soul, always ready to share his great learning. "Tap the doctor at any time," a friend said, "he will flow." Jefferson called him "the Congressional dictionary," and his congressional colleagues, their "Stalking Library." It was his practice to share his impressions of the Congress by letter with his wife in New York. Burr figured frequently in these reports. On 13 February the senator-scientist leaned forward from his scarlet chair with its lining of morocco leather, the better to take in the face of the Vice President as he broke the seals on the electoral-college ballots and proclaimed the next President to be Thomas Jefferson, and the next Vice President, George Clinton.

Unlike Plumer, Mitchill found no cracks in the surface. Of Burr's demeanor that day, he wrote his wife that, "hard and trying as such a task must have been to a man of keen sensibility and to one who feels that the most outrageous wrongs have been done him, he . . . acted his part with so much . . . composure . . . you would not have seen the least deviation from his manner . . . He has been for some years disciplined in the school of adversity, and really has learned to behave like a stoic. All the difference I discerned was that he appeared rather more carefully dressed than usual."

Like Plumer, many of the Federalists in the Senate kept the Vice President at arm's length, eschewing conversation with him whenever possible. Not so the Republicans, or the Democrats, as they were beginning to style themselves. "Burr is still with us," Plumer noted in December. "He is avoided by federalists, but caressed and flattered by democrats from the President to the door keeper." Confronted with this volte-face, the Hampshire senator could only assume it to be an outgrowth of Democratic delight at the passing of Hamilton. Again, Plumer had identified a phenomenon correctly. Again, he appears to have missed its real animus. Hatred of Hamilton had little to do with it. Behind the Administration's incredible change of attitude toward Burr was another motive altogether.

At the turn of the year, Jefferson's long power struggle with the Federalist-dominated judiciary was fast approaching a climactic moment. Still at the forefront of the President's thinking was the conviction that the will of the people would be frustrated were the federal courts to exercise the right to nullify an act of Congress by declaring it unconstitutional—a right that Chief Justice Marshall had already articulated in the landmark case of *Marbury v. Madison*. As the national judges served for life, only impeachment could achieve the President's ends. One federal jurist had already gone that route: John Pickering of the United States Court for the District of New Hampshire. But Pickering was admittedly insane, and his conviction and removal from office could not be cited as a precedent for proceeding in the same manner against Marshall and the other four Federalists still sitting on the six-man bench of the United States Supreme Court.

Now one of those Federalists—Associate Justice Samuel Chase of Maryland—was under impeachment. An aging giant of a man, fleshy and flushed of visage—people spoke of him as "Bacon Face"—Chase had supplied his enemies with ample ammunition. He was arrogant and arbitrary. On at least one occasion, he had used the bench as a platform from which to air his own political ideas. The Democratic majority in the House had indicted him during the closing days of the preceding session. By the end of 1804, the articles of impeachment were before the Senate, and the Jeffersonians were keenly aware of the pivotal role that Burr would play in the upcoming trial. As presiding officer of the Senate sitting as a court of impeachment, he would be called on for numerous rulings. What evidence should be admitted, what not—his decisions on such questions could affect the outcome of the hearings.

The Administration's wooing of the man they had long treated as a pariah was blatant to the point of being comic. Jefferson, Plumer observed in late December, has "shown more attention and invited Mr. Burr oftener to his house within this three weeks than ever he did in the course of the same time before. Mr. Gallatin . . . has waited upon him often at his lodgings . . . The Secretary of State, Mr. Madison . . . accompanied him on a visit to . . . the French Minister." The President's "whip" on the floor of the Senate, William Giles of Virginia, drafted a petition to Governor Bloomfield of New Jersey and got most of the leading Democratic senators to sign it. It asked the governor to quash the murder indictment against Burr in his state. Within a few years, that indictment would fade away and be forgotten. So would the one in New York. But in early 1805 Bloomfield, although a close friend to Burr, could only point out to the senators that his powers did not permit him to interfere with the procedures of a duly constituted grand jury.

For three years, Burr's patronage recommendations had for the most part been ignored. All at once, his wishes in this regard became the Administration's commands. Three of his closest friends were named to high posts. Stepson Bartow Prevost was appointed judge of the superior court of New Orleans. Brother-in-law Joseph Browne was given the office of secretary of the Louisiana Territory, meaning the upper of the two administrative districts into which that vast area had been divided. General Wilkinson was not only made governor of the same territory; he was also allowed to retain his post as commanding general of the army, an amalgam of civil and military powers that Thomas Jefferson would never have condoned under ordinary circumstances. No doubt, Burr dictated these appointments. If so, his desire to see all three friends in the Southwest can be taken as a measure of how fully crystallized in his mind were the schemes that would soon take him into that area and in time bring him before a federal court to face charges of high misdemeanor and treason. Quietly he nursed his still unrevealed projects and kept his own counsel. He was not taken in by the unprecedented flow of warmth from the Jeffersonians. How little that affected his thinking is shown by an incident in late February when for the last time he was called on to give his casting vote in the Senate. The bill before the body was one that the Administration wanted. A political maverick to the end, Burr blandly voted against it.

11

FOLLOWING A FEW PRELIMINARIES of a mostly technical nature, the trial of Samuel Chase opened on 4 February 1805. Fresh in American memories was the long impeachment trial in England of Warren Hastings, first governor general of British India. On Burr's orders and under his supervision, the two-story Senate chamber took on much the same physical appearance that the House of Lords had assumed for the Hastings hearings. Vividly colored cloths went over everything: crimsons, greens, and blues. Out went the senators' tables. In came a large number of chairs and tiered benches. Underneath the public balcony, a smaller temporary balcony was erected and lavishly adorned. The plan was for ladies only to occupy it, but, to quote the official record, "this feature of the arrangement made by the Vice-President, was at an early period of the trial abandoned, it having been found impractical to separate the sexes!" A passageway ran from the chair of the presiding officer to the door. To either side of it stood a low stall, its balustrades and the chairs within covered with blue cloth. One of these pens was for the seven managers named by the House to conduct the prosecution. The other was for the defense attorneys, headed by Luther Martin of Maryland. The alterations in the sedate and classic chamber of the Senate, take them all in all, gave it the look of one of the royal fields of England set up as a list for a jousting match between dueling knights.

From time to time during the preliminaries, Burr had exhibited a noticeable degree of ill temper. Plumer took note of these uncharacteristic eruptions. When the elderly and ailing defendant appeared in the chamber for the first time, the Vice President was slow about letting him have a chair. He was heard to remark that in England, when an impeached officer appeared before the House of Lords, he was obliged to fall on his knees, "and rises not till the Lord Chancellor directs him." The sergeant at arms having brought the justice an armchair, Burr adamantly refused a plea that he be given a table as well. When Chase rose to begin reading his answer to the charges against him, Burr interrupted him frequently. "Reprehensible," was Plumer's comment on these actions. "It is indeed a humiliating scene to behold an *aged man, a Judge* of the Supreme Court of the United States . . . Arraigned before a Court, the president of whom . . . stands indicted as a MURDERER!"

Eight articles of impeachment had been drawn up. When the recently elected young senator from Massachusetts, John Quincy Adams, read them, he was taken aback. They contain "in themselves," he explained, "a virtual impeachment of the Supreme Court!" What Adams knew, many of the spectators who crowded the two balconies throughout the ordeal also knew. In the person of Samuel Chase, the high court as a whole was on trial. Were Chase convicted, similar actions could be expected against most, if not all, of his fellow justices, perhaps even against the great John Marshall himself.

But if the Jeffersonians hoped that Burr would lean their way, they were in for a disappointment. On the other hand, if they feared he might lean in the opposite direction, they were to have no cause to say so. Burr conducted the impeachment trial of Associate Justice Chase with such fairness, and with so correct a handling of its legal permutations, that what had begun as a political inquest ended as a memorable example of judicial procedure at its best. On this judgment the newspapers of both parties were in accord. Burr, one of them reported, performed his duties during the trial "with the dignity and impartiality of an angel, but with the rigour of a devil." By the time the hearings ended, Chase having been acquitted on all counts, even Senator Plumer had joined the ranks of the Vice President's admirers. "Mr. Burr," he conceded, "has certainly, on the whole, done himself, the Senate and the nation honor by the dignified manner in which he has presided over this high and numerous Court."

12

THE TRIAL ENDED on 1 March 1805. By the next morning its colorful trappings had gone and the members of the upper house, a little limp after the tension of the preceding weeks, were in executive session when Burr rose from his chair to say that the time had come to bid them goodbye. He apologized for not finishing out the day, but noted that he had a "slight indisposition (sore throat)." As he later explained to Theodosia, he realized that as this was to be his formal leave-taking, it would be "decent and proper" of him to make a talk. But what about? "There was nothing written or prepared, except it had been some days on my mind to say something." He now proceeded to say it.

There are no verbatim reports, only some paraphrases. The Washington *Federalist* published one of them. Based on the recollections of some of those who had heard the speech, it was "rather awkwardly and pompously told," according to Burr. Plumer essayed a paraphrase. So did John Quincy Adams. Later a synthesis of these contemporary accounts would be placed in the official records.

Burr spoke quietly and conversationally. None of his known

speeches contains any of the literary allusions so much used in his day. In this talk, as in others, he relied principally on the epigrammatic statement. Plumer quoted two such stylistic devices: "Error often is to be preferred to indecision." "To be prompt is not to be precipitate." He began by citing a couple of rules of order that he thought the Senate ought to change. Then he said that he realized that he had made some errors in his rulings from the chair. He had made no effort to rationalize these decisions, "because a moment of irritation is not a moment for explanation." Next he said that in his conduct of his office he had "known no party, no cause, no friend, had always tried to be fair and impartial." Finally, he thanked the senators for their support and asked them not to eliminate the rules and decorum he had established, even though "the ignorant look upon such matters as unnecessary and trivial."

John Quincy Adams got the impression that Burr's original intent was to confine his valedictory to these matters of senatorial business. Perhaps so. Perhaps his closing remarks were an afterthought. Plainly, they came from some deeper part of his being. At this point, he spoke of his country and the constitution. We have no way of identifying the feelings that made him do so. We can assume that they were the perhaps ambivalent feelings of a man who had lost his mother in infancy, had lost the wife who had taken her place in the prime of his marriage, and now had reason to feel that his only remaining mother, his country, was no longer treating him very well. Still, he loved her. He spoke of the Senate as "a sanctuary; a citadel of law, of order and of liberty . . . and if the Constitution be destined ever to perish by the sacrilegious hands of the demagogue or the usurper, which God avert, its expiring agonies will be witnessed on this floor."

Having finished, Burr walked across the room and through the door into the lobby. In the chamber behind him, grown men wept. Senator Mitchill shared the moment with his wife. "There was a solemn and silent weeping for perhaps five minutes," he told her. "For my own part, I never experienced anything of the kind so affecting me . . . My colleague, General Smith, stout and manly as he is, wept as profusely as I did. He laid his head upon his table and did not recover from his emotion for a quarter of an hour more."

Thus did the subject of our strange tale bring his Vice Presidency to its conclusion. His past lay behind a door that had closed, and for the moment his future was no more than plans and hopes in his head. His political career lay in ruins around him, Hamilton was dead, and the fates that had brought them together were now free to concentrate on Burr.

Sources and Notes

Sources and Notes

ABBREVIATIONS FREQUENTLY USED

AB	Aaron Burr
AH	Alexander Hamilton
AH, Papers (Syrett)	*The Papers of Alexander Hamilton*, Harold C. Syrett, editor; Jacob E. Cooke, associate editor
DAB	Dictionary of American Biography
Davis, *Burr*	*Memoirs of Aaron Burr* by Matthew L. Davis
HSP	Historical Society of Pennsylvania
LC	Library of Congress
MHS	Massachusetts Historical Society
NYHS	New-York Historical Society
NY–JA	Journal of the General Assembly of New York
Parton, *Burr*	*The Life and Times of Aaron Burr* by James Parton
PVG	Peter Van Gaasbeek
Schachner, *Burr*	*Aaron Burr, a Biography* by Nathan Schachner
SHM	Senate House Museum, Kingston, New York
Theo Sr.	Mrs. Theodosia Bartow Prevost Burr
Theo Jr.	Mrs. Theodosia Burr Alston
TJ	Thomas Jefferson
Yale	Yale University Library

Sources and Notes

PAGE

PREFACE

xi "Burr's life, take it all together." *Memoirs of John Quincy Adams*, IX, 429.

xv "the Fates." Burr Family Papers, Yale.

1. VISIBLE SAINTS

3 "unexpectedly." Esther Burr's Manuscript Diary, Beinecke Rare Book Lib., Yale. Unless otherwise indicated, all quotes attributed to Esther are from this source.

3 "famous, infamous." *The Gentleman's Magazine*, LX, pt. 1, 86.

4 Burr-family background. Donald Line Jacobus, ed., *History and Genealogy of the Families of Old Fairfield*, I, 124, 482 passim; Fairfield, *1779–1879, Centennial Commemoration of the Burning of Fairfield, Connecticut, by the British troops*, map of Burr block; Charles Burr Todd, *A General History of the Burr Family in America*, 146 passim; Frank Samuel Child, *An Old New England Town*, 77; Elizabeth L. Child, *Fairfield, Connecticut Tercentenary 1639–1939*, 20; Kate E. Perry, *Old Burying Ground of Fairfield . . . epitaphs on the 583 tombstones*, passim; Mary Depue Ogden, ed., *Memorial Cyclopedia of New Jersey*, 47; Nathaniel Goodwin, *Genealogical Notes*, passim; Suzanne Burr Geisler, "The Burr Family, 1716–1836" (unpublished doctoral thesis, 1977), passim.

6 "sermon-proof." Perry Miller, *The New England Mind from Colony to Province*, 34.

6 "half-way covenant." Samuel Perkins Hayes, "An historical study of the Edwardsean Revivals," *American Journal of Psychology*, VIII (Oct. 1902), 552.

6 "You can and you can't." Ibid., 557n.

7 "eighty-two opinions," etc. Ibid., 552.

7 Growth of Episcopalians, Arminians, etc. H. E. Parkes, "New England in the Seventeen-Thirties," *The New England Quarterly*, III (July 1930), 414–15.

PAGE

7 "three hundred souls." S. Austin, ed., *The Works of President Edwards*, III, 234–35.

8 "This year God saw fit." Caleb Smith, *Diligence in the Work of God, and Activity During Life. A Sermon occasioned by the . . . Death of the Reverend Mr. Aaron Burr*, 22–23; Jonathan French Stearns, *First Church in Newark*, 153.

8 "meek and unoffending." Frank John Urquhart, ed., *A History of the City of Newark, New Jersey*, I, 193.

9 "8 students." Rev. AB to Rev. Joseph Sterrett, 9 Nov. 1751, Simon Gratz collection, HSP.

9 "lenient byass . . . small man." Franklin B. Dexter, *Biographical Studies of the Graduates of Yale College*, 532.

9 look no further than Esther Edwards. Sally Prince to Mr. and Mrs. Shippen, Boston, 1 May 1758, Shippen Family Papers, LC. This hitherto overlooked letter details the courtship of Rev. AB and Esther. Cited hereafter as Burrissa Letter.

10 "insight into science." Perry Miller in the foreword of the Meredian Books edition of his *Jonathan Edwards*. In his fifteenth or sixteenth year Edwards discovered water to be a compressible fluid, a fact that was not given to the world by scientists until 1763, and one that if Edwards had pursued it further might have led him to Benjamin Franklin's theory of electricity before Franklin discovered it, according to Sereno Dwight, ed., *Works of President Edwards*, I, 53.

10 homicidal madness in Edwards family. Ola Elizabeth Winslow, *Jonathan Edwards*, 19–20; Perry Miller, *Jonathan Edwards* (American Men of Letters Series), 36. Hereafter the citations to Miller's biography are to this edition.

10 "From my childhood up." Dwight, *Edwards Works*, I, 60–1.

11 "not a means to an end." Winslow, ed., *Jonathan Edwards: Basic Writings*, xxvii.

11 "handfuls of silver and gold." Dwight, *Edwards Works*, I, 30.

11 "proud, overbearing and rash." Miller, *Edwards*, 210.

12 six-sided desk. Sarah Cabot Sedgewick and Mrs. Christina Sedgewick Marquand, *Stockbridge 1739–1939, a Chronicle*, 84.

PAGE

13 "formed to please." Samuel Hopkins, *The Life and Character of . . . Jonathan Edwards*, 93.

13 Student's remarks on the marriage. Parton, *Burr*, 38.

14 "No apologies." AB to Theo Jr., 20 Jan. 1804, Davis, *Burr*, II, 272–73.

14 Account book. Original at Princeton University. Quoted in Paul Van Dyke, "An Old Book," *Magazine of American History*, XXVIII, 186–88.

16 Eighteenth-century Puritans on sex. Parkes, "New England in the Seventeen-Thirties," 397, 407–9.

18 "into a . . . covenant with God." Davis, *Burr*, I, 21–24.

19 "vapid, sizzy." Dwight, *Edwards Works*, I, 565.

19 Dr. William Shippen. Often called "the elder" to distinguish him from his son, the Dr. Shippen who ran the hospitals for the Continental Army during the Revolution. The elder William Shippen was a great-uncle of Peggy (Margaret) Shippen, who married Benedict Arnold.

19 "seemingly without any disease." Electa Fidelia Jones, *Stockbridge, Past and Present*, 160; Hopkins, *Edwards*, 93.

19 "scrupled" in her mind. Burrissa Letter.

20 Rev. AB's mother living 1757 and guardianship papers issued. George E. McCracken, "Who was Aaron Burr?," *The American Genealogist*, XL (Apr. 1964), 69, 65.

2. RESOLUTE BOY

21 Timothy Edwards, character, etc. William Henry Edwards, comp., *Timothy and Rhoda Ogden Edwards of Stockbridge, and Their Descendants*, 20. Some of Burr's biographers and a current encyclopedia mistakenly identify Timothy as a minister.

22 three little tales. Davis, *Burr*, I, 25–26.

22 Timothy reproached himself. Edwards, *Timothy and Rhoda Ogden Edwards*, 27.

22 A surviving legal document. "An Agreement between Aaron Burr on the behalf of Timothy Edwards and Timothy Edwards and Sons . . . and Divers Creditors," 11 June 1791,

PAGE

Burr Papers, NYHS; see also Sedgewick and Marquand, *Stockbridge*, 162, 180.

23 Matthew Ogden, description, etc. George Theodore Thayer, *As We Were: the story of old Elizabethtown*, 166; Bertha Baldwin Bigelow, comp. & ed., *Record Book of First Presbyterian Church of Elizabeth, New Jersey*, 51.

23 "noble and commanding face." Henry Childs Merwin, *Aaron Burr*, 5.

23 Scolding letter to sister. AB to Sally Reeve, 31 Jan. 1774, Burr Family Papers, Yale.

24 examination father had drafted. Minutes of the Trustees of the College of New Jersey, I, from Minutes of 9 Nov. 1748, in Burr Additional Papers, Princeton University Lib.

24 traveler from across the sea. Isaac Weld, *Travels through the states of North America*, I, 259.

24 "the meanest mechanick." "On Music," n.d., Gratz collection, HSP.

25 Witherspoon's notice. New Jersey *Archives*, 1S.26, pp. 426–28.

26 Eighteenth-century Princeton. Philip Vickers Fithian, *Journal and Letters 1767–1774*, I, 8, 9, 18; V. L. Collins, *President Witherspoon*, I, 106.

27 "quite virtuously." Samuel H. Wandell and Meade Minnigerode, *Aaron Burr*, I, 31.

27 William Paterson, character, etc. Julian P. Boyd, "William Patterson: Forerunner of John Marshall," in William Thorp, ed., *The Lives of Eighteen from Princeton*, 1 passim.

28 "*stealing* through life." Davis, *Burr*, I, 212.

28 letter enclosing "notes on dancing." Ibid., 36–37. A version of the essay is in the Dreer collection, American Statesmen, HSP.

28 Paterson wrote them all. William Paterson, "Aaron Burr or William Paterson, Which?," *New Jersey Law Journal*, XX (June 1897), 166–71.

29 The societies and their doings. Wallace J. Williamson III, *The Halls: A Brief History of the American Whig-Cliosophic Society of Princeton University*, 6–9, 39; William Paterson, Glimpses of colonial society and the life at Princeton College, 18.

PAGE

29 "I . . . shall conclude." William E. Curtis, "An Unpublished Essay on 'Honor' by Aaron Burr," *Cosmopolitan Magazine*, XXI (Sept. 1896), 557–59.

29 faculty awarded him . . . honors, etc. Wandell-Minnigerode, *Burr*, 27; Holmes Moss Alexander, *Aaron Burr, The Proud Pretender*, 14; *General Catalogue of Princeton University, 1746–1906*, 48–49; John McLean, *History of the College of New Jersey*, I, 302.

30 "Building Castles in the Air." Ibid.; Benjamin Rush to John Adams, 3 Apr. 1807, L. H. Butterfield, ed., *Letters of Benjamin Rush*.

31 such "was the prayer." Davis, *Burr*, I, 43.

31 "suffocating odor of sanctity," Gamaliel Bradford, "Aaron Burr," in *Damaged Souls*, 87.

32 Has "the doctor . . . under" his thumb. Davis, *Burr*, I, 47.

32 "Just been over to the tavern." 17 Jan. 1774, Burr Family Papers, Yale.

32 "act your pleasure." Davis, *Burr*, I, 45.

33 On deism. T. A. Burkill, *The Evolution of Christian Thought*, 304–5.

33 "the road to Heaven." Davis, *Burr*, I, 45.

33 seldom allowed "a moment alone." Todd, *Burr Family in America*, 77; Samuel G. Drake, *Some Memoirs of the Life and Writings of the Reverend Thomas Prince*, 105.

34 "a certain Miss ———." Davis, *Burr*, I, 50.

34 "*Steadily*, Aaron." Ibid., 55.

34 "several hundred persons." Ibid., 48–49.

35 Reed to Washington. 24 July 1775, Reed Papers, NYHS, as quoted in George A. Boyd, *Elias Boudinot: Patriot and Statesman*, 26.

3. GENTLEMAN SOLDIER

36 "not more than 9 rounds a man." Washington to president of Congress, 4 Aug. 1775, John Hancock Papers, LC.

37 walked the sixty miles. AB to Sally, 13 Sept. 1775, Burr Family Papers, Yale.

37 "join'd with anything of the gentleman." Ibid.

PAGE

38 AB's military record and ranks. Berthold Fernow, *New York in the Revolution*, 239; Mark M. Boatner, *Encyclopedia of the American Revolution*, article on AB; Congress, instructions to Washington [17 June 1775], John Hancock Papers, LC; Bryce Metcalf, *Original Members . . . Society of the Cincinnati*, 70; AB to Theodore Sedgwick, 17 Feb. 1791, Sedgwick Papers, MHS; Francis B. Heitman, *Historical Register of Officers of the Continental Army*, AB entries.

38 "The establishment which cadets hold." James Wilkinson's order book, Record Group 94, Adjutant General's office, p. 219, National Archives (hereafter NA).

38 "as sound as I left you." AB to Sally, 13 Sept. 1775, Burr Family Papers, Yale.

38 "The very name is prosperous." Ibid.

38 "obliging" to a soldier. 24 Sept. [1775], Ibid.

39 "winter approaching." Extracts from Matt's journal in *Proceedings of the New Jersey Historical Society*, XIII (Jan. 1928), 24. The ms. journal is in the collections of the Washington Assoc. of N.J., Morristown, N.J.

39 craft plunged them twenty feet. Samuel L. Knapp, *The Life of Aaron Burr*, 21.

40 "ever intended any ill." John Joseph Henry's jrnl in Kenneth Roberts, *March to Quebec*, 343.

40 Preparations for and attack on Quebec. John Coats to Maj. David Hopkins, 10 Jan. 1806, Samuel Smith Papers, LC; Return J. Meigs, "Journal of the Expedition Against Quebec . . . ," in Charles I. Bushnell, ed., *Crums for Antiquarians*, I, 21–32; Lt. Col. Strange, "Historical Notes on the Defence of Quebec in 1775," *Transactions of the Literary and Historical Soc. of Quebec . . . 1876–1880*, N.S. 12–14, pp. 22–29, 37–38, 101.

40 Lack of "gentlemen." Isaac Q. Leake, *Memoir of the Life and Times of General John Lamb*, 120.

41 Montgomery's last words. William Dunlap, *Diary of . . .* , I, 737.

42 "Dirty, ragged . . ." 2 Feb. 1776, Burr File, Henry E. Huntington Lib. (Hereafter, Huntington.)

42 "promotion, the caresses of the great." Davis, *Burr*, I, 81–82.

PAGE

42 mentioned in Congress. Edmund C. Burnett, ed., *Letters of the Members of the Continental Congress*, I, 319.
43 "I go on public business." AB to Sally, 26 May 1776, Burr Family Papers, Yale.
44 Hancock's role. Herbert Sanford Allan, *John Hancock: Patriot in Purple*, 238.
44 22 June orders. War of the Revolution Orderly Book, Book 12, p. 20, RG 93, NA.
45 "My good old general." Davis, *Burr*, I, 109.
45 "A girl of fourteen." Parton, *Burr*, 89.
46 "*Ginrale* Putnams compliments." Ibid., 94.
48 enlarging the population. AB to Sally, 1 July 1776, Burr Family Papers, Yale.
48 Inspects Long Island and in retreat therefrom. Davis, *Burr*, I, 106, 122.
48 Conference near N.Y. Public Library. Martha J. Lamb, "Historic Homes and Landmarks," *Mag. of Amer. Hist.*, XXI (Jan. 1889), 12.
49 Rescue of the brigade. AB's story is in Thomas Jones, *History of New York During the Revolutionary War*, I, 606; see also Henry P. Johnston, "The Campaign of 1776 Around New York and Brooklyn," in *Memoirs of the Long Island Historical Society*, III, 40. For Flexner's view that the incident never occurred, see his *The Young Hamilton*, 112n.
51 "The most important revolution." Davis, *Burr*, I, 107.
51 "Pr. of Leathern Drawers." AB to Sally, 26 Oct. 1776, Burr Family Papers, Yale.
51 Crossing Hudson and in Philadelphia. Peter Force, *American Archives*, 5th series, III, 634; *Pennsylvania Colonial Records*, XI, 463.
51 "as to 'Expectations of promotion.' " Davis, *Burr*, I, 19.
52 "honour done me." 21 July 1777, Force, *American Archives*, 5th series, III.
53 "You shall have the honor." Davis, *Burr*, I, 112.
53 recruiting drive. War of the Revolution Book 121, Supplies Recvd and Delivered, AGO, 1 Feb. 1778, RG 93, NA.
54 no intention of running. Davis, *Burr*, I, 113.
54 "night of terror" and account of it. Frances A. Westervelt, ed., *History of Bergen County, New Jersey, 1630–1923*,

PAGE

107; statement of Judge Gardiner, dated Newburgh 20 Dec. 1813, Force, *Archives*, 5th series, III.

55 regiment to join Washington. Putnam to AB, 27 Sept. 1777, Ibid.

55 Incident at Gulph. William S. Baker, "The Camp by the Old Gulph Mill," *Pa. Mag. Hist. Biog.*, XVII (1893), 414–29.

56 AB at Monmouth, and the controversy over Lee's conduct there. William S. Stryker, *Battle of Monmouth*, 210–11; Theodore Thayer, *The Making of a Scapegoat: Washington and Lee at Monmouth*, passim; Davis, *Burr*, I, 135.

58 On shores of Hudson, gathering information. Ibid.; John C. Fitzpatrick, ed., *The Writings of George Washington . . . 1745–1799*, XI, 133.

58 Malcolms to West Point. Davis, *Burr*, I, 131.

59 Asks to retire from pay, and His Excellency's answer. Ibid., 137.

59 "repaired forthwith." Parton, *Burr*, 109.

59 "I shall bring a French master." 15 Nov. 1778, Burr Family Papers, Yale.

60 Washington Irving. In his "Wolfert's Roost and other Papers," as quoted in John Lockwood Romer, *Historical Sketches of the Romer, Van Tassel and Allied Families, and Tales of the Neutral Ground*, 90–91.

60 in charge of the Westchester Lines. AB to Gen. McDougall, 13 Jan. 1779, Force Transcripts, LC; AB's orderly book in "Aaron Burr in Westchester County, January–February 1779," *Westchester County Historical Bulletin*, VIII; Davis, *Burr*, I, 158–66; Charles Felton Pidgin, *Theodosia*, 138; Davis, *Burr*, I, 168.

4. LOVE AND LAW

64 "Mrs. Prevost Presents." As quoted in Dorothy Valentine Smith, "Mrs. Prevost requests the honor of his company . . . ," *Manuscripts*, XI (Fall 1959), 27–31.

65 "we talked and walked." Bernard C. Steiner, *The Life and Correspondence of James McHenry*, 22–23.

PAGE

65 Background on Stillwells, De Vismes, Bartows, and Prevosts. Dr. John E. Stillwell, *The History of Captain Richard Stillwell, Son of Lieutenant Nicholas Stillwell, and His Descendants*, passim. Evelyn Bartow, *Bartow Genealogy*, passim; T. C. Elliott, "The Surrender of Astoria in 1818," *Oreg. Hist. Soc. Quar.*, XIX (Dec. 1918), 271–82; Dorothy Smith, "An Intercourse of the Heart: Some little-known letters of Theodosia Burr," *NYHS Quar.*, XXXVII (1953), 41–53; Mabel Lorenz Ives, *Washington's Headquarters*, 183–84; Lamb, "Historic Homes and Landmarks," 1–23.

66 "the Provost Patent." Ruth M. Keesey, "Loyalty and Reprisal; the loyalists of Bergen County, New Jersey, and their estates" (unpublished doctoral thesis, 1957), 97n.

67 "I have had the opportunity." Davis, *Burr*, I, 204–5.

68 "She had the truest heart." As quoted in Smith, "Mrs. Prevost requests," 31.

68 "Chesterfield himself." Parton, *Burr*, 63.

69 "The indulgence you applaud." Davis, *Burr*, I, 224–25.

69 At Titus Hosmer's. See Albert E. Van Dusen, *Middletown in the American Revolution*, 11–12.

69 "will bear no imposition." Davis, *Burr*, I, 194.

69 "this wrangling world." Ibid., 214

70 "inclined to *hypo*." Ibid., 194.

70 "forfeiting act." Keesey, "Loyalty and Reprisal," 57–68; New Jersey, *Votes and Proceedings of the General Assembly*, 27 Nov. and 8 Dec. 1778.

70 Prevost in America. *Royal Georgia Gazette*, 11 Mar. 1779; Justin Winsor, ed., *Narrative and Critical History of America*, VI, 470.

70 Prevost in England and Jamaica. J. M. Prevost to Jeffrey Amherst, 22 Dec. 1779; same to same, 26 July 1780, Amherst Papers, Public Records Office, London.

70 Paterson writes on behalf of Theo Sr. Davis, *Burr*, I, 188.

70 Troup on her behalf. Smith, "Mrs. Prevost requests," 29.

71 Theo Sr. served with inquisition. N.J., *Votes and Proceedings*, 24 Dec. 1779.

71 "as a British subject." Ibid.

71 Prevost suggests Theo Sr. join him. E. B. Duval to Theo Sr., 3 Nov. 1779, Gratz collection, HSP.

PAGE

71 "Your health." 16 June 1780 (misdated 1770), Burr Family Papers, Yale.
72 Takes Theo Sr. to Sharon. Tapping Reeve to AB, 4 Mar. 1781, Burr File, Huntington.
72 "even on Saturday nights." Davis, *Burr*, I, 191.
72 "three years." Ibid., 193.
73 "I must have a retired place." 26 Apr. 1780, Gratz collection, HSP.
73 Hosmer died. *Biographical Directory of the American Congress;* Peter Colt to AB, 17 Sept. 1780, Gratz collection, HSP.
73 Study with Paterson, both broke, AB not rich, and privateer chased ashore. Davis, *Burr*, I, 207, 209; Thaddeus Burr to AB, 1 Mar. 1781, Gratz collection, HSP; Davis, *Burr* I, 215; Samuel H. Wandell, *Aaron Burr in Literature*, 48; Thaddeus Burr to AB, 29 May 1780, Gratz collection, HSP; Davis, *Burr*, I, 205, 207.
74 "the beginning of April." Davis, *Burr*, I, 222.
75 "fit" them "for submission to the bar." Ibid., 223.
75 Not sure Troup will make it. Ibid., 225.
75 "master of the friendly hint." Dixon Ryan Fox, *The Decline of Aristocracy in the Politics of New York*, 15.
75 Old supreme court ruling. Dorothy Rita Dillon, *The New York Triumvirate*, 22.
76 Letter to Chief Justice. Davis, *Burr*, I, 231.
76 "à la rustique." Ibid., 228.
76 Hobart's assurance. Ibid.
76 "Yates is playing the fool with me." Ibid., 237.
77 "A sick headache." Ibid., 236.
77 Albany in 1781. Joel Munsell, *The Annals of Albany*, III, 118n.
77 "inelegant." Davis, *Burr*, I, 237.
78 "I know you to be ill." Ibid., 242
78 Franklin stoves. Ibid., 234, 238
78 "You write me too much." Ibid., 242.
78 blanket edict. Dillon, *Triumvirate*, 23; Julius Goebel, Jr., ed., *The Law Practice of Alexander Hamilton*, I, 42 (hereafter AH, Law Papers).

PAGE

79 "if you have not seen the York Gazette." Gratz collection, HSP.

79 Had known Prevost not expected to live. Author is indebted to Mary-Jo Kline for calling his attention to evidence to this effect.

79 "fitter for Chelsea." To Amherst, 26 July 1780, Amherst Papers, PRO.

80 "annihilation." Ibid.

80 "the squire." AB to Sally, 28 Jan. 1777, Burr Family Papers, Yale.

80 "I wish you to study for your own sake." Davis, *Burr*, I, 227. The date Davis puts on this letter, May 1781, is in error, as it was obviously written after the death of Col. Prevost in October 1781. Mary-Jo Kline points out that since Theo Sr. mentions Burr's "studies," indicating that the letter was written prior to his admission "to practice as an attorney in the New York Supreme Court 19 January 1782," it can safely be dated "December 1781–January 1782." (Letter to author, 18 Aug. 1976.)

81 Ceremony by Rev. Van Der Linde. Certificate of marriage, Worthington C. Ford, "Some Papers of Aaron Burr," *Proc. Amer. Antiquarian Soc.*, N.S. XXIX (9 Apr.–5 Oct. 1919), 92.

81 "particulars of our wedding." July 1782, Burr Family Papers, Yale.

82 "This resolution." 5 Nov. 1783, Ibid.

5. THE SCARLETT OF THE AMERICAN BAR

83 New York City, winter 1783–1784. I. N. Phelps Stokes, *The Iconography of Manhattan Island, 1489–1909*, V, passim; William B. Hatcher, *Edward Livingston*, 8; Richard B. Morris, ed., *Select Cases of the Mayor's Court of New York City*, 48.

85 Hamilton admitted to bar. AH, Law Papers, I, 47.

85 "in the last years of the eighteenth century." Henry W. Taft, *A Century and a Half at the New York Bar . . .*, 9.

85 "Very able." AH, Law Papers, II, 83n.

PAGE

85 "never undertaken . . . a cause . . . under £40." Schachner, *Burr*, 87.

85 Didn't always charge that much. AH, Law Papers, I, 160–61.

85 Range of cases. Ibid., II, 49.

86 *Le Guen v. Gouverneur & Kemble* cited over a hundred times. Ibid., 49.

86 "Scarlett of the American Bar." David McAdam, ed., *History of the Bench and Bar of New York*, I, 274.

86 "As a lawyer." Eugene L. Didier, "Aaron Burr as a Lawyer," *The Green Bag*, XIV (Oct. 1902), 452.

86 "wax to receive" etc. Ibid., 452–53.

87 Case of the earlier will. McAdam, *History*, I, 109.

87 Instructions to clerks. Todd, *Burr Family in America*, 124 passim. In *The Common Law*, Oliver Wendell Holmes, Jr., writes (pp. 1–2) that the "substance of the law at any given time pretty nearly corresponds, so far as it goes, with what is then understood to be convenient . . ."

88 "got out the paper." Allan McLane Hamilton, *The Intimate Life of Alexander Hamilton*, 71; "Coleman" in DAB.

88 AH's published confession. See chap. 11 of this book.

88 Attorney for Abraham Yates. Alfred F. Young, *The Democratic Republicans of New York: the origins 1763–1797*, 165.

88 no "pleasure to himself." Didier, "Aaron Burr as a Lawyer," 453.

89 a nose "inclined to the right." Dr. John Edwin Stillwell, *The History of the Burr Portraits*, 2.

89 "Under the medium height," etc. Todd, *Burr Family in America*, 116.

89 "that urbanity." John Davis, *Travels of Four Years and a Half in the United States of America*, 25.

90 "In his manner of listening." A. M. Hamilton, *Intimate Life*, 366n.

90 *People v. Levi Weeks*. AH, Law Papers, I, 693–705; Liva Baker, "The Defense of Levi Weeks," *Amer. Bar. Assoc. Jrnl.*, LXIII (June 1977), 818–24.

93 Parton's tale. In his *Burr*, 149.

94 Comments of Root and Yates, Davis, *Burr*, II, 20.

PAGE

94 "charity cases never." John C. Miller, *Alexander Hamilton: Portrait in Paradox*, 332.
95 "a man of honor." Ibid., 356.
96 "He is a . . . strange sort of animal." De Alva S. Alexander, *A Political History of the State of New York*, I, 45.
96 Troup on AH's temper. AH, Law Papers, II, 86.

6. NOTHING BUT THE BEST

98 "O, my Aaron." Davis, *Burr*, I, 271.
98 "Read the Abbé Mably's little book." Ibid., 266–67.
99 "Will you believe me, Reeve." 19 Aug. 1783, Tapping Reeve Papers, Yale.
99 another daughter. AB to Bernard Gratz, 21 June 1785, Gratz collection, HSP.
99 "unfortunate lying in." 3 Aug. 1788, Burr Papers, NYHS.
99 "Variegated . . . my scenes of anguish." 20 Mar. 1789, Burr Family Papers, Yale.
100 "Give Johnstone." Davis, *Burr*, I, 255.
100 "Tell one of the boys." Ibid.
100 "step into the office." Ibid., 291.
101 "Bartow . . . to the surveyor-general." Ibid., 257.
101 "waggons and horses." Stokes, *Iconography*, V, 1200.
101 Hudson River travel. Munsell, *Annals of Albany*, III, 116–34.
101 "Pensive." Davis, *Burr*, I, 247–48.
101 "Tell me, Aaron." Ibid., 279.
102 "Homesick." Ibid., 263.
102 "Let T." Ibid., 262–63.
102 "To hear . . . no time . . . wasted." Ibid., 264.
102 "Bartow never quits." Ibid., 256.
102 "Never pass a word." Ibid., 308.
102 Rousseau-like letter. Ibid., 256.
103 "I tell everyone." Ibid., 254–55.
103 "Little Theo." Ibid., 248.
103 "Few parents." Ibid.
103 "over delicate." Winslow, *Edwards*, 20.

PAGE

103 "near . . . insanity." Undated. Tapping Reeve Papers, Yale.
104 "I hope you persevere." Davis, *Burr*, I, 204.
104 "too good for some works," etc. Theo Sr. to AB, 13/16 July 1791. Burr Family Papers, Yale.
104 "You don't recollect." Ibid.
105 "a great character." Maunsell to Mrs. Watkins, 14 Dec. 1783, in A. M. Bradhurst, *My Forefathers*, 40.
105 "*on the day that I was arrested*." Schachner, *Burr*, 92.
105 AB in suit against Maunsell. Copy of "Superior Court Case, 5 May 1792, Lewis Morris . . . v. . . . Maunsel [sic]," in collection of the late J. W. Marino in Weehawken, N.J.
105 "never more." Charles Felton Pidgin, *Theodosia: The First Gentlewoman of Her Time*, 117.
105 "distressing family." Wandell-Minnegerode, *Burr*, I, 112.
106 "Gloom." Davis, *Burr*, I, 257.
106 "When Aaron smiles." Ibid., 268.
106 "Oh, Theo!" Ibid., 282–83.
107 "little chariot." Pidgin, *Theodosia*, 263.
107 "paltry object." Davis, *Burr*, I, 297.
107 "cannot control necessity." Ibid., 283.
108 largest frontage. Stokes, *Iconography*, V, 1230–31.
108 by 1790 moved again. N.Y. *Daily Advertiser*, 5 Jan. 1790; Stokes, *Iconography*, V, 1260.
108 "*Big* Symmon's house." Pidgin, *Theodosia*, 118.
108 On Richmond Hill. Arthur Pound, *The Golden Earth*, 270; Stokes, *Iconography*, V, 1254.
108 "Grand and sublime." To Mrs. Shaw, 27 Sept. 1792, in C. F. Adams, ed., *Letters of Abigail Adams*, 399–400.
109 Leases Richmond Hill. Stokes, *Iconography*, V, 1340; Liber Deeds (register's office), LXV, 512, in Bancker Papers, N.Y. Public Lib. (hereafter NYPL); Davis, *Burr*, I, 385, 387; New York City Directory, 1794.
109 "a spacious hall." Stokes, *Iconography*, V, 1254.
110 Helps Davis. Davis, *Travels*, 9–23.
110 "Genius from Obscurity." 21 June 1795, PVG Papers, SHM.
111 "hampered by Money Matters." AB to PVG, 14 Apr. 1795, Ibid.

PAGE

111 "in the hands of usurers." 9 Apr. 1796, Ibid.

112 Loan to Van Gaasbeek in 1793. AB to PVG, 19 Apr. 1793, Ibid. This letter is not clear, but when read with others about to be cited, it leaves the impression that AB had arranged a loan for PVG. In a work in progress entitled "Van Gaasbeek Research Project" (Senate House Historic Cite, 16 May 1976), Kate Mearns of SHM provides a picture of PVG's deteriorating finances at the time of his death at the age of forty-three in 1797. "Tradition," she writes, "suggests . . . that Peter may have died from worry over his debts."

112 "impotent distress." 23 Apr. 1796, PVG Papers, SHM.

112 "on the subject of money." 9 Apr. 1796, Ibid.

112 a "very great" thing. 23 Apr. 1796, Ibid.

112 "Sure it will not be sold." 30 Aug. 1799, Burr Papers, NYHS.

113 Goes surety on a friend's debt. AH, Law Papers, II, 17n.

113 "any hopes of recovering." Mary Hilton Le Guen to Thomas Ludlow Ogden, 1826, Burr–Le Guen letters, Huntington.

113 "brave but turbulent." George Pellew, *John Jay*, 29.

114 "a mere boy," etc. Isaac Q. Leake, *Memoir of the Life and Times of General John Lamb*, 125–26.

114 Sale of furnishings. Schachner, *Burr*, 124–25.

114 "release you from your offer." Ibid.

115 Four thousand acres in one country. "Some Aaron Burr Papers," *Vineland Historical Magazine*, XIX, 117–19.

115 "about 80,000 dollars." AH, Papers (Syrett), XXI, 312n.

115 "establishment" at Richmond Hill. AB to Theo Jr., 25 Apr. 1804, in Pidgin, *Theodosia*, 203–4.

116 Henry and Washington pressed for cash. Alfred Jeremiah Beveridge, *The Life of John Marshall*, II, 61n.

116 "scarcely dared leave house." George Dangerfield, *Chancellor Robert R. Livingston of New York, 1746–1813*, 246.

116 Inept manager of own affairs. AB to Tapping Reeve, 22 May 1779, Tapping Reeve Papers, Yale.

116 "twenty-six acres." Stokes, *Iconography*, V, 1310.

117 Sublets four lots. Indenture, 20 June 1797, Burr Papers, Yale. Burr had a number of rental properties, but there is no evidence that these were a part of the Richmond Hill

PAGE

estate. See extract of Manhattan Company records in *Vineland Hist. Mag.*, XIX, 99.

117 Sale to Astor and fate of house. Arthur Pound, *The Golden Earth*, 274.

7. COURTESY OF HAMILTON

118 "a private gentleman." Schachner, *Burr*, 83.

119 Assembly career. NY-JA, 12 Oct. 1784–27 Apr. 1785.

120 One of Burr's biographers. Schachner, *Burr*, 85.

120 "vague and ridiculous." Ernest Wilder Spaulding, *New York in the Critical Period, 1783–1789*, 107.

120 "the mighty . . . ones." Ibid.

121 "Gentlemen, I will live . . ." Alexander, *Burr*, 173.

121 Handbills. Parton, *Burr*, 173.

122 "The Anti-Federalist politicians in the ratifying conventions." The quote is not from Wood's book but from p. 91 of the portion of it reprinted in Wood, *The Confederation and the Constitution: The Critical Issues*.

123 "Republican government . . . beyond the compass of state boundaries." Elkins and McKitrick, "The Founding Fathers: Young Men of the Revolution," pamphlet reprinted with variations from *Pol. Sci. Quar.*, LXXVI (June 1961), 21.

124 "the eighteenth-century assumption." Wood, Gordon, *The Confederation and the Constitution*," 90.

124 "struggle over . . . Constitution . . . social." Ibid., 92.

125 Colden's report. To the Lords Commissioners of Trade, 20 Sept. 1764, *The Colden Letter Books*, in NYHS, *Collections* (vols. 9 and 10, 1867–77), I, 363–64. For a vivid picture of political shifts in New York during the Revolution, see Young, *The Democratic Republicans of New York*, chap. I.

128 "the propriety of Swimming with a Stream." R. R. Livingston to William Duer, 22 June 1777, R. R. Livingston Papers, NYHS, as quoted in Young, Ibid., 15.

128 Highlights of N.Y. constitution. See Charles Z. Lincoln, *The Constitutional History of New York;* Allan Nevins, *The*

PAGE

	American States During and After the Revolution, 1775–1789.
130	"virtuous . . . brave." Schuyler to Jay, 14 July 1777, in Henry P. Johnston, ed., *The Correspondence and Public Papers of John Jay, 1763–1826*, I, 147 (hereafter Jay, Papers [Johnston]).
131	"services . . . for sale." Alexander, *Political History*, I, 41.
131	Schachner's defense. In his *Burr*, 103.
131	"something . . . impossible." Worthington C. Ford, *Some Papers of Aaron Burr*, 48.
132	Mechanics federalists. Young, *Democratic Republicans*, 100–3.
132	"Equivocal." AH, Papers (Syrett), V, 524.
133	"numerous and respectable." N.Y. *Daily Advertiser*, 13 Feb. 1789.
135	"masterly . . . study." Schachner, *Burr*, 97.
136	A few statistics. Young, *Democratic Republicans*, 296.
137	neglecting his duties. Alexander, *Political History*, I, 41.
137	AB managed to buy two hundred thousand acres. Young, *Democratic Republicans*, 242.
137	AH and Schuyler "interested." N.Y. *Journal and Patriotic Register*, 16 June 1792; *Daily Advertiser*, 21 June 1792.
139	a gentleman's agreement. John C. Miller, *Alexander Hamilton: Portrait in Paradox*, 354 (hereafter Miller, *Hamilton*).
139	"art of holding together." Ibid., 355.
139	"some . . . unfit character," and AB using mails. AH to Rufus King, 15 July 1789, AH, Papers (Syrett), V, 262.
139	Clinton also pushing King. Young, *Democratic Republicans*, chap. I.
140	Livingstons quit Federalists, join Clinton, elect AB to Senate. Young, Ibid., 187–93; Broadus Mitchel, *Alexander Hamilton: The National Adventure*, 11 (cited hereafter as Mitchel, *Hamilton*, II), AH, Papers (Syrett), VII, 614–16, 616n.; Hammond, *History*, I, 50; Miller, *Hamilton*, 344–55; *Daily Advertiser*, 6, 15, 19, and 20 Jan. 1791.
142	"supple jack." Edgar S. Maclay, ed., *Journal of William Maclay*, 389–90.
142	Schuyler refuses to quit council. Hammond, *History*, I, 46–47.

PAGE

142 "formed for unpopularity." DAB.
142 "This Person (C.B.)." Hazard to AH, 25 Nov. 1791, AH, Papers (Syrett), IX, 537.
143 "always sedulous." Miller, *Hamilton*, 355.
143 "twistings." Troup to AH, 19 Jan. 1791, AH, Papers, (Syrett), VII, 455.
143 "sucked into his Excellency's vortex." James Tillary to AH, Jan. 1791, Ibid., 615.
143 Lewis to get attorney generalship. William B. Hatcher, *Edward Livingston: Jeffersonian Republican and Jacksonian Democrat*, 161.
144 "principal." 29 Jan. 1792, AH, Papers (Syrett), X, 579–81.

8. "COMMENCE POLITICIAN"

146 "smothered the . . . fire of Antifederalism." Irving Brandt, *James Madison: Father of the Constitution*," 332.
146 AH's fiscal policy and the argument over it. See Buel, *Securing the Revolution*, chap. 1, and Brandt, *Madison: Father of the Constitution*, chap. 23.
149 AB on the bank. Letter to Sedgwick, 3 Feb. 1791, Sedgwick Papers, MHS.
150 Duer's plaint. 19 Jan. 1791, AH, Papers (Syrett), VIII, 443; Troup's plaint, Ibid., VII, 455.
150 "that great fat fellow." Davis, *Burr*, I, 307.
151 "Clintonia borealis." S. E. Morrison and H. S. Commager, *Growth of the American Republic*, I, 343.
151 "passionate courtship." 15 June 1791, AH, Papers (Syrett), XI, 201.
151 "no inkling." Schachner, *Burr*, 101.
151 "Burr . . . easily fooled." Marquis James, *The Life and Times of Andrew Jackson*, 117.
151 "my election." 20 Jan. 1791, Sedgwick Papers, MHS.
152 "commence politician." Davis, *Burr*, I, 298.
152 "Dissipation & Ease." 3 Feb. 1791, Sedgwick Papers, MHS.
152 "Clinton is staggered." 30 Sept. 1791, AH, Papers (Syrett), XI, 246.

PAGE

153 still attorney general. New York State, *Opinions of the Attorneys General*, opposite p. viii.
154 "tolerable winter quarters." Davis, *Burr*, I, 303.
154 "commodious." Ibid., 306.
155 "the most inhospitable region." 23 Mar. 1792, Burr Papers, NYHS.
156 "a very plain chair," etc. "Historic Philadelphia," Amer. Philosophical Soc., *Transactions*, N.S. XLIII, pt. 1 (1953), 28n.
157 quantitative analysis. Mary P. Ryan, "Party Formation in the United States Congress, 1789–96," *The William and Mary Quar.*, 3d series, XXVIII (Oct. 1971), 530, 532.
158 "sufficient apology." Davis, *Burr*, I, 331.
159 "reports on my life style." Ibid., 314.
159 three brief notes to . . . Van Gaasbeek. 23 Feb., 27 Apr., and undated, 1794, PVG Papers, SHM.
160 TJ used cipher. For example, TJ to Madison, 20 June 1787, Julian P. Boyd, ed., *The Papers of Thomas Jefferson*, XI, 481, 484 (hereafter TJ, Papers [Boyd]).
160 "I accept your challenge." 22 June 1792, AH, Papers (Syrett), XI, 545.
160 "Savius." A. Pauly and others, *Real Encyclopadie d. Classicken Altertumwissenschaft.*
161 Theo Sr. on Catherine the Great. Davis, *Burr*, I, 301.
161 "spoken of with a coldness." Ibid., 363.
161 Dolley in financial straits, etc. Paul G. Sifton, " 'What a Dread Prospect . . .' Dolley Madison's Plague Year," *Pa. Mag. of Hist. and Biog.*, LXXXVIII (Apr. 1963), 182–87.
161 "trusted friend and adviser." Irving Brant, *James Madison, Father of the Constitution*, 406.
161 Dolley's will and "Thou must come to me," etc. Ibid., 406–7.
162 "Devil's own incomprehensibles." Frank Monaghan, *John Jay, defender of liberty . . .*, 325.
163 Yates can't afford to run. Schuyler to AH, 29 Jan. 1792, AH, Papers (Syrett), X, 589.
163 Troup temporarily for AB. Troup to AH, 7 Mar. 1792, Ibid., XI, 158.
163 Watson to AH. 2 Feb. 1792, Ibid., XI, 6–7.
164 Burrites under AB neither numerous nor strong. Jerome

PAGE

Mushkat, "Matthew Livingston Davis and the Political Legacy of Aaron Burr," *New-York Historical Soc. Quar.*, LIX (Apr. 1975), 123–48.

164 Charter Burrites. Young, *Democratic Republicans*, 285–86.

165 Ledyard's proposition. AH, Papers (Syrett), XI, 2–3.

166 Hamilton replied. Ledyard to AH, 17 Feb. 1792, Ibid., 38.

167 *Albany Gazette* article. As quoted in *New York Journal*, 22 Feb. 1792.

167 Ledyard to AH. 17 Feb. 1792, AH, Papers (Syrett), XI, 38.

9. REPUBLICAN AT LARGE

169 Election statute. *Laws of the State of New York*, 10th sess., chaps. 1 and 15.

169 "Was Richard R. Smith the sheriff?" Davis, *Burr*, I, 333–36.

170 Canvassers preponderantly pro-Clinton. Schuyler to AH, 9 May 1792, AH, Papers (Syrett), XI, 378–79; draft, same to ?, 19 May 1792, Schuyler Papers, LC.

170 Disputed election arguments and counter-charges. Young, *Democratic Republicans*, 300–1, 386.

171 "We conferred." 15 June 1792, Davis, *Burr*, I, 355–56.

171 King's opinion. Ibid., 336–38; Burr's opinion, Ibid., 339–41.

172 Troup's prediction. To Jay, 10 June 1792, Jay, Papers (Johnston), I, 428.

172 "obliged to give an opinion." Davis, *Burr*, I, 356.

172 Jay to his wife. Jay, Papers (Johnston), I, 289.

173 Demonstration for Jay. Young, *Democratic Republicans*, 311.

173 "to give him an honorable retreat." Oliver Wolcott, Sr., to his son, 2 Dec. 1792, in George Gibbs, ed., *Memoirs of the Administrations of Washington and John Adams, Edited from the Papers of Oliver Wolcott*, I, 84 (hereafter Gibbs, *Memoirs*).

173 "a greater menace—Burr," etc. AH to ———, 21 Sept. 1792, John C. Hamilton, ed., *The Works of Alexander Hamilton*, V, 527 (hereafter AH, *Works* [Hamilton]).

PAGE

174 AH recommends AB to high post. AH to Jay, 12 Feb. 1799, AH, Papers (Syrett), XXII, 476.

174 "private letter" to Washington. 26 Sept. 1792, Dreer Collection, HSP.

175 "Clinton . . . uncertain." To Jeremiah Wadsworth, 22 Sept. 1792, Jeremiah Wadsworth Papers, Conn. Hist. Soc., as quoted in "Turner, New-York in Presidential Politics," 101.

176 "Nothing . . . occurred in New York." 17 Oct. 1792, Madison Papers, NYPL, as quoted in Ibid., 103.

176 "Aaron Burr . . . puisne Judge." William Johnson, *Reports of Cases Adjudicated in the Supreme Court of Judicature of the State of New York*, I, xix.

176 Senate per diem. Jonathan Roberts, "Memoirs of a Senator from Pennsylvania," PMHB, LXXII, 239.

176 Edwards's report to Hutchinson, PMHB, XII (Oct. 1888), 372–73.

178 Attempt to ban bankers from Congress. *Annals*, 3d Cong., 1st sess., 31–32.

178 Attempt to censor Washington. Ibid., 3d Cong., 2d sess., 794.

178 Gallatin unseated. Ibid., 3d Cong., 1st sess., 58.

179 Jay's Treaty and AB's attitude toward. Samuel Flagg Bemis, *A Diplomatic History of the United States*, 5th ed., 90–95, 103; Monaghan, *Jay*, 367; *Annals*, 3d Cong., 1st sess., 83; *Ibid.*, 4th Cong., special sess., 8 June–26 June 1795; John C. Miller, *The Federalist Era*, 168; Stokes, *Iconography*, V, 1322; Jerald A. Combs, *The Jay Treaty: Political Battleground of the Founding Fathers*, passim. For a brilliant discussion of both the foreign-policy debate and the treaty, see Richard Buel, Jr., *Securing the Revolution*, chaps. 2 and 3.

183 Washington questions AB's "integrity," etc. Davis, *Burr*, I, 408–9.

183 Sedgwick's view of turndown of AB. 19 Nov. 1796, AH, Papers (Syrett), XX, 405.

185 "Correspondent" in *Albany Gazette*. 4 Dec. 1794.

185 Farewell Address published. In *American Daily Advertiser*.

186 AH's subterranean campaign. Douglas Southall Freeman, *George Washington: A Biography*, VII, 424.

PAGE

186 "struggling to get his walls up." Malone, *Jefferson*, II, 79.

186 AB guest at Monticello. Deposition of J. J. Monroe and Thomas Bell, 17 Oct. 1796, TJ Papers, LC.

186 Federalist paper on visit. *Virginia Gazette and General Advertiser*, 12 Oct. 1796, as quoted in Malone, *Jefferson*, III, 277.

187 TJ favors Madison. Davis, *Burr*, II, 77.

187 William L. Smith's impressions. Smith to Ralph Izard, 18 May 1796, in U. B. Phillips, ed., "South Carolina Federalist Correspondence, 1789–97," *Amer. Hist. Rev.*, *XIV* (July 1809), 780.

187 "totally unfit." To Judge Henry Tazewell, 11 Oct. 1796, Burr Papers, Yale.

188 Apology to Eustis. 30 Nov. 1796, Eustis Papers, MHS.

188 TJ consents to serve. Jay to Rufus King, in Charles R. King, ed., *The Life and Correspondence of Rufus King*, II, 102 (hereafter R. King, *Correspondence*).

188 PVG reports "interview" with "H." 25 Nov. 1796, PVG Papers, SHM.

188 PVG gets letters suggesting last-minute action for AB. [T. L. Witbeck?] to PVG, 2 Dec. 1796, and ——— to ———, no date, PVG Papers, 2766–146 and 2973–153, SHM.

188 Code drafted by Burrites. 12 Nov. 1796, PVG Papers, SHM.

189 Promises by Southern electors. Raymond Walters, Jr., *Albert Gallatin: Jeffersonian Financier and Diplomat*, 125; Gibbs, *Memoirs*, II, 488.

190 "I have watched the movements." Ibid., I, 379–80.

10. THE THEODOSIAS

191 "It was a knowledge." Davis, *Burr*, I, 362.

192 "attachment not . . . common." Ibid., 270.

192 "Miss Prissy." Ibid., 371.

192 "Augusta Louisa," etc. Ibid.

192 "*mere* fashionable woman." Ibid., 361–62.

192 "averse." Ibid., 433.

PAGE

192 "impeachment of my taste." Theo Jr. to Frances Prevost, 24 Mar. 1802, Burr Papers, NYHS.
192 "intercourse of the heart." Theo Jr. to Bartow Prevost, 18 Mar. 1810, Ibid.
192 "thinking of my dear brother." Same to same, 15 Jan. 1799, Ibid.
192 "giddiness." Same to same, 1795, Ibid.
193 "greatest sacrifice." Same to same, 25 Feb. 1798, Ibid.
193 "resign politics," "can love her too," and "Have you seen a few verses?". Same to same, 27 June and 13 Jan. 1799, and 18 Dec. 1794, Ibid.
194 "disagreement" with landlady. Sifton, " 'What a dread prospect,' " 187n.
194 "easy place to live in." 1794, Burr Papers, NYHS.
194 dreams of carriage "oversetting." Theo Jr. to Frances Prevost, 17 July 1801, Ibid.
194 "how I love a riot." 1794, Ibid.
194 "grand source of female folly." Mary Wollstonecraft, *A Vindication of the Rights of Woman*, 96–97.
194 "women have souls." Davis, *Burr*, I, 361–62.
195 "my adopted daughter." 25 or 26 Jan. 1801, Eustis Papers, MHS.
195 On Nathalie. See South Carolina *Daily Item*, 75th anniversary ed., 15 Oct. 1969.
195 "you write *acurate* for *accurate*," etc. Pidgin, *Theodosia*, 193.
195 Utilizes sentence from one of her letters. Davis, *Burr*, I, 374.
196 AB on Stuart portrait of Theo Jr. AB to Theo Jr., 23 Jan. 1797, in Pidgin, *Theodosia*, 202.
197 Offers to quit Senate. David, *Burr*, I, 369.
197 Céleste affair. Ibid., II, 222–32.

11. AFFAIRS OF STATE

199 Schuyler resigns from Senate. NY-JA, 2 Jan. 1798.
199 AB nominated for state Senate. Broadside, 19 Apr. 1796, New York State Lib., Albany.
200 Troup baffled. 2 Oct. 1798, R. King Papers, NYHS.

PAGE

201 "You red-headed son of a bitch." E. Millicent Sowerby, "Thomas Jefferson and His Library," Biblio. Soc. of Amer., *Papers*, L (1956), 221–22.

201 $13 million in claims. Bemis, *Diplomatic History*, 114–15.

202 TJ's 17 June 1797 letter to AB. TJ Papers, LC; Paul Leicester Ford, ed., *The Works of Thomas Jefferson*, Federal ed., VIII, 309–13 (hereafter TJ, *Works* [Ford]).

203 "His conduct." Franklin B. Sawvel, ed., *The Complete Anas of Thomas Jefferson*, 26 Jan. 1804 (hereafter TJ, *Anas*).

204 AB's answer to TJ. 21 June 1797, TJ Papers, LC.

204 Conference in Philadelphia, Malone, *Jefferson*, III, 324.

204 The Reynolds affair. TJ, Papers (Boyd), XVIII, Appendix; AH, Papers (Syrett), XXI, "Introductory Note," 121–44 (Boyd favors Callender's view that AH's love letters to Maria were forgeries. Syrett argues that too many questions remain unanswered to warrant such a view); Miller, *Hamilton*, 461; Robert C. Alberts, "The Notorious Affair of Mrs. Reynolds," *American Heritage*, XXIV (Feb. 1973), 91; AB to Monroe, 13 Aug. 1797, Burr File, Huntington.

209 Burr pushes emancipation. NY-JA, 4 and 31 Jan., 7 Feb., and 28 Mar. 1797.

209 On the Swartwouts. Walter Barrett, *The Old Merchants of New York City*, 3d series (1864), 248–51; see also Arthur James Weise, *The Swartwout Chronicles*.

211 "absurd to suppose." Letter to Randolph Harrison, 3 Mar. 1816, as quoted in Fox, *Decline*, 126.

211 On Peck. Throop Wilder, "Jedidiah Peck, Statesman, Soldier, Preacher," *New York History*, XXII (1941), 290–300; Hammond, *Political History*, I, 123–25.

215 Adams to Lloyd. *Works*, X, 123–26.

216 AH to Wolcott. [28 June 1798], AH, Papers (Syrett), XXI, 521–22.

216 Troup amazed. Troup to R. King, 2 Oct. 1798, R. King Papers, NYHS.

216 "he despised Washington," etc. Miller, *Hamilton*, 480.

217 AH asks Jay to give post to AB. AH, Papers (Syrett), XXII, 476.

218 AB ducks vote on Addison-Foote. NY-JA, 4 Jan. 1799;

PAGE

James Cheetham, *A View of the Political Conduct of Aaron Burr, Esq.*, 26–27 (hereafter Cheetham, *View*).

218 Holland Company Affair. Paul D. Evans, *The Holland Land Company*, passim; Laws of New York, chap. 58, 19th sess.; Ibid., chap. 36, 20th sess.; Davis, *Burr*, I, 418–23; Schachner, *Burr*, 156; Laws of New York, chap. 72, 21st sess.; Troup to R. King, 2 Sept. 1799, R. King Papers, NYHS.

221 Manhattan Company Affair. Beatrice G. Reubens, "Burr, Hamilton, and the Manhattan Company," *Pol. Science Quar.*, LXXII (Dec. 1957), 578–607; Ibid., LXXIII (Mar. 1958), 100–25; Stokes, *Iconography*, I, 387–88; Dangerfield, *Chancellor Livingston*, 291; AH to James A. Bayard, 16 Jan. 1801, AH Papers, LC.

12. PRESIDENT-MAKER

231 Alien and Sedition Acts and Virginia and Kentucky Resolutions. Adrienne Koch and Harry Ammon, "The Virginia and Kentucky Resolutions: An Episode in Jefferson's and Madison's Defense of Civil Liberties," *The William and Mary Quar.*, 3d series, V (1948), 145–76; Richard E. Welch, Jr., *Theodore Sedgwick, Federalist: A Political Portrait*, 197; Leonard W. Levy, *Jefferson and Civil Liberties: The Darker Side*, 258; AB to TJ, 3 Feb. 1799, TJ Papers, LC; Alexander, *Political History*, I, 89–90; Hammond, *History*, I, 132; Wandell-Minnegerode, *Burr*, I, 189; Hatcher, *Edward Livingston*, 59.

237 "April contest" a popular Presidential election. Turner, "New-York in Presidential Politics," 171.

238 Sedgwick and others disliked Adams. Troup to R. King, 1 Jan. 1800, R. King Papers, NYHS.

238 Adams "unfit." Morris to Washington, 9 Dec. 1799, in Jared Sparks, *The Life of George Washington*, III, 123.

238 "would do credit." Hammond, *History*, I, 90.

239 Tammany not AB's creature. Peter Paulson, "The Tammany Society and the Jeffersonian Movement in New York City, 1795–1800," *New York Hist.*, XXXIV (1953), 72–84; Mushkat, *Tammany: The Evolution of a Political Machine, 1789–1865*, 26–29.

PAGE

239 Extent of suffrage in 1800 in NYC. Turner, "New-York in Presidential Politics," 171; and see Richard Patrick McCormick, *The Second American Party System.*

240 Legislator's salary and AH's problem. NY-JA, 24th sess., 2d meeting, p. 30; M. L. Davis to Gallatin, 24 Mar. 1800, Gallatin Papers, NYHS.

241 "Now I have him all hollow." John Adams to James Lloyd, 17 Feb. 1815, Adams, *Works*, X, 125.

241 AH's tally. Miller, *Hamilton*, 152.

241 "gentlemen are not worth their salt." Ibid.

241 AB's slate and Clinton's reluctance. N.Y. *American Citizen*, 22 Apr. 1800; William Peter Van Ness, *An Examination of the Various Charges Exhibited against Aaron Burr*, 35; N.Y. *Commercial Advertiser*, 26 Apr. 1800.

244 "Col. Burr kept open house." Journal of Benjamin Betterton Howell, 118–19, NYHS.

244 a "would be Vice President." *Daily Advertiser*, 28 Apr. 1800.

244 "Hamilton harangues." *Commercial Advertiser*, 3 Apr. 1800.

244 "I have been night and day." Letter to Peter Van Schaack, 2 May 1800, as quoted in Turner, "New-York in Presidential Politics," 177.

244 "storm of rain." *Commercial Advertiser*, 25 Apr. 1800.

245 "brimstone." *American Citizen*, 15 Apr. 1800.

245 "elegant chariot." Ibid., 1 May 1800.

245 flotilla of "carriages," etc. *N.Y. Gazette*, 13 May 1800.

245 watch "leading Federal gentlemen." Davis, *Burr*, II, 61.

245 TJ "will have 12 votes for President." *Daily Advertiser*, 12 May 1800.

246 "Intervention of a Supreame Power." James Nicholson to Gallatin, 6 May 1800, Gallatin Papers. NYHS.

246 "beat you by superior *Management*." Miller, *Hamilton*, 531.

246 "Shadows, fiends and darkness." Letter to R. King, 1 Oct. 1800, R. King Papers, NYHS.

246 "in times like this." AH to Jay, 7 May 1800, Jay, Papers (Johnston), IV, 270–72.

247 "Proposing a measure." Ibid., 272n.

PAGE

248 AB "the least selfish." Dangerfield, *Chancellor Livingston*, 298.

248 "If we carry this election." Davis to Gallatin, 24 Mar. 1800, Gallatin Papers, NYHS.

248 three "characters . . . contemplated." Same to same, 5 May 1800, Ibid.

249 "the New York election has engrossed . . . us." Gallatin to Hannah G., 6 May 1800, Henry Adams, *The Life of Albert Gallatin*, 240–41.

250 Nicholson's two letters to Gallatin. 6 and 7 May 1800, Gallatin Papers, NYHS.

251 "Burr . . . no confidence in the Virginians." Hannah Gallatin to G., Adams, *Life of Gallatin*, 243.

251 two documents drafted three years later. G. Clinton to D. Clinton, 13 Dec. 1803, and Nicholson's deposition of 26 Dec. 1803, DeWitt Clinton Papers, Columbia University.

254 Nicholson gets federal office. Schachner, *Burr*, 180.

254 Both parties pledge electors to vote equally for candidates. Miller, *Federalist Era*, 259; MHS, *Collections*, 7th series, I, 77; Gibbs, *Memoirs*, I, 347; Uriah Tracy to James McHenry, 30 Dec. 1800, Steiner, *Life and Corres. of James McHenry*, 483.

255 "support *Adams* and *Pinckney* equally." 4 May 1800, Henry Cabot Lodge, ed., *The Works of Alexander Hamilton*, X, 371 (hereafter, AH, *Works* [Lodge]).

256 "my mind is made up." AH to Sedgwick, 10 May 1800, Sedgwick Papers, MHS.

256 AH's pamphlet against John Adams. Hammond, *History*, I, 60, 150; Miller, *Hamilton*, 518, 520, 523–24; Adams, *Works*, IX, 277.

259 "a kind of suppurative tumors." AB to Eustis, 13 June 1800, Eustis Papers, MHS.

259 Miss Binney. AB to Eustis, Ibid.

259 AB's visit to R.I. and Conn. and belief TJ will get a R.I. vote. Theo Jr. to F. Prevost, 26 Aug. 1800, Burr Papers, NYHS; AB to Eustis, 10, 16, and 26 Aug. 1800, Eustis Papers, MHS; AB to R. R. Livingston, 7 and 24 Sept. 1800, R. R. Livingston Papers, NYHS; Troup to R. King, 14 Sept. 1800, R. King Papers, NYHS; AB to TJ, 23 Dec. 1800,

PAGE

TJ Papers, LC; AB to James Madison, 9 Oct. 1800, Burr Papers, Yale.

260 "uneasy lest the Southern States" be untrue "to their duty." Madison to Monroe, date unknown, *Madison's Writings*, Cong. ed., II, 160.

261 "expresses much anxiety." Same to TJ, 12 Oct. 1800, Ibid., 162.

261 "Mr. Gale handed me your letter." AB to Willett, 11 Sept. 1800, Burr Misc. Papers, LC.

261 AB's reliance on Green and Hampton. AB to Eustis, 9 Dec. 1800, Eustis Papers, MHS; Green to Denniston and Cheetham, 11 Oct. 1802, quoted in Van Ness, *Examination*, 76–77.

262 On DeWitt Clinton. Stokes, *Iconography*, V, 1191; DAB; Dorothie Bobbé, *DeWitt Clinton*, 62–67; Van Ness, *Examination*, 42.

265 AB "in very high glee." Troup to R. King, King, *Life and Corres.*, III, 290.

266 "rumors . . . alarm us." 18 Nov. 1800, Edwards Family Papers, Yale.

266 AB on S. Carolina electors. Letters to Eustis, 7 and 9 Dec. 1800, Eustis Papers, MHS; to Charles Biddle, 10 Dec. 1800, Fuller Collection, II, A, 1, Princeton U. Lib.

267 One Federalist amused. Uriah Tracy to James McHenry, in Steiner, *Life and Corres. of James McHenry*, 483.

13. DILEMMA: THE TIE FOR PRESIDENT

269 Federalist Dent a Jeffersonian but Md. evenly divided. Edward G. Roddy, "Maryland and the Presidential Election of 1800," *Md. Hist. Mag.*, LVI (Sept. 1961), 263.

269 McKean's threat. Letter to TJ, 19 Mar. 1801, TJ Papers, LC.

269 Less than twenty congressmen for usurpation. Adams, *Life of Gallatin*, 247–51.

270 AH calls AB "*selfish*," and Sedgwick's comment thereon. AH to James A. Bayard, 16 Jan. 1801, Hamilton, *Works* (Hamilton), VI, 487; Sedgwick to AH, same date, Ibid., 511–15.

PAGE

270 AB's choice of Smith as confidant unwise. Suggested by Mary-Jo Kline in letter to author, Dec. 1977.

271 AB's disclaimer letter to Smith. Contemporary copy in Burr File, Huntington. This copy carries a postscript, reading "We think J. has one vote at least (Col. Dewey) in Vermont, but as yet nothing certain has transpired."

271 "I could hardly forgive any democrat." AB to Smith, 24 Dec. 1800, U. of Va. mss. 5789.

272 Tie appears certain to Washingtonians on 15 Dec. 1800. Dangerfield, *Chancellor Livingston*, 301; Brant, *James Madison, Secretary of State 1800–9*, 26; Edw. Livingston to R. R. Livingston, 16 Dec. 1800, R. R. Livingston Papers, NYHS.

272 "From South Carolina," etc. TJ to AB, 15 Dec. 1800, TJ Papers, LC.

273 AB willing to fill "chasm." Letter to TJ, 23 Dec. 1800, TJ Papers, LC.

274 "My dear Colonel." Harper to AB, 24 Dec. 1800, U. of Va. mss. 5789; *Niles Register*, 4 Jan. 1823.

274 AB's angry letter to Smith. 24 Dec. 1800, Burr File, Huntington.

275 "Burr deserves immortal honor." Letter to Joseph H. Nicholson, 3 Jan. 1801, J. H. Nicholson mss., LC.

275 "cordially cooperate." Morton Borden, *The Federalism of James A. Bayard*, 81.

275 Burr not "committed." Letter to R. King, 21 Jan. 1801, R. King Papers, NYHS.

275 the "cunning" Burr. Steiner, *Life and Corres. of James McHenry*, 483.

275 *Washington Federalist*'s comment. 1 Jan. 1801.

276 "language of the democrats." Robert G. Harper to AB, 24 Dec. 1800, U. of Va. mss. 5789; *Niles Register*, 4 Jan. 1823.

276 The Philadelphia get-together. Hitchborn to TJ, 1 Jan. 1801, TJ Papers, LC; Christie to Smith, 19 Dec. 1802, S. Smith Papers, LC; TJ, *Anas*, 223.

278 "a stand taken by the Democrats." 11 Jan. 1801, S. Smith Papers, LC.

PAGE

279 "purely on private business." N.Y. *Chronicle Express*, 25 Nov. 1802; Davis, *Burr*, II, 76–77.

279 AB asks "history of an evening's amusement," and Smith's reply. AB to Smith, 29 Dec. 1800, Burr File, Huntington; Smith to AB, 11 Jan. 1801, S. Smith Papers, LC.

280 "Demo's . . . uneasy." Bayard to Bassett, 3 Jan. 1801, Elizabeth Donnan, ed., "Papers of James A. Bayard, 1796–1815," *Annual Report of the American Historical Association for the Year 1913*, II (1915), 116 (hereafter Bayard, Papers [Donnan]).

280 TJ records rumors. His *Anas*, 209–10.

281 AH's letter-writing campaign. To Wolcott, 16 Dec. 1800, AH, *Works* (Hamilton), VI, 486; to Bayard, 16 Jan. 1801, Ibid., 419–24; to Rutledge, 4 Jan. 1801, Edward Carey Gardiner Collection, misc. sec., HSP.

282 McKean for letting TJ and AB decide. McKean to TJ, 27 Jan. 1801, TJ Papers, LC.

282 *Aurora* on AB. 1 Jan. 1801.

283 On Alston. Anthony Q. Devereux, *The Rice Princes: a rice epoch revisited*, 37, 399; Arney R. Childs, *Rice Planter and Statesman: The Recollections of J. Motte Alston, 1821–1909*, 17; Davis, *Burr*, I, 282.

283 Courtship and marriage of Alston and Theo Jr. AB to Eustis, 10 Aug. 1800, Eustis Papers, MHS; Theo Jr. to F. Prevost, 26 Aug. 1800, Burr Papers, NYHS; Madison to TJ, 21 Oct. 1800, *Madison Writings*, II, 162; Theo Jr. to Alston, 13 Jan. 1801, Burr Family Papers, Yale; Davis, *Burr*, II, 244.

286 AB hears from TJ and replies. 1 Feb. 1801, and 12 Feb. 1801, TJ Papers, LC.

286 AB aware TJ is heeding rumors. Smith to AB, 11 Jan. 1801, S. Smith Papers, LC.

287 Gallatin's request and AB's reaction. Herbert S. and Marie B. Hecht, *Aaron Burr: Portrait of an Ambitious Man*, 163–65; Jrnl of Benjamin Betterton Howell, pp. 117–23, NYHS (Betterton writes: "Sometime after the appearance of the first Vol. of Burr's life by M. Davis, I met Davis. Mr. Townsend . . . was with me. He inquired of D. why the pre-

PAGE

ceding fact [that Gallatin had urged AB to come to Washington and fight for the Presidency] had not been used in the Life. D. replied in substance that it would appear in the 2d. Vol. . . . however it did not appear in the 2d Vol. Townsend subsequently told me that he had once intimated his knowledge of the subject to Gallatin who replied, you must be mistaken, I was always for Jefferson . . ."); AB to Gallatin, 12 Feb. 1801, Adams, *Life of Gallatin*, 246; same, Gallatin Papers, NYHS.

289 Eve of House election and the election. Plumer, *Memorandum*, 30 Dec. 1805, p. 261; Bayard's 1805 deposition in Bayard, *Papers* (Donnan), 122n; Bayard to Andrew Bayard, Ibid., 121; Roddy, "Maryland and the Presidential Election of 1800," 264; *Annals*, 6th Cong., 2d sess., pp. 1021–34; Bayard's 1806 deposition in Bayard, *Papers* (Donnan), 128n; Bayard to Bassett, 16 Feb. 1801, Ibid., 126; Washington *National Intelligencer*, 13, 16, and 18 Feb. 1801; Davis, *Burr*, II, 113–14; Bayard to AH, 8 May 1801, AH, *Works* (Hamilton), VI, 522–24.

14. VICE PRESIDENT BURR

296 "your very amusing history." 25 Feb. 1801, Gallatin Papers, NYHS.

296 Appearance of Senate chamber. Glenn Brown, *History of the United States Capitol*, 27.

297 "We behold our hero." Parton, *Burr*, 297.

299 AB's patronage recommendations and TJ's handling of them. Noble E. Cunningham, Jr., *Jeffersonian Republicans in Power: Party Operations 1801–1809*, 38–44; Malone, *Jefferson*, IV, 34; Schachner, *Thomas Jefferson: A Biography*, 669, 673, 675–76; AB to Gallatin, 28 June 1801, Gallatin Papers, NYHS; AB to Smith, 18 May 1801, U. of Va. mss. 5789; Gallatin to TJ, 12 Sept. 1801, Henry Adams, ed., *The Writings of Albert Gallatin*, I, 47–48; same to same, 14 Sept. 1801, Ibid., 51–53; Howard L. McBain, *DeWitt Clinton and the Origin of the Spoils System in New York*, 126–37; John Armstrong to Gallatin, 7 May 1801, Gallatin

PAGE

Papers, NYHS; TJ to AB, 18 Nov. 1801, TJ Papers, LC; same to Gallatin, 18 Sept. 1801, Ibid.; TJ to AB, 18 Nov. 1801, Ibid.; Samuel Osgood to Madison, 24 Apr. 1801, Madison Papers, LC; TJ to George Clinton, 17 May 1801, TJ, *Writings* (Ford), VIII, 53.

300 NY State patronage and the 1801 constitutional convention. McBain, *DeWitt Clinton*, 84–85; AB to George Clinton, 22 July 1801, George Clinton, *Public Papers*, XXVI, 6858, as quoted in McBain, Ibid., 131–32; Ibid., 122–25; Davis, *Burr*, II, 158; Schachner, *Burr*, 212.

307 AB's inferior position in Administration and the Judiciary Act repeal debate. Sedgwick to R. King, 20 Feb. 1802, R. King, *Works* (King), IV, 74; D. Clinton to Horatio Gates, Feb. 1802, Emmett collection, NYPL, as quoted in Schachner, *Burr*, 219; Bayard to Bassett, 25 Jan. 1802, Bayard, *Papers* (Donnan), 147; Morris, *Diary and Letters*, II, 147, 426; Davis, *Burr*, II, 169, 171; Beveridge, *Marshall*, III, chap. VIII; *Annals*, 7th Cong., 1st sess., 7, 12, 14, 15, 19, 26, and 27 Jan., and 2 and 3 Feb. 1802.

313 Washington's birthday toast. *American Citizen*, 12 June 1802; Bayard to AH, 12 Apr. 1802, AH, *Works* (Hamilton), VI, 539; Schachner, *Burr*, 225–26.

314 Pamphlet War. Davis, *Burr*, II, 182n, 183, 205, 215; *Evening Post*, 26, 27, and 31 May and 1, 2, 4, and 22 June 1802; Wandell, *AB in Literature*, 251; "John Wood" in DAB; "James Cheatham" in DAB; Alan Nevins, *The Evening Post: A Century of Journalism*, 25, 51; Cheatham to TJ, 10 Dec. 1901 and same to same, 29 Dec. 1801, TJ Papers, LC; TJ to Cheatham, 17 Jan. 1802, TJ, *Works* (Ford), IX, 347–48; same to same, 23 Apr. 1802, MHS, *Proceedings*, 1907–8, 3d series, I, 58; Parton, *Burr*, 324n; Hammond, *History*, I, 141, 189–90; AB to Joseph Bloomfield, 21 Sept. 1802, and AB to Eustis, 13 May 1801, Eustis Papers, MHS; *American Citizen*, 28 May 1802; Schachner, *Burr*, 226–33; *Chronicle Express*, 2 May 1803, and 19 and 23 Jan. and 6 and 28 Feb. 1804; Alexander, *Political History*, I, 122–27; Fox, *Decline*, 58–60.

323 AB's life in Washington. Schachner, *Burr*, 224; Davis, *Burr*, II, 172, 176, 185, 189, 218; Plumer to Judge Smith, 21

Feb. 1803, in William Plumer, Jr., *Life of William Plumer*, 256–57.

324 Relations with women and friends. Pierpont Edwards to AB, 8 Aug. 1785, Gratz collection, HSP; AB to Eustis, 21 Mar., 18 and 27 Apr. 1801; Eustis Papers, MHS; Eustis to AB, 11 and 13 Aug. 1803, and 25 May 1804, Gratz collection, HSP; Mrs. Hayt to AB, 29 Sept. 1803, Ibid.

327 Becomes a grandfather. Davis, *Burr*, II, 163, 170, 196–97; Theo Jr. to F. Prevost, 18 July 1802, Burr Papers, NYHS; F. Prevost to Theo, 6 Aug. 1802, Ibid.; Schachner, *Burr*, 237.

15. TRAGEDY AT WEEHAWKEN

331 Harry Croswell case. Levy, *Jefferson and Civil Liberties*, 59; AH, *Law Papers*, I, 757–77, 785, 789, 793; Hammond, *History*, I, 205–6.

332 G. Clinton does not want another term. DeWitt Clinton to TJ, 26 Nov. 1803, TJ Papers, LC.

332 G. Clinton lets leadership know he is available. G. Clinton to TJ, 20 Jan. 1804, Ibid.

332 Clinton nominated. Cunningham, *Jeffersonian Republicans in Power*, 212.

333 AB plans Western tour. Davis, *Burr*, II, 318.

333 Burrites buttonholing Federalists. Troup to R. King, 4 Jan. 1804, King, *Papers* (King), IV, 340.

333 AB to spend time in NY. Davis, *Burr*, II, 271.

334 AB-TJ interview. TJ, *Anas*, 224–28.

335 AB to NY and back. Davis, *Burr*, II, 275–76.

336 The 1804 gubernatorial election and the New England Secession movement. Schachner, *Burr*, 241, 244; Spaulding, *George Clinton*, 273; Hammond, *History*, I, 208; AH, *Works* (Lodge), VII, 325, 609; AB to Sedgwick, 10 July 1804, Sedgwick Papers, MHS. Davis, *Burr*, II, 277, 281, 284; *Chronicle Express*, 22 Feb., 17, 20, 24, and 29 Mar., and 2 and 6 Apr. 1804; Plumer to Jeremiah Smith, 25 Feb. 1804, Plumer Papers, LC; Maclay, *Journal*, 22 Feb. 1790, 331–32; Plumer to John Quincy Adams, 20 Dec. 1828, in

PAGE

Henry Adams, *New England Federalism*, 144–46; Malone, *Jefferson*, III, 405; Plumer, *Memorandum*, 517–18; Van Ness to Van Buren, 22 Feb. 1804, and Van Buren to Van Ness, 13 Mar. 1804, Van Buren Papers, LC; *Civil List, State of New York 1887*, 166; John Randolph to Joseph H. Nicholson, 1 July 1804, J. H. Nicholson Papers, LC; Griswold to Wolcott, 4 Mar. 1804, in Adams, *New England Federalism*, 354–56; J. C. Hamilton, *History of the Republic of the United States*, 781ff.; Fox, *Decline*, 64–65; Alexander, *Political History*, I, 137.

344 The duel. James F. Risher, Jr., *Interview with Honor*, 48 passim; *Virginia Globe*, 21 Nov. 1968; Malone, *Jefferson*, III, 421; Edwin Brockholst Livingston, *The Livingstons of Livingston Manor*, 342; Plumer, *Memorandum*, 213; Charles Biddle, *Autobiography*, 305; Miller, *Hamilton*, 569; TJ, *Anas*, 224; Harold C. Syrett and Jean G. Cooke, eds., *Interview in Weehawken*, passim; AB to Charles Biddle, 18 July 1804, Charles Biddle Papers, HSP (Burr's letters to Biddle, previously overlooked, are valuable in that they reveal his motives for challenging, his version of what happened on the dueling ground, and his reactions on learning of Hamilton's expressed resolve to withhold his first and perhaps even his second fire); Davis, *Burr*, 290, 324–26; A. M. Hamilton, *Intimate Life*, 409; Merrill Lindsay, "Pistols Shed Light on Famed Duel," *Smithsonian*, VII (Nov. 1976), 96; photo of AH's death certificate, NYHS; Randolph to Joseph H. Nicholson, J. H. Nicholson Papers, LC; AB to Dr. Hosack, 12 July 1804, collection of autograph letters, principally to Dr. David Hosack, owned by John Hampton Barnes, Jr.—American Philosophical Society has privilege of copying.

357 AB's flight. Davis, *Burr*, II, 327–29, 332, 331, 334, 171, 345, 352, 347–48; John Swartwout to Charles Biddle, 18 Oct. 1804, Fuller Collection, IV, a, 6, Princeton U. Lib.

363 Chase trial and AB's last days in Senate. Plumer, *Memorandum*, 213, 244, 239, 310, 313; Plumer to Daniel Treadwell, 6 Nov. 1804, Plumer mss., LC; O'Neill, *Great God Brown*, II, 3; S. L. Mitchill, "Dr. Mitchill's Letters from Washington: 1801–1813," *Harper's Magazine*, LVIII (Apr. 1879),

740, 749–50; *Annals*, 8th Cong., 2d sess., 13 Feb. 1805 passim; Plumer to Jeremiah Smith, 6 Dec. 1804, Plumer mss., LC; Beveridge, *Marshall*, III, 159, 179; *Trial of Samuel Chase*, I, 23; John Quincy Adams, *Memoirs*, I, 223; Gordon L. Thomas, "Aaron Burr's Farewell Address," *Quar. Jour. of Speech*, XXXIX (Oct. 1953), 278, 313, 277n; Davis, *Burr*, II, 360; *Annals*, 8th Cong., 2d sess., 23 Feb. 1805.

Bibliography

Index

Bibliography

I. Manuscripts

American Philosophical Society
Collection of autograph letters, principally to Dr. David Hosack, owned by John Hampton Barnes, Jr.
Charles Wilson Peale Letterbook

Columbia University Libraries
Papers of DeWitt Clinton and the Jay Family

Henry E. Huntington Library
Burr File and Burr–Le Guen Correspondence

Historical Society of Pennsylvania
Papers of John Barclay, Charles Biddle, and Col. Clement Biddle
Dreer Collection
Edward Carey Gardiner Collection
Simon Gratz Collection

Library of Congress
Papers of Aaron Burr, Alexander Hamilton, John Hancock, Thomas Jefferson, James Madison, James Monroe, Joseph H. Nicholson, William Plumer, Samuel Smith, Jeremiah Wadsworth, Oliver Wolcott, and Martin Van Buren
Peter Force Transcripts
Shippen Family Papers

Massachusetts Historical Society
William Eustis's letters to Aaron Burr and Theodore Sedgwick Papers

National Archives
James Wilkinson's Order Book, Record Group 94, Adjutant General's Office
War of the Revolution Orderly Book, Book 12, Record Group 93

New–York Historical Society
Papers of Aaron Burr, Albert Gallatin, Horatio Gates, Rufus King, John and Anthony Lamb, and Robert R. Livingston
Broadside: B775. New York, 1791. Election Proclamation
The Journal and Scrapbook of Benjamin Betterton Howell

Princeton University Library
Papers of the Rev. Aaron Burr and Jonathan Edwards
Burr Additional Papers, Thomas Foxcroft Manuscripts, and Manuscripts from the C. P. G. Fuller Collection

Public Records Office, London
Jeffrey Amherst Papers (microfilm available)

Franklin D. Roosevelt Library
Peter Van Gaasbeek and De Peyster Papers in FDR's Collection of Hudson River Valley Manuscripts and FDR's Collection of Historical Manuscripts

Senate House Museum, Kingston, N.Y.
Peter Van Gaasbeek Papers

University College Library, University of London
Jeremy Bentham Papers

University of Virginia Library
U. of Va. Manuscripts 5789—relating to the election of 1800
McGregor Collection

II. Printed Sources

Adams, Abigail. *Letters of*, Chas. F. Adams, ed., 1840.
Adams, Henry. *New England Federalism*, 1877.
Adams, John Quincy. *Memoirs of*, Chas. F. Adams, ed., 12 v., 1874–77.
Annals of the Congress of the United States, Gales and Seaton, eds., 1849.
Bayard, James A. "Papers of," Elizabeth Donnan, ed., American Historical Association, *Annual Report for 1913*, II.
Biddle, Chas. Autobiography of, 1883.
Boston News-Letter obituary of the Rev. Aaron Burr, 20 Oct. 1757.

Burr, Aaron. *An Impartial Statement Respecting the Decision of the late Committee of Canvassers* (pamphlet [Nov. 1792]).

———. "Orders of, 15 Jan.–28 Feb. [1779], while in command at White Plains, of a detachment on the lines in Westchester County," *Quarterly Bulletin of the Westchester County Historical Soc.*, VII (Oct. 1932), 169–73.

———. "Some Papers of," W. C. Ford, ed., *Proceedings of the American Antiquarian Soc.*, 1919.

———. "Some . . . papers [of], *Vineland Hist. Mag.*, XIX, 95–100, 114–19; XX, 173–75, 211–15, 233–37, 287.

Burr, Rev. Aaron. *A discourse Delivered at New-Ark in New Jersey, January 1, 1755.* Being a day set apart for *solemn Fasting* and *Prayer*, on Account of the late Encroachments of the French, and their Designs against the *British Colonies in America.*

———. *A Servant of God dismissed from Labour to Rest.* A Funeral Sermon Preached at the Interment of . . . Jonathan Belcher, Esq.; Governor of . . . New Jersey [1758].

———. Letter to Mr. Hogg, Edinburgh merchant, 3 Dec. 1755, *The Gentleman's Mag.*, XLIIV, N.S. (July 1855), 50–51.

Chase, Samuel. *Trial of . . .* , an associate justice impeached by the House of Representatives for High Crimes and Misdemeanors before the Senate of the United States, taken in shorthand by Samuel H. Smith and Thomas Lloyd, 2 v., 1805.

Chastellux, François Jean, Marquis de. *Travels in North America in the Years 1780, 1781, and 1782*, 2 v., 1786.

Cheetham, James. *A Narrative of the Suppression by Col. Burr of the History of the Administration of John Adams, 1802.*

———. *An antidote to John Wood's Poison*, 1802.

———. *A view of the Political Conduct of Aaron Burr*, 1802.

———. *Nine Letters on the subject of Aaron Burr's Political Defection*, 1803.

———. *A Reply to Aristides*, 1804.

Chesterfield, Philip Dormer Stanhope, Fourth Earl of. *Lord Chesterfield's Letters to his Son and others*, 1774.

Coglan, Mrs. Margaret. *Memoirs of*, 2 v., 1795.

Coleman, William. *Cases of Practice Adjudged in the Supreme Court of the State of New York, together with the Rules and Orders of the Court, from October Term 1791 to October Term 1800*, 1801.

DAVIS, John. *Travels of Four Years and a Half in the United States*, 1909 reprint.
DAVIS, Matthew L., *Memoirs of Aaron Burr*, 2 v., 1836–37.
DUNLAP, William. *Diary of*, NYHS, *Collections*, 1929–30.
EDWARDS, Jonathan. *Basic Writings*, Ola E. Winslow, ed., 1966.
———. *The Works of*, Sereno Dwight, ed., 10 v., 1830.
Elizabeth, New Jersey, *Record Book of First Presbyterian Church of*, Bertha Baldwin Bigelow, comp. and ed., 1916.
EVANS, Charles. *American Bibliography*, 1639 through 1820, 13 v., 1903.
FITHIAN, Philip Vickers. *Journal and Letters 1767–1774*, John Rogers Williams, ed., 1900.
FORCE, Peter. *American Archives*, 5th series, III, 1853.
GALLATIN, Albert. *The Writings of*, Henry Adams, ed., 3 v., 1879.
HAMILTON, Alexander. *Letter from, concerning the Public Conduct and Character of John Adams, Esquire, President of the United States*, 1800.
———. *The Law Practice of*, Julius Goebel, ed., 2 v., 1964–
———. *The Papers of*, Harold C. Syrett, ed., 23 v., 1961–
———. *The Works of*, John C. Hamilton, ed., 7 v., 1851.
———. *The Works of*, Henry Cabot Lodge, ed., 12 v., 1904.
HUNT, John. *A Sermon occasioned by the death of Mrs. Sarah [Prince] Gill*, 1771.
JAY, John. *The Correspondence and Public Papers of*, H. P. Johnston, ed., 4 v., 1970 reprint.
JEFFERSON, Thomas. *The Papers of*, Julian P. Boyd, ed., 18 v., 1950– .
———. *Works of*, Federal Edition, Paul L. Ford, ed., 12 v., 1904–5.
———. *The Writings of*, Monticello Edition, A. A. Lipscomb, ed., 20 v., 1904.
———. *The Writings of*, H. A. Washington, ed., 9 v., 1861.
———. *The Complete Anas of*, Franklin B. Sawvel, ed., 1903.
KING, Rufus. *The Life and Correspondence of*, Chas. R. King, ed., 6 v., 1894–1900.
LIVINGSTON, William. *Funeral eulogium on [Rev.] Aaron Burr*, 1758.
LOCKE, John. *An essay concerning Human Understanding*, 1690.
MACLAY, William. *Journal of*, Edgar S. Maclay, ed., 1890.

MADISON, James. *Letters and other Writings of*, Congress Edition, 4 v., 1865.

———. *The Writings of*, Gaillard Hunt, ed., 9 v., 1900–10.

Mass. Hist. Soc. Proc., 1907–8, 3d series, I.

MEIGS, Return J. "Journal of the Expedition Against Quebec under . . . Col. Benedict Arnold," in Charles I. Bushnell, ed., *Crums for Antiquarians*, I, 1964.

MITCHILL, Samuel Latham. "Letters from Washington: 1801–1813," *Harper's Mag.*, LVIII (Apr. 1879), 740–55.

MONROE, James. *Autobiography of*, Stuart Gerry Brown, ed., 1959.

MORRIS, Gouverneur. *The Diary and Letters of*, Anne C. Morris, ed., 2 v., 1888.

New Jersey, *Votes and Proceedings of the General Assembly of*, 1779.

N.Y. (City), *Minutes of the Common Council*, 1784–1831, A. Everett Peterson, ed., 1917; Analytical Index, 1930.

———, Mayor's Court, *Select Cases of*, 1674–1784, Richard B. Morris, ed., 1935.

N.Y. (State). *Laws of*, 1777–1801, 7 v., 1886.

———. Opinions of the Attorneys General of, to Feb. 1782, Hiram E. Sukels, comp., 1872.

———, *Votes and Proceedings of the General Assembly of*, 1784–85, 1788–89, 1801.

———, Supreme Court of Judicature, *A digest of the reports of cases determined in . . . from . . . 1794–1843*, 2 v., 1850.

———, Supreme Court of Judicature, *Reports of Cases Adjudicated in* [1799–1803], by William Johnson, 1846.

———, Supreme Court, "Rules Respecting the Admission of Attornies," 28 October 1797, copy of broadside, Harvard University Library.

Newark, N.J., Records of the town of, 1666 to 1836, 1864.

Officers of the Continental Army, Historical Register of, by Francis B. Heitman, 1914.

OGDEN, Matthias. "Journal of, 1775, in Arnold's Campaign Against Quebec," in *Proc. of the N.J. Hist. Soc.*, XIII, no. 1 (January 1928), 17–30.

PATERSON, William. *Glimpses of Colonial Society and the Life at Princeton College, 1766–73, as described in the Letters of*, W. Jay Mills, ed., 1903.

PLUMER, William. *Memorandum of Proc. in the U.S. Senate, 1803–07*, E. S. Brown, ed., 1923.

Presbyterian Church in the United States, *Records of*, 1706–1788, 1841.

Princeton University. *General Catalogue of*, 1746–1906, 1908.

———. *General Catalogue of the American Whig-Cliosophic Society of*, 1954.

ROBERTS, Jonathan. "Memoirs of a Senator from Pennsylvania," *Pa. Mag. of Hist. & Biog.*, LXI, 446–52; LX, 11, 64–97, 213–48, 361–409, 502–51.

ROBERTS, Kenneth. *March to Quebec: Journals of the Members of Arnold's Expedition*, 1938.

ROCHEFOUCAULD-LANCOURT, François Alexandre Frédéric, Duc de La. *Travels through the United States of America*, 4 v., 1800.

RUSH, Benjamin. *Autobiography of*, Geo. W. Corner, ed., 1948.

———. *Letters of*, L. H. Butterfield, ed., 2 v., 1951.

SMITH, Caleb. *Diligence in the Work of God and activity During Life. A Sermon occasioned by the . . . Death of the Reverend Mr. Aaron Burr*, 1758.

STILES, Ezra. *The Literary Diary of*, F. B. Dexter, ed., 3 v., 1901.

SYRETT, Harold C. and Jean G. Cooke, eds. *Interview in Weehawken*, 1960.

U.S. Senate, *Journal of the Executive Proceedings of*, 3 v., 1828.

VAN NESS, William Peter (Aristides). *An Examination of the various charges exhibited against Aaron Burr*, 1803.

WELD, Isaac. *Travels through the states of North America*, 1795, 1796 and 1797, 2 v., 1807.

WASHINGTON, George. *The Writings of*, John C. Fitzpatrick, ed., 39 v., 1934.

WEEKS, Levi. *An Important Account of the Trial of*, by James Hardie, 1800.

WOLCOTT, Oliver. *Memoirs of the Administrations of Washington and John Adams*, edited from the papers of, by George Gibbs, 2 v., 1846.

WOLLSTONECRAFT, Mary. *A Vindication of the Rights of Woman*, 1792.

———. *A Correct Statement of the Various Sources from which the History of the Administration of John Adams was Compiled, and the Motives for its Suppression by Col. Burr*, 1802.

———. *The Suppressed History of the Administration of John Adams*, 1802.

Yale University. *Catalogue of Graduates of*, 1701–1892, 1892.
———. *Historical Register of*, 1701–1937, 1939.

III. Newspapers

Albany Centinel, 1798, 1804
Albany Gazette, 1792, 1794
Albany Register, 1802–4
Baltimore American, 1801
Boston Centinel, 1801
Boston News-Letter, 1757
New York American Citizen, 1802–4, 1809
New York Chronicle Express, 1802–4
New York Commercial Advertiser, 1800–4
New York Daily Advertiser, 1792, 1800–4
New York Evening Post, 1800–4
New York Gazette, 1780
New York Journal, 1792
New York Sun, 9 July 1846
Philadelphia Aurora, 1800–4
Philadelphia, Gazette of the United States, 1792–97
Sumpter (S. Car.) Daily Item, 15 Oct. 1969
Vienna (Va.) Globe, 21 Nov. 1968
Washington Federalist, 1800–4
Washington National Intelligencer, 1800–5

IV. Other Related Works

Adams, Henry. *History of the United States of America*, 9 v., 1898.
———. John Randolph, 1882.
Ahlstrom, Sidney E. *A Religious History of the American People*, 1972.
Alexander, De Alva S. *A Political History of the State of New York*, 4 v., 1906–23.

ALEXANDER, Holmes Moss. *Aaron Burr: The Proud Pretender*, 1937.

ALLAN, Herbert Sanford. *John Hancock: Patriot in Purple*, 1948.

ANDERSON, F. M. "Contemporary Opinion of the Virginia and Kentucky Resolutions," *Am. Hist. Rev.*, V, 1900.

ANTHONY, Katherine Susan. *Dolly Madison: Her Life and Times*, 1949.

ATKINSON, John A. *Duelling Pistols and some of the affairs they settled*, 1966.

BAKER, Liva. "The Defense of Levi Weeks," *Amer. Bar Assn. Jrnl*, LXIII, June 1977.

BAKER, William S. "The Camp by the Old Gulph Mill," *Penn. Mag. of Hist. and Biog.*, XVII, 1893.

BARRETT, Walter. *The Old Merchants of New York City*, 3d series, 1864.

BARTOW, Rev. Evelyn. "The Prevost Family in America," *N.Y. Genealogical and Biographical Record*, XIII, 1882.

———. *Bartow Genealogy*, 1879.

BEARD, Charles Austin. *Economic Origins of Jeffersonian Democracy*, 1915.

BEMIS, Samuel Flagg. *A Diplomatic History of the United States*, 5th ed., 1965.

BEVERIDGE, Albert Jeremiah. *The Life of John Marshall*, 4 v., 1916–19.

Bicentennial Committee, *Suffern: 200 Years, 1773–1973*, 1973.

BINKLEY, Wilfred E. *American Political Parties: Their Natural History*, 1962.

BOATNER, Mark B. *Encyclopedia of the American Revolution*, 1966.

BOBBÉ, Dorothie. *DeWitt Clinton*, 1933.

BOGERT, Frederick W. *Paramus: A Chronicle of Four Centuries*, 1961.

BOLES, John B. "Politics, Intrigue and the Presidency: James McHenry to Bishop John Carroll, May 16, 1800," *Md. Hist. Mag.*, LXIX, Spring 1974.

BORDEN, Morton E. *The Federalism of James A. Bayard*, 1955.

BOWERS, Claude G. *Jefferson and Hamilton: The Struggle for Democracy in America*, 1925.

BOYD, George Adams. *Elias Boudinot: Patriot and Statesman*, 1952.

BRADFORD, Gamaliel. "Aaron Burr," in *Damaged Souls*, 1923.

———. *The Journal of*, Van Wyck Brooks, ed., 1933.
BRADHURST, A. Maunsell. *My Forefathers*, 1910.
BRIGHAM, Clarence S. *History and Bibliography of American Newspapers, 1690–1820*, 1947.
BROOKS, James Wilton. *History of the Court of Common Pleas of the City and County of New York*, 1896.
BROWN, Glenn. *History of the United States Capitol*, 1900.
BUCHANAN, Roberdeau. *Genealogy of the Descendants of Dr. Wm. Shippen, the Elder*, 1877.
BUEL, Richard Jr. *Securing the Revolution: Ideology in American Politics, 1789–1815*, 1972.
BULKELEY, Alice T. *Historic Litchfield*, 1907.
BURKILL, T. A. *The Evolution of Christian Thought*, 1971.
BURR, Samuel Engle Jr. *Colonel Aaron Burr: The American Phoenix*, 1961.
BYINGTON, Ezra Hoyt. *The Puritan in England and New England*, 1896.
CASSELL, Frank A. "General Samuel Smith and the Election of 1800," *Md. Hist. Mag.*, LXIII, December 1968.
Celebration of the Rededication of Congress Hall: Addresses of Hon. Woodrow Wilson and Hon. Champ Clark at Philadelphia, Pa., Oct. 25, 1913, 63d Cong., 1st sess., Document 672, 1913.
CHARLES, Joseph. *The Origins of the American Party System*, 1956.
CHESTER, Alden. *Courts and Lawyers of New York*, 4 v., 1925.
———, ed. *Legal and Judicial History of New York*, v. 1, 1911.
CHILD, Elizabeth. *Fairfield, Connecticut Tercentenary*, 1940.
CHILD, Frank Samuel. *An Old New England Town*, 1895.
———. *Fairfield, Ancient and Modern*, 1909.
CHILDS, Avery R. *Rice Planter and Statesman: The Recollections of J. Motte Alston*, 1953.
COLLINS, V. L. *President Witherspoon*, 2 v., 1925.
COMBS, Jerald A. *The Jay Treaty*, 1970.
CUNNINGHAM, Noble E. Jr. *Jeffersonian Republicans in Power: Party Operations 1801–1809*, 1963.
DALLINGER, Frederick W. *Nominations for Elective Office in the United States*, 1897.
DANGERFIELD, George Dan. *Chancellor Robert R. Livingston of New York*, 1960.
DANIELS, Jonathan. *Ordeal of Ambition: Jefferson, Hamilton, Burr*, 1970.

DAUER, Manning J. *The Adams Federalists*, 1953.

DEVEREUX, Anthony Q. *The Rice Princes*, 1973.

DEXTER, Franklin Bowditch. *Biographical Sketches of the Graduates of Yale College*, 1885.

DIDIER, Eugene L. "Aaron Burr as a Lawyer," *The Green Bag*, XIV, Oct. 1902.

DILLON, Dorothy Rita. *The New York Triumvirate*, 1949.

DIX, Rev. Morgan. "Loyalty to Our Country," *Mag. of Amer. Hist.*, XXVII, April 1892.

DRAKE, Samuel G. *Some Memoirs of the Life and Writings of the Rev. Thomas Prince*, 1851.

DUER, William A. *Reminiscences of an Old Yorker*, 1867.

EDWARDS, George William. *New York as an eighteenth century municipality*, 1968 reprint.

EDWARDS, William. *Memoirs of Col. William Edwards*, 1847.

EDWARDS, William Henry. *Timothy and Rhoda Ogden Edwards of Stockbridge, Mass.*, 1903.

EGBERT, Donald Drew. *Princeton Portraits*, 1947.

EISMAN, Harry Paul. *O'er Aaron Burr's Grave*, 1948.

ELKINS, Stanley, and Eric McKitrick. "The Founding Fathers: Young Men of the Revolution," pamphlet reprinted with variations from *Pol. Sci. Quar.*, LXXVI, June 1961.

ELLIOTT, T. C. "The Surrender at Astoria in 1818," *Oreg. Hist. Soc. Quar.*, XIX, Dec. 1918.

ESSARY, Jessie Frederick. *Maryland in National Politics*, 1932.

EVANS, Paul D. "The Holland Land Company," *Buffalo Hist. Soc. Pub.*, XXIV, 1924.

FERNOW, Berthold. *New York in the Revolution*, 1887.

FISKE, John. *The Critical Period of American History*, 1888.

FLEXNER, James Thomas. *The Young Hamilton*, 1978.

FOOTE, Katherine Adelia. *Ebenezer Foote, the founder*, 1927.

FOX, Dixon Ryan. *The Decline of Aristocracy in the Politics of New York*, 1919.

FREEMAN, Douglas Southall. *George Washington: A Biography*, V (1951) and VI (1953).

GAUSTAD, Edwin Scott. *The Great Awakening in New England*, 1957.

GEISSLER, Suzanne Burr. "The Burr Family, 1716–1836," unpublished doctoral thesis, Syracuse University, 1977.

General Society of Mechanics and Tradesmen of the City of New York, 1785–1914, *Historical sketch and government of*, 1914.

GESSFORD, J. Douglas. "Motoring after Aaron Burr," *N.J. His. Soc. Proc.*, LV, 1937.

GOLDBLOOM, Maurice J. "How They Indicted a Vice President," *The Washington Post*, 30 Sept. 1973.

GOODWIN, Nathaniel. *Genealogical Notes*, 1856.

GROVES, Joseph A. *The Alstons and Allstons of North and South Carolina*, 1901.

HAGEMAN, John F. *History of Princeton and its institutions*, 2 v., 1879.

HAMILTON, Allan McLane. *The Intimate Life of Alexander Hamilton*, 1910.

HAMILTON, John C. *History of the Republic of the United States*, 7 v., 1857–64.

HAMMOND, Jabez Delano. *The History of Political Parties in the State of New York*, 2 v., 1842.

HATCHER, William B. *Edward Livingston*, 1940.

HAYNES, Samuel Perkins. "An historical study of the Edwardsean Revivals," *Am. Jour. of Psych.*, XIII, Oct. 1902.

HENDERSON, H. James. "Quantitative Approaches to Party Formation in the United States Congress: A Comment," with a Reply by Mary P. Ryan, *Wm. & Mary Quar.*, XXX, Apr. 1973.

HODGE, Charles. *The Constitutional History of the Presbyterian Church in the United States*, 2 v., 1840.

HOPKINS, Vivian C. "The Empire State—DeWitt Clinton's Laboratory," *N.Y. Hist. Soc. Quar.*, LIX, 1975.

HOTCHKISS, Thomas D. Jr. "Glimpses of the College of New Jersey," *Mag. of Amer. Hist.*, XXVIII, Dec. 1892.

HUFELAND, Otto. *Westchester County During the American Revolution*, 1926.

IVES, Mabel Lorenz. *Washington's Headquarters*, 1932.

JACOBS, James R. *Tarnished Warrior: James Wilkinson*, 1938.

JACOBUS, Donald Lines. *History and Genealogy of the Families of Old Fairfield*, v. I, 1930.

JENKINSON, Isaac. *Aaron Burr, his personal and political relations with Thomas Jefferson and Alexander Hamilton*, 1902.

JOHNSTON, Henry F. "The Campaign of 1776 around New York and Brooklyn," *Memoirs of the L.I. Hist. Soc.*, III, 1878.

JONES, Electa Fidelia. *Stockbridge, Past and Present*, 1854.

JONES, Thomas. *History of New York During the Revolutionary War*, v. I, 1879.

KASS, Alvin. *Politics in New York State 1800–1830*, 1965.

KEESEY, Ruth M. "Loyalty and Reprisal; the loyalists of Bergen County, New Jersey, and their estates," unpublished doctoral thesis, Columbia University, 1957.

KENYON, Cecelia M. "Men of Little Faith: The Anti-Federalists on the Nature of Representative Government," in Gordon S. Wood., ed., *The Confederation and the Constitution: The Critical Issues*, 1973.

KNAPP, Samuel L. *The Life of Aaron Burr*, 1835.

KOCH, Adrienne and Harry Ammon, "The Virginia and Kentucky Resolutions: An Episode in Jefferson's and Madison's Defense of Civil Liberties," *Wm. & Mary Quar.*, 3d series, V, 1948.

LAMB, Martha J. "Historic Homes and Landmarks," *Mag. of Amer. Hist.*, XII, Jan. 1889.

LEAKE, Isaac Q. *Memoir of the Life and Times of General John Lamb*, 1850.

LEE, Francis Bazley. *New Jersey as a Colony and as a State*, v. III, 1902.

LEVIN, David, ed. *The Puritan in the Enlightenment: Franklin and Edwards*, 1963.

LEVY, Leonard W. *Jefferson and Civil Liberties: The Darker Side*, 1963.

———. *Legacy of Suppression: Freedom of Speech and Press in Early American History*, 1960.

LEVY, Samuel Jacob. *Chester, N.Y.: A History*, 1947.

LEWIS, William Draper, ed. *Great American Lawyers: A History of the Legal Profession in America*, 8 v., 1907–9.

LINCOLN, Charles Z. *The Constitutional History of New York*, 5 v., 1906.

LINGLE, Walter L. *Presbyterians: Their History and Beliefs*, 1928.

LIVINGSTON, Edwin Brockholst. *The Livingstons of Livingston Manor*, 1910.

LODGE, A. C. *Life and letters of George Cabot*, 1877.

LOSSING, Benson John. *The Hudson, from the Wilderness to the Sea*, 1866.

LYNCH, Denis Tilden. *An Epoch and a Man: Martin Van Buren and His Times*, 1929.

MCADAM, David, ed. *History of the Bench and Bar of New York*, 2 v., 1897–99.

MCBAIN, Howard Lee. *DeWitt Clinton and the Origin of the Spoils System in New York*, 1967.

McCormick, Richard Patrick. *The Second American Party System*, 1966.

McCracken, George E. "Who Was Aaron Burr?," *The American Genealogist*, whole number 158, v. 40, no. 2, April 1964.

Maclean, John. *History of the College of New Jersey*, v. I, 1877.

Magill, Frank N., ed. *Masterpieces of Christian Liberty in Summary Form*, v. 2, 1963.

Malone, Dumas. *Jefferson and His Time*, 5 v., 1948–70.

Marsh, Philip. "Philip Freneau and His Circle," *Penn. Mag. of Hist. and Biog.*, LXIII, 1939.

Merwin, Henry Childs. *Aaron Burr*, 1899.

Miller, John C. *Alexander Hamilton: Portrait in Paradox*, 1959.

———. *The Federalist Era, 1789–1801*, 1960.

Miller, Perry. *Jonathan Edwards*, in the American Men of Letters Series, 1949.

———. *The New England Mind from Colony to Province*, 1953.

Mitchell, Broadus. *Alexander Hamilton*, 2 v., 1957, 1962.

Monaghan, Frank. *John Jay, defender of liberty*, 1935.

———. *The Results of the Revolution*, 1934.

Moore, George H. *The Treason of Charles Lee*, 1858.

Morgan, H. R. "Colonel Aaron Burr," *Daughters of the American Revolution Magazine*, XVI.

Munsell, Joel. *The Annals of Albany*, 10 v., 1850–59.

Murray, Nicholas. *Notes Historical and Biographical Concerning Elizabeth-Town*, 1844.

Mushkat, Jerome. "Matthew Livingston Davis and the Political Legacy of Aaron Burr," *New-York Hist. Soc. Quar.*, LIX, April 1975.

———. *Tammany: The Evolution of a Political Machine, 1789–1865*, 1971.

Myers, Gustavus. *The History of Tammany Hall*, 1901.

Nevins, Allan. *The American States During and After the Revolution, 1775–1789*, 1924.

———. *The Evening Post: A Century of Journalism*, 1922.

Nissenson, Samuel G. *The Patroon's Domain*, 1937.

Nye, Russel Blaine. *The Cultural Life of the New Nation 1776–1830*, 1960.

Ogden, Mary Depue, ed. *Memorial Cyclopedia of New Jersey*, 1915.

Pancake, John. "Aaron Burr: Would-Be Usurper," *Wm. & Mary Quar.*, 3d series, VIII, April 1951.

Papers in Honor of Andrew Keogh, Librarian of Yale University, by the Staff of the Library, 1938.

PARKES, H. B. "New England in the Seventeen-Thirties," *New England Quar.*, III, July 1930.

PARMET, Herbert S. and Marie B. Hecht. *Aaron Burr: Portrait of an Ambitious Man*, 1967.

PARTON, James. *The Life and Times of Aaron Burr*, 1857.

———. "Theodosia Burr," in *Famous Americans of Recent Times*, 1867.

PATERSON, William. "Aaron Burr or William Paterson, Which?," *N.J. Law Journal*, XX, June 1897.

PAULSON, Peter. "The Tammany Society and the Jeffersonian Movement in New York City, 1795–1800," *N.Y. Hist.*, XXXIV, 1953.

PEELING, James Hedley. "Governor McKean and the Pennsylvania Jacobins," *Penn. Mag. of Hist. and Biog.*, LIV, 1930.

PELLEW, George. *John Jay*, 1890.

PENFOLD, Saxby Vouler. *Romantic Suffern*, 1955.

PERRINE, William. "The Beautiful Daughter of Aaron Burr," *Ladies' Home Journal*, XVIII, Feb. 1901.

PERRY, Kate E. *The Old Burying Ground of Fairfield, Conn.*, 1882.

PIDGIN, Charles Felton. *Theodosia: The First Gentlewoman of Her Time*, 1907.

POCOCK, J. G. A. "The Classical Theory of Deference," *Amer. Hist. Rev.*, LXXXI, June 1976.

POMERANTZ, Sidney I. *New York: An American City, 1783–1803*, 1938.

POUND, Arthur. *The Golden Earth*, 1935.

PRATT, Julius. "Aaron Burr and the Historians," *N.Y. Hist.*, XXVI, October 1945.

RANKIN, Jeremiah Eames. *Esther Burr's Journal*, no date (largely fictionalized and of little value).

REUBENS, Beatrice G. "Burr, Hamilton and the Manhattan Company," *Pol. Sci. Quar.*, LXXII (Dec. 1957), LXXIII (March 1958).

REYNOLDS, James B., Samuel H. Fisher and Henry B. Wright, eds. *Two Centuries of Christian Activity at Yale*, 1901.

RODDY, Edward G. "Maryland and the Presidential Election of 1800," *Md. Hist. Mag.*, LVI, September 1961.

ROMER, John Lockwood. *Historical Sketches of the Romer, Van Tassel and Allied Families and Tales of the Neutral Ground*, 1917.

ROOSEVELT, Theodore. *Gouverneur Morris*, 1916.

ROSENKRANS, Allen, comp. *The Rosenkrans Family in Europe and America*, 1900.

RUTTENBER, Edward M. *History of the County of Orange*, 1875.

RYAN, Mary P. "Party Formation in the United States Congress, 1789 to 1796: A Quantitative Analysis," *Wm. & Mary Quar.*, 3d series, XXVIII, 1971.

SABINE, Lorenzo. *Notes on Duels and Duelling*, 1885.

SCHACHNER, Nathan. *Aaron Burr: A Biography*, 1937.

SCOTT, Henry Wilson. *The Courts of the State of New York*, 1909.

SEDGWICK, Theodore J. *A Memoir of the Life of William Livingston*, 1833.

SEDGEWICK, Sarah Cabot and Christina Sedgewick Marquand. *Stockbridge 1739–1939: A Chronicle*, 1939.

SHAW, Peter. *The Character of John Adams*, 1976.

SHAW, W. H. *History of Essex and Hudson*, 2 v., 1884.

SHELLABARGER, Samuel. *Lord Chesterfield and His World*, 1951.

SHIPPEN, Rebecca Lloyd. "Inauguration of President Thomas Jefferson, 1801," *Penn. Mag. of Hist. and Biog.*, XXV, 1901–2.

SIFTON, Paul G. "What a Dread Prospect . . . : Dolly Madison's Plague Year," *Penn. Mag. of Hist. and Biog.*, LXXXVII, April 1963.

SMITH, Dorothy Valentine. "An intercourse of the Heart: Some little-known letters of Theodosia Burr," *New-York Hist. Soc. Quar.*, XXXVII, 1953.

———. "Mrs. Prevost requests the honor of his company," Manuscripts, Fall 1959.

SMELSER, Marshall. *The Democratic Republic, 1801–1815*, 1968.

SMITH, Arthur D. H. *John Jacob Astor: Landlord of New York*, 1931.

SOWERBY, E. Millicent. "Thomas Jefferson and His Library," Bibliographical Society of America Papers, L, 1956.

SPARKS, Jared. *The Life of George Washington*, 1902.

SPAULDING, Ernest Wilder. *His Excellency George Clinton: Critic of the Constitution*, 1938.

SPONSELLER, Edwin H. "Northampton and Jonathan Edwards,"

Faculty Monograph Series, Dilys M. Jones, ed., v. 1, no. 1, March 1966.

STEARNS, Jonathan French. *First Church in Newark: Historical discourses*, 1853.

STEINER, Bernard C. *The Life and Correspondence of James McHenry*, 1907.

STEVENS, John Austin. *Albert Gallatin*, 1883.

STILLWELL, Dr. John Edwin. *The History of the Burr Portraits: Their Origin, Their Dispersal and Their Reassemblage*, 1928.

———. *The History of Captain Richard Stillwell, Son of Lieutenant Nicholas Stillwell, and His Descendants*, 1930.

STOKES, Isaac Newton Phelps. *The Iconography of Manhattan Island*, 1489–1909, 6 v., 1926.

STRANGE, Lt. Col. "Historical Notes on the Defence of Quebec in 1775," *Transactions of the Lit. and Hist. Soc. of Quebec*, 1876–1880.

TAFT, Henry. *A Century and a Half at the New York Bar*, 1938.

THAYER, Theodore G. *As We Were: The Story of Old Elizabethtown*, 1964.

———. *The Making of a Scapegoat: Washington and Lee at Monmouth*, 1976.

THOMAS, Gordon L. "Aaron Burr's Farewell Address," *Quar. Jrnl of Speech*, XXXIX, Oct. 1953.

THORP, William, ed. *The Lives of Eighteen from Princeton*, 1946.

TODD, Charles Burr. *A General History of the Burr Family in America*, 1878.

TOMPKINS, Hamilton B. *Burr Bibliography: A List of Books relating to Aaron Burr*, 1892.

TUCKERMAN, Bayard. *Life of General Philip Schuyler, 1733–1804*, 1903.

TURNER, John James, Jr. "New-York in Presidential Politics," unpublished doctoral thesis, Columbia University, 1968.

URQUHART, Frank John, ed. *A History of the City of Newark, New Jersey*, 3 v., 1913.

VAN DER LINDEN, Frank. *The Turning Point: Jefferson's Battle for the Presidency*, 1962.

VAN DUSEN, Albert E. *Middletown in the American Revolution*, 1950.

VAN DYKE, Paul. "An Old Book," *Mag. of Amer. Hist.*, XXVIII, Sept. 1892.

VAN RENSSELAER, Rev. Maunsell. "Lieutenant-General John Maunsell," *Mag. of Amer. Hist.*, XXVII, June 1892.

WALTERS, Raymond, Jr. *Albert Gallatin: Jeffersonian Financier and Diplomat*, 1957.

———. "The origins of the Jeffersonian Party in Pennsylvania," *Penn. Mag. of Hist. and Biog.*, LXVI, Oct. 1942.

WANDELL, Samuel H. *Aaron Burr in Literature*, 1936.

WANDELL, Samuel H. and Meade Minnigerode. *Aaron Burr*, 2 v., 1927.

WARREN, Charles. *The Supreme Court in United States History*, rev. ed., 2 v., 1892.

WEISE, Arthur James. *The Swartwout Chronicles*, 1899.

WEISS, Harry Bischoff. *Life in Early New Jersey*, 1964.

WELCH, Richard E., Jr. *Theodore Sedgwick, Federalist: A Political Portrait*, 1965.

WESTERVELT, Frances A., ed. *History of Bergen County, New Jersey, 1630–1923*, 1923.

WERTENBAKER, Thomas Jefferson. *The Founding of American Civilization: The Middle Colonies*, 1963.

———. *Princeton 1746–1896*, 1948.

WHEELER, William Ogden, comp. *The Ogden Family in America: Elizabethtown Branch*, 1907.

WHITELEY, Emily Stone. *Washington and His Aides-de-Camp*, 1936.

WILDER, Throop. "Jedidiah Peck, Statesman, Soldier, Preacher," *N.Y. Hist.*, XXII, 1941.

WILLIAMS, William Carlos. "The Virtue of History: Aaron Burr," in *In the American Grain*, 1925.

WILLIAMSON, Wallace J., III. *The Halls: A Brief History of the American Whig-Cliosophic Society of Princeton University*, 1947.

WINSLOW, Ola Elizabeth. *Jonathan Edwards*, 1940.

WINSOR, Justin, ed. *Narrative and Critical History of America*, 8 v., 1884–1889.

WOOD, Gordon S. *The Creation of the American Republic 1776–1787*, 1969.

———, ed. *The Confederation and the Constitution: The Critical Issues*, 1973.

Index

Index

Index